THE PROGRESS OF THE

JESUITS (1556-79)

by

JAMES BRODRICK, S.J.

AUTHOR OF *The Origin of the Jesuits*

A Campion Book

LOYOLA UNIVERSITY PRESS

CHICAGO

Loyola University Press
3441 North Ashland Avenue
Chicago, Illinois 60657
ISBN 0-8294-0523-2

Trustees of Roman Catholic Purposes Registered is the legal
title of the English Province of the Society of Jesus which now
holds all rights to Father Brodrick's work. This Loyola Request
Reprint is done with their permission.

A LOYOLA REQUEST REPRINT, 1986

We gratefully acknowledge the help of the Cudahy Memorial
Library of Loyola University of Chicago in obtaining copies of
the original edition.

Originally published in 1940

LONGMANS, GREEN AND CO. LTD.

39 PATERNOSTER ROW, LONDON

LONGMANS, GREEN AND CO. LTD.

215 VICTORIA STATION, TORONTO

LONGMANS, GREEN AND CO. LTD.

55 FIFTH AVENUE, NEW YORK

DE LICENTIA SUPERIORUM ORDINIS

Nihil obstat:
REGINALDUS PHILLIPS, S.T.L.

Censor Deputatus

Imprimatur:
E. MORROGH BERNARD

Vic. Gen.

Westmonaterii: die 1a Junii 1946

Library of Congress Cataloging in Publication Data
Brodrick, James, 1891-
    The progress of the Jesuits (1556-79)

    Sequel to: the author's The origin of the Jesuits.
    Reprint. Originally published: 1st ed. New York:
Longmans, Green, 1947.
    Includes index.
    1. Jesuits—History—16th century. I. Title. BX3706.B72
1986   271'.53'009031   86-2864
ISBN 0-8294-0523-2

PREFACE

THIS book is the long overdue sequel to a shorter one entitled, *The Origin of the Jesuits,* published in 1940, when the Society of Jesus attained its fourth centenary. Though it deals with only a brief period of time, roughly the generation between the death of St. Ignatius in 1556 and the election of his fourth successor, Claudio Aquaviva, in 1581, it covers, at least in a geographical sense, a great deal of ground. The process of adjusting the rival claims of space and time brought home the wisdom of Mary Mitford, who confined her explorations to a village, and roused black envy of Xavier de Maistre, who made a masterpiece of a tour around his room. "Even in books," wrote Miss Mitford, "I like a confined locality. Nothing is so tiresome as to be whirled half over Europe at the chariot-wheels of a hero, to go to sleep at Vienna and awaken at Madrid." Alas, in this book the reader will sometimes go to sleep in Yamaguchi and awaken in Pernambuco. It could not be helped, because the Jesuits of those days were such inveterate wanderers.

Prefaces, we all know, are a mere vanity, but it is better to be vain than unjust, and a protestation must here be made, however lame and inadequate it may seem. One of the grave and sad limitations of a book such as this is that the work of other orders, and of the greatest of all orders, the secular priesthood, has to be passed over or only perfunctorily treated, with a consequent displacement of the true historical perspective. To take the missions to the heathen alone, the Franciscans, Dominicans and Augustinians were ahead of the Jesuits in every field east and west, except those of China and Japan. In Europe, as engineers of the Counter-Reformation, the Capuchins, once in their stride, yielded nothing to the Jesuits, except in the domain of education. Many flattering words about the Jesuits from the lips of great, and sometimes holy, men are cited in the following pages, and the picture given, usually in their own words, of the fathers at work and prayer is inspiring enough and true enough to life and history, provided we remember that other

v

religious orders at the time presented as fair a face to God, and were equally good architects of the Church's temporal destinies.

Even within its narrow compass some readers may consider that the book is out of focus and gives a disproportionate amount of space to the family differences of the Jesuits, especially in Spain. Very probably they will be right, but so surely was Boswell when he wrote in his *Journals:* "There is a tragic beauty in the *whole* truth that no degree of decorative evasion can ever supplant or conceal." The author may humbly plead that he was aiming at the whole truth. Anyhow, he professes to be writing history and "sin in some shape or other is the great staple of history," so, as was well said a century ago, its students must expect "to hear more of one turbulent prelate or one set of factious or licentious monks than of a hundred societies or a thousand scattered clergy living in the quiet decency suited to their profession."

The book is based very largely on the letters of the Jesuits themselves, now being published officially in the series entitled, *Monumenta Historica Societatis Jesu,* which is approaching its seventieth volume. For convenience' sake the series is referred to in the notes by the initials M.H. These notes are many and various, and the reader in his charity ought not entirely to neglect them, or he will be tempted to accuse the author of even more sins of omission than the large number already weighing upon his conscience. Owing to the abundance of foreign words and names in the book, the printing of it must have been a peculiarly difficult task, especially in present circumstances, and the author would like to record his gratitude to the firm which carried it out so efficiently, as well as to his ever friendly and helpful publishers.

J. B.

Stonyhurst
July 1946

CONTENTS

CHAPTER I

GROWING PAINS

THE first of countless crises in their troubled history came upon the Jesuits immediately after the death of St. Ignatius Loyola in July 1556. For more than twenty years he had been all in all to them, a visible providence, a father, protector, stimulator, guide, and perfect friend. "As an eagle stirreth up her nest, fluttereth over her young, spreadeth abroad her wings, taketh them, beareth them on her wings," so with vigorous, bracing affection did Ignatius teach his sons to take to the air, the four winds of the world, and to be afraid of nothing. He had begun with nine companions whose names stand beside his in the Papal bull of 1540 that created the Society of Jesus, and he died sixteen years later the superior of close on two thousand disciples scattered over the earth westward from Japan to Brazil.[1]

It is interesting to observe how those men reacted to the death of their founder. He had taught them that they ought not to grieve when God called one of their number away, as it meant a new intercessor in Heaven, but they were not stocks or stones and felt the blow intensely. "I was stricken to the soul," wrote the Saint's *alter ego*, Father Jerome Nadal, whom he had constituted vicar-general or vice-superior of the entire order two years before. Father Juan Polanco, its secretary, was a more stoical type, but even he had to wrestle with

[1] According to the testimony of the Saint's secretary, the new order had a membership of 1500 by the year 1554. This was rapid growth, perhaps too rapid, but Ignatius controlled it by severely restricting the number of those admitted to the highest of the several grades of which the order is composed, that of the solemnly professed who make a fourth vow to the Pope to go unhesitatingly and without provision from him wheresoever his Holiness may direct them on the Church's business. This vow, which perhaps had more relevance in the fluid conditions of the sixteenth century than it has today, though it is still sometimes invoked, sent St. Francis Xavier speeding to India and Japan, and many others of similar spirit on missions or nunciatures involving the entire Pauline list of perils and miseries. At the time of Ignatius's death the order numbered only forty-two professed fathers, including five survivors of the original nine companions (*Monumenta Historica Societatis Jesu,* Polanco, *Chronicon,* iv, 476; vi, 40).

his tears: "We strive as best we know how to accept this passing of our Father from the hand of the Lord with composure and thankfulness." The most eminent of the dead Saint's disciples, Father Francis Borgia, avowed that he experienced "a feeling of loneliness and sorrow beyond the power of words to express."[1] So it was with all of them whose letters have survived, but their grief invariably merges into a great new hope, for they at once canonize Ignatius in their hearts and rejoice to think of him as their advocate before God. Pedro Ribadeneira, his protégé from boyhood, was in Flanders at this time. He used to describe himself ruefully as another Josue fighting a long and losing battle with the Amalek of Spanish bureaucracy which thwarted his every effort to obtain a legal footing for his order in the Low Countries. "Three days after our Father mounted to Heaven," he says, "the King at last signed the letters-patent and Josue brought off a handsome victory."[2] Ignatius had become the Moses of his people, and such he has remained in their love and reverence from that day to this. Many besides the Jesuits mourned him, and the sweetest flower laid on his grave came to the fathers in Rome from the Barnabites of Milan: "The news of the death of venerable Father Ignatius has grieved us sorely, both on your account and our own, for he was our father also. . . But he has not withdrawn entirely from us, because, wherever in the wide world the name of Christ has penetrated, even to the Antipodes, his dear and gracious memory will remain always green. His was the inspiration and guiding hand behind the latter-day apostles and martyrs who have created in our time new Christianities to rival those of the primitive ages. Now the Father has followed his heroic sons, not less than they a martyr by the long-drawn-out martyrdom of care and solicitude for the whole Church of God. Not your great family alone but many others also have leaned for long on the heart of this common father of all good men, who was ever a foot to the lame and an eye to the blind, and the sure shield and comfort of any man bearing the titles of poverty or affliction. . . We beg you of your charity to accept these tears of our love and reverence, and to love us in return and be mindful in your prayers of our littleness."[3]

[1] M.H., *S. Franciscus Borgia*, iii, 266.
[2] *Cartas de San Ignacio*, vi, 351 (Madrid 1889).
[3] M.H., *Lainii Monumenta*, i, 344–5.

The Jesuits needed their advocate in Heaven, for conspicuous among those from whom no message of sympathy seems to have come was Pope Paul IV, the octogenarian Gian Pietro Carafa, co-founder with St. Cajetan of the Theatines.[1] This tall, lean, fiery-tempered, cheerful, imperious old man, born to wealth and station in a rocky castle of Calabria, spoke five languages fluently and was reputed to know the whole of Homer, Virgil and the Bible by heart. He possessed the spirit of a Homeric hero and, like Goliath, was a man of war from his youth, much addicted to crossing swords and issuing challenges. He bore down the gentle St. Cajetan but found in St. Ignatius Loyola one as strong-minded and unyielding as himself, which did not increase his love for the Jesuits. He had been a favourite of both Alexander VI and Julius II, and under Leo X spent three years as nuncio in England. After his return, he stayed in Flanders and became, as a Neapolitan, a member of the privy council of the King of Spain. In temperament he was much more Spanish than Italian, and that may well have been the general reason why he learned so thoroughly to detest these other autocrats and politicos, Charles V and his son, Philip II. But there were good specific reasons too, for he and his Theatines had been victimized by their brutal, drunken soldiery during the terrible sack of Rome in 1527.

[1] Cardinal Carafa, who had been bishop of Chieti and archbishop of Brindisi, resigned both sees on joining up with St. Cajetan, but Pope Clement VII required him to retain the title of Bishop of Chieti. This, adjectively, in Latin is *Theatinus,* and as Gian Pietro was the driving power in the foundation of the new order, as well as its first provost or superior, its members became known as the Theatines. His partnership with Cajetan, one of the sweetest and most lovable of the saints, was the strangest imaginable, that of an eagle with a nightingale. Founded in 1524, the Theatines constituted a new departure in the religious life of the Church, that of "Clerks Regular" or priests living according to a specific community rule. Unlike the monastic orders of monks, friars and hermits, the primary object of the clerks regular is the sacred ministry, the salvation of souls by means of the sacraments, preaching, teaching, attending the sick, etc. The Jesuits were only the fifth order of clerks regular, the three others antedating them being the Clerks of the Good Jesus, who afterwards died out (1526), the Barnabites (1530) and the Somaschi (1532). The Theatines, who were later constantly confused with the Jesuits, even by such a knowledgeable person as St. Teresa, did not entirely break with the older monastic tradition, for they continued to chant office in choir, though in a simpler manner than the monks. A fixed rule with them, especially dear to Cardinal Carafa, was that superiors might only be elected for a period of three years.

To his dying day Gian Pietro never got over that nightmare experience of the *furor Hispanicus*. The chief wrong, however, that envenomed him against Spain was not personal at all, but a nobleminded concern for the vanishing liberties of Italy and of the Church. Spain held in her paralysing grip both the Duchy of Milan and the Kingdom of Naples, between which upper and nether millstones lay the defenceless Papal States. Was the Holy See, then, to become an appanage of the Spanish crown? Neither Charles nor Philip could see any good reason against such a happening, since, to their mind, Spain was the faith and the faith was Spain.

Paul is a genuinely tragic figure, a Lear among the Popes, ruined by the defects of his own very great qualities, his unbounded courage, his boyish optimism, his wholehearted love of the Church, his glowing patriotism, his high personal integrity and austerity. All his life long he strove with his volcanic temper but never learned to control it. He was very witty and fond of puns but had little sense of humour. The strong virtues were his in abundance, but he appears to have lacked almost completely the gentler ones which gave such a radiance to the character of his friend and victim, St. Cajetan. It might be said without too much injustice that he lacked St. Paul's thirteenth chapter to the Corinthians, for he was not patient nor kind, and he was easily provoked to anger, and readily thought evil, and had hardly any forbearance. The Florentine ambassador at his court described him as a man of iron who if thwarted or in the least denied his wishes caused sparks to fly from the very stones under his feet. The Jesuits, as will be seen, were responsible for some of those sparks. Paul had not forgotten three encounters with St. Ignatius from which he had emerged unvictorious. He never forgot such incidents, which was one of his fundamental weaknesses. He might bury the hatchet for a time, but he gave the impression of always carefully marking the spot. It is true that he received Ignatius very cordially after his election as Pope, but not many months later he gave orders that the Saint's own house was to be searched for weapons of war, as though the Jesuits, with their Spanish connections, might be meditating an assault on the Vatican.

Before the first year of his pontificate had passed it became evident that only a miracle could keep Paul and the Spaniards from one another's throats. Neither side wanted the conflict and both sides contributed about equally to render it inevitable, the Spaniards or their Italian *protégés,* the Colonnas and Sforzas, by irritating acts of aggression, and the Pope by the extreme violence of his language. But the chief villain of the tragic story was Paul's nephew and evil-genius, Carlo Carafa, a typical soldier of fortune turned churchman and director of Vatican policy, who delighted, as his unscrupulous abettor, Farnese, wrote, "to fan the flames of his Holiness's righteous anger." It was characteristic of his Holiness that he should have chosen for his motto a bellicose verse of Psalm xc: "Thou shalt walk upon the asp and the basilisk, and thou shalt trample under foot the lion and the dragon." Nobody needed to be told that the other names of those beasts were Charles and Philip. In open consistory, for all the world to hear, the Pope denounced the Spaniards as "that accursed nation, the spawn of Moors and Jews, the dregs of the earth," and referred to the Emperor, just then about to say farewell to all his greatness, as "this miserable and sorry creature, this cripple in body and soul, the worst man born into the world for a thousand years."

Hard words break no bones, and what precipitated the war was not the invective of the uncle but the intrigue of the nephew, who succeeded in obtaining Lutheran help for the Pope and in securing the backing of France, Spain's traditional enemy. As France was allied with the Grand Turk, that courteous potentate also professed himself willing to lend a hand in this little Christian imbroglio. King Philip could stand no more provocation. Made easy in conscience by the *nihil obstat* of his leading theologians, including Friar Melchior Cano, he instructed his viceroy in Naples, the famous and ruthless Duke of Alva, to issue an ultimatum to the Pope towards the end of August 1556. A few days later, before the Holy Father had time to consider or draft his reply, the impatient Alva crossed the frontier and seized the Papal town of Pontecorvo. The war had begun. Against its lurid background of hatreds and daily alarms, the seven score of Jesuits resident in Rome tried to continue their peaceful pursuit of study and prayer. From their letters, which are numerous, one could never guess at the storm that whirled around them, for they refer to it only as "questi tumulti," the "troubles" of the time. They represented a Pentecostal variety of nationalities, Spanish, Italian, German, French, English, Irish, Bohemian, Flemish, Greek, Scandinavian and Slav. Most of them were fledglings, novices or students, and all lived in that cheerful state of destitution which St. Francis de Sales used to call "poverty really poor." Their principal house, the *casa professa,* which was also the novitiate and had attached to it the little church of Santa Maria della Strada, subsisted entirely on alms, nor could the priests living there accept any stipend for Masses or other services. St. Ignatius was so particular about this that he required the rectors of the other two houses, the Roman and German Colleges, to testify on oath before secular witnesses at the beginning of each year that they had not transferred any sums received by them to the house of the professed.[1] It became an easy oath to take when Pope Paul discontinued the subsidies granted to the Colleges by his predecessor, for they had no other resources and fell into extreme poverty. Everybody except Ignatius himself believed them doomed, but he refused to despair and committed them as his dearest trust to the love and fidelity of his sons. For the sake of the Roman College, which was to grow into the Pontifical Gregorian University and spread its influence over the whole Catholic world, he sent away to Spain as its advocate the man he most trusted and needed, Father Jerome Nadal, just as at an earlier time he had surrendered to the missions the best-loved of all his family, St. Francis Xavier.

With Nadal gone and out of reach, there remained in Rome only four professed fathers to weather the crisis caused by the death of Ignatius and the approach of war. As their natural leader, Diego Laynez, himself lay at death's door, the responsibility passed to the sturdy shoulders of Father Juan Polanco, who seemed born for such burdens. Juan belongs to the great army of the unrecognized, of the quiet heroes who "labour and pass and leave no signs," except a vast collection of business letters and domestic memoranda. Most Jesuits even would score poor marks in an examination on his career. Yet for a quarter of a century, the first vital and formative quarter, this unknown Atlas seemed to one who knew him well and watched him at work "to carry the entire Society of Jesus on his back." He was born of a good family at Burgos in the year that Luther nailed up his theses on indulgences. Detractors maintained, whether rightly or wrongly it is now impossible to say, that he had

---

[1] M.H., *Polanci Complementa,* i, 116.

Jewish blood in his veins. Perhaps his complete freedom from the usual Spanish prejudice about *limpia sangre,* or racial purity, may have given rise to the story. After taking a master's degree at Paris while still in his teens, he went to Rome to become one of the numerous clerks at the Vatican. There he made the acquaintance of Laynez, whom ever after he worshipped. The Spiritual Exercises under this best of interpreters determined his vocation, to the great disgust of the proud family in Burgos, who hoped, no doubt, to see him a cardinal. Some years later, after his ordination, a younger brother, Luis, who lived in Italy, waylaid the astonished Juan on one of his missionary journeys and carried him off protesting to a house in Florence, where he was forcibly detained. After enduring what he calls "insultos diabolicos" from his fraternal abductor, he escaped by a window in the best Pauline tradition, but was soon recaptured and locked up again under guard. This time it required all the diplomacy and influence of St. Ignatius to get him out. He was exceedingly angry and wrote letters to and about Luis, in which the sentiments of the Sermon on the Mount struggle rather unsuccessfully with the comminations of an injured Spanish hidalgo. Juan had plenty of spirit. For his greater security St. Ignatius brought him to Rome, and there, in 1547, made him secretary of the Society of Jesus.

Then for twenty-six years, during the lifetime of three successive generals, Polanco remained contentedly chained to his desk and the slave of his pen. St. Francis Borgia, who was addicted to nicknames, christened him "Pater Cobos," in allusion to a fabulously industrious secretary of Charles V. In his careful legible hand he drafted thousands of letters, often in duplicate or triplicate, to Jesuits and others in various parts of the world, kept six great ledgers always up to date, and in spare moments compiled a vast day-by-day history of his order down to 1556, which when published in our time ran to six volumes of nearly a thousand pages each.[1] As if that were not enough, he wrote nearly a dozen books on ascetical theology, in-

---

[1] This is the work called the *Chronicon Societatis Jesu,* issued in the *Monumenta Historica* series. It displays little art, but is scrupulously faithful to sources, as much when they tell against as for the Jesuits. The work was not meant for the general public. It is a private family history, packed with the homely details and sometimes even trivialities characteristic of this type of litera-

tended chiefly to help confessors and missioners. He was himself an indefatigable confessor and preacher during all the years of his secretaryship, and he did more than any other to keep the doors of the Roman College open by being its champion beggarman through the entire European postal system. Some of his brethren became irritated with his everlastingly outstretched hand, as did others, because to him fell the invidious task of passing on to the right address rebukes and admonitions from the Father General. But for those drawbacks and the rumour of his Jewish blood he would almost certainly have been elected general himself. Those who lived close to him and knew the truth had a different tale to tell. He was "affabilissimo," they said, "ever serene and imperturbable, and abounding in beautiful Spanish courtesy." We can judge this for ourselves by observing the real delicacy with which he conveys the General's admonitions to offenders, whether they be subjects or superiors. The aggrieved subject is advised of the difficulties of his superior and exhorted to remember the bargain that he made when he took his third vow; the superior is told to remember that his subject has feelings and begged to be sparing with his reprehensions. "For the love of Christ," writes Father Juan to the somewhat choleric rector of the college in Prague, "*show* to all the love for them which you really possess. . . Employ a little dexterity in your government, turning a blind eye to faults where you can, and bearing in mind that, if you must order penances, the manner in which this is done is often more resented than the penance itself." There are hundreds of such passages in the Secretary's dry official correspondence, revealing a genial sympathetic heart behind the handsome but somewhat austere façade of the bureaucrat.

---

ture. Polanco loved his Jesuits, and to one who loves nothing is trivial. His deep attachment to his order and his brethren comes out on almost every artless page. This was well known. Nadal, wishing to emphasize the devotion of the Infante of Portugal to the Jesuits, could think of no stronger way of putting it than to say, "Not even Master Polanco, in my opinion, has a greater love for the Society nor a keener desire for its increase" (M.H., *Epistolae Nadal,* i, 173). His promptitude in answering letters had also become proverbial. When St. Francis Borgia as general fell a little behindhand with his correspondence, he remarked ruefully: "They will say at once that it is obvious Father Polanco is not now in Rome" (M.H., *S. Franciscus Borgia,* iv, 508).

During his last days on earth, when he was racked with pain, St. Ignatius had committed the government of the order into the hands of Father Juan, since Nadal could not be recalled in time from Spain. Immediately after the Saint's funeral, Juan took counsel with the only other professed fathers within reach, Martin Olave, André des Freux, Nicholas Bobadilla and Ponce Cogordan. Cogordan, the procurator of the Society, was, so to say, only three-quarters professed, as he had been permitted at his own earnest entreaty to take the three ordinary vows in solemn form, but failed to attain to the honour of the fourth through defects of character and tended to regard himself as a martyr on that account. Owing to the turmoil in the city and the imminence of war, some quick decision as to government seemed imperative in view of the grave issues that would depend on the first general assembly of the order, such as the ratification of the constitutions. Polanco took the only course open to him. He put the matter to the vote of his *bijou* cabinet, who, having learned that Laynez was past the crisis of his illness, unanimously and joyously elected him vicar-general. Out of consideration for the invalid, whose antipathy to office or dignities was a byword among his brethren, they withheld the news from him for three days. When at length informed, he wept bitterly and protested that they had chosen a man not only morally unfitted but physically barely alive.[1] However, he submitted, and empowered Polanco to issue in his name the writ convoking the congregation, which was fixed provisionally to meet in Rome in November.

Meantime, Father Jerome Nadal, the vicar-general of St. Ignatius's own appointment, pursued his difficult, humiliating quest for alms in an impoverished Spain, which was beginning to suffer from the curse of Midas. The country, as their motherland, already num-

---

[1] In his first promotion of cardinals, Pope Paul IV definitely intended Laynez, already twice famous at Trent, to be among the number. Paul required him to live at the Vatican for a time in order to help with the reform of the Datary and other such business, but he secured permission to return to his brethren at Santa Maria della Strada each evening. In the matter of the cardinalate he showed such distress and worked so energetically to secure intercessors against the scheme that the Pope, who had a soft place in his heart for him, desisted. Four years earlier, when St. Ignatius appointed him the first provincial superior of the Jesuits in Italy, he urged a dozen objections, including the bouts of malaria from which he suffered all his life. But Ignatius remained firm.

bered three provinces of Jesuits, Aragon, Castile and Andalusia, each having its own superior and, with Portugal included, all four presided over by the genial authority of St. Francis Borgia. On a previous visit to Spain to promulgate the constitutions, Nadal had himself enjoyed plenary jurisdiction, but this time he came only in an advisory capacity, his power as vicar having been suspended out of regard for St. Francis, the former duke and viceroy. Francis and his provincials, all very sensitive on the point of their authority, interpreted this to mean that Nadal became subject to them while on Spanish soil, but Father Jerome held the proof in his pocket, in the shape of a letter of Ignatius, that such was not the case. He might have flourished the letter on many an occasion and so saved himself from snubs and contradictions, only that he was not that sort of person. Francis, the ruler born, did not entirely cease to be a grandee while he progressed towards heroic sanctity, and in his conduct as Jesuit "commissary-general" for Spain and Portugal there are occasional flashes of the portly nobleman who once used to chase bandits through the Catalan mountains on foot and hang them when he caught them.[1] The vocation of this great-grandson of Pope Alexander VI and King Ferdinand the Catholic to the rawest and least distinguished of religious orders, which stirred aristocratic Europe as few things had done since the conversion of St. Paulinus of Nola in the sixth century, was due very largely to the burning eloquence and austere life of Father Antonio Araoz, a nephew of St. Ignatius and the first Jesuit to appear as such in Spain. Afterwards, if anyone could have made Francis abandon his vocation, it was this same Antonio, become provincial of Castile and the bane of the Saint's existence. He and the equally cantankerous Francisco Estrada, provincial of Aragon, had become illustrious as preachers, and both suffered from the touchiness which is supposed to be the peculiar infirmity of illustrious preachers. They were excellent men within their somewhat narrow range, prayerful and zealous, but devoid of any sense of humour or proportion, hard on themselves and hard on everybody else. They were also among the

---

[1] "You can guess what a business it has been for my paunch!" he wrote after one of those expeditions to his friend Cobos, the secretary of Charles V (M.H., S. Franciscus Borgia, ii, 391).

very few Jesuits who betrayed symptoms of what would now be
called nationalism and tended to despise or cold-shoulder the non-
Spanish breeds of mankind.   One of Araoz's grievances against
Borgia was the twelve thousand ducats which in two years he had
collected and transmitted across the sea for the upkeep of the Roman College.   The good man also felt his native Castilian caution
outraged by the precipitancy with which Borgia planted Jesuit
foundations all over Spain, twenty of them in a bare seven years.
Borgia, on the other hand, though he inclined to be too peremptory
and too much of a dictator, belonged to the family of lovable saints,
the smiling debonair ones who keep their austerities to themselves
and do not think a joke a mortal sin.

   All three men, however much at variance among themselves,
combined in a sort of united front against the unfortunate Nadal.
They resented and refused his advice, snubbed him, ordered him
about, and generally made him feel somewhat like a worm that had
blundered into a private altercation of blackbirds.   But Jerome
Nadal was no worm.   During his first visit to Spain he had tried
to help the moody Estrada, who hated being provincial, by appointing him an assistant to do the work whenever he felt disposed to
retire into contemplation.   At first Francisco liked this arrangement,
which anyhow was of his own choosing, but afterwards he began to
consider it an injustice.   The fact is that he hardly knew what he
wanted, except possibly a tall pillar in a desert on which to climb
away from this bad world altogether.   He and others in Spain
were intent on turning the Society of Jesus into a purely contemplative order and had so far succeeded that two hours' meditation
daily, apart from other prayers, was already the custom in that
country, as against one hour or less everywhere else.   Those men
of sincerely holy aspirations smouldered with opposition to Nadal
who had the mind of St. Ignatius in this as in all other matters, and
was the determined foe of their plan, though himself by inclination
far more of a Mary than a Martha.   Jerome kept a diary, his
Ephemerides, in which he jotted down in a sort of shorthand Latin
the heads of his doings, sufferings and offendings.   The little book,
one of the most candid and self-depreciatory ever written, is simply
a prolonged examination of conscience, with such entries as that he
craved for the possession of a good horse or haggled over the price

of a partridge.[1] The following passage shows that saints are human and that very good and prayerful men often have uncertain tempers:

"Father Araoz does not get on very well with Father Francis. He has lost heart for government because Father Francis takes practically everything into his own hands. Francis summoned him to Simancas, and there, with Father Barma and myself present, severely reprimanded him about many things. . . He gave me a rub, too, for my importunity in visiting him, but I pretended not to notice, as I knew that I was not his subject. On one occasion, when we were in a little library together, I told him that it was the wish of our Father that he should not afflict himself with flagellations and penances, whereupon he retorted heatedly, 'Between you, you will drive me into retiring to the Carthusians.' With Father Antonio I had a warm dispute as to the time allowed by the constitutions for prayer. I found that they had as good as abolished the arrangements made by me on my first visitation. Father Ignatius had told me to help Father Francis and to join forces with him for the transaction of more important business, but when I saw that he did not like my interfering in his government, I kept my distance. I also stopped admonishing him, after two or three unsuccessful experiments which he took badly. . . While here I perceived that Estrada was incensed with me. He gave me a hostile reception, but when he started to upbraid me about that assistant I had provided for him I retorted so sharply that he has left me alone ever since. Father Barma made his profession here, on which occasion Araoz preached and Father Francis invited the principal religious of all orders in the town to dinner.[2] In the midst of the proceedings he suddenly bade me go into the pulpit and tell the diners something in Latin about the Society's institute. It was no difficulty for me to speak unprepared, but I resented his compelling me to do so by an order and without notice. However, the business succeeded well enough." [3]

[1] It is published in the *Monumenta Historica* series, *Epistolae P. Hieronymi Nadal,* ii (Madrid 1899), 1–97.

[2] He also invited the Princess Regent, Prince Carlos, and the Papal nuncio. The affair was not an ordinary dinner but a banquet, and it formed the subject of one of Nadal's unsuccessful admonitions. St. Francis's idea was to impress on his distinguished guests the importance of last vows in the Society of Jesus.

[3] M.H., *Epistolae P. Nadal,* ii, 42–3.

The first intimation of the death of St. Ignatius to reach Spain came in a letter from Flanders, which said nothing about the appointment of Laynez as vicar-general. Nadal at the time had just recovered from one of his frequent bouts of illness. On hearing the news he recorded his sorrow in the Diary, and then continued: "I thought that I was vicar and so did the other fathers here, the three provincials and the commissary. On their advice I wrote to the Portuguese fathers, telling them to prepare for the journey to Rome. Father Francis said that he could not go, as the doctors were against it, and Araoz and Bustamante had the same story, only Estrada showing any inclination to set out. A few days later we received notice from Father Polanco that Laynez had been made vicar. This news did not ruffle me."

Meantime, in Italy, Alva and his forces had approached almost to the walls of Rome, leaving in their track beautiful little towns ruined and depopulated. The Pope, defiant as ever, set about preparing his city for siege and required that the Jesuits and other religious should help with the fortifications. Bands of them were to be seen daily marching to work with picks and shovels on their shoulders, at their head Father Alfonso Salmeron, one of the five remaining Jesuit patriarchs, who had distinguished himself at Trent and was but recently returned from a grimly uncomfortable Papal mission to semi-heretical Poland.[1] Tivoli and Ostia had both fallen

---

[1] Salmeron was inured to hardship by earlier dangerous Papal missions to Scotland, Ireland and Germany, but this one to Poland beat anything in his wide experience of suffering and frustration. He made the journey from Augsburg to Warsaw and Vilna as companion and adviser to the Papal nuncio, Luigi Lippomani, Bishop of Verona. From Warsaw, on 10 October 1555, he wrote as follows to St. Ignatius: "Since our arrival in Poland we have been provided for and accommodated as nicely as I think I was in Ireland. A man who has once passed through this Kingdom has done his Purgatory in my opinion, satisfied for all his sins and gained a plenary indulgence. There is no wine, and beer is difficult to procure. But water is plentiful, and we would prefer it to the Polish beer even if it tasted like the Tiber. As for beds, I will say no more than that an armful of straw on which to lie on the ground without any covering is a luxury not easily acquired. . . I am very sure that by the time we shall have left this country we shall be seasoned to bear any labour and to carry anything sent to us of the cross of Christ our Saviour." The winter journey homewards from Vilna to Vienna nearly deprived Alfonso of his toes through frostbite. He said that his whole body felt "like a book that had been pulped" (M.H., *Salmeronis Epistolae*, i, 130–1, 135).

by 19 November, cutting off Rome to the east and to the west, and leaving the Pope dependent for his safety on a band of Lutheran mercenaries hired by Carlo Carafa to defend the Holy See against the only genuinely Catholic monarch remaining in the world. The irony of history could go no further than that. Carafa appealed for a truce, not from honourable motives of which he was incapable, but to give his French allies time to arrive at the scene of operations, and King Philip obliged the reluctant Alva to concede it. It was set for forty days, during which time optimistic Jesuits from many parts made their painful way to Rome to attend the congregation, postponed until the spring of 1557. But the Spanish fathers, naturally enough in the circumstances, felt no desire for the Seven Hills, to the disappointment and annoyance of Nadal, as he explains in his Diary:

"Seeing that the fathers were disinclined to go, I asked them what they thought about myself setting off. They held a consultation and informed me through Bustamante that in their opinion I ought not to leave but to stay in the province of Aragon until such time as the congregation had assembled. This wish of theirs was not to my liking, and I began to entertain all sorts of suspicions that they were not being open and honest in dealing with the question. It afterwards occurred to me that already they were nursing hopes of the election being held away from Rome, a scheme which the following year they worked strenuously to bring about. I therefore spoke my mind plainly to them and roundly condemned their idea, without at all trying to conceal my disgust with it. I told them that I wished to go that very day, and go I did. Father Francis and the others were angry with me for my outspokenness, but so far from that making me more subdued, I let Father Francis know, as he went on urging his point, that I revered, not the duke he had been, but the Jesuit he now was."

The good Jerome was a little less than fair to St. Francis on that occasion. Without any ties himself except to the Church and his Jesuits, he could not appreciate the difficulties of one who had long been a valued friend and counsellor of "the worst man born for a thousand years." A short time after Nadal's outburst Francis was invited to the famous hermitage at Yuste in the Estremadura mountains to receive the sad Emperor's intimate confidences and be shown all his latest inventions and acquisitions in clocks. Charles told him of his hopes and misgivings about the future of Spain and Europe, but especially his hope that he might himself find at last the peace which had so persistently eluded him when he was ruler of half the world. "My prayer," wrote Borgia to Laynez, "is that God may grant His peace to one whom I love and have always loved." [1]

St. Francis was invited to remote and inaccessible Yuste twice the following year, made one of the two trustees of the Emperor's will, and sent by him on a delicate secret mission to the court of Portugal. He had no liking for such high responsibilities, which in Portugal nearly cost him his life, but undertook them out of his wholehearted devotion to the man whom Pope Paul so wholeheartedly detested. Paul, for all that, was an admirer of Francis, and had he appeared in Rome would undoubtedly have wanted to give him a cardinal's hat. That, in the eyes of Jesuits, was a very good reason for his staying away, even had there been no paralysing gout or tertian ague to act as deterrents. If he could not go to Rome himself Francis did try very hard to shepherd thither his unwilling provincials. They also alleged illnesses, but it is to be feared that they were of the kind called strategic, and the Saint in the end found himself compelled to suggest to Laynez the rather dangerous alternative of holding the congregation in Spain at Barcelona, or in France at some southern and neutral town such as Perpignan, Narbonne or Avignon. When a little later Laynez cautiously sounded the Pope on this project, his Holiness asked with some sarcasm: "Why do you want to go to Spain? Is it to join the heresy and schism of King Philip?" Early in the new year, 1557, the ambiguous truce between Pope and King collapsed owing to French intervention, and then Philip solved any remaining scruples of the Spanish provincials by proclaiming Rome a forbidden city for all his subjects under pain of high treason.

Once more the congregation was postponed and the eleven fathers who had succeeded in reaching Rome from France, Germany and other distant parts again took the long road home. Nadal remained, to be the prop and stay of his supplanter, Laynez, in the

---

[1] M.H., *S. Franciscus Borgia*, iii, 272. The intimacy between Francis and Charles led to an extravagant rumour in Italy that the Emperor had become a Jesuit (Polanco, *Chronicon*, vi, 193).

crisis that soon supervened. An early writer on Jesuit affairs, the very honest and open-minded Italian, Francis Sacchini, avowed that he could not understand by what right Nadal had been deprived of his authority as vicar-general, and Laynez, as his letters show, was himself troubled with some misgivings as to the legality of the proceedings. Commenting on the election, Sacchini says: "Anybody viewing simultaneously the happenings in Rome and in Spain would doubtless have expected sedition and civil war among the fathers." [1] It came to that later, but with Nadal fighting like a Trojan in defence of the authority of Laynez. Typical of him, too, was his change of front on the question of holding the congregation in Spain. From being its doughtiest opponent, he became its most ardent champion when he perceived that he had misjudged the point of view of Borgia. No wonder that Borgia loved him, in spite of his free tongue.

When next Laynez, with his heart in his mouth, approached the Pope about going to Spain, he found to his delight a great change come over his Holiness. The Duke of Guise and his Frenchmen had disappointed Paul. For three weeks now they had been blazing away with their big guns at the little Neapolitan border town of Civitella, and failed to reduce it. The women of the place played as gallant a part in its defence as the men, knowing very well the fate that awaited them if the dissolute, war-maddened Gascons broke in. Heavy rains half drowned the invaders, until Guise, who was no angel, exclaimed in exasperation that God must have turned Spaniard. Seeing his chance, Alva moved up to Pescara, whereupon the frustrated French leader decided to cut his losses and retire to Ascoli. He blamed the Pope for his misfortunes and the Pope was not slow to return the compliment with interest. For once in a way the old man's optimism abandoned him. He became a chastened Paul, ready even to listen without an explosion to the plea of the bewildered Jesuits. He received Laynez with the greatest cordiality and intimated to him that he had in mind to use the offices of the Spanish fathers, particularly Borgia, in bringing about an understanding with King Philip, who plainly could not be thrown out of Italy. As for holding the congregation away from Rome,

[1] *Historia Societatis Jesu*, pars ii (Antwerp 1620), lib. i, n. 26.

he would pray about the matter and give the vicar an answer after he too had again pondered it and commended it to God.[1]

At this point, June 1557, when their sky seemed blue, there suddenly broke on the heads of the Jesuits a most fearful storm, conjured by one of the first companions of St. Ignatius and the most fractious of his children, that Nicholas Bobadilla who is pictured to the life in the following lines written by him to Ignatius from the court of Charles V at Ratisbon: "It is the unanimous opinion of this Court that if all members of our Society were Bobadillas, then indeed would it be a fortunate Society. They rank me above everybody else in the order, and of some I could mention have a very poor opinion. Of course I am aware that men may be deceived in this matter, but nevertheless I thank Christ *quod sine querela conversor ita ut modestia mea* y talento *notum sit hominibus.*" The Spanish talent is an amusing addition to St. Paul, whose epistles are much quoted in the letter to justify its writer's persistent infringements of rule. Father Nicholas was perfectly serious in believing himself to be a paragon of Jesuits, and it exasperated him to find that his beloved brethren did not share his conviction. He ends the letter by asking Ignatius to pray that he may patiently support his labours in Germany, "which are other than those of your garden and kitchen in Rome."[2] He was ill at Tivoli at the time of Laynez's election as vicar-general but sent a message that he desired his vote to be cast for the man of Polanco's choice. Laynez was that man, yet Bobadilla contested his authority almost from the first moment, on the ground that, until the constitutions had been ratified, the government of the order belonged by right and equity to all five "founder-fathers," as he liked to call them, who still remained of St. Ignatius's original band. An able and indefatigable propagandist, Father Nicholas won some converts to his views, in which there was just enough reasonableness to make them plausible. But he never could resist over-playing his hand, and when he began openly to criticize both the constitutions and the Saint who wrote them, he soon found that he had only one dour ally left, the Frenchman Ponce Cogordan, still brooding over his unattainable

[1] M.H., *Epistolae P. Nadal,* ii, 14.
[2] M.H., *Bobadillae Monumenta,* 102.

fourth vow and planning how to clip the wings of his Spanish brethren. Like Bobadilla, who was a demon for work, Cogordan possessed very valuable qualities and did his order great service in France at a later period, but during the autumn of 1557 he came within an ace of wrecking it altogether.

The conspiratorial pair wielded a good deal of influence, for Bobadilla had the ear of the Pope, whom he resembled in character, and Cogordan basked in the favour of numerous cardinals. Through the intermediary of two of these, Père Ponce conveyed to the Holy Father a secret memorial in which he alleged that Laynez and his abettors, meaning Polanco and Nadal, were seeking to have the congregation transferred to Spain for no other reason than to be more independent of his Holiness's control. The Pope, who by nature was an intensely suspicious and credulous man, smouldered with indignation, and kept Laynez cooling his heels for hours, when, ignorant of the manœuvre, he returned to the Vatican for the promised answer to his petition. At length, the perplexed and anxious Vicar begged some passing cardinals to remind the Holy Father of his existence. They were quickly back to say that the Pope commanded him to deliver at once for examination the constitutions and other title-deeds of the order, and to submit a list of all Jesuits then present in Rome, none of whom was to leave the city without express permission from his Holiness.[1]

Not to be outdone, Bobadilla also favoured the Pope with a memorial, which was in the following terms: "Every best and perfect gift is from above. Almighty God has not permitted our Society to go to Spain for its general congregation as the devil eagerly desired and plotted that it should, in order to destroy it. For the Holy Spirit inspired your Holiness to prohibit this move and to command that the congregation be held in Rome, the seat of the Apostolic See. The bull establishing our Society laid down that the constitutions were to be made by the first ten founders, but, in spite of this, Master Ignatius alone had any say in their composition, for he was an uncontrolled father and master, and did whatever he liked.[2] The constitutions which he made, with their accompanying

[1] M.H., *Epistolae P. Nadal,* ii, 14.

[2] This is a complete misrepresentation. In the first place, Ignatius was expressly commissioned by the other fathers, including Bobadilla, to draw up the

declarationes, are a labyrinth of utter confusion, so much so that neither subjects nor superiors can understand them, much less observe them. They are full of difficulties, irrelevancies, and things contrary to the regulations observed by Holy Church. The Society has so many Apostolic bulls conferring favours, privileges and exemptions — exemptions even from the jurisdiction of ordinaries — that they have made the name of Jesuit odious, as in Spain to the late archbishop of Toledo of happy memory,[1] and in France to the bishop of Paris. Indeed, the Faculty of Theology of Paris has issued a defamatory decree against the Society, and also against the Apostolic See for granting those bulls. . . After the death of Master Ignatius, two or three persons, wishing to imitate and ape him in everything, have brought the Society into bad odour throughout Rome. . . From those three men all our domestic troubles have proceeded, for they want everything done or thought by Master Ignatius to be regarded as inspired by the Holy Ghost. No doubt Ignatius was a wise man, but still a man, and, as your Holiness knows, wedded to his own ideas. Let us take what was good in them, and not obstinately defend the bad, so that ultimately error may not prevail over truth. Such is my hope in Christ and in your Holiness, whom may Christ happily preserve. Amen." [2]

The cause of the Pope's sudden anger with them soon became known to Laynez and his brethren, and resulted in a certain amount of resentment against Cogordan and Bobadilla. One indignant soul even muttered the name "Judas," but this was not because the pair

---

constitutions. In the second place, he called those fathers into consultation at every stage of his work, and revised it repeatedly in accordance with their judgment. In the third place, he submitted the completed constitutions to the experience of the entire order, and did not permit them to become binding in his lifetime, nor until they had been examined and approved by a general congregation, though the Jesuits at large accepted them as their rule of life immediately. Bobadilla knew all this very well, and he knew also the travail of soul through which Ignatius had passed while engaged on the work, so that a single word sometimes cost him days of prayers and tears and penances.

[1] Cardinal Juan Martinez Guijarro, Latinized Siliceo, who regarded the Jesuits as heretics, and endeavoured to have the Spiritual Exercises of St. Ignatius condemned by the Inquisition. One of his grievances against the fathers was their unwillingness to subscribe to his rabid anti-semitism.

[2] M.H., *Epistolae P. Nadal,* iv, 732–4.

had gone to the Holy Father above the heads of superiors, which is the right of every Catholic. It was because they had maligned St. Ignatius and misrepresented the motives of Laynez. Nothing was done to Bobadilla, but for his share in the plot Cogordan received a microscopic penance, which his confederate magnified, when reporting it to the Pope, into rigorous persecution and treatment worthy of one guilty of some enormous crime. He went on to advise the Holy Father how to frustrate the machinations of Laynez, Polanco and Nadal. The Jesuit constitutions and other charters ought to be submitted to diligent examination by four cardinals belonging to old monastic orders and then revised by a board of canonists which Nicholas thoughtfully nominates. His Holiness should stringently command all professed fathers of the Society, except the sick and foreign missionaries, to come to Rome, and it would be well also to summon thither the Faculty of Theology of Paris. Even the title of the Pope's hoped-for decree overhauling all Jesuit affairs is suggested to him: "Reformatio omnium bullarum apostolicarum Societatis Jesu per Paulum Quartum Pontificem Maximum."

Knowing the Holy Father's autocratic temper, easy gullibility, and small affection for their order, the Roman Jesuits were sorely anxious lest this storm should portend disaster to St. Ignatius's enterprise. Certainly there was menace in the words of Paul to Laynez: "Trust not in your bulls, for what one Pope has done another Pope can undo." So, like the Israelites of old, the men concerned "cried to the Lord with great earnestness and they humbled their souls in fastings, and the priests put on haircloths and cried to the Lord, the God of Israel, with one accord, that their children might not be made a prey." [1] Bobadilla expressed distaste for those proceedings

---

[1] Judith iv. 7–9. Bobadilla cited 3 Kings xii to the Pope as an argument against Laynez and his advisers. There it is told how Roboam, the son of Solomon, came to grief and caused a rebellion by rejecting the counsel of the elders to speak gently to the people and following that of the young men of his court who recommended him to say to the restive tribes: "My little finger is thicker than the back of my father. And now my father put a heavy yoke upon you, but I will add to your yoke. My father beat you with whips, but I will beat you with scorpions." The parallel is not as neat as Nicholas obviously thought, because Nadal, the principal adviser of the Jesuit Roboam, was two years older than Bobadilla and a great counsellor of gentleness. Nadal always found it difficult to speak harshly of anybody. The Cardinal of Toledo who,

as savouring of contempt of court. Heaven, he felt, might have
been left out of it, but Nadal, for his part, was perfectly willing to
meet him on lower ground.

Nadal is the hero of the whole sad story. In a series of vivacious
ripostes he tore to shreds Bobadilla's pretensions to be a founder
of the Society of Jesus, and made hay of his claim to a voice in its
government. He calls him "Bo" for short, which seems a happy
abbreviation, and addresses him in the following style: "Before I
come to your case with justice and charity, to use your favourite
phrase, will you answer me this, Father Bo — Why in everything
that you write, as well as in all the many sermons, letters and handbills preached and published on behalf of your aristocratic, or rather
monarchical, cause, is the whole tone so secular and profane? Leaving aside other things so full of the spirit of the world and the contentions of worldly men that not a spark of religion seems to remain, I confine myself to your main point, your claim *ex justitia* to
be superior. Were such a way of thinking permitted to creep in
among religious, Father Bo, the whole institution of monasticism
would perish in a day. In true monasticism, Father, there is no
wrangling after your fashion for dignities, but rather does each
one strive by humility, and knowledge and contempt of self, to show
that he is so unfitted, so evil and worthless a man, that he could not
in justice, nor even in equity or common prudence, be made superior. . . But you will protest that we misjudge you, that justice
and charity are your only motives, that you rely on the authority
of the Papal bulls and from them draw your arguments. Well,
then, Father Bobadilla, let us see whether we do you any wrong.
In the first place, the bulls do not give the original companions of
Father Ignatius jurisdiction over the Society, as I shall make abun-
dantly clear before I finish, but even if such was the case they would
not and could not give *you* any jurisdiction, . . . a man so seditious
and restless that alone among us you backed and approved Cogordan
when he delated our peaceful and youthful Society to a Pope who,

---

judging by his actions, would seemingly have liked to skin Jesuits alive, is for
him *hic bonus archiepiscopus,* and even for Melchior Cano, the enemy of enemies, he has only the kindliest epitaph, believing him to have been so determined a Jesuit baiter *ex zelo religionis et pietatis.* He said many Masses for
him in life and after death, as was indeed the right and Christian thing to do.

as both you and he openly testified, was bent, if possible, on its destruction. . . But all this is to go for nothing. Regardless of the common law and of the authority of our bulls, you proclaim throughout the City by means of advocates and lawyers that in justice you ought to be superior, even though there is not a man amongst us who wants you, or who does not deny and repudiate your pretension. . . And you cry out, God save the mark, that we overwhelm you with words! Oh no, Bobadilla, it is not our words but your own deeds that overwhelm you, your — but I refrain lest what I might truly say in my zeal for Father Ignatius and our Society should be interpreted too darkly by those who do not know you. You see, Bobadilla, that I treat you with the freedom which a superior uses towards a subject, for, you know, you *were* my subject these three years agone. You remember my election as vicar or commissary of the whole Society? Why, none other than your very self presided at it by order of Father Ignatius, who thereby, as you will not have forgotten, constituted me his second in command. . . If Father Laynez is not now vicar by right as you contend, then I am, and I have a patent signed by Father Ignatius to prove it." [1]

[1] M.H., *Epistolae P. Nadal,* iv, 131-3. The conclusion of the document is missing, and the last sentence above has been taken from Nadal's "Ephemerides" (*Epistolae,* ii, 59). He is a peculiarly difficult writer to translate owing to his disregard of grammar and his indulgence in etceteras. But of course he never anticipated that anybody would want to translate him. A different interpretation of the facts of this case, more favourable to Bobadilla and Cogordan, has been suggested to the author by a Jesuit friend, and he most gladly appends it in this place: "Bobadilla and Cogordan appear to have been blamed, and the latter penanced, for having appealed to the Holy See against Laynez and his party. That the penance was a trifling one does not touch the question of principle; and the fact that Paul IV was 'bent on the destruction of the Society,' as Nadal puts it, is also irrelevant. The subject has always the right to appeal to the supreme tribunal, and his manner of making such appeal is not subject to correction by lower superiors — least of all when they themselves are the respondents in the case. The constitutional position was really very difficult, and allowance should be made for Bobadilla on this ground. His criticism that the constitutions were a 'labyrinth' sounds like a *cri du cœur*. Very many things remained to be cleared up, the question of the legitimate vicar being one of them. There were several possible claimants, (1) Nadal, whose appointment by St. Ignatius some years before his death had never been rescinded, except perhaps orally by (2) Ignatius's nomination of Polanco on his death-bed. Polanco then convoked

As the Pope's war with Spain went from bad to worse so did Paul inversely show himself less hostile to the Jesuits. On the anniversary day of King Philip's ultimatum, 27 August 1557, the Spaniards, with English assistance, captured the key fortress of St. Quentin in northern France, thereby compelling the Duke of Guise to retreat hastily from Italy for the defence of Paris. That spelt doom to the last hopes of his Holiness, who had willy-nilly to sue for peace and make the best of an impossible situation. To King Philip's undying credit as a Catholic he rendered the procedure as painless as was in his power, which caused the indignant Alva to exclaim that the terms might have been "dictated by the vanquished rather than by the victor." It is satisfying to know that the haughty Duke was required to kiss the Pope's toe and publicly ask pardon for having borne arms against the Holy See. Rome went mad with joy, all except the Jesuits whose domestic struggle still showed no signs of abating. In September Laynez humbly begged the Pope to appoint a cardinal to adjudicate between himself and Bobadilla. The Pope not only agreed, but even invited the Vicar to name his preference, which of course that sensible man declined to do. The Holy Father then appointed Cardinal Ghislieri, the austere and high-minded Dominican who afterwards became known to history as Pope St. Pius V. All the Jesuits except Bobadilla and Cogordan were delighted. Summoned before the Cardinal, Nicholas again expressed his dissatisfaction with the constitutions, his sympathy with the confessor and martyr Cogordan, and his desire to be given his rights as one of those who founded the Society of Jesus. "The government of the Society, *sede vacante,*" he told his judge, who heard him out in silence, "ought to devolve on those founder-fathers, though he would be content for the sake of peace and charity that Master Diego Laynez should retain the office of vicar *ex benevolentia,* provided that, until the election of a general, he acted in conjunction with the other founder-fathers,

---

a congregation which elected (3) Laynez. If Polanco was indeed vicar-general, then he had no right to make a tacit abdication by proceeding to the election of another vicar. If he was not vicar, then Nadal's authority was perhaps still in possession and his acquiescence in Laynez's election would have been illegitimate." That is excellently argued, but it does not meet the point that Bobadilla did not want a vicar at all but government by a cabinet of equals.

and accepted the decision of a majority among them. If others, not founders of the Society, were required for consultation, they could be called in, and so everything would be done with justice and charity, unto the edification of the Society." [1]

Cardinal Ghislieri's counsels to Bobadilla are not known, but they seem to have been effective, for he showed a disposition immediately after the interview to abandon his campaign and retire from Rome. No doubt, Nadal's good controversy also had something to do with the change. One of Nicholas's friends, Cardinal Guido Sforza, who appears to have believed in spiritual homoeopathy, invited him to undertake the reform of some Silvestrine monasteries in the district of Perugia. Nicholas was nothing loath. As he could not reform the Jesuits, those monks would do instead. Seven weeks later Laynez received the following letter from him: "Very Reverend Father in Christ, *Gratia et pax Xti Domini sit semper nobiscum. Amen.* I did not write to your Reverence sooner because I was going about on my visitation. With the grace of Christ I hope to hold a chapter-general this week, and shall then begin the reform of the monks. This is certainly an enterprise requiring the favour of God, so I beg your Reverence to assist me with your prayers to Him and all His saints. . . Will you order Master Polanco to write me a large bulletin telling me how the Society fares, and also get him to send me on my satchel at once. It is at Signor Romulo's house and I have urgent need of it for my sermons and lectures in Foligno. . . I am sick, as usual. Good-bye. I shall let you know

---

[1] Document in Astrain, *Historia de la Compañía de Jesús en la Asistencia de España,* ii (Madrid 1905), 611-12. Nadal spoke for all normal Jesuits then and since when he replied as follows to Bobadilla's pretensions: "We acknowledge no other founder than Father Ignatius. It is true that he had nine companions who with him petitioned the Apostolic See to confirm the Society and establish it as a new religious order, but these nine he had won from life in the world by means of his Spiritual Exercises, and from him they had imbibed the spirit of religion, of which he gave them example and proof in his own conduct before he called them. It was under his leading and inspiration that the nine governed the Society before it was confirmed, while after that event he became entitled by the Church's law to the obedience of all. We have therefore always known only one father and founder of the Society" (M.H., *Epistolae P. Nadal,* iv, 134-5).

how I am getting on from time to time. At the service of your Reverend Paternity, Bobadilla." [1]

One or two of the fathers continued to dislike and distrust the jaunty Nicholas who so easily put the past behind him and forgot to express any regret for its misdemeanours. They wished that he might be severely punished by the forthcoming congregation "per esempio perpetuo della Compagnia," or in French, "pour encourager les autres." It is pleasant to record, as Nadal does, that their commination completely failed of effect, for when the time came not a word of censure was breathed on either of the culprits. As for the oppression and persecution of Cogordan which so wrung Nicholas's heart, we have the following contemporary account of its savagery: "At his examination before Cardinal Ghislieri, Ponce announced that he had four charges to make against those fathers, the first being, quoth he, that Father Vicar imposed a penance on me for having, without his knowledge, sent that memorial to his Holiness the Pope. . . What penance did he impose upon you? interpolated the Cardinal. That I should say one Hail Mary, replied Ponce; whereupon the usually gentle Cardinal became angry and would not listen to another word from him, but sent him packing in disgust." [2] After that rebuff Ponce, to the joy of his brethren, retired to Assisi, where he achieved excellent results as a missioner. Later, in his own country, he was to have his finest hour in combat with that same Faculty of Theology of Paris for whose views on the Jesuits Bobadilla had shown so much tenderness. And so the domestic storm died away. Pope Paul lifted his ban on departures from Rome and even sent the fathers a hundred ducats to help them on any journeys which they felt disposed to make. He also returned the constitutions and other title-deeds of the order without comment or criticism of any kind, though Nadal relates that one of those appointed to examine them, Cardinal Capodiferro, did not seem to like the abandonment of choir duties by St. Ignatius. Therein lay the omen of another storm.

The much-postponed congregation had been finally fixed for June 1558, when it was hoped that the Spanish fathers might have

[1] M.H., *Bobadillae Monumenta*, 185–6.
[2] M.H., *Epistolae P. Nadal*, ii, 57–8.

recovered from their various illnesses.   As the time approached, however, it became evident that none of them was likely to appear,
though St. Francis Borgia again did his best to set them in motion
and they made a great bustle booking passages on ships or plotting
routes by land.   Indeed, less than half the professed fathers in the
order managed to reach Rome, some being overseas and others
detained by the hazards of the Church in northern Europe.   Of the
twenty men who formed the congregation ten were Spaniards, among
them, innocent as any lamb, Nicholas Bobadilla.   When this time
Laynez went to the Pope for a blessing on their work he had a
kindly reception, but was somewhat disconcerted to hear the good
old man suddenly burst into a panegyric of St. Mary Magdalen
whom, said he, angels used to visit and levitate at the canonical hours
of Matins, Lauds, Prime, and so on.   "He always had that matter
of choir in his head," explains Nadal, which is not surprising, for
the Jesuits' discarding of it was a tremendous innovation.

On 28 June, after a week of preliminary discussions and investigations, the fathers began a solemn four days of prayer and penance
to obtain God's blessing on their election, which was fixed for 2
July, and conducted very much in the manner of a Papal conclave.
In the low and narrow room consecrated by the labours and death
of St. Ignatius, Father Peter Canisius, provincial of the Jesuits of
upper Germany, himself to-day a saint and doctor of the Church,
made a brief exhortation to his brethren gathered round Cardinal Pacheco, the representative of the Pope.   Then followed another hour
of prayer, after which the ballot took place in the Cardinal's presence.   Laynez received thirteen votes at the first scrutiny, Nadal
four, and three other fathers, including the absent Borgia, one
apiece.   Father Paschase Broet as the longest-professed in the gathering then formally declared Laynez elected general in the name of the
whole order, whereupon the others proceeded to do him homage,
and that finished, all with thankful hearts recited the *Te Deum.*

After the election, three days were given up to decorous festivi-
ties for which the Pope lent the Church of the Rotunda.   Thither
eight cardinals and a host of other dignitaries flocked to enjoy the
rare spectacle of a sacred play, and to hear young eloquence trying
its wings in the stratosphere of Cicero, Demosthenes and the Hebrew
Prophets.   The staid fathers of the congregation took an elder-

brother pride in those feats of their nurselings, many of whom before they died would have to wrestle with the swarming ideographs
of Japanese or with the fearful sounds and symbols of Indian tribes
on the Orinoco. On 6 July the Congregation was received in audience by the Holy Father, who in a speech of extraordinary warmth,
congratulated them on the election, promised their "beata Societas"
his continuing favour, and exhorted them to bear the cross manfully,
for "unto labour, contumely, persecution, and even death were they
called for the name of Jesus and the exaltation of His Church." He
confirmed all the graces, indults, and privileges granted to them by
previous Popes, and then dismissed them with other affectionate
words and manifold blessings.[1] It seemed to the fathers as though
summer had come in their fortunes — but it was as brief as an Indian summer.

Much reassured and comforted, they next settled down to the
grave task of giving the sanction of law to the constitutions, which
was achieved without making more than minor verbal alterations
in St. Ignatius's text. By a special decree or self-denying ordinance
the fathers removed it from their own or any future congregation's
power to change or even discuss the substantial features of their
founder's great work. It was this brave and filial decision of
twenty obscure men which gave the Society of Jesus stability to
weather the storms of centuries and even energy to rise from the
dead. The constitutions had foreshadowed the creation of a sort of
cabinet or curia to aid the general in the work of government, and
this was now provided by the division of the order into four "assist-
ancies" or administrative areas, Italian, Spanish, Portuguese, and
Northern, for each of which a representative was elected. Nadal
became the Northern assistant, charged with the business of his
brethren in France, Flanders and Germany. He had already
travelled much in Germany and left his apostolic heart there, as the
following letter, written to Ignatius three weeks before that Saint
died, touchingly shows: "God gives me no greater consolation than
to see the Society increase in Germany, nor greater sorrow than to
hear of its trials and dangers in that land. May He grant that
your Paternity be not troubled because I have a few times confided
to you my longing for Germany. It is a longing utterly dependent

---

[1] M.H., *Lainii Monumenta*, viii, 665–9.

on the divine will and on the desire of your Paternity. Blessed be God, I feel as detached as ever, with much sweetness. Since I entered the Society I have never cherished a private inclination, that is to say, I have not willingly opened the door to any bias towards one thing rather than another. Only in this matter of Germany do I seem unable to achieve indifference, though I know that if your Paternity pointed me to something else, I would find complete contentment in it. I speak to you, Father, as I would to God whose I am and whose I always will be by His grace, whether in life or death, in Germany or in any other place or ministry. Well I know that there are two things I could ambition in the Society, the missions of China and Germany, and Germany would always come first, though I see that it is mere pride to think of it as my destination, or that I could be of any use to the country if sent there." [1] The good Father was to have his fill of Germany before he died, and to render the stricken Catholic Church of the Empire inestimable services.

Towards the end of August 1558, when the Jesuits gathered in Rome had begun to grow anxious about their work in other places and were feeling, as Nadal says, "a vehement desire to bring the congregation to a close," they received sudden orders from the Vatican to deliberate whether it would not be well for them to fall into line with traditional monasticism by the adoption of choir and the restriction of their general's term of office to three years. Great was the surprise and consternation of the twenty men who had been expressly assured by Cardinal Pacheco on the day of the election that the Pope preferred the general's office to be for life, and by the Holy Father himself a few days later that he approved their institute and confirmed it unreservedly. Of Paul the judicious Pastor remarks that "as a true son of Naples he was very susceptible to sudden impressions, hasty and changeable in his decisions." Also, as a true son of Vesuvius he had a volcanic temper which erupted on the slightest sign of contradiction. The Jesuits knew this only too well, so the action which they took was not altogether wanting in courage. After earnest prayer, they dutifully discussed the two changes proposed and voted unanimously that they could not in conscience adopt them except at the explicit order of his Holiness. This conclusion they set forth with much respect and many careful

[1] M.H., *Epistolae P. Nadal,* i, 341.

circumlocutions in an official document signed by all save Laynez, whose own cause was in question. It ended with the following sentence: "We are the sons of obedience and absolutely ready to carry out whatsoever your Holiness shall command."

Now the Pope had taken his name of Paul out of regard for the memory of Paul III, to whom he owed his cardinalate and other favours. Not wishing, then, to abrogate officially any privileges or immunities approved by his revered predecessor who had established the Society of Jesus, he hoped to obtain from the fathers a voluntary surrender of the rights that irked him. For the Jesuits, on the other hand, it was a case of to be or not to be, since to turn them into choir monks and require triennial elections would destroy their flexibility and mobility, and render impossible the special type of service to the Church which they were founded to provide. One can sympathize with both parties, with the Pope who loved the old ways and was born in the wrong century, and with the Jesuits, who felt in their very bones the appeal and the claim of a new epoch. Their unwillingness to be abolished *qua* Jesuits exasperated the Pope, who remembered his encounters with St. Ignatius in the flesh, and was not now going to be thwarted by the shadow of Ignatius. On 6 September Laynez was summoned to the Vatican. The Holy Father began in a low voice, as though muttering to himself. The rule of St. Ignatius, he said, had been a tyranny. It would be better if the general's term of office were for three years, after which he might be re-elected for another three. It would rest with the Holy See to confirm the re-election or to appoint a new superior. Then the question of choir came up, at which point Vesuvius completely erupted. Paul stormed at the unfortunate General and his companion in misery, Father Salmeron, who knelt before him, saying that they were rebels and helpers of the heretics by their attitude towards choir. He feared lest one day some devil might emerge from the Jesuit ranks. Choir was of the essence of the religious life, and divinely ordained according to the words of the Psalmist, *septies in die laudem dixi tibi.* He was determined that they should adopt it, and would no longer tolerate so great an evil as its omission. If they did not fall in with his wishes they would all be accounted heretics. And let them not imagine themselves excused on the score of their studies, "accursed studies for the sake of which the divine office is neglected." When at length the Pope calmed down and bade Laynez speak, that dazed man contented himself with saying that so far from wanting his office to be prolonged for life, he would be very happy to be relieved of it altogether by his Holiness then and there. As for the choir, how could he and his brethren fairly be accounted rebels until they had been given an order against which to rebel? [1]

Two days after that threatening audience the Pope's youthful nephew, Cardinal Alfonso Carafa, delivered the order by word of mouth, whereupon Laynez instructed his men to do all in their power to carry it out. He expressed doubt as to what sort of *grandes maestros* they would prove at the psalmody, and cautioned them against trying to emulate the beautiful *Canto figurato* of the Benedictines, as was the temptation of some aspiring rectors. Their congregations were not too pleased with the effect, but as Polanco remarked drily, "the important thing was to please the Pope." When the constitutions were printed for the first time that same year, 1558,[2] his Holiness ordered the insertion of a slip at the end bearing

---

[1] M.H., *Lainii Monumenta,* viii, 673–5. It need hardly be said that the Jesuits did not neglect the divine office. They said it privately, each priest for himself, as had been fully sanctioned by Pope Paul III and Pope Julius III. Moreover, the non-priests were accustomed to recite the Little Office of the Blessed Virgin on all Saturdays, Sundays and feast days, the Office of the Dead every Monday, and other offices the remaining days of the week.

[2] A printing-press had already been set up at the Roman College. The idea of it came from St. Ignatius, who wished to provide poor students with classical texts at the lowest possible price and all students with texts purged of lines offensive to decency. He hoped at first that he might obtain as a gift a press in the possession of Duke Cosimo dei Medici, with whom Laynez was very friendly. That failing, the Saint instructed his men at Venice and other places to be on the watch for a set of type at a reasonable price. Alas, when it was acquired, just two months before he died, it disappointed him, the letters being too small (M.H., *Monumenta Ignatiana,* series 1a, xi, 321). Finally, in the autumn of 1556, Laynez, then vicar-general, acquired a press in Rome, and had it installed at the Roman College. The first fruits of this first of a multitude of Jesuit printing-presses was a set of academic theses. The first *book* to come from the new press seems to have been the *Epigrams of Martial,* expurgated by Father André des Freux and edited by Father Edmund Auger in 1558. At the same time, the Jesuit *Constitutions* were printed. After that date, books of all kinds began to appear. In 1564, Pope Pius IV presented the Roman College with a set of Arabic type, whereupon Father Gian Battista Eliano, a Jesuit con-

a record written by the fathers themselves of his instructions concerning choir and the office of general. Everywhere in Europe the new choir duties seriously hampered the work of Jesuit preachers, teachers, missioners and confessors, to which in most cases they were bound by agreements with bishops or other dignitaries. However, they did their best and kept cheerful, remembering the Pope's great age. When the old man came to die in his unlucky month of August, 1559, he summoned Laynez and said to him in a voice so different from that of the last interview: "O Father Laynez, how sadly did flesh and blood deceive me, precipitating me into the misfortunes of a war from which so much sin has resulted in the Church of God! From the time of St. Peter there has not been a pontificate more unhappy than the one now closing. I am truly sorry for all that has happened. Pray for me, because I love your Society with all my heart. . . You see that coffer. In it I have accumulated funds for the endowment of the Roman College. . ." [1] After the Pope's death, on 18 August, Laynez consulted five eminent canonists about the choir obligation, who declared to a man that a spoken order did not and could not abrogate written bulls and briefs promulgated in full legal form. Such an order lapsed with the death of him who had issued it, and ought not to be any longer obeyed if the Jesuits wished to avoid possible complications arising out of custom and tacit consent. Thus fortified, the General made a protestation before a public notary, and at the same time issued instructions to the various provinces that the singing of office in choir was to cease.[2]

---

verted from Judaism, who will recur in these pages, translated the canons and decrees of the Council of Trent into Arabic. This version was printed at the Roman College in 1566 and widely disseminated among the Christians of the Near East. The college printed also an Arabic version of the New Testament, as well as a grammar and dictionary of the language to help students to learn it more easily, "for the glory of God and the salvation of souls" (M.H., *Polanci Complementa*, i, 560). In 1577 the press acquired a set of Hebrew characters.

[1] Manare, *De Rebus Societatis Jesu Commentarius* (Florence 1886), 125–6. Father Oliver Manare was a Flemish Jesuit living in Rome at the time of Paul IV's death. Though not a particularly exact or critical writer, Father Oliver had good opportunities for knowing what occurred between the dying Pope and Laynez. However, the Roman College was not endowed.

[2] M.H., *Lainii Monumenta*, viii, 676–80.

CHAPTER II

THE TRAVAIL OF FRANCE

WHILE the fathers in Rome were struggling to preserve their constitutions, the few pioneers of the order in Paris were fighting a hard battle with the bishop of that city for the bare right to exist. This however was only a preliminary skirmish, leading soon to the age-long conflict with the University of Paris, which might be described as the Hundred Years' War of the Jesuits. It must be admitted that they were innocent in history to have gone to the capital of monk-shy France hopeful of a welcome. Did they know nothing of the reception accorded to the Dominicans and Franciscans there three hundred years earlier? "They were treated as 'blacklegs' are treated in a great strike. It was dangerous for a friar to be seen abroad: it was not only the clerks they had to fear, but a section, at all events, of the lay mob was equally hostile. No sooner was a friar caught sight of than he was surrounded by the human swarms that poured forth from every house and hostel in the narrow street. . . Filthy rushes and straw off the floors of those unsavoury dwellings were poured upon the cowled heads from above; mud, stones, sometimes blows, greeted them from below. Arrows had even been shot against the convent, which had henceforth to be guarded night and day by royal troops. Bulls commanding the readmission of the Mendicants and denouncing every possible penalty upon transgressors now follow one another in bewildering profusion. From the way in which these bulls succeed one another it is evident that, entrusted as they were to secular prelates who secretly sympathized with the university, they must have been very tardily and partially executed, and such execution as they obtained must have been attended with very partial success." [1] It was under those circumstances that St. Thomas

---

[1] Rashdall, *The Universities of Europe in the Middle Ages*, i (1895), 386–7 (new ed., 389–90). The account is based on a report of the Dominican Master-General from Denifle's *Chartularium*, of which Rashdall writes: "When every allowance is made for the exuberance of medieval rhetoric and the tendency of a

Aquinas took his degree and endeavoured to begin lecturing. Though the privileges of both the University and the religious orders derived from the same source, the Apostolic See, the secular Masters of Paris were determined to bring the newcomers under their own authority and wielded sufficient power of boycott and passive resistance to attain their object in spite of suspension, excommunication, deprivation, and every other weapon available to Rome. One grave result of the struggle was the growth of anti-Papal feeling in the University, which developed during the Conciliar Age into full-blown Gallicanism.

In the sixteenth century the worst possible way for a man to recommend himself to Paris was to come armed with a Papal brief or bull. Yet that is precisely what the Jesuits did. They thought that the world was their oyster, to be opened at once with that magical piece of parchment, and they soon discovered that the world of Paris at least was not an oyster at all, which is an inoffensive creature, but a hornets' nest. It is very dangerous indeed to be without a sense of history. To anyone with the slightest knowledge of academic life in sixteenth-century Paris it must seem strange at first sight that the Jesuits, who were not altogether devoid of worldly wisdom, should have been so eager to avail themselves of its advantages. *Non sum qualis eram boni sub regno Thomae!* The University, once the chief glory of Christendom and treasure-house of its culture, had degenerated under the impact of many disasters, including the Black Death, into a mere logic-chopping institution, and very bad logic at that. The Jesuits knew this as well as anybody. Very many of them had been through the dusty mill, including St. Ignatius and his first nine companions, and if some of them, notably Laynez and Salmeron, became genuinely learned men, it was not Paris that made them such but their own hard reading. Why then did St. Ignatius conceive what was little short of a cult for Paris? Why did he persist in thinking of it as the ideal place of studies for the brighter spirits among his young men? At that time the really live universities were to be found in his own Spain, at Salamanca

---

friar, with the evangelical blessing of the persecuted ever in his ears, to make the most of his own or his brethren's sufferings, there can be no doubt that the friars whose lot it was to beg their bread from door to door in the Quartier Latin during the winter of 1255–6 must have had a decidedly hard time."

and Alcalá, where a trio of Dominican geniuses, Vitoria, Cano and Soto, had resuscitated the long-buried glories of scholasticism. Ignatius knew this too, for he had once elbowed his way into the thronged and buzzing lecture-halls of both places. It was in fact the throngs and anarchical syllabuses of Spain which caused his preference for Paris, where if the masters had little to teach they at least taught it to manageable groups and according to an orderly graduated system. The system of Paris, the division of the students into classes of ascending difficulty, the well-devised *horarium,* these were the great attractions. Given them, the Jesuits, being young and sanguine, felt equal to supplying flesh and blood for the shapely skeleton out of their own resources.

And so they came, the first small band of hopefuls as early as the spring of 1540, some months before the official establishment of the Society of Jesus by Pope Paul III. They joined the undistinguished Collège du Trésorier, which however was well sited for theological students, being about midway between the famous Dominican Convent of St. Jacques, where St. Thomas used to teach, and its great medieval rival, La Sorbonne. From time to time St. Ignatius reinforced them with fresh contingents until they outgrew their cramped quarters and migrated to the more commodious Collège des Lombards. Among their number in those early days were our friends, Ponce Cogordan, Antonio Araoz, Francis Estrada and Pedro Ribadeneira. Pedro, aged fifteen when he set out, tells how the journey was made from Rome: "They all travelled on foot, dressed in whatever clothes they could find, as the Society had then no common habit. But their various outfits had this in common that they were all very poor and threadbare. They lived on alms and lodged at public hospices when such places would give them shelter. Only if they could find neither hospice nor alms were they free to use the small sum of money which they carried with them for such emergencies. . . They were very happy together even in the midst of great trials, because they felt it a privilege to suffer something for the love of God. Father Ignatius had given express orders that the weakest member of the company was to walk in front and set the pace each day for the others. . ." In Paris they were not molested, for they kept their secret to themselves and took care not to be seen too much together.

But the inevitable happened. In July 1542 there began another of those dreary interminable wars between France and the Empire, as usual over Europe's then favourite apple of discord, the Duchy of Milan. At once the French King issued an edict ordering all Spaniards and Flemings to quit his realm within eight days on pain of death. Father Domenech, the Spanish superior of the Paris Jesuits, and nine of his young countrymen, including the boy Ribadeneira, accordingly made post-haste for the Flemish frontier, well over a hundred miles away, and reached Arras more dead than alive, only to be turned away from every door. There was nothing for it then but to plod on, footsore, hungry, faint from want of sleep, over the almost equally long and hard road to Louvain. At any rate, there was a university at the end of the journey. Wars might lay waste the nations, but studies must continue, and the "Athens of Brabant" would be some compensation for the lost advantages of the City of Light on the Seine. From that little band of tattered, half-starved refugees sprang, after many a hard fight for recognition,[1] the sturdy Belgian province of the Jesuits, the province which produced three hundred years ago and maintains to this day the unique Society of the Bollandists. To have sponsored the *Acta Sanctorum* and carried on that gigantic work of learning over so long a period and in the teeth of so many obstacles is certainly one of the greatest things achieved by the Jesuits of any country.

The few French and Italian Jesuits left in Paris while the war between his Most Christian and his Most Catholic Majesty proceeded to the advantage of nobody except Dr. Martin Luther, attracted to their modest orbit for a brief period the most brilliant and most eccentric star of the Paris academic world. He was William Postel, professor of mathematics and Oriental languages at the ungodly Collège de France, which the godless Francis I had recently founded as a challenge to the dreaming University. From Pierre de la Ramée or Ramus, the virulent hater of Aristotle, to Alfred Loisy, the Modernist, this place was to prove a nursery of anti-Catholics, but Wil-

---

[1] The foundation of each college and mission in Belgium involved something in the nature of a small war between the Jesuits and the local communes. In 1578 they were driven out of their houses in Antwerp, Bruges, Douai, Maastricht, Tournai and Cambrai. But they returned, and to-day there are two Belgian provinces.

liam Postel did not belong to that tradition.   His trouble was Ham-
let's, too much speculation.   Marguerite de Valois called him the
"merveille du monde," and that, coming from so unbalanced a lady,
ought to have been a warning to the Jesuits.   They accepted him into
their noviceship in Rome, and there, worn out by long travels in the
East searching for ancient manuscripts, he began to have grandiose
visions, one being of a universal monarchy for the rightful heir of
the ages, the King of France, lineal descendant of Japhet, son of
Noah.   He found no sympathy for his dreams among the puzzled
fathers, who were mostly Spaniards anyhow, so he retired disappointed, but remained on the friendliest terms with them to the day
of his death.

The Peace of Crespy, signed in September 1544, caused a lull in the
hostilities of sufficient duration to enable Paul III to open at last
the much-postponed Council of Trent.   Among the half-dozen
French prelates who came to the Council in its first stages was the
Bishop of Clermont, Guillaume du Prat, a good man of illustrious
ancestry seriously concerned about the religious state of his native
Auvergne.   He was also, like Postel, much concerned for the glory
of France.   What a human affair, as well as divine, was the Council
of Trent!   This admirable bishop, one of the most devout and
zealous of his generation, held up business at the very first meeting
with a demand that his sovereign, the promoter of Lutheranism in
Germany and the ally of the Turks, be mentioned by name in the
decree ordering prayers for the Emperor and all Christian princes.
Shortly afterwards he caused what the diarist of the Council, Massarelli, describes as "un gran disturbo" when he found that the letters
destined for the Emperor and the King of the Romans were going
to be read to the Fathers before the one addressed to the King of
France.   He and his two countrymen, the Archbishop of Aix and
the Bishop of Agde, maintained with heat that the King of France
was the first and worthiest prince in Christendom, whereas the King
of the Romans was a mere shadow-monarch, without an acre to his
high-sounding name.   The Cardinal of Trent, host of the Council,
and a strong imperialist, repudiated the contention scornfully in a
long speech illustrated with provocative examples.   That night the
three unhappy Papal legates who presided over the Council stayed

up until 2 A.M., "trying to find some way of calming this great storm." [1]

But good Monseigneur du Prat's nationalism was a small thing compared with his love of the Church. He had long been an ardent advocate of reform, and at Trent his was the voice most often raised in condemnation of pluralism and absenteeism on the part of bishops and others charged with the care of souls. The French Church lay sick unto death of such evils, which gave those sombre undertakers, the Calvinists, good hopes of soon arranging for her funeral. Often at his residence, the Château de Beauregard, Bishop du Prat would hold anxious conferences long into the night with a saintly friar of the Minims, Simon Guichard, as to ways and means of halting the progress of heresy in Auvergne. One step which he contemplated taking was to revive at the town of Billom in his diocese its ancient but long-moribund academy of higher studies. To ensure a supply of professors for the project, he determined, with the Pope's permission, to turn a property of his diocese at Paris, the Hôtel de Clermont, into a hostel for students from Auvergne. But where in that tough, bucolic province, a surviving patch of Caesar's Gaul, was he to find his students? While he puzzled over this problem, Friar Simon, in reminiscent mood, kindled his interest with a story of some priests he had known in Rome who lived together in a tumbledown house close to the convent of the Minims. They were all graduates of Paris, he said, and full of zeal for whatever sacred cause might need them. They would make very good professors.

Then at Trent, on an auspicious morning, the Bishop fell in with one of those very priests, his first Jesuit, Father Claude Le Jay, from Savoy, who was acting as proxy in the Council for the main prop of the Catholic resistance in Germany, lordly, spendthrift, lovable Cardinal Otto Truchsess, Bishop of Augsburg. The type of man Le Jay was may be guessed from the conclusion of the letter in which he tells St. Ignatius of his meeting with Monseigneur du Prat: "I humbly desire to be remembered to our Reverend Father in Christ, Misser Pietro Codacio. Though I have not written to him separately that does not mean that he is not written in the middle of my heart. Every day of my life I pray God to preserve him and to keep him

---

[1] Merkle, *Concilii Tridentini Diariorum*, pars prima (Freiburg 1911), 398.

always written in the book of His elect." [1]   The Emperor's brother
and successor, Ferdinand, King of the Romans, thought so well of
this friendly genial priest that he exerted all his great influence with
the Holy See to have him promoted to the bishopric of Trieste, and
only desisted when he saw how miserable the prospect of such an
honour made him.   Trieste was a small comfortable diocese, a
gentleman's post, and Claude had long since given his heart to a
larger flock, the humble folk, sick or sinful, of every land.   The
King's agent in the affair was Bishop Weber, of Laibach, a most
persistent and eloquent prelate who gave Le Jay no peace at Trent
for several months.   But the Father found a staunch ally in Leonora,
wife of Juan de Vega, the Emperor's ambassador to the Holy See,
who had seen him at work among the numerous beggars and
vagrants visiting the Council.   "The day that Monsignor of Laibach
arrived here," Claude told St. Ignatius, "he was nearly drowned in
the Adriatic Sea, and the following day he tried to drown me in the
sea of episcopal grandeur.   Praise be to God that we both escaped
the tempest.   It gives me special pleasure to owe my escape to the
good Lady Leonora, who much prefers to see me at the hospital than
as a bishop."   To Monseigneur du Prat's eager questions about his
order, he replied by showing him printed copies of letters recently
received from St. Francis Xavier and others in India and beyond,
electrifying letters which shortly before had caused Jerome Nadal to
bang the table in his Majorcan hermitage and decide to investigate
these Jesuits.   He also put in the Bishop's hands a copy of Pope
Paul's bull establishing the Society of Jesus and setting forth its aims
— "the propagation of the faith by means of public sermons, retreats,
works of charity, in particular the instruction of children and un-
lettered adults in Christian Doctrine, and the provision of spiritual
comfort to souls by the hearing of confessions."   It was the simplest
programme and contained not a word about professors or colleges,
except in the sense of mere hostels at universities where young Jesuits
might live while studying for their degrees.

As is clear from the Pope's bull, the Jesuits, according to the first
intention of their founder, were meant to be primarily roving
mission-priests, with no greater educational ambitions than to preach
a good sermon and to teach the catechism.   But circumstances proved

[1] M.H., *Epistolae Paschasii Broeti, Claudii Jaii,* etc., 309.

too strong for St. Ignatius. The first concession was wrung from him by his best-beloved son, St. Francis Xavier, who petitioned that some of his men be allowed to take classes in the College of Holy Faith at Goa, founded for Hindu students by a Portuguese secular priest, but unprovided with a staff. Then the exiled Archbishop of Armagh, Robert Wauchope, speaking on behalf of the entire academic body, begged for the services of Father Le Jay as a lecturer at the University of Ingolstadt, and shortly afterwards the Duke of Bavaria sent his famous and shady chancellor, Leonhard von Eck, to Rome to secure for the same institution the great abilities of Father Salmeron and Father Peter Canisius. In Spain the Duke of Gandia wanted not merely a college properly so called, but an entire university under Jesuit supervision, while in Sicily the viceroy, Juan de Vega, one of the order's most generous friends, pleaded the educational needs of Messina and Palermo. Besieged on all sides, Ignatius slowly gave way, recognizing in the human voices an echo of the will of God.

At the time, early in 1546, when Monseigneur du Prat first met Le Jay, the evolution of the original college as hostel, catering exclusively for Jesuits, into the mixed college which accepted external students also, had already begun, but it was a slow process and did not blossom into the college devoted entirely to the education of secular youth until after the year 1550, when Pope Julius III, by a new bull removing certain restrictions on the recruitment of the order, made such a development possible. Having no youths of his own to barter with the Paris Jesuits, Bishop du Prat decided after some hesitation to risk his hopes for Auvergne in the hands of the fathers, and accordingly offered them the use of the Hôtel de Clermont without conditions, if also without ownership and without endowments. It was no great gift, but it had great consequences.

In their new home the young religious, their superior, a somewhat irascible Italian named Father Viola, and his assistant, a large-hearted Fleming, Father Everard Mercurian, who had recently joined the order and was destined to become its fourth general, all suffered from poverty so dire that at times they had to sell some of their scanty wardrobes to obtain a little food. They were totally dependent on alms, for St. Ignatius, who was himself in the same predicament, had nothing to send them except his prayers and pity.

To beg they were not ashamed, but a rule of the University forbade it. During one black month their total receipts amounted to three francs and ten sous. Now and again, when he remembered, Monseigneur du Prat might send them a small donation. Another bishop whom Father Viola timidly approached replied that they and regulars in general would be much better employed tilling the soil. But hunger was easier to bear than daily petty persecution. Hitherto, lost in the crowd and unknown to be religious, they had enjoyed the blessings of obscurity, but as a separate group, addicted to devotional practices not in the common tradition of undergraduate life, they quickly fell under suspicion. Then they were subjected to the same treatment that had enlivened the studies of the Angelic Doctor. They were traduced, preached against, maltreated in public, and threatened with flogging through the streets. But two religious families stood by them through thick and through thin, the Carthusians and the Benedictines. In 1551 yet another war between the usual parties reduced the little community to four by compelling the Spanish and Flemish members of it to migrate. To the forlorn quartette, the half of a broken hope, St. Ignatius, invincible optimist, sent his old companion, Father Paschase Broet, not merely as superior of the Hôtel de Clermont but as provincial of the non-existent province of France. It was the gesture of a soldier: "Mon centre cède, ma droite recule. . . J'attaque!"

Father Broet was a veteran of many difficult campaigns and had even been imprisoned as a spy, but the hardest of his life's tasks now lay before him, a contention with the Bishop, the Parlement, and the Theological Faculty of Paris, which lasted until his death ten years later. The Bishop, Eustache du Bellay, cousin of the famous Pléiade poet of that name and a true-blue Gallican, scenting a new religious order not of native growth in the Clerks of Clermont, hardened his heart against them from the first. It only made matters worse when Broet, who was no diplomatist, exhibited his bulls and other authentications. The Bishop refused to ordain any Jesuits and forbade those among them who were already priests to hear confessions, preach or exercise their ministry at all, on the ground that they had no legal right of existence in the country. "If you dare to mount a Paris pulpit," said one of his officials to the astonished Paschase, "you will bring upon your heads the wrath of all the doctors of theology and of the four orders of Mendicants." This was far from being an idle threat as a trial or two proved, so the defeated Broet turned to the Gentiles, to the inauguration of that college in rustic Auvergne, where happily the writ of Bishop and Theological Faculty did not run. But here the Barbary Pirates delayed operations by seizing Père Jean de la Goutte, one of the two professors assigned by St. Ignatius to start the college, and carrying him captive to Tunis. His brethren stormed Heaven and starved themselves to ransom him, but each time the Pirates advanced their price until the poor man was dead of his privations and sufferings. Many another Jesuit of those days shared his grim fate, for to sail on the Mediterranean, as they had constantly to do, was to take their lives in their hands.

Despite that tragedy and other setbacks, the College of Billom was triumphantly opened in July 1556, just five days before St. Ignatius died, with seven Jesuits, all Frenchmen, on its staff, five hundred pupils who received their education free on its roll, and an endowment from Monseigneur du Prat of twelve thousand *livres* a year in its books. It was the first Jesuit school in the full modern sense of the word, for its predecessor, opened by Nadal in Sicily in 1548, "in spite," as he feelingly expressed it, "of all the devils of Messina," was a mixed college with Jesuit as well as extern students. Billom consequently makes something of a landmark in the history of education. It enjoyed success from the first moment, and within a few years had increased its numbers to the astonishing figure of 1600. Owing to shortage of masters, the classes remained for some time fearsomely large, but the Jesuits overcame that defect to some extent by setting their more proficient scholars to practise what they had learned on beginners. It is an interesting footnote to history to know that the new order's new departure of teaching boys Latin, Greek, mathematics and their mother tongue met with frowns from many eminent brows besides those of such prejudiced parties as the Paris dons. In his *Life of St. Ignatius* Ribadeneira felt it necessary to devote a whole chapter to the defence of his brethren in this matter, and in a later book on the Jesuit institute, published at Madrid in 1605, returned to the charge, having listed the following objections: "The Society's opening of schools for boys is frowned upon in some quarters for four principal reasons. The first is that no other religious order does the like.[1] The second is that this occupation would appear to be repugnant to religious gravity. The third, that it is a most tedious, troublesome and anxious task to drive, teach and control a mob of boys, who by nature are giddy, restless, garrulous, lazy creatures, so that not even their parents can restrain them at home. The consequence is that our young men engaged in instructing them lead a very hard life, fritter away their strength, and lose their health. Nor is that all, for many of these men are gifted and might make great progress in learning were they not prevented by having to attend to childish trifles of no consequence. The fourth reason is that St. Gregory sharply rebuked Bishop Desiderius for teaching grammar to some pupils and explaining to them the effusions of the poets." Ribadeneira begins his refutation well back, with Origen, who kept a school at Alexandria in the third century, and works his way through the Fathers and ecclesiastical writers down to the Council of Trent. What was good enough for Clement of Alexandria and his disciple, Origen, for St. Jerome and St. John Chrysostom, is good enough for the Jesuits. The martyr, St. Cassian, kept a school,[2] and the monks of St. Basil and St. Benedict taught boys in their monasteries. So Father Pedro proceeds, steadily missing the point that all the schools to which he refers were either taught by non-order men, or open only to adults, or intended exclusively to prepare boys for the monastic life. The first objection must therefore be sustained. The Jesuits as an order were unquestionably innovators in the assumption of schoolmastering as a large and normal part of their ministry. Ribadeneira himself doubted whether any other work done by his order rendered greater service to God than the education of youth, and that is an opinion for which there is much to be said.

Leaving the other objections of which Pedro easily disposes — they can be easily disposed of by anybody with a grain of sense — let us return to Paris, where we left the Clerks of Clermont heading

[1] The Brethren of the Common Life had famous schools in the fifteenth century, but they were not a religious order and, in any case, did not themselves do the teaching.

[2] According to the legend, he was handed over by his judges to the tender mercies of his pupils, who stabbed him to death with their styluses.

for a collision with the Bishop and the Parlement.[1] It happened four years before St. Ignatius died. In 1550 Ignatius had secured for his sons in France the patronage of a very powerful, if youthful, churchman, Cardinal Charles de Guise, who had come to Rome that year for the conclave leading to the election of Pope Julius III. On his return to France the friendly magnificent Charles, who meantime had inherited his famous title of Cardinal of Lorraine, put in a good word for the Paris Jesuits with his quixotic master, Henry II, and obtained from his Majesty letters patent entitling them to own property and exercise other ordinary citizen rights. The letters ended with the new and sinister formula, "Car tel est nostre plaisir," which was to be recast a hundred years later in the more pithy shape of "L'état, c'est moi." But under Henry II the Parlement of Paris still had a mind of its own, and refused obstinately to register the King's ordinance, an attitude warmly supported by the Faculty of Theology which regarded the famous "liberties and immunities of the Gallican Church" as being at stake. To be Pope's men, as so unashamedly were the Jesuits, meant to Parlement and Faculty a subtle form of treason to France.

Father Broet, who was a straightforward simple soul, could not understand this at all. It is even possible that he knew nothing of the Pragmatic Sanction of Bourges or of the Concordat of 1516. Throughout the year 1553 he continued to write such bewildered letters as the following to St. Ignatius, and to trail his bulls round Paris: "I have been to present the King's new injunction and our bulls to Messieurs of the Parlement. Most of them, especially those of greatest influence, were exceedingly hostile. They told me that there were more than enough religious orders already without start-

[1] The French Parlements of the *ancien régime* were more in the nature of courts of justice than of legislative assemblies. There were thirteen of them and each claimed supreme jurisdiction within its own province. In the course of time they had come to be regarded as the custodians of the laws of the realm, and no new law or ordinance of the king might be effective until they had registered it. If they did not approve the new law or considered it incompatible with traditional rights they addressed *remonstrances* to the king. The Jesuits were to account for a large number of such wordy and irate things. The Paris Parlement tended to be anti-king, but the provincial ones, and especially that of Toulouse, which was composed mostly of lawyers, rather favoured absolutism.

ing new ones, and in any case it was contrary to the holy Councils.
. . . On the feast of the Purification I visited several advisers of
the Parlement at their private addresses, hoping to secure their
assistance with our affair. Some showed a certain readiness to
help, but others were so opposed that they said to me it was the devil
who had founded this Society of Jesus. . . One man told me in a
terrible temper that we were superstitious, proud, puffed-up, vain-
glorious people. I did not know what to answer him, he was in
such a rage, and nothing that I could have said would have made any
difference. . . Humanly speaking, with things as they are, we have
no prospect of obtaining our object, but I keep hoping that God our
Lord will fulfil the holy desires of His Society, if not now at some
future time of His good pleasure. The more contradiction I find
the more does my hope increase, but that will not prevent me from
continuing to prosecute the business by all and every promising
means which the Lord may inspire. Once more yesterday I spoke
to the first president, begging him for the love of God to expedite
our business, so that if sentence is given against us we may again
have recourse to the King by means of the Cardinal of Lorraine, who
has just arrived here and will be staying eight or ten days. I received a scolding for my pains, the president complaining that there
are already too many religious orders, and that if we wanted to be
religious, why couldn't we enter the Franciscans or the Carthusians
or some other recognized order. I answered that our institute is
quite different as to the way of living, whereupon he retorted very
angrily, 'What, do you people work miracles and think yourselves
superior to these others?' Then he said that he would expedite our
affair, but in a tone that I felt boded us no good. Will your Reverence please pray that God may bless our labours, because for a
month and a half now I have been doing nothing except running
around trying to get the matter settled. . ." [1]

The upshot of all poor Paschase's interviews was that the wily
Parlement, being sure of their men and anxious to avoid conflict
with the King who had issued a second injunction, remitted the
whole affair to the judgment of Bishop du Bellay and the Faculty
of Theology. Still undaunted, Broet made another attempt to open
the Bishop's eyes to the fact that the Jesuits had been approved by

[1] M.H., *Epistolae P. Paschasii Broeti*, 83–5.

both the Pope and the King. "The Pope," retorted Monseigneur, "has no power to approve an order in this country, but only in his own States. Neither has the King such power, the matter being spiritual. As for myself, I shall never permit you to become naturalized." Besides his ardent Gallicanism, Eustache du Bellay had a more personal reason for antipathy to the Jesuits as being the *protégés* of Lorraine, a man whom he detested. He kept Broet and his brethren on tenter-hooks for a year more before pronouncing his judgment, which appeared in eleven parts, each a condemnation of some aspect of the Society of Jesus. The good Bishop had a vein of irony in him like his cousin of the Pléiade, and finished his document with the following words: "If these new clerks desire the right to establish houses, let them go and build them on the rim of Christendom where they will find the Turks more accessible to their much-vaunted zeal than from Paris, the centre of Christendom." [1]

Then, on 1 December 1554, came the climax. After a Mass of the Holy Ghost the doctors of the Theological Faculty met in plenary session at the Sorbonne [2] and proceeded to pass a solemn sentence of canonical extermination on the Jesuits. The principal author of their decree was Père Jean Benoit, O.P., whose nephew, Jacques Forestier, had become a Jesuit, and a fine one, much against his distinguished uncle's will. The decree begins with a long protestation of the doctors' love and reverence for the Holy See. Their only desire as good Catholics is to save the Holy See from the consequences of its own imprudence in sanctioning "this new society which arrogates to itself the unheard-of title of the name of Jesus, and receives into its bosom without any attempt at selection all kinds of persons, however base their extraction or disreputable their previous record." The good doctors and their scribe, who had no first-hand knowledge whatever of the Jesuits, were indebted for that opening to the German Protestants. They continue: "This society, which has been endowed with so many and such various privileges, indults, and liberties, especially in the administration of the sacraments, and in the office of preaching, lecturing and teaching, to the prejudice of bishops, of other religious orders, and even of princes and temporal

---

[1] D'Argentré, *Collectio Judiciorum*, ii, 192.
[2] The Faculty of Theology was not yet identical with the Sorbonne, though most of its members belonged to that college.

authorities, as well as to the detriment of universities, and the great grievance of people in general, appears to us to violate the honour of monasticism. It impairs the devout and necessary practice of abstinence and mortification, gives occasion for apostasy from other religious orders, denies to bishops due obedience and subjection, and deprives both ecclesiastical and temporal dignitaries of their just rights, disturbing the spheres of both and being the cause of innumerable complaints, quarrels, contentions, hatreds, rebellions, and schisms among the people. Having diligently examined and pondered the matter, we consider this society to be in *negotio fidei periculosa, pacis Ecclesiae perturbativa, monasticae religionis eversiva, et magis in destructionem quam in aedificationem.*" [1]

Some of the fathers in Rome wanted to answer this public attack, but St. Ignatius would not allow it. The following speech put into his mouth by Ribadeneira may be of the Thucydidean kind but it certainly represents his sentiments. "We must remember, brothers," he said, "the parting words of our Lord to His disciples: My peace I leave with you, My peace I give unto you. Nothing is to be written or done that might occasion bitterness or bad feeling, or diminish the authority of the Faculty of Theology of Paris. Great though it is, that authority will not prevail over the truth, which may be oppressed and opposed but can never be overwhelmed. If need be, which God avert, we shall find a less dangerous remedy for this wound and a sweeter medicine to cure it." [2] The Saint in the event adopted two remedies, the first being of a private character. He instructed his provincials in various parts to solicit testimonials from a number of eminent men as to the work of the Jesuits in their midst. Among those who replied in the most eulogistic terms were the King of the Romans, the King of Portugal, the Viceroy of Sicily, the Dukes of Tuscany, Ferrara and Bavaria, the Universities of Ferrara, Valladolid, Coimbra, Louvain and Vienna, several archbishops and bishops, and four Dominican inquisitors, one of whom

---

[1] *Cartas de San Ignacio de Loyola*, v, 478-80. "Had the Jesuits been atheists or Turks it would hardly have been possible for bishop and theologians to have condemned them more roundly or more rudely" (Evennett, *The Cardinal of Lorraine and the Council of Trent*, Cambridge 1930, 59).

[2] Ribadeneira, *Vida de San Ignacio de Loyola* (1602), lib. iv, c. 11. Also in M.H., *Monumenta Ignatiana*, ser. 4a, i, 426.

threatened major excommunication against disseminators of the
Paris decree in his domain of Saragossa.[1]

The other measure taken by Ignatius was to appoint four of his
men for an amicable discussion with four Paris theologians, including the redactor of the decree, who came to Rome on a political
mission in 1555, and to permit Father Martin Olave, himself a former
doctor of the Sorbonne, to state the Jesuit case in writing for the
benefit of his old colleagues.   One point made by Olave in his very
temperate and courteous statement is that the title, Society of Jesus,
which used to offend many people and perhaps still offends a few,
was not meant to be a challenge to anybody except to the men who
bore it.   "The title," he continues, "is not so uncommon as sometimes
thought, for in Italy there are some congregations bearing it or its
equivalent, e.g., the Jesuati [2] and the Knights of Christ.   In the
kingdom of Aragon the Friars Minor are called *fratres Jesu*.   Besides,
is there any reason why this title should cause more heart-burning
than titles borne by religious orders named after the Blessed Trinity
or the Holy Ghost or the Blessed Virgin?   It ought surely to be
counted for humility and wisdom in the founder of the order that
he wished his own name forgotten and the name of Jesus assumed,
purely as a reminder to his sons not to let their eyes ever wander from
Him who is the way, the truth, and the life of all men." [3]

Meantime, in Paris, the Theologians' decree had been the signal

[1] These documents are to be found in the *Acta Sanctorum,* vol. vii of July,
513 *sqq.*

[2] Founded in the fourteenth century by Blessed John Columbini of Siena, a
surprising and fascinating man of God, whose feast, curiously, is on the same
day as that of St. Ignatius, 31 July.   The Jesuati did not thrive as did the Jesuitae
and were suppressed for lack of numbers just a hundred years before the others
suffered the same fate, for very different reasons.

[3] *Cartas de San Ignacio de Loyola,* v, 494–512.   The allegation, urged with
especial heat by Melchior Cano in his great book, *De locis theologicis,* that the
Jesuits had arrogated to themselves a name common to all Christians, as though
they alone were to be accounted companions of Jesus, was rather neatly turned
by Ribadeneira.   "By the same token," said he, referring to Cano's religious
family, "the sons of St. Dominic might be charged with arrogance for calling
themselves the Order of Preachers, as though that office belonged to them exclusively and nobody else had a right or the capacity to give a sermon."   Nadal had
used this same argument in 1553, replying to an attack on *The Spiritual Exercises* by a Dominican of Toledo (Polanco, *Chronicon,* iii, 527–39).

for renewed attacks on the unhappy Clerks of Clermont. They were denounced from various pulpits, held up to ridicule in the schools, and even lampooned on handbills affixed to the doors of churches. One great friend stood by them through all their troubles, the Prior of the famous Benedictine abbey of Saint-Germain-des-Prés, who, though threatened and persecuted himself, continued to allow them to hear confessions, preach and teach the catechism in a chapel of the monastery church. As Saint-Germain was an exempt abbey [1] he had a perfect right to do this, but it exasperated Eustache du Bellay, who saw the detested Clerks thus escaping his pestle. Father Broet explains the situation in a letter to St. Ignatius of 9 June 1555: "This is to tell your Reverence about the tribulations which the Lord is sending us through Monseigneur the Bishop of Paris and the doctors. . . Every day they become heavier. Having striven by their censure to destroy our Society altogether, at least in Paris, . . . the doctors went a second time to Saint-Germain to dissuade the Prior from allowing us to hear confessions and administer Holy Communion in the monastery church. He must know, they protested, that we had been condemned by the Faculty of Theology, and were reprobated by the Parlement and the Bishop. . . Unable to shake the Prior, they returned to the Bishop who cited me to appear before one of his officials on 27 May. I complied, and was strictly forbidden by this man to hold *conventicles,* as he called them,[2] or to administer the sacraments in any place whatsoever . . . under pain of immediate excommunication and of imprisonment. . . . Our friends have advised us to refrain from going to Saint-Germain while the storm lasts, as the Bishop, though without juridical right, is quite capable not only of excommunicating us but of posting his sentence all over the city, with scandal to the people. . . . If I thought that your Reverence would prefer us not to follow this advice, we would go to Saint-Germain and carry on as usual, prison or no prison. Indeed, we are not worthy of such an honour

[1] What is known in canon law as an *abbatia nullius* (*diœcesis*), that is, a miniature diocese under the jurisdiction of the abbot of a monastery, situated within the boundaries of another ordinary diocese. By entering the territory of such an abbey a priest or layman is understood to have left the territory of the surrounding diocese and thereby becomes released from the obligation of its laws.

[2] A term of opprobrium, applied by the Catholics to the meetings of the Calvinists.

in this cause. Pray for us, your unworthy sons, that we may have strength from God our Lord to bear with true patience all the adversities and contradictions which He sends us." [1]

Though often disheartened and full of forebodings about the future of France, Broet carried on the struggle alone for two years more.[2] Then, in 1558, on his way back from the general congregation, he was given a great lieutenant. "As we passed through Assisi," he reported to Laynez, "we dug out (*havemo cavato*) Father Ponce, to the vast discontent of the principal citizens." Ponce Cogordan had certainly made his mark in Assisi. "With his ardour," wrote one man, "he set the whole town on fire." To believe the mayor and other worthies who deluged Laynez with protests against his removal, religion in the town of St. Francis was doomed without Ponce or some of his brethren to support it, but they were angling for a Jesuit school and this cajolery constituted the bait. On their way north, through Modena, Broet and Cogordan called on the superior of the college in that city, Father David Wolfe, Ireland's first contribution to the Society of Jesus, who was to return to his afflicted country as Papal nuncio two years later. Broet took an interest in Ireland, where for a hectic month he had been nuncio himself, but the purpose of his visit was to borrow six crowns from Father David if he possessed so much money, which Father Paschase doubted. They were all desperately poor, and their letters are full of the problems attendant on long journeys with nothing to cover expenses.

But the poorest, the most straitened of any Jesuits were the men of the beleaguered fort of the Hôtel de Clermont. The coming of Ponce Cogordan there was as the arrival of a relieving army, for he was a man of inexhaustible energy and loved nothing better than an atmosphere of battle, the thunder of the captains and the shouting. Once dedicated to a task, he flung himself upon it with a cheerful disregard of sleep, rest, hunger, cold, or any other inconvenience.

---

[1] M.H., *Epistolae P. Paschasii Broeti,* 101–3.

[2] With legal assistance he drew up an appeal from the Bishop to the Pope, but was curtly notified by the episcopal chancery that it would be an infringement of law to send the document out of France. He then, poor harassed man, made several handwritten copies of Olave's apology and distributed them among the doctors. These had some effect but not sufficient to secure any public avowal of mistaken judgment. The dignity of the Sorbonne had to be considered.

As intermediary between Father Broet and the various participants in the Jesuits' struggle for existence, whether friends or foes, he hurried daily from one critical point of the field to another, from Paris to the travelling royal Court at Fontainebleau or Amboise or Orléans or Rheims; from the Court back to the Parlement, the Bishop's palace, and the Sorbonne. These incessant journeys were made on foot and alone in every kind of weather, through a France on the verge of civil war, to bring appeals to the King,[1] the King's commands to the Parlement, supplications to the Bishop, and explanations to the doctors of theology.

Ponce's perambulations might be called heroic were he not the last man alive to pose as or deem himself a hero. While he strove so valiantly with the theological and magisterial array, soon to be powerfully reinforced by the adhesion to the anti-Jesuit cause of the University at large, his brethren succeeded in finding a ministry compatible with the liberties and immunities of the Gallican church in the prisons and hospitals of Paris. Sometimes, too, a curé short of ideas for a sermon might even offer one of the censured fathers the honour of his pulpit. Life was diversified by such mild excitements as the arrival of Father Ribadeneira, all penniless and unshaven, from London, where he had witnessed without much comprehension the first enigmatic moves of Queen Elizabeth, or of other Jesuit birds of passage with tales of the great swaying battle being fought for the Catholic soul of the Netherlands, Germany, Austria and Poland, or of letters from India and Japan which filled the nine younger members of the community with longings for the wings of a dove or the decks of a caravel. For three years their champion Ponce toiled like a Sisyphus to obtain them legal recognition. Again and again, at great labour and some cost, for he had to pay various officials exorbitant fees, he secured *lettres de jussion* from the King to the Parlement couched in the most peremptory terms: *"Nous*

---

[1] Cogordan had three kings to deal with in quick succession: Henry II, who died as the result of an accident on 10 July 1559; Francis II, his son, who died at the age of sixteen on 5 December 1560; and Charles IX, brother of Francis, who came to the throne at the age of eleven. Both the boy-kings were ruled by their clever, well-meaning, unscrupulous Italian mother, Catherine de Medici, whose policy of appeasement during her regency for Charles was destined to drown France in blood and misery.

désirons singulièrement le dicte ordre et religion estre receu et approuvé. . . We order, command, and expressly enjoin by these presents that you proceed forthwith to publication, registration, and homologation of the said bulls, as though they had emanated from our Person. . . *Car tel est nostre plaisir."* [1]

Such, however, was not the pleasure of the Parlement which, entrenched behind a rampart of custom and privilege, knew that it could safely disregard those high-sounding missives from the Louvre. Part at least of the determination not to register the royal letters patent was due to political motives rather than to any particular distrust or dislike of the Jesuits, who as yet were too small fry to disturb august breasts with such emotions. With the Bishop and the doctors it was different. "The Bishop," wrote Cogordan to Laynez, "is like a viper in his hostility to us, and he cannot bear the sight of me personally." But he had to bear it, because no amount of snubs, delays or insults sufficed to keep Ponce at bay. Wave aside the new letter he brought from the King, and he would be back next day with one from Catherine de Medici. Show him the door with that and he would reappear on the morrow with one from the Duke of Guise, or, miracle of miracles how he secured it, with one from Chancellor de l'Hôpital himself, leader of the *politiques,* the party of peace at any price, who stood for everything that the Jesuits most reprobated. Among his acquisitions were testimonials from all the French cardinals except Odet Châtillon, the brother of Admiral Coligny, who shortly afterwards apostatized from the Catholic faith, married a wife, and went to England as ambassador of the Huguenots, where he died and was buried in Canterbury Cathedral. By such means as these the importunate Cogordan wore down the unfortunate Du Bellay. Eventually, for much the same reason as that given by the unjust judge in the Gospel of St. Luke, the Bishop pronounced in favour of recognizing the Jesuits on condition that they changed their name, surrendered all their Papal privileges, and put themselves unreservedly under the jurisdiction of himself and his successors. Even that small measure of tolerance, which looked more like an invitation to commit corporate suicide, was refused by the Parlement. In an *arrest* of 22 February 1561,

---

[1] M.H., *Epistolae P. Paschasii Broeti,* 235.

this body required the fathers, in true Gallican fashion, to obtain the approval of the forthcoming General Council before again applying to be admitted to citizenship.

While waiting on Providence in Paris the Jesuits had not been idle in other parts of the country. The news of the success of Billom and the effective preaching in rural districts to which sermons were a novelty of Fathers Broet, Claysson and Le Bas led to many petitions for colleges and missions. The appeal from Périgueux, which was not exceptional in its revelations, throws some light on the religious condition of provincial France at this critical period. "Would to God," it ran, "that Father Ignatius might be inspired to send hither some of his brethren. They would achieve more for the glory of God in these parts than in India itself. . . In matters of religion our people are more ignorant than many savage tribes. There is a forest near Bordeaux thirty leagues in depth whose denizens live like the beasts of the field. Persons of fifty years and more are to be found who have never heard Mass in their lives, nor learned a single syllable of the faith." [1] One of the places most endangered by the rapid spread of heresy was Pamiers, the capital of the County of Foix, whose suzerain, the formidable lady, Jeanne d'Albret, had recently become an enthusiastic convert to Calvinism. The Bishop of Pamiers, confirmed absentee though he was,[2] felt that something should be done to counteract Queen Jeanne's missionary zeal and accordingly invited in the Jesuits. But he was a niggardly person and did not so much as provide the fathers appointed to start the college with money for their journey. Pamiers proved to be a small Jesuit purgatory. The men were denied the use of the buildings intended for them by his missing Lordship, and while he instituted a long-distance and leisurely suit against the usurpers of his rights, they were obliged to take refuge from the biting Pyrenean winds in an abandoned hovel that had neither door nor windows. Some kind soul had given them a bed in which

---

[1] M.H., *Litterae Quadrimestres,* ii, 368. These letters were official reports addressed to the general every four months by local superiors in Europe.

[2] About forty of the French bishops resided permanently in Paris, leaving their dioceses to be governed or misgoverned by surrogates. Father Broet expressed a wish that they might all be excommunicated if they did not return to their flocks.

they slept by turns until a certain Master Arnold took sick and monopolized it altogether.

But somehow they managed to keep up their spirits, if we may judge by the cheerful letter which young Père Edmund Auger posted to Laynez. Edmund was used to hardships. As a boy he had walked from Troyes to Paris, from Paris to Lyons, and from Lyons to Rome, all at one stretch, in quest of an education. Ponce Cogordan found him penniless and forlorn in the Campo di Fiori, where he had set up a letter-writer's booth but attracted no customers. The practical Ponce took him home to the Jesuit professed house and put him to work in the kitchen. The novices deputed to help the cook noticed the very unusual scullion and spoke about his manners and wit with such enthusiasm that the story reached the ears of St. Ignatius, who promptly rescued Edmund and arranged for him to continue his studies. At the age of twenty he begged to be received into the Society of Jesus, which reckons him among the three or four best pulpit orators it ever produced. He first made a name for himself at the new college in Padua, where he was immensely happy inspiring an international team of young Spaniards, Germans, Poles, Italians, and Englishmen with his own enthusiasm for the literature of Greece and Rome. "All are striving to progress in the spirit and the letter," he informed Laynez. "They compose verses and orations, and they are as quiet as mice. It seems as if God were blessing us very specially, perhaps that we may suffer later on for His glory."

Edmund had prophesied when he wrote those words. He describes their abode in Pamiers as being "twenty times worse" than a notorious old shack which they had once occupied in Perugia. But some of the local clergy were good to them, sending them daily a pint of wine and occasionally even a square meal, which caused this optimist to describe his condition as having nothing and possessing all things. In common with many Jesuits of the time, he had cherished a secret hope of being sent on the foreign missions. Pamiers he discovered to be no bad alternative — "questo è una buona India." While waiting for something to be settled about their college, Auger and his genial superior, Père Jean Pelletier, devoted themselves to mission work in numerous towns and villages whose neglected Catholics were drifting towards Calvinism. Then, at the beginning of winter, 1559, they decided to start the college on their own account, and had the good fortune to find a house small and mean enough for the twenty-seven francs of rent which they could afford. After the other place, Auger deemed it a palace. We are not told how many pupils came, but only that they arrived with Calvin's Catechism in their satchels. This discovery inspired Auger to set to work on his Catholic Catechism, which afterwards became almost as widely diffused in France as that of St. Peter Canisius in Germany. He also wrote stage pieces for his boys, dramatic eclogues and dialogues that were regarded "as miracles in this last land of the Pyrenees." [1]

In spite of the most strenuous efforts of the universal provider, Ponce Cogordan, the fathers in Pamiers went hungrier every month, until Laynez in his pity for them was driven to issuing the Bishop an ultimatum. This, however, he had not the heart to carry into effect when the time-limit of three months expired, owing to the gravity of the situation in France, but the Huguenots solved the problem for him shortly afterwards by driving out his men and suppressing their college. Nearly seventy years were to pass before they had an opportunity to return. They seemed to take such setbacks, which were of common occurrence, as all in the day's business, and calmly moved their tents elsewhere. Pelletier and Auger went on crusade, one in Toulouse and the other in the dangerous town of Foix. An attempt was made to poison Père Jean, but Père Edmund was given a new shirt and suit of clothes by the predestinarians, whose liking for a good sermon prevailed over their antipathy to a Jesuit. At the same time, Père Louis du Coudret, a secular canon turned Jesuit, was carrying on a laborious, single-handed campaign against the embattled Calvinists of Savoy and Provence, and the Mantuan-born Antonio Possevino had begun, at twenty-seven, in the Maritime Alps, his extraordinary career of roving Papal ambassador, which

---

[1] M.H., *Lainii Monumenta,* iv, 527-33. Plays were adopted as a regular feature of Jesuit education from the beginning. The comedies and tragedies acted were not for mere amusement or diversion, but had a severely practical intent. The purposes of them, as one of the most prolific Jesuit dramatists, Father Luis da Cruz, expressed it, was "to promote the studies, to give authority and renown to the school, and to foster piety and good conduct among the scholars." For this last reason the subjects of the plays, their plots as we might say, were nearly always taken from Scripture, Church History, or the Lives of the Saints.

culminated at the court of Ivan the Terrible as peacemaker between Poland and Russia.

We are at the kaleidoscopic year of French history, 1560. The country was bankrupt,[1] hungry and full of restless, proselytizing Huguenots whom the Guise brothers, Duke and Cardinal, in power by virtue of their avuncular influence with the girl-queen, Mary of Scotland, wife of the new boy-king, Francis II, strove unavailingly to suppress. The Bourbon brothers, Anthony, King of Navarre, and Louis, Prince of Condé, heirs to the throne should the House of Valois fail, had both gone over to the heretics and watched with smouldering resentment the growing prestige of the semi-foreign intruders from Lorraine. Condé engineered a plot to seize the young King and the Guises during their stay at Amboise in March 1560, and to set up his rather unco-operative brother, Anthony, as regent. This famous Conspiracy or Tumult of Amboise miscarried, but it gave the Court a terrible fright and caused Catherine de Medici to turn from the Guises to other advisers, Admiral Coligny, a good man and Calvinist of honest conviction, and Michel de l'Hôpital, the *politique,* a nominal Catholic who had brought up his children as Protestants and probably believed in nothing much except keeping the peace. With L'Hôpital as Chancellor, the Huguenots found themselves much less embarrassed, and quickly shed the pacific mask which the cautious Calvin had at first instructed them to wear. Each fresh measure of toleration only made them the more belligerent, until the anxious appeasers, Catherine and Michel, felt that nothing but a national council of the Gallican Church would suffice to stop the drift towards civil war. Their plan had the support of the Cardinal of Lorraine, who was opposed to the resumption of the Council of Trent, and he optimistically undertook to secure for it the sanction of the new Pope, Pius IV. But the Pope, though a benevolent and conciliatory man, friendly to France, was much too experienced in the ways of the world and of worldly churchmen not to recoil in horror from such a proposal, especially as he was about to reassemble the still unfinished General Council. However, he agreed to Lorraine's petition that he should send the Dean of the

[1] So was Spain, and that was the real reason why Philip II and Henry II had to call off their Italian wars by the Peace of Cateau-Cambrésis the previous year. They could no longer pay for them.

Sacred College, Cardinal de Tournon, as legate to France, but with secret instructions not at all according to the mind of the petitioner.

The old Legate's journey up the Rhône Valley to his archiepiscopal see of Lyons was rendered sorrowful by the evidence on all sides of Calvinist infiltration and Calvinist aggressiveness. Even his own town of Tournon, on the banks of the Rhône near Valence, and the fine college which he had built there after his retirement from the post of Lieutenant-General of France had become infected with Genevan doctrines. That discovery decided him to offer the college to the Jesuits, with whom he had been on the friendliest terms ever since he had rescued Fathers Broet and Salmeron from prison in Lyons and given them the hospitality of his palace, on their return from Ireland in 1542. Two other eminences, Lorraine and Armagnac, wanted Jesuit colleges at this time, the first, who was a fearful pluralist with an income equivalent in modern money to about £30,000 a year, in his bishoprics of Metz and Verdun; the other at Toulouse and Rodez. All four places and a dozen besides were to be satisfied later when there were enough French Jesuits to go round, but at the moment Laynez felt that Tournon had the best claim on his scanty resources.[1] The college there opened under the new *régime,* in June 1560, with Père Auger at its head and an attendance of seven hundred pupils. Among the masters, teaching logic, was young Père Claude Matthieu, destined afterwards to equivocal fame as a chief fomenter and standard-bearer of La Sainte Ligue, while in the opposite camp would stand Père Auger, the first of that long line of uncrowned martyrs, the Jesuit confessors of the Kings of France.

The interpretation which has been imposed so successfully on the events of the past by Whig historians naturally inclines us to sympathize with the tolerant intentions of Queen Catherine, and to frown on the "reactionary" policy of the Jesuits, who deprecated the habit of truckling to the Huguenots as being about as useful as trying to placate a jungle tiger. But that is to read history through

---

[1] Père Pelletier twitted Laynez a little on the question of man-power: "Many of us wonder what becomes of all those fathers and brothers whom the Roman College, that great generator of men, produces. I believe that one day, like the Trojan Horse, it will launch them forth to overrun and conquer the wicked world. May our Lord Jesus Christ bring it to pass, soon, soon" (Letter of 10 May 1561).

very modern spectacles, in fact to invent history, and to imagine that we are being enlightened when we are only being myopic. The Jesuits knew more than we can ever know about the tiger. They had seen him loose in the churches of France, destroying and desecrating. They had felt his hot breath on their own faces, and they are scarcely to be blamed if they thought the best place for him was behind bars. It was not a Jesuit or a Catholic who wrote a short time ago that the consequence of Catherine de Medici's and L'Hôpital's sweet reasonableness was inevitably "to encourage the growth of the Huguenot movement, increase the bitterness of religious feeling everywhere, and make the religious problem graver than ever." [1] It led directly, in March 1562, to the so-called Massacre of Vassy, which was "the Sarajevo of the Civil Wars." The mere fact that these wars lasted off and on to the end of the century and then after a lull continued for a good part of the following century is sufficient proof of the Calvinists' power and of the narrow margin by which the Catholic Church in France escaped with its life, though with wounds that were never to heal. After Vassy the sectaries flew to arms and found to lead them many bold captains of the lesser nobility whose motives were not exclusively religious. None of these men inspired more terror than the priest-eating François de Beaumont, Baron des Adrets, who laid waste Dauphiny and captured Valence. Among his prisoners was Père Auger, there to preach the Lent and immediately sentenced to be hanged. But the Calvinist ministers, who lived for sermons and appreciated the father's oratorical gift, begged a stay of execution in hopes of making so precious a recruit see the light that streamed from Geneva. While the excellent men thus wasted their time, the Catholics managed by a clever ruse to spirit their difficult catechumen out of prison and away to the college of Billom. There he found his community of Tournon assembled, with a story as lurid as his own of siege and pillage and hairbreadth nocturnal escapes. Not for sixteen months did the fortunes of war permit them to steal back and resume their schoolmastering functions. The colleges of Rodez, Mauriac, Avignon, Toulouse, Chambéry, Lyons, Verdun and Nevers, all started within the following decade, all had similar initial histories of alarm and adventure, and some of them suffered from poverty so dire that a windfall of two pigeons, cooked

[1] Neale, *The Age of Catherine de Medici* (1943), p. 53.

very amateurishly with a small piece of mutton, was considered a sumptuous banquet for seven desperately hungry men. Their usual fare consisted of stale bread, plums and water. In the winter they had no fuel except some rotten wood, the smoke of which nearly suffocated them, and they went to bed, after a hard day with hundreds of boys, in a dormitory open to all the winds of heaven. But they kept the flag flying on their dilapidated walls till the magic of their courage transformed them into splendid colleges which did more to save the faith of France, though not its Catholic throne, than the myriad flashing swords of the Leaguers.[1]

Meantime, in Paris, neither Jesuit history nor the larger kind had ceased to be written. Monseigneur du Prat died in October 1560, bequeathing the bulk of his considerable property as endowments for the Hôtel de Clermont and for the two *auvergnat* colleges of Billom and Mauriac. It was a brave thing to do, a magnificent gesture of confidence, seeing how insecure as yet was the foothold of his legatees in the country. At first they could not, as aliens, enter into their inheritance, for which all sorts of other aspirants, including the Paris hospitals, began immediately to compete. The situation that arose was too much even for Ponce Cogordan, and he momentarily lost heart. "Never was there such contradiction and tribulation as we are enduring," he told Laynez. "The misery and weariness of the whole thing have reached their limit. For two or three months now I have had to be off to the Louvre at dawn and to hang about there all day, weighed down with my years and asthma and other infirmities. . . I think I shall have to go to the Court again. God in His mercy grant me soon the grace to go to the court of Heaven. . . Everybody wants that money bequeathed to us, and we have to fight, not one lawsuit, but five or six. Day and night I must work drafting replies to these claimants. . . Would your Reverence for the love of God please take me out of Paris and put me wherever else you like in France. . . If ever I worked for the salvation of my own and other men's souls in Portugal or Italy, I promise you I would work twice as hard then, with God's assist-

---

[1] When Father Oliver Manare visited the College of Rodez in 1564, he found that this place, which had begun without a penny of revenue or so much as an inkpot, was catering for no less than eight hundred boys (Manare, *De Rebus Societatis Jesu Commentarius,* p. 83).

ance. Again I beg you to do me this favour for the love of God. Pontio." [1]

When he penned that *cri du cœur* Pontio was nearer than he could have guessed to the prize of citizenship for which he had so long and patiently striven. By the irony of circumstances the Jesuits would be indebted for it to that national council which every man among them was doing his small best to hinder. But not even the Pope was able to hinder it, though he sent another Legate, a grandson of Alexander VI, and with him the General of the Jesuits, to try. Catherine de Medici and L'Hôpital went their appeasing way, summoned the bishops and, to encourage them to come, pretended that the assembly was to be merely in the nature of an *aperitif* for the goodly banquet of Trent. At the same time, the scheming pair, who held a pathetic belief in the mollifying effects of bringing dissident parties together, were in busy negotiation with the Calvinist leaders. It deterred them nothing at all that such colloquies or conferences had been tried again and again in Germany without other result than to make the Protestants more intransigent and the Catholics more depressed. Catherine herself wanted Calvin invited, but that was considered too dangerous and she had to be content with issuing a welcome to his great lieutenant, Theodore Beza, who accepted it graciously. She also insisted on inviting her countryman, the apostate monk Vermigli, known to history with fantastic inappropriateness as Peter Martyr, though the other plotters would have preferred a team exclusively French. Cardinal Odet Châtillon constituted himself host of the twenty-two Huguenot ministers and lay delegates who arrived, and courteously permitted them a wide liberty of preaching and proselytizing along the banks of the Seine. The French hierarchy as a whole behaved very well, for only forty-six bishops out of 113 obeyed Queen Catherine's summons, and these, with four notorious exceptions headed by Châtillon, came in no mood to fraternize with the Calvinists. The little village of Poissy, near Paris, where St. Louis was born, had been chosen as the meeting place of the Assembly, which Charles IX, St. Louis's entirely worthless successor, opened on 31 July 1561. L'Hôpital then addressed the bishops and urged the importance of avoiding conten-

[1] M.H., *Lainii Monumenta*, v, 406-8. Ponce writes expansively and in even worse Italian than Broet.

tion, of fighting the battles of the Lord with the weapons of charity, prayer, persuasion, and of eschewing such party names as Huguenot and Papist, which were mere slogans of sedition. It was magnificent, but assuredly not war as the men of Geneva understood the business. Almost it was possible to see the oil run down this dear old Aaron's beard, but the bishops saw too that his speech, despite its deliberate vagueness, amounted to a plea for the repudiation of the Council of Trent.[1]

Beza joined the "Protestant house-party" on 22 August, whereupon Catherine sprang her mine and compelled the unhappy bishops to grant him a hearing. Whether we like to call it arrogance or fine courage, he preached at them as though in one of his own conventicles and shocked even Admiral Coligny by his want of tact. The bishops, perturbed and indignant, decided to adopt one measure of retaliation which Queen Catherine from her previous action was certain not to oppose. They would pass a decree legalizing the Jesuits. But the circumstances of the hour warned them to tread warily, so they left the drafting of the decree to their brother of Paris, who could be trusted to avoid any dangerous enthusiasm in its terms. What the good man did in effect was to serve up practically unchanged his own recent recommendation to the Parlement. "The Assembly," it ran, "receives and approves the said Society as a corporation and college, not as a new religious order, on condition that the members thereof take another title than that of the Society of Jesus or Jesuits; that the diocesan bishop have complete jurisdiction over them with power to expel from their ranks criminals and evildoers; that they refrain from all courses, spiritual and temporal, to the prejudice of bishops, chapters, curés, parishes, universities, and other religious orders; that they become subject in every respect to the common law, without any private rights or jurisdiction; and, finally, that they renounce in express terms all privileges granted to them by their bulls which are contrary to the aforementioned stipulations." [2]

---

[1] Far the best account in English of the Assembly and subsequent Colloquy of Poissy is to be found in H. O. Evennett's masterly study, *The Cardinal of Lorraine and the Council of Trent,* pp. 235-393.

[2] Text from the Archives nationales in Fouqueray, *Histoire de la Compagnie de Jésus en France,* i (1910), 254-5.

This was no bouquet of roses for the sons of St. Ignatius, but by its author's intention more in the nature of a brickbat. Even so, it met with opposition from Châtillon and his three brethren in Calvin, and, though passed unanimously by the other bishops, was not registered by the Parlement until five months later. Then, on 13 February 1562, the Jesuits came into legal existence in France under the title of "la Société du Collège de Clermont," whereupon Ponce Cogordan, entirely recovered from his fit of depression, purchased with the legacy of Monseigneur du Prat a fine property in the University quarter, having its own garden and well. It was called the Cour de Langres, but rechristened the Collège de Clermont, and there, only two years later, the same Ponce proudly counted from his window more than a hundred excited students flocking to the lectures of the brilliant young professor from Salamanca, Father Juan Maldonado, or Maldonatus.[1] It seemed almost as if the days of St. Thomas had returned, for the lectures dealt with that insuppressible Arab, Averroes, whose theories of the soul, smitten by the Angelic Doctor, were again being propagated in the schools of Paris. But the days of St. Thomas returned in another sense also. Early in 1564, the rector of the University, a broad-minded man, had admitted the new Jesuit College to all academic rights and privileges, but unfortunately he held office only for three months, and his successor in 1565, aggrieved by the extraordinary popularity of Maldonatus, cancelled the concessions and stringently forbade any more lecturing. From then on it was war to the death between the University, the fortress of Gallicanism, allied with the Collège de France, the nursing mother of sceptical humanism, and the Clerks of Clermont, whose conception of themselves was set forth as follows by Ponce Cogordan at the demand of the University authorities: "Messieurs, as you require to know who we are, and as there are various opinions abroad, we shall tell you the truth briefly. We are children of our holy Mother, the Catholic, Apostolic, and Roman Church, in whose bosom we protest our determination to live and to die. If need be, and with the grace of God, we are prepared to die not only in her but for her. As to our condition in France we are such as the decree of the Parlement and our approbation by the synod of Poissy declare us to be, namely a

[1] Before 1570 the number of students had increased to more than a thousand.

collegiate body and society calling itself the College of Clermont.
This you can read for yourselves in the said decree and in the act of
Poissy. The nature of our society over and above this is no concern
of the present assembly. To those whom it does concern, the Holy
Apostolic See and our sovereign lord the King, we are always ready
to give an account of ourselves as set forth in our institute and bulls.
. . . We very humbly supplicate to be incorporated in the Univer-
sity, promising you our obedience and all the little services in our
power. Ponce Cogordan, Procurator of the Society of the College of
Clermont, Paris." [1]

A chief grievance of the University against the College was the
number of foreigners on the staff. This was true enough, even the
rector being a Scotsman, Father Edmund Hay, but it was a curious
complaint to come from a body that boasted before all the world of
its great sons, Alcuin the Englishman, Scotus Erigena the Irishman,
Peter the Lombard, Albertus Magnus the German, St. Thomas and
St. Bonaventure the Italians. The deepest cause of the hostility was,
however, like all human motives in the long run, theological, as the
University authorities readily admitted: "The University knows
the Jesuits to be monks and regulars who pronounce, in addition to
the three vows, a fourth which makes them the vassals of the Pope.
As the University with the Gallican Church ranks the Council above
the Pope, it cannot receive any society or college which puts the
Pope above the Council. Let the Jesuits, if they like, betake themselves in the quality of Papal vassals to the unbelieving pagans whom
they were founded to evangelize." The Jesuits betook themselves
instead to the Parlement, which, flattered by this attention, at first
sided with them against the University. Father Oliver Manare,
Broet's successor in Paris,[2] tells of the conflict that ensued: "The

---

[1] Prat, *Maldonat et l'Université de Paris* (1856), pp. 100–1. This lively and
learned old book brings the story down to the death of Maldonatus in 1583, at
the early age of fifty. His constant preaching and his many great tomes on philosophy, theology, and the Scriptures, which are still appreciated (several volumes of his Scripture commentaries were translated into English under Anglican
auspices), wore him out in his prime.

[2] In 1562 the plague made one of its fiercest descents on Paris, which caused
Broet to hurry his young men out of the city, first to Saint-Cloud and then to
Noyon, under the charge of Ponce Cogordan. Ponce implored him to come
too, but he could not be persuaded to leave while so many dying people needed

masters and theologians regarded us as heretics and maintained that if we were received we would prove more pernicious to France than the very Huguenots. They went from house to house spreading every sort of tale and rumour that might serve to discredit us . . . and finally decided to fight the matter out before the court of the Parlement with all the power at their disposal. Then indeed did everyone think that we were lost; but no, for with the exception of a few who lodged in other colleges and were there forcibly detained by their masters, our pupils remained faithful to us. . . The next rector worked up the *curés* and friars against us to such an extent that on one day alone we were the theme of twelve hot and long-winded sermons. . . In these circumstances it was decided that I should go to Toulouse to see the King, who was then making a tour of his realm." At Toulouse Manare found himself simultaneously in the presence of Charles IX and of the future Henry III and Henry IV, but from their youth and the fact that they were all dressed alike judged them to be mere pages. He had not Jeanne d'Arc's powers of detection and shifted from one foot to the other in great embarrassment until one of the smiling boys came forward, kissed him, and asked what was his trouble. That soon was told and Charles then said many kind things and made many large promises of about the same lasting value as the fireworks-display to which his Majesty next proceeded.

---

his ministrations. Four of the Jesuits succumbed despite the precautions, and Broet and Cogordan had a last meeting in the Bois de Boulogne to provide for further eventualities. Paschase himself died at his post on 14 September, whereupon Cogordan hastened to Paris without a thought for his own safety. People warned him not to enter the Hôtel de Clermont, for all within, "down to the very cat," had been carried off by the pestilence. Enter, however, he must, to rescue a sum of three thousand *livres,* which had been carefully husbanded to repay a debt to a certain merchant. On Broet's desk he found a note in the dying man's hand carefully listing all the objects which he or his one companion, Frère Jean Bourgeois, "qui estoit quasi ung second Jehan Baptiste," had touched and also saying where he had hidden the money. Ponce searched high and low but could not find it. He tells the sequel in old French to Laynez: "On disoit que le marchant me vouloit faire arrester à Paris pour estre poyé. Je luy respondu . . . quil seroit poyé, et quil ne pouvoit perdre les deulx mill cent livres; mays moy je perdoys les personnes qui me son plus chers que toux les biens. . ." No wonder that he signed another letter "Le pauvre Ponce Cogordan" (M.H., *Lainii Monumenta,* vi, 422–8; vii, 567).

The great law-suit which has echoed down the ages, the University of Paris *v.* the Jesuits, began on 29 March 1565. It proved in fact to be eight law-suits all at once, for the University men had persuaded seven other interested parties, including the bishop and curés of the city, and certain claimants to the legacies of Monseigneur du Prat, to enter the fight by their side. As their leading advocate they briefed Étienne Pasquier, a man of thirty-six still unknown to fame except by some love lyrics of a mildly Rabelaisian flavour. Later Jesuit writers, including Père Fouqueray in his *Histoire,* have brought much heavy artillery to bear on those lyrics, but their author seems to have been in real life a rather engaging character, a Cyrano of the bar who boasted much of his escapades and kept to old-age his "gaillardises d'esprit." His *Plaidoyer* before the Parlement was a remarkable effort compounded of wit, irony, scorn, pathos, appeals to prejudice both national and ecclesiastical, jugglery with facts, and all the other famous tricks of the trade. Among Pasquier's titles to renown is his invention of the secret disguised Jesuit who was to prove such a godsend to the novelists.[1] But the *Plaidoyer* and a catechism of Jesuit morals which the enterprising Étienne wrote

[1] One of the funniest examples of the type is to be found in that distinguished contemporary novel, *The Magic Mountain.* The second half of the long, long story is taken up with the wrangles of a Herr Naphta and a Herr Settembrini, patients at the sanatorium in Switzerland. Settembrini, who belongs to the Carbonari, visits Naphta's rooms accompanied by the hero, Hans Castorp. Castorp, impressed by the taste and furnishing, surmises that the owner must be pretty well off:
 " 'Herr Naphta,' Settembrini answered, 'is personally as little of a capitalist as I am.'
 " 'But?' queried Hans Castorp. 'There is a but in your tone, Herr Settembrini.'
 " 'Well, those people never let anyone lack who belongs to them.'
 " 'Those people?'
 " 'The Fathers.'
 " 'The Fathers? What Fathers?'
 " 'Why, Engineer, I mean the Jesuits.'
 " 'What! Good Lord! — You can't mean it! You don't mean to say the man is a Jesuit!'
 " 'You have guessed aright,' Herr Settembrini said with punctilio."
Herr Thomas Mann, evidently a believer in the existence of such wildfowl, disposes of his disguised Jesuit, who for good measure is also an atheist, by means of a dramatic suicide in the snow.

as a pendant to it have served widely different causes, such as Jansenism and various types of anti-clericalism, even unto the days when the romantic apostle of the Revolution, Jules Michelet, preached it all again from the rostrum of the Collège de France.[1]

In spite of their advocate's eloquence, the University men did not secure the suppression of the College of Clermont, but neither did the Jesuits obtain the incorporation of the college into the University. The Parlement discreetly gave judgment for the *status quo,* whereupon the University's ancient and well-tried weapons of passive resistance and active annoyance were resumed. "It would take too long," writes Manare, "to tell the story of what we had to endure. Countless were the tracts which they issued against us in both French and Latin. Again and again the college underwent a regular siege. Our windows were smashed with stones, and filth from the streets thrown into the house. Often we ourselves were stoned when we ventured out of doors. They declaimed against us incessantly, and held us up to ridicule in their dramatic representations. . . *Benedictus Deus!*" Finally, they received peremptory orders to cease teaching, and at the same time an ukase from the Sorbonne forbidding any more theological lectures under pain of mortal sin. Manaré felt that there was nothing to do but close down until tempers had cooled, at which proposal the tempers of the Clermont students boiled over. If the Jesuits would not fight, others knew how, window for window, mud for mud, stone for stone. The situation became so threatening that the Parlement offered Manare a permanent guard of five hundred soldiers for the college, but he wisely refused them, and instead sent Antonio Possevino, the born diplomat, on a new mission to the King. The University appealed for help to no less a person than Condé, the sword of the Huguenots; the Pope intervened on behalf of Clermont with Condé's brother, the Cardinal de Bourbon; and as a result of all the high manœuvring the college was allowed to live. It lived and, like a hardy Highland pine, actually throve on the storms that seemed must inevitably uproot it, until presently it became the most famous Catholic college in the world, the nursing mother of such diverse geniuses as St. Francis

[1] Among scores of amusing "howlers" in the *Plaidoyer* perhaps the best is Pasquier's transmogrification of Pope Paul IV, whom he detested on Gallican instinct, into a Jesuit — Paul IV of all people in the world!

de Sales, Cardinal de Bérulle, Descartes, Corneille, Molière and Voltaire. We must leave it for the moment and look Romewards to study the man who was the driving inspiration behind its activities, and all Jesuit activities.

CHAPTER III

PORTRAIT OF LAYNEZ

I T WAS a custom of Father Polanco, the Secretary, to compile from time to time large news-letters of Jesuit doings in Rome which he would then patiently multiply with his own hand and dispatch for the information and encouragement of the brethren in other lands. These bulky bulletins are so many monuments to the good Secretary's charity, for they must have given him great trouble to put together and he had no telephone. They are strictly family papers and record, as is their intimate right, how the baby is getting on from day to day, its appetite, its growth, the wonderful things it says and does, what people think of it. Naturally, it is the finest baby in the world. All babies notoriously are. Of swift growth there are numerous indications. In April 1559 the Roman Jesuits numbered 190. By November of 1560 they are 250. In five months of the following year another forty recruits arrived from such diverse directions as Flanders, Poland, Estonia, Hungary, Albania and Spain. The Roman College looked like a tiny replica of Europe, *mundi quasi compendium,* and not one of its students, Polanco is happy to say, but could preach in two languages or make himself sufficiently understood in four or five. They practised preaching in Arabic regularly, with an eye to the Moslem world which had been the first missionary dream of St. Ignatius. Over their studies presided a notable group of very youthful professors, themselves all recent recruits to the Society of Jesus. The leader of this team was Diego Ledesma, who had joined the Jesuits after gathering to himself the scholastic laurels of Alcalá, Paris and Louvain. Classical scholar, eminent theologian and one of the most popular confessors in all Rome, it was he who did the "devilling" for Laynez during his great days at Trent, but his best title to remembrance within his order is that he contributed more than any other to the shaping of educational methods which resulted ten years after his death in the first *Ratio Studiorum.*[1] With him, teaching theology at twenty-three,

[1] An excellent selection of Ledesma's letters and opinions on education is

was his fellow-Spaniard, Juan Mariana, destined to become one of
the classical historians of his native land, an expert on economic problems, and an absolute torment to his long-suffering order.[1]   The
professor of philosophy, Francis Toledo, was yet another Spaniard,
a man of Jewish descent, aged twenty-eight, who five years earlier
had held the same post at the University of Salamanca.   The exacting Montaigne spoke of him as a man of "extraordinary ability" when
he met him in Rome two decades later, and Pope Clement VIII
created him a cardinal, but the Jesuits themselves have never been
particularly fond of this dour genius, the first of their number to be
incarnadined, even if he did bring them glory.   A very different
type was the Portuguese professor of Scripture, Manuel da Saa,
whose commentaries are still appreciated by the learned, but whose
innumerable forgotten sermons won him a dearer prize, the love
and reverence of the humble folk of Tuscany.   Among the pupils
of those men, two Tuscan cousins, nephews of Pope Marcellus II,
are particularly noticed by Polanco, especially the younger, who is
described as "a boy of seventeen, *buen humanista y muy inginioso.*"
The very ingenious humanist was Robert Bellarmine, now Saint
and Doctor of the Church.   Another student at the time who has
left a permanent if unsigned impress on history was the Bavarian
youth, Christoph Clau, Latinized as Clavius, one of the principal
architects of the Gregorian Calendar.   The hundred resident Jesuits
and 650 day pupils of the College made many friends but none better
loved or more teased than a humble Capuchin lay brother, who
taught them the tunes that came into his head as he tramped the
streets in quest of alms and countered their merry chaff "with a
gaiety equal to their own."   That beloved Fra Felice is known
now as St. Felix of Cantalice.[2]

---

given in *Renatae Litterae in Scholis S.J. stabilitae*, by T. Corcoran, S.J. (Louvain
1927), pp. 72–143.

[1] Mariana's divagations from the path of Jesuit orthodoxy happily belong to a
later period, outside the scope of the present pages, but it may be said in general
that he exasperated the Court of France by his views, carefully guarded though
they were, on tyrannicide, maddened the King of Spain, who imprisoned him
for several years, by opposition to that monarch's economic measures, and wrote
a criticism of the government of the Society of Jesus which became a sort of
Bible of the order's enemies.

[2] Cuthbert, *The Capuchins* (1928), i, 176.

In the Lent of that same year, 1560, the young Jesuits went, as was their custom, to visit the various Roman prisons and bring what comfort they could to the condemned. At the Castle of St. Angelo, Rome's Bastille, they found awaiting execution a man for whom all the guns of the same Castle had thundered a salute only a few years before. Giovanni Carafa, Duke of Paliano, Captain General of the Church, was to die for the murder of his wife, the beautiful Violante d'Alife. Even Renaissance Italy has few murders to compare with this one in sheer horror. Giovanni, the elder brother of Cardinal Carlo Carafa and the maker of that miscreant's career, was in many ways a worse miscreant, a tempestuous, overbearing, evil-living man, whose only religion had been the advancement of his family's fortunes. How such a person came to ask the young Jesuits for a priest is a mystery of the infinite mercy of God. Laynez sent him Father John Baptist Peruschi, a fearless and ruthless physician of souls, who for eleven days on end fed his penitent with the bitter medicine of the First "Week" of St. Ignatius's Spiritual Exercises. The results were extraordinary. The wild beast became a lamb within a fortnight and vowed, according to Polanco, who had it from Peruschi, that were Pope Pius to give him his life he would immediately become a Jesuit. The Pope spared Laynez some embarrassment by refusing a pardon, and Giovanni, attended to the last by the faithful Peruschi, died clasping his crucifix and breathing the name of Jesus.[1]

A constant feature of Polanco's bulletins is naturally the work and the worries of his life's greatest hero, Laynez. If Diego, or plain James, Laynez has not been beatified it must be because he took steps in Heaven to prevent it, as in this world he tried so hard but vainly to keep away from the notice of men. He had a sort of passion for

[1] M.H., *Polanci Complementa*, i, 256–61. Polanco enclosed copies of the letters which the Duke had written in his last hours to his sister and his only son, those letters of which the unemotional Pastor says: "One cannot but read them with deep emotion." The letter to the son, which Pastor reproduces, begins with these lines: "Praised be the name of our Lord Jesus Christ for all eternity. This paper contains, I believe, the last words and advice I shall be able to address to you in this life; I pray God that they may be such as a father should address to his only son. As the first and most necessary thing, I would remind you that in all your dealings and inclinations you must prove yourself a true servant of God and show that you love His Divine Majesty far above yourself. . ." (*History of the Popes*, English tr., xv, 168–9).

the shadows, to be unknown and esteemed a nobody, which constantly kept breaking out and was a great anxiety to his Jesuit sons. He was a genuinely learned man by the standards of any age and fabulously so for his own pettifogging period, but he made nothing of it, and, except for two undesired intervals of glory at Trent, loved to spend his days traversing Italy from end to end as a missioner. That in the main was how he passed the twenty-two years of his life among the Jesuits before they elected him their general, preaching the Gospel to the poor in Venice, Rome, Parma, Piacenza, Vicenza, Bassano, Perugia, Gubbio, Montepulciano, Siena, Pisa, Reggio, Padua, Brescia, Genoa, Monreale, Naples, Bologna, Florence, Palermo, and "a camp in Africa." It was a common experience for him in those places to have no time for a meal until night, owing to the demands of the sick or dying on his compassion or to the pressure of souls in trouble who besieged him for advice and absolution from their sins. Of course he often fell a victim to his two chief and lifelong enemies, gout and malaria, and he suffered torments periodically from "the stone." He says that he found rhubarb good for his malaria, which may be a surprise to doctors. Let us watch him at work in Pisa in April 1551, just when Polanco wrote to say that Julius III had designated him to be again one of the Papal theologians at the resumed meeting of the Council of Trent. Italy in those days abounded in picturesque unwashed tramps and vagrants, who lived entirely by their wits. Trent's theologian discovered a hundred of the fraternity in Pisa, collected them by promise of a reward, and proceeded to try and teach them the Pater Noster and Creed. They learned the prayer well enough as far as the petition, "Give us this day our daily bread," but beyond that they refused to go, protesting that the rest was a Spanish addition, never heard of in Pisa. Their instructor then had recourse to bribery. Any man who learned the prayer in full and could repeat it right down to Amen received an extra penny. This scheme was successful, except for some conservative old gentlemen who could not be persuaded to move further than their daily bread. "In consideration of their age and poverty," says Laynez, "I let them have a penny notwithstanding." Polanco was amused by his hero's methods and chaffed him a little: "His Holiness is of opinion that you are capable of higher things than teaching the Pater Noster on a system of payment by results. Speaking recently with two cardinals about the theologians to be sent in his name to the Council, he mentioned some eminent men of various religious orders whom he was considering, but said that he had already made up his mind as regards your Reverence and Father Salmeron. He said much else about you, too, and made certain comparisons, but as these would be distasteful to you I am not repeating them." [1]

Wherever Laynez walked and worked colleges seemed to spring up as if by magic, the thanksgiving of such places as Padua, Venice, Florence, Perugia, Genoa, Palermo, for his devoted apostolate among them. It is interesting to know that while so engaged, largely with children or people of no education, he was also working at a compendium of theology, for which he seems to have received innumerable requests. It was to be in six parts, of which he had finished three by August 1553. Alas, it turned out to be no compendium but a huge expansive affair, and what became of it nobody knows. Sad to say, his handwriting was about the most illegible of any Jesuit's in history, which is saying a great deal, and the result has been oblivion for much that it would be precious to possess. Here, however, are a few extracts from a long dissertation on preaching which this indefatigable preacher composed: "The whole purpose of a preacher's office is to win souls, not to acquire a name for himself as an orator, or to gain a following, or to practise profundities on the people. He is before all a fisherman. . . As to the means he will employ, the first and foremost is a vehement love of God, for without this he will not be able to bear the heavy labours of his office nor to touch the hearts of his listeners. . . This was what our Lord implied when He three times asked of Peter, 'Lovest thou Me?' before He said, 'Feed My sheep.' . . . From this love springs a right

[1] M.H., *Monumenta Ignatiana*, series prima iii, 413–4; Polanco, *Chronicon*, 11, 175–6. The adventures of Laynez at Trent in its middle phase are amusingly related by himself in a letter translated in the companion volume to this. There also the reader will find the story, slightly but unavoidably expurgated, of his celebrated encounter with Melchior Cano at the Council, and the wonderful letter which he addressed to St. Ignatius after being severely reprimanded by him for a trifling fault. As is well known, Ignatius, following the Divine example, perhaps without warrant, treated hardest the sons he loved best. He regarded Laynez as his greatest son (*The Origin of the Jesuits*, 1940, pp. 228–37).

intention, by which the preacher is preserved from having an inflated opinion of himself because he fills the church, and it also gives him constancy to bear the disappointments and trials which sooner or later will visit every earnest minister of the Word. 'If they persecuted Me so also will they persecute you,' said Jesus. . . Zeal and fervour in preaching can only come from the love of God, and if we would kindle the fire of divine charity in the hearts of others, it must first burn brightly in our own. And so a great familiarity with God is essential to the preacher . . . for if, as the Apostle teaches, we cannot breathe the name of Jesus as we ought without the help of the Holy Spirit, that same help will be much more necessary to a man who has to talk on sacred subjects for a solid hour. The saints used to tire out Heaven with their prayers before they preached, and surely it is a rash man who thinks that he knows better than they. . . But that granted, I would also insist, that no one will become a perfect preacher who does not start with some natural ability. It is true that God once spoke by the mouth of an ass, but that was a miracle, and it is not for us to tempt God, presuming miracles, as would a man who hoped to become a preacher by the power of prayer alone. . . Religious men under obedience must not be frightened by such a statement, even though acutely conscious of their ignorance and inability. Let them not be downhearted, for if only they burn with zeal for the glory of God and take the necessary pains they will see their deficiencies vanish. . . God, who is noble and liberal of mind, will not deny His help to a suppliant anxious to perform worthily the duty set him by obedience. . ."

Laynez then proceeds to give preachers the benefit of his own long experience. They must have the Scriptures and the Fathers of the Church at the tips of their tongues. They must not rant in the pulpit, nor on the other hand drone on monotonously until the people are asleep. "Some imagine that their sermon will freeze unless they shout like lunatics and make any amount of noise. Others know not how to pause even to fetch a breath, but hasten on until they choke. . . Others again pause too often and too long, dragging out their syllables until the sermon congeals. . . There are two rules about this matter. First, the preacher ought to begin with his natural voice, taking care to raise it sufficiently to be heard. Let him imagine that he is speaking with two or three of his congregation on some matter of business. . . Nothing is to be gained by shouting as though the rafters were the congregation, . . . but anyone will listen willingly to a speaker who talks sense, and from his heart, and in the voice that God gave him. . . The second rule flows from the first, namely, that it must be a preacher's chief care to speak with conviction, for that, as we know well, leads of itself in the case of learned and simple alike to a proper use of voice and gesture. Watch a peasant talking to another as they walk along a road. He has never heard of such a thing as rhetoric, yet if he is telling a story he speaks with an even voice, but if he would persuade his companion to some course, up goes his tone, and his arms and hands come into action spontaneously. . . It must be the same with the preacher. Let him take all care that his zeal suffers no diminution, let his sole concern be the good of those whom he addresses, and then he need not be very anxious about other qualifications, for it is impossible that they should be wanting to him. Constant prayer, solid arguments, the right tone of voice, these three things will be his certain passport to the hearts of his people. . ."

Finally, here is a glimpse of Laynez himself preaching in Italian in Rome, as he did not cease to do week after week to the day of his death, burdened though he was with the care of nearly three thousand Jesuits: "You will find some good men waiting for you at the church door. Give them a generous alms, for they know how to distribute it to the best advantage. They go about Rome and see and know that such and such poor fellows are dying of hunger. To one they give a *giulio,* to another three, to others four or six, according to their need, and so these *poverelli* have a chance to breathe and to be grateful to God. Open your purses now, as these hard times require of you. When I go through the City myself what do I see? In one *piazza* bread is on sale, and in the next and the next there are men ready to commit murder in order to be able to buy a little. Look where I may I find abundance of nothing except mud and mire, and I think to myself that God has done this because He sees in our souls nothing except mud and mire. He sends us poverty, scarcity, inundations and other tribulations to make us cleanse our muddy souls.[1] And how are we to go about this? Well, besides

[1] This probably refers to the great inundation of the Tiber on the night of 14 September 1557, of which Polanco writes: "Never in my life have I seen any-

prayer, fasting and confession there is another grand means, and that is almsgiving. . . I recommend to you the Hospital for Incurables. Owing to everything being so damp these days, it is impossible to have all the patients in one ward, and the more wards used the more nurses are needed, and that means more money for salaries. Great are the expenses and great is the need, but, owing to our sins, little is the charity. People with money say that they have to buy their bread now. When they were able to bake it at home they willingly set aside some for the poor but now they declare this to be impossible. Oh, for the love of our liberal God let us remember that good times will come again and that there is hope of a good harvest. By His grace let us take a little risk. Look at the brave way the gambler puts down his stakes, or see that priest investing his savings in order to purchase a benefice. . . If they venture their money for a sinful end, will you not be bold enough to give a little alms to win the high stake of Heaven? Hurry, hurry, I beseech you by the Passion of our Lord Jesus Christ. . ."[1]

---

thing so extraordinary and terrifying." The Roman College and the Church of Santa Maria della Strada were both flooded. The fathers spent the night in upper rooms praying, Laynez leading off with the Seven Penitential Psalms (M.H., *Polanci Complementa,* ii, 607).

[1] Grisar, *Jacobi Lainez Disputationes Tridentinae,* etc., ii (Innsbruck 1886), 506–42, 558. Besides the strictly Tridentine dissertations, this very interesting book contains also the brilliant disputation "On Usury and the Various Transactions of Merchants," which Laynez wrote for the benefit of the business men of Genoa. "To decide such questions of commercial justice exactly," he says, "one would need to be an Argus with a hundred eyes," but he makes a very gallant attempt in a hundred closely argued pages. The knowledge of canon law, not then neatly codified, which he displays in this and the subsequent treatises on Simony, Taxation, Ecclesiastical Benefices, and the Duties of Bishops, is truly impressive, but modern ladies would not care much for his thirty-five pungent pages, *De Fuco et Ornatu Mulierum.* He is the declared enemy of lipstick and the powder-puff, and he detests the use of perfumes, though perhaps not sufficiently taking into account that in those bathless days it may have been the lesser of two evils. "Man," he says, forgetting his genders, "ought to be content with the ornamentation which nature provides, just as the cock is with his comb and the lion with his mane." If the ladies will not believe what he has to say about the dangers and evils of make-up and servitude to fashion let them read Clement of Alexandria, Tertullian, Cyprian, Jerome, Augustine, Chrysostom, Boethius, *et omnes fere alios,* and see what they have to say! While somewhat rigorous, the dissertation is full of shrewd remarks and curious learning. It is a social

While at Genoa, in 1554, preaching incessantly and endeavouring to instruct the free and easy consciences of the city's merchants and stockbrokers, Laynez received copies of letters from Jesuits working at the eastern and western ends of the world. "God knows how profoundly they thrilled me," he told St. Ignatius. "From time to time in my own cold way I find inexplicable longings arising in my heart to go to Jerusalem. I know that the way to die well is to live well, and seeing myself a poor hand at living well, I crave our Lord to let me die well out of His sheer mercy, which might come about if it were permitted to me to die for the faith. But may He dispose of me as it best pleases Him, whether in life or in death, and give us all the grace to fulfil His holy will." Among many others, Father Simon Rodriguez, the founder of the Portuguese province and a much-loved but wayward man, had also hankered for Jerusalem until given permission to go there, whereupon he said he would prefer to return to Portugal. Laynez wrote to him at Venice, encouraging him in his first design: "By going eastwards you would find benefit for both body and soul, and also perhaps be the means of opening a door through which the Society could pass into those parts. But what chiefly moves me to write is seeing how greatly our Father desires this course. Be it known and certified to your Reverence that if you were the son and brother and father of our Father Ignatius and monopolized all the love given to ones so near and dear, he would not counsel you otherwise than to go on with your journey. . . Would to God that I might be ordered to keep you company on it! . . . Remember me when there is mention of a college in Jerusalem and beg our Father to do me the favour of allowing me to participate in such a work. . ."[1]

---

document of real value, so far neglected or overlooked by the historians. From it emerges that Laynez's deepest objection to beauty-parlours was part of his great love for the poor. The money which women spent on their hair and faces could be so much more profitably invested in the eternal unfading beauty reserved in Heaven for the charitable. On the other hand, our man protested strongly against the theory preached in Genoa by his brother Jesuit, Father Manoel Gomes, that it was a mortal sin to wear a wig or to shave (M.H., *Lainii Monumenta*, i, 263–4).

[1] M.H., *Lainii Monumenta*, i, 250–1, 258–9. By a bull dated 6 October 1553, Pope Julius III proclaimed his intention of establishing three Jesuit colleges in Jerusalem, Cyprus and Constantinople, with a view to helping the oppressed

It was not to be, and Laynez, instead of finding a swift and glorious end at the hands of the Turks, was destined to nine years of hidden martyrdom at the hands of the Jesuits. As has been finely said, "the true martyr is he who has become the instrument of God, who has lost his will in the will of God, and who no longer desires anything for himself, not even the glory of being a martyr." [1] Such a one by all the evidence was James Laynez. He had faults in plenty. He was hot-tempered, as Melchior Cano and others, including even such friends as Nadal and Salmeron, knew to their cost.[2] He was impulsive and exacting, requiring so much physical and intellectual perfection in the men sent to the colleges of which he was the superior that St. Ignatius, exasperated, told him on one occasion to stop assessing his acquisitions by the principles of mathematics. Later, as general, he changed his views when confronted with other Jesuits imbued with the same principles, Father Bouclet of Tournai, for instance, who complained that he was being deluged with invalids. "If it is gladiators you want on your staff," replied Laynez tartly, "such paragons of fitness are not to be found in our Society." Sometimes he could also be strangely insensitive and tactless. Before the day of the ballot from which he emerged general, an unfortunate rumour reached the congregation that the first

---

Christians of the Levant. Nothing, however, came of the project until many years later. The bull itself disappeared until 1896 when it was discovered in a Viennese library and published with a commentary in *Études*, t. 70 (1897), 72–86.

[1] From Becket's Christmas Day sermon in Eliot's *Murder in the Cathedral*.

[2] "After the election of Laynez as general," writes Nadal, "Cano came to Rome to pursue his cause about the provincialate against his brother Dominican, Peter Soto. He pursued it and won it. On this occasion Father Laynez had a lively encounter with him in the house of Cardinal Pacheco. Cano launched out in his usual fashion against us, whereupon our man rated him in no measured terms. 'What a joke,' said he, 'to find one little mannikin up in arms against a whole religious order!' Before leaving Rome, Cano thought he would make his peace with Father Laynez and accordingly invited him through an official named Alvarado to come for a settlement of their differences. This method of approach offended the Father, and he refused to go" (M.H., *Epistolae P. Nadal*, ii, 46). When Cano died in 1560 Polanco considered it highly probable that he would receive more requiem Masses from the Jesuits than even from his own Dominican brethren (M.H., *Epistolae Salmeronis*, i, 411).

Jesuit of Belgian nationality, a saintly but most eccentric priest named Cornelius Wischaven, had prophesied the election of Nadal. The tale naturally disturbed Laynez who, as vicar, was responsible for the canonical validity of the election, but he need hardly have acted as though he suspected a plot by questioning all the fathers, including Nadal. Nadal was angered by the investigation. "He neither knew nor cared," he said, "what other people gossiped about him. The fathers might believe what they liked. He would not lose his peace of mind, God helping him, before whom he protested against the injustice of the suspicion." [1]

A more surprising instance of tactlessness in one so generally and justly beloved was Laynez's inconsiderate treatment of his friend from boyhood, Father Alfonso Salmeron. These two had been bosom companions at Salamanca and Paris, and together they had joined St. Ignatius. They were together at the Council of Trent in all its three phases, and their names are almost as inseparable in Jesuit memories as those of Castor and Pollux. In 1552 St. Ignatius recalled Salmeron from his labours in Germany to start off the Jesuits in the Kingdom of Naples. There this quondam Papal nuncio and luminary of Trent was to be seen with a hod on his shoulder or a pick in his hands helping to dig the foundations and build the walls of the new college, which had among its first pupils the eight-year-old Torquato Tasso, greatest of Italian poets after Dante.[2] Naples at that time needed her Salmeron, for the semi-heretical Spaniard, Juan Valdes, and his two friends, the out-and-out apostates, Bernardino Ochino and Pietro Martire Vermigli, all three brilliant men, had recently been evangelizing the impressionable children of Vesuvius. Lutheranism was in the air, and its doctrine of faith alone had attractions for many hot-blooded folk who found good works inconvenient. Salmeron went from church to church, preaching or lecturing every day and for two hours at a time. He made such an impression that when the Pope sent him to the

---

[1] M.H., *Epistolae P. Nadal,* ii, 61. Laynez's doubts, if doubts they were, must have been of the most transient kind, for we soon find him regarding and treating Nadal as the most loyal, trustworthy and important man in the order.

[2] Ribadeneira, *Vita P. Jacobi Laynis, Alphonsi item Salmeronis* (1604), p. 237.

Diet of Augsburg in 1555 and subsequently to Poland, important people described as "Li electi della fidelissima città di Napoli," wrote earnestly begging St. Ignatius to see that such a thing did not happen again. They expressed their "great affection and love for the Reverend Father Don Alfonso . . . who has been a very trumpet of the Gospel in this Most Faithful City," and "desired with all their hearts to be assured of not losing any more the great spiritual benefit of his devout, solid and fruitful preaching and teaching." [1]

Salmeron was one of the few to whom Laynez continued to write in his own baffling hand after his election as general. This old friend had learned to decipher the hieroglyphics. The letters are affectionate and full of the odds and ends characteristic of an intimate correspondence. There is much about a small black boy named Peter, a little slave from Africa bequeathed to the college in Naples. Salmeron taught him his letters: "He is now thirteen and a lively lad, engaged in making grammatical concordances and often discordances. If he applies himself he will do well." Laynez liked to hear of Peter and applauded his progress. In due course Salmeron manumitted him with full legal formality and gave him the handsome sum of twelve ducats to enable him to return to his mother. Another matter often and anxiously discussed was a certain consignment of Spanish wine which Salmeron made great efforts to obtain for the thirsty brethren in Rome. In return will Laynez kindly lend him his manuscript writings, which he does, saying, however, "che stanno confussi." Laynez is also asked to pronounce on the claims of the alchemists. "In spite of the fact of our Father being so burdened with business that your heart would bleed for him," replied Polanco, "he has stolen a little time to study alchemy, in order to satisfy your Reverence." More serious was the concern of the two friends about poor Archbishop Carranza, the Dominican Primate of Spain, who had been very good to the Jesuits in Toledo and for that among other reasons, including plain base jealousy, incurred the lasting enmity of his brother in religion, Melchior Cano. Carranza's sad story is one of the chief blots on the record of that over-zealous, nationalistic and unlovable body, the Spanish Inquisition. It arrested him in August 1558 on suspicion of Lutheranism because of a few ambiguous or carelessly worded statements in a

---

[1] M.H., *Epistolae P. Salmeronis*, i, 592.

huge commentary on the Catechism [1] which he had brought out in Spanish at Antwerp earlier that year. In the zeal of his heart, zeal plain to all the world from his good work at the Council of Trent and in England under Mary Tudor, he had wanted to educate the common people in their religion as a protection against Lutheranism, and his reward was to be nearly seventeen years in the cells of the Inquisition. The Archbishop succeeded in getting a messenger through to Salmeron and a letter to Laynez asking for a testimony as to the orthodoxy of his book, which incidentally was written during his residence in Oxford as visitor of the University. Laynez's opinion has not come to light, perhaps because he did not express one, but we have Salmeron's and it is well worth recording: "I remember having read the entire book at Liége, and very carefully too. As is my way when I read other men's books, I extracted some good things out of it. I say sincerely that I found nothing to offend in it, except that the matter of the union and annexing of benefices is treated in too free a manner. Even in this there were so many limitations and reservations that the doctrine seemed to me beyond reproach. As for the rest, it appeared to me to be the common teaching, and to be taken almost entirely from St. Thomas." [2] Salmeron sent this testimony to Laynez for censorship, but though the General wrote to console Carranza he did not dare to enclose a certificate which might easily have brought his old friend Alfonso also to the dungeons of the Inquisition.[3] That tribunal was controlled by King Philip II and Philip did not like the Jesuits. In any case, Salmeron's testimony would have availed the Archbishop nothing. At Trent three years later a whole array of prelates and theologians pronounced in his favour without doing him the slight-

[1] "He who has fastened a bad name on this book is Friar Master Melchior Cano. I know not why, but suspect that among other causes was the welcome I gave to members of the Society in Toledo" (Carranza to Laynez, December 1558, in M.H., *Lainii Epistolae,* iv, 20).

[2] M.H., *Epistolae P. Salmeronis,* i, 256–7.

[3] Shortly afterwards a celebrated professor of Salamanca, Martin Azpilqueta, known as the "Doctor of Navarre," and dearly loved uncle of St. Francis Xavier, was arrested at his own house, though full of years and infirmities, because he had publicly expressed his conviction of Archbishop Carranza's innocence. The doctor was quite right. Carranza was almost certainly a saint and practically a martyr.

est good, and not even the Pope himself had the power to wrest the unfortunate man out of the hands of the Inquisition. They were King Philip's hands, grasping hands, into which fell, as long as Carranza remained in prison, the rich revenues of the diocese of Toledo.[1]

Laynez and Salmeron had one topic of close personal interest to discuss, the ague. Laynez was the more experienced in this matter as his was the tertian variety, with a paroxysm every other day, whereas Salmeron suffered from the quartan, with a paroxysm only every third day. In the early winter of 1558 poor Alfonso fell ill of a "double quartan," which meant that he had only one free day in six, with a complete failure of appetite and all other simple joys of living. "Ho perduto il gusto d'ogni cosa," he told his confidant. Laynez at once wrote to him as follows: "We heard the news of your quartan with some feeling, especially myself who know the sort of company it provides. But I trust in our Lord that He came with the illness which He sent for the greater good of your soul, and that in body too you will presently be all the better for the visitation. I am hoping also that you will escape more lightly than I do, because you are a sturdier man and have the mild air and other amenities of Naples. Now as to remedies. Apart from patience while the disease runs its course and the remembrance that the quartan gives you a legitimate holiday from all worry about study, sermons or fatiguing occupations, I have found the following things helpful, a warm bed, clysters, broths and especially chicken-broth, a certain amount of exercise. Beware of foods that induce melancholy, and see that you have good wine. Dark wines are better I think, or a white one of a moderately generous kind. If too old, these wines are said to become dry and to make one heated, with after ill-effects. In my experience medicines do a man with the ague more harm

[1] This was the time when Philip had to patch up his age-old dispute with France because he had exhausted his treasury and could no longer finance the war. How like under the skin, and whether Catholic, schismatic or Protestant, were all those kings and queens of the sixteenth century! St. Francis Borgia loved and befriended the persecuted Archbishop at the cost of antagonizing both King Philip and his Inquisition. The whole story stinks, for the Grand Inquisitor was the Archbishop of Seville, who could not forgive Carranza the crime of having been preferred before him for Toledo, the primatial see of Spain.

than good, yet will he try all that are recommended to him, and people will recommend him three hundred. So do we delude ourselves. I think it is better not to eat much except on your free day, and it helps to get up for a little exercise and congenial conversation. That is the sum of what occurs to me. May it please our Lord to restore you to health speedily in order that you may be able to serve Him by helping the colleges. Meantime you are not to worry about anything. Our Lord who made the colleges out of nothing will preserve and increase them, to His greater glory." In spite of all this medical advice the patient did not recover. His paroxysms sometimes lasted four or five hours and left him completely exhausted. "I had not the firmness," he confesses, "to refuse various remedies, some of which were prescribed by the doctors, and some forced on me by the entreaty of well-meaning visitors." In January 1559 Laynez wrote again expressing his sympathy. "I feel so sorry for you," he said, "knowing as I do so well the heaviness and nausea that accompany the quartan. But I am putting my hopes in the coming of summer. You might then think of a change of air if the doctors advise. It is my belief that when you have once ridded yourself of the disease you will feel better than ever before, and that you will do our Lord great service. Meantime we must serve Him with our patience which is the best shield during this exile wherein that good old gentleman Adam landed us [1] . . . As for myself I am middling well and so busy with the importunate demands of this burden or task which has been placed upon me that all day long I seem to do nothing but listen like Moses to somebody or other, indoors or out of doors. I haven't even time to continue with the bits of sermons (*sermoncillos*) which I was preaching in that rhetorical style you know of. So I too have need of that shield I mentioned, and do you help me to obtain it from our Lord. . . I commend myself to the prayers of all the brethren, among them to Geoffrey and his flowers, about whose blossoming I have doubts with the quartan occupying him." [2]

Laynez, so genial and sympathetic in those letters, showed himself

---

[1] "*Donde nos puso aquel buen viejo Adam.*"

[2] M.H., *Epistolae P. Salmeronis*, i, 259–60, 269–70. The Geoffrey mentioned was Father Salmeron's lay brother infirmarian, who also did some gardening and spent other spare moments *en governar una mula.*

less careful of the courtesies when he dispatched Father Christopher Madrid to inspect the Neapolitan Jesuit province in November 1560. Madrid, a man of barely four years' standing in the order, was made assistant for Italy before being well out of the noviceship. He must have had great administrative ability, but that did not compensate the veteran Salmeron for his rawness in the religious life. The two men were soon at loggerheads. Madrid found fault with the Provincial for allowing some sodalities to meet in the house instead of in the church, though St. Ignatius had given leave for the practice and it was productive of much good. He seems to have behaved throughout in a peremptory and tactless manner. There was, for example, the question of the flies. "During the hot season," wrote Salmeron to Laynez, "our church is so infested with flies that it is almost impossible to say Mass there. They are vicious flies and one gets tired out and exasperated fighting them. For this reason I felt it necessary to install a large fan which is operated by the sacristan. Other well-kept and devotional churches have the same device, but Father Madrid says that it is a new rite, introduced without the leave of the General. I think that if he was here in July or August and experienced for himself the might of those flies, he would introduce the fan without the slightest scruple. . ." On the report of his visitor Laynez appears to have addressed to Salmeron a number of reprimands which wounded him sorely. His reply is a very human document, much too long, unfortunately, to quote in full. "I had made up my mind," he says, "to keep silent and write no more about this matter, but your Reverence seems to force me to answer, and I believe that you will be better pleased if I do. . . You say that I have taken the visitation and correction badly. I am sorry about that. There had been no visitations in the time of good Father Ignatius nor since. I am the first to be sent a visitor, so was it strange if I felt that your Reverence had no good opinion of me or that you thought this college must be going to perdition? . . . The visitor made it his whole business to search out all the faults he could find, and as we are all faulty men, *in multis offendimus omnes,* he found them, but by God's mercy only trifling ones. It can hardly be said, then, that you did not send him to correct me. I have not complained nor do I now complain at the correction, . . . but I think I have some reason to resent the manner in which it was delivered.

It seems to me that it pertains to your Reverence as general to correct your provincials, instead of committing the duty to somebody else. . . On this delicate mission you sent to me who have lived in the Society since its foundation a man of the eleventh hour, not himself yet proven in the crucible of obedience. . . Father, I confess my ignorance, but this appeared to me hard, and I doubted whether if Father Ignatius were alive he would have done such a thing. . . Moreover, according to what I have heard the methods employed in this visitation were harsh. It may be a laudable and charitable deed to investigate the faults of one's neighbour in order to help him, but strictly to demand confession of them in virtue of holy obedience and by means of a charge-sheet containing thirty or forty articles, I seriously doubt whether even a criminal would be proceeded against with so much rigour. O Father, is that the simplicity with which our Society has hitherto pursued its way? Is it surprising that I should feel some resentment after being so treated in my declining years? [1] . . . Believe me, your Reverence, it would be an easy thing to convict those fathers-assistant themselves by a similar process. I was affronted also by the way the visitor avoided me during the whole of his stay here, for he seemed to show by his never-ending questions and inquiries of others that he had come to indict me. That hurt, and he knew it. O Father, who is so perfect as not to feel such a wound? Why so big a gallows for so tiny a thief? I confess my frailty, but when your Reverence wrote to say that you were sending a visitor and that I must take him as I would a dainty dish, I rather feared that there would be arsenic (*rexalgar*) in it. . . You accuse me of writing angrily, . . . and I admit that I wrote as one aggrieved and bewildered, but is it not so that all sons lament to their fathers? . . . I do not think that my letter to your Reverence was nothing but admonitions, without, as you say, any salt or vinegar. A son who complains to his father cannot be said to admonish him, and you ought not to think so of me who put myself in your hands and seek from you a remedy. . . May God keep and advance your Reverence in His holy grace. Your Reverend Paternity's son and servant, Salmeron." [2]

That letter is valuable as showing how genuinely humble and holy

[1] Salmeron was forty-five and lived to be seventy.
[2] M.H., *Epistolae P. Salmeronis*, i, 420–6.

men can sometimes stand on their dignity and make a great deal of fuss about nothing in particular. Salmeron's humility is unmistakable and nearly everybody who knew him regarded him as a saint, but still he was a child of *"aquel buen viejo Adam,"* as it seems to be the useful function of the Madrids of this world to prove. A few weeks later he is again writing huge bulletins of news to Laynez as though no shadow had ever come between them. "You will not forget your promise to me about the alchemy," he says in the last line of a letter running to nearly four thousand words. But Laynez had to beg release from his promise to write against the alchemists because he could not find time enough even to deliver a short lecture to which he had committed himself. He was harassed with a thousand cares, for the Society of Jesus was spreading fast and, naturally enough, meeting with plenty of opposition. His sons are by no means all angels and he has a difficult time keeping some of them within the traces. Good ladies who found colleges are occasionally the problem, as, for example, the excellent Maria Frassona del Gesso of Ferrara, whose name constantly occurs in the letters. The fact quite plainly was that she had lost her heart to the charming Père Jean Pelletier, rector of the college. After trying by other means to abate the lady's ardour, Laynez wrote to her as follows: "Molto magnifica Signora, From the greatness of the debt which our college and all of us owe to you, you can estimate the strength of my desire to serve and console you in our Lord, to the utmost of my ability. So I do hope you will take the order which I have given to Father John in good part, as it was inspired solely by my earnest desire for the highest good and eternal happiness of your Highness and of him. . . Though I am convinced that you both mean well, yet the friendship between you and your familiar conversations are proving an offence to secular persons and may be the cause of scandal. For instance, your custom of sending the Father food cooked specially for him alone is not well thought of, and as we are in duty bound to set a good example to our neighbour as well as to keep our own consciences pure before God, I have told Father John not to go to your house so often nor to accept private presents from you. I beg your Highness to try, not only to acquiesce in this, but to divest yourself interiorly of any extraordinary affection for one spiritual father rather than another. Such attachments impede our holy affections towards God and eternal things. If you do this and make your confession now to one father now to another, loving them all in Christ our Lord without clinging to one in particular, believe me, you will soon find yourself greatly helped in soul. It is a common experience to find that our love for God diminishes in proportion as we give our hearts to any creature." [1]   As we have seen, Laynez was obliged to cut this particular knot eventually by returning Père Jean to his native land, where, first as rector and then as provincial, he received very different attentions from the Calvinists of Toulouse. From there he writes on the feast of SS. Peter and Paul, 1561, to report that an urgent letter from the General had taken more than nine months to reach him, and discloses the reason for the delay when he asks his Paternity's prayers "per il povero Pelletario, che sta in prigione propter verbum Dei et testimonium Jesu Christi."

That intercepted letter has an interesting history. It will be remembered that Pope Paul IV had made two vital changes in the Jesuit constitutions by insisting on the adoption of choir and the reduction of the general's term of office to three years. On the death of the Pope, Laynez, following legal advice, had countermanded his oral instructions about choir, but left in abeyance the question whether he was himself to have a life-sentence as general or to be reprieved after three years of servitude. He seems always to have been brooding over it, and at one point actually decided to summon the professed fathers to Rome for a new election at the end of his third year of office. But his confessor vetoed such a course until he had discovered the mind of the Society on the subject. His own mind was clear. He wanted more than anything in the world to be released from his burden. When appointed provincial of Italy in 1552, he had pleaded earnestly with St. Ignatius to spare him, adducing his *quartana,* his want of dignity, his hot temper, his exactingness, and other deficiencies, as so many witnesses for the defence. "I entreat you, therefore," he concluded, "to be content that I remain as long as I live the servant of your Reverence and of the Society, without obligation to govern others, at least until I have changed my own skin, which is not to be done in a day." To discover the mind of the brethren, the General addressed himself in

[1] M.H., *Lainii Monumenta,* iv, 143–4.

September 1560 to each of the sixty professed fathers of Europe,
solemnly adjuring them "in nomine Domini Nostri Jesu Christi et
in virtute sanctae obedientiae" to give their candid considered opinion, after earnest prayer, as to whether or no there should be a new
election the following summer, when he would have completed
three years of office. No father might discuss the question with
another, and each was to sign and seal his *votum,* which would not
be read by the General himself but by his assistants. Thus, he would
not know in what sense any particular father had written, but only
the majority view, and so, he said, "I hope that no bitterness nor
cooling of the charity which I owe to all will be found in me, by
the grace of our Lord." To help the fathers he gave a list of the
pros and cons as they appeared to himself, of which the following
are a few: "It seems to me that I ought to bear the cross which
God has imposed on me, and that to refuse it might proceed from
self-love seeking a more peaceful occupation than to be condemned
to read and write letters and to give ear and thought to the troubles
of other people for the remainder of life. . . In favour of a new election the first and principal reason which occurs to me, and one sufficient by itself, is that, having pondered upon the qualities required
by the constitutions in the general, I find I possess practically none
of them, either interiorly or exteriorly, except perhaps a little good-
will and fidelity to the Society, and a little learning, spoilt by want
of steady application. . . In these its beginnings the Society has need
at its head of men of great parts and qualities. By a fresh election
we might secure such a man, and I think it would show a great want
of love for our Lord and the Society if I were to close the door
against him. . . If I were released from office I could become more
recollected, and more freely serve our Lord and the Society hearing
confessions, explaining our institute and vocation to the brethren in
the colleges, and teaching the people Christian doctrine, all at the
direction of obedience. By the goodness of our Lord I would be
able to do this in Italy and Spain, as also, after a little refreshing
of memory, in France. . . I humbly beseech each and all of you, if
the service of our Lord is unaffected, to relieve me of this burden
which is too great for my shoulders." [1]

[1] M.H., *Lainii Monumenta,* v, 224-9. The letter needs to be read unabridged

The answers of the sixty men are extant, some but a few emphatic
lines long, many running to several eloquent argumentative pages.
Père Pelletier in his very belated letter advances twelve reasons
against any change, one being this: "The office of general is a burden, so much so that I would consider him to be a great lunatic
(*un gran matto*) who showed a preference for it over the office of
cook in the curial kitchen." One father only voted outright for a
new election on the ground that Paul IV's mandate still held good,
whatever the canonists might think. This man, an Italian named
Francis Adorno, scion of a ducal house and intimate of St. Charles
Borromeo, had a poor opinion of canonists and attributed to them
"not only contentions among religious but universal schisms in the
Church." Ponce Cogordan judged that it would be better to have
new generals every six years, except in the case of Father Laynez
who ought to be kept on for life because, among other reasons, "he
has always been a pattern of goodness and holiness, a most learned
man who has brought the Society renown, very spiritual-minded and
experienced, one greatly loved by the whole Society and the world
at large as the kindest of men, easy to deal with, approachable, and
a promoter of peace." [1] As for Nicholas Bobadilla this is what he
wrote: "Very Reverend and most Honourable Father in Christ. My
vote is that the generalate be always for life, according to the constitutions. In the case of your Reverence I wish the office to be so
firmly established that it may last for a hundred years, and that if
you die you may immediately be resurrected and confirmed in
office until the day of universal judgment. I beg you to accept it for
the love of Jesus Christ. . . I write this from my heart, according
to truth and reason, with my own hand, *ad perpetuam rei memoriam*.
God keep your Reverence. . . With this a hearty farewell. From
Ragusa. Your Paternity's son in Christ, Bobadilla." One good

---

in the original troubled Spanish in order to appreciate to the full its sincerity and
freedom from any taint of affectation.

[1] "De bonissima natura, tratabile, communicabile et pacifico." It may be
wondered how Cogordan came to be among the professed, a position for which
he had so long and vainly striven. It was Laynez's own doing, his mark of
appreciation of Ponce's services in France. He made his solemn profession in
the church of Saint-Germain-des-Prés on St. Catherine's day, 1560.

man, the Portuguese father, Manoel Alvares, later to be known, and perhaps execrated, by generations of Jesuit schoolboys all over the world as author of a celebrated Latin Grammar, took Laynez's self-depreciation in a very literal fashion: "Father General's contentions may be answered in the words of St. Paul — What they were afore-time, it is nothing to me. God accepteth not the person of man. While still in this life God made of Simon the Fisherman St. Peter the most holy and prudent Pope." Practically all the fathers felt as did Bobadilla, though they expressed themselves less pictur-esquely. Four, including St. Francis Borgia, urged that the new Pope, Pius IV, be asked to rescind in set terms the orders of his predecessor, and this suggestion Laynez seized as might a drowning man a straw. He let it be known that he was determined to carry out his *gran rifiuto* on the third anniversary of his election unless by that date Pope Pius had explicitly abrogated the decree of Pope Paul and commanded him to remain in office. Nadal and the other assistants met this fresh crisis by hastily drawing up a petition to the Holy Father. Then, a good fortnight before the ominous anniver-sary, they were able to present the General with a document duly signed and sealed by Cardinal Ippolito d'Este testifying that on 22 June 1561, in his presence, the Pope had annulled the contentious decree, and approved and confirmed the constitutions in their pris-tine Ignatian form. *Causa finita est.* The Jesuits kept their be-loved General, but it is possible that they deprived the Catholic Church of a very great theologian.[1]

In his government Laynez followed very closely the firm, sym-pathetic, encouraging methods of St. Ignatius. He guarded the constitutions as the apple of his eye, knowing them to be the order's best treasure, and had no patience with any slackness in their ob-servance. Even eminent rectors who indulged their liturgical bent with High Masses and choral services beyond the law were obliged to do penance for their enthusiasm. But given good will or bad health, there was none so unfailingly kind as Laynez. He did not approve of rigorous superiors, however excellent might be their other qualifications. One of his favourite words when addressing such men is *destrezza,* dexterity. In the words of the modern Jesuit

[1] M.H., *Lainii Monumenta,* viii, 748. The fifty *vota* are given in this volume, pp. 696–745. Laynez survived under his burden only another four years.

poet he would have them dress the days of their men "to a dexterous and starlight order." Let them use the Nelsonian technique of the blind eye when the fault is of little consequence. Let them beware of the parade-ground style when exercising their authority, for "often subjects are more put out by the manner in which an order is given than by the thing they are told to do." The rector of the new college in Prague, Father Ursmar Goisson, was a "molta bona persona," but, like so many good people unfortunately, not exactly amiable. Laynez writes to him as follows: "I believe that Father Canisius will have counselled your Reverence to deal with your subjects, who are your brethren, in such a way that even when you reprehend them and give them penances they may easily see that you are actuated by charity. Nothing in your words or tone or attitude ought to betray a suspicion of passion, anger, irritation or ill-will. . . You are by nature and habit somewhat irascible, as you gave proof when you were here at the German College. For the love of Christ our Lord cherish and show that love and charity to all which is certainly in your heart. If occasions arise when it seems to you impossible to overlook somebody's misbehaviour appoint another person to deal with him if you cannot trust yourself to refrain from getting into a temper." Ursmar's *bête noire* in the Prague community was the professor of philosophy, Father John van der Linden, and here we can sympathize with him, for the uniformly kindly and generous Peter Canisius told Laynez that he doubted whether there was a more cantankerous man in the whole Society than Father John. John did not stop short with mere criticism of his superior. He formed a regular league against him and denounced him to the ecclesiastical authorities of Prague. On one occasion he even resorted to violence. A chief cause of his wrath was the rector's refusal to let him have certain baths at a spa which he considered necessary for his health. It seems never to be safe to deny the waters to a man bent on having them. Laynez was appealed to by both parties. To Linden he wrote a stern letter reminding him of his vows. To Goisson he said: "Do show him love as one who is his father and the *locum tenens* of Christ. Remember that this is the way to maintain your authority and to keep the affection of your subjects. . . If the doctors advise it let him have his baths, and see to it that he is not overburdened with work." To another rector, Father Adriaens-

sens of Louvain, who belonged to the school of those whose principle is, We have a law and according to that law he ought to die,
Laynez wrote: "I commend to your Reverence care for the health
of Master Adrian Witte. He sadly needs your sympathy. If you
hesitate as to extremes, I beg you to choose the extreme of indulgent
charity rather than that of severe repression." Such is the spirit of
Laynez's instructions all the way through. To give one last example out of a multitude, here he is smoothing by means of Polanco's elegant pen the ruffled feathers of Father Juan Vitoria, a
ruthless Spanish superior of German Jesuits who believed that everybody ought to be as vigorous and iron-willed as himself. In the letter the hand is the hand of Esau but the voice is the voice of Jacob:
"Padre mio, for the love of God, do not become so easily dispirited
because of a light admonition addressed to you. These reminders
are given to you as from friend to friend, so take them in good
part if you find that they apply and if not, console yourself with
the proverb that by them you have lost nothing except what you
had to lose.[1] If you become so upset by them I think I shall resolve
never to write you anything of the kind again, because the disadvan-
tage of making you sad would weigh more heavily with me than
any advantage that might come of the admonitions. I can truly
say that I have dealt with you openly and simply, in a manner *vere
fraterna,* as I would wish to be dealt with by you and others who
love me in the Lord. In Him I beg your Reverence to enlarge your
heart and to find the consolation of your life in the practice of
obedience. As far as you can, strive to be more equable in your
conduct . . . and to win the love of the brethren. That is what
will help you best. . . May God help us all and supply for my
deficiencies." [2]

The dog days of 1561 brought a new responsibility to Laynez.
Pope Pius IV, anxious about the trend of events at the Assembly of
Poissy, had appointed a third legate to France, in addition to Lor-
raine and Tournon, and this man, Cardinal Ippolito d'Este, son of
Lucrezia Borgia and uncle of the Duke of Guise, asked that the
Jesuit General be given him as his principal theologian. Very

[1] "Haga cuenta que no se pierde sino la hechura." This is a Spanish "ex-
presión jocosa."
[2] M.H., *Epistolae P. Nadal,* ii, 634.

reluctantly the Pope, who used him as his own principal theologian, bade Laynez go. It meant leaving a hundred threads of business floating in the air but that could not be helped. Laynez appointed Salmeron to rule the order in his absence and characteristically included in his instructions to him this item: "If Father Bobadilla comes to Rome treat him well." Accompanied by Polanco, the French Jesuit, Annibal du Coudret, and a lay brother, he set off in the deadly July sun to find the legate at Ferrara. On his way he was asked to preach in the cathedral of Perugia before Cardinal della Corna, the Bishop, and all the city's notables. "It made him ill," says Polanco, "and no wonder after being out in that sun, sleeping in wretched conditions, and having to eat unsuitable food." Wherever he went he was called upon to preach, Ameria, Montepulciano, Siena, Florence, Bologna, all places with Jesuit colleges that expected his fatherly attentions. At Ferrara he was laid low with his tertian ague, but recovered sufficiently after a blooding by the ducal physicians to be able to ride away with the Cardinal Legate on 7 August. The Jesuits bestrode mules, which at any rate is not a dull method of covering the ground, and carried straw for their bedding, meaning the Jesuits' bedding, on a pack animal. In the mountains they lay on "talking beds" — *letti di parlamento* — composed of dry leaves which crackled and rustled at every movement. "But they were clean and comfortable," reported Father du Coudret, "and life high up was far better than might have been anticipated." The worst affliction of the journey was the immoderate Italian rain which drenched them all the way to Mont Cenis and endangered their lives at the fords of swollen rivers. France was not so bad, though it too provided adventure in the shape of prowling Huguenots. They reached Paris on 17 September, having been a month and ten days with the mules. After a happy day with the brethren of the Hôtel de Clermont, they went on to Saint-Germain which the Legate had made his headquarters because of the presence of the Court there. For the four of them this *magnifico,* grandson of Alexander VI and inheritor of his easy conscience, provided "una cambretta molto piccola," without beds, except two mattresses on the floor, or even a chair. The Cardinal himself lived in great state at the King's palace, where he used to invite Laynez to breakfast in order to obtain his advice.

The Assembly of Poissy had developed or degenerated into the Colloquy of the same name by the time that Ferrara with his hundreds of gaily clad retainers and four shabby Jesuits arrived on the scene. Beza's defiant speech before the Assembly on 9 September, in which he attacked the Catholic doctrines of the visible Church, Purgatory, and the Real Presence, had been eloquently answered by the Cardinal of Lorraine a week later, whereupon the Calvinists clamoured for a second round of the debate, seeing in it a golden opportunity to broadcast the ideology of Geneva.[1] It was at that crucial moment that the cavalcade from Italy entered. "Unasked and unwanted, the legate of the supreme fisherman at Rome came to cast his line into troubled waters which Catherine de Medicis had reserved for herself. He came not only to ruin her tackle and to rob her of her prize, but also to serve her with a notice of trespass, intimating that the owner of the fishing rights, angry at her unwarrantable poaching, bade her haul in her line and turn her energy into more desirable channels."[2] Catherine was not pleased and neither was the Cardinal of Lorraine, keen now after his first win on points for another bout with Beza. Between them they arranged for the continuance of the discussions privately, as the bishops obstinately refused to listen to the Calvinists again in public. The first of the two resultant conferences took place on 24 September in a large room of the old Dominican convent of Poissy. The Catholics were represented by five cardinals, three bishops, and as many theologians, including Angelo Giustiniani, a Franciscan who had become Laynez's bosom friend on the journey from Rome. Laynez himself was there too, the picture of disapproval, appraising Beza and his eleven supporters with anything but friendly eyes. To

---

[1] The curious and interesting resemblance between the propagandist technique of the sixteenth-century Calvinists and the modern Communists has been stressed by Professor Neale in his little book on Catherine de Medici: "Communist and Fascist states have shaken the world by the enthusiasm they have aroused in other countries; and also, it must be added, by the detestation. The same contagious emotional quality belonged to Calvin's Geneva. To Puritans in every land it represented the New Jerusalem. . . The missionary value of this model state can hardly be exaggerated. Making allowance for the differing scale of the world, its influence was perhaps more formidable than that of Communist Russia in our own day" (p. 22).

[2] Evennett, *The Cardinal of Lorraine*, p. 337.

honour the occasion came Catherine and her Calvinistic guests, the King and Queen of Navarre, Condé, and Coligny, but young King Charles was mercifully permitted to find a more congenial pastime.

Beza again led for his party and was answered by two Catholic Claudes, D'Espence, amiable and liberal, and De Sainctes, fierce and uncompromising. As the day wore on and the texts and interpretations flew this way and that, others joined in until the babel became too much even for optimistic Lorraine. Laynez kept silence, but stamped on his face as plain as could be were the words, "I told you so!" At length Lorraine jumped up and commanded attention. It was perfectly useless for them to range the whole field of theology, all talking at once and ambushing and sniping one another like so many implacable enemies. The purpose of the Colloquy was to restore harmony and good-will, and it could not continue unless they found some common and agreed basis for their discussions. As Beza had caused the Real Presence of Christ in the Blessed Eucharist to become the principal subject of contention, the Calvinists must be prepared to make some allowance for the Catholic view, and he therefore proposed that they sign their assent to an article on the Eucharist which he had extracted from that unimpeachably Protestant source, the Confession of Augsburg.[1]

This skilful move of the Cardinal put Beza and his men in a very awkward position. They felt that all Protestants ought to hang together in face of the common enemy and so were most reluctant to repudiate the famous Confession publicly, though it retained far too much of the ancient faith for their liking. Anticipating some such manœuvre on the part of the Catholics, the shrewd Calvin had warned Beza to avoid Eucharistic controversy altogether, but the man's overweening self-confidence led him into temptation. On the other hand, to sign the article proposed with its acceptance of the Real Presence in the Catholic sense would be tantamount to surrendering one of the fundamental tenets of Calvinism. Beza could

---

[1] There are two versions of this Confession, both mainly the work of Melanchthon, and reflecting his vacillating mind. In the original version of 1530 the Real Presence is taught in the full Catholic sense, with, however, an implied rejection of Transubstantiation. The version of 1540 could be interpreted in a Catholic or a Zwinglian sense. Melanchthon seems not to have known himself what precisely he believed.

not sign. In his dilemma Queen Catherine, anxious for the fate of her Colloquy, came to his rescue and begged Lorraine to find some formula more considerate of the Calvinist conscience. Lorraine, an obliging man, tried and tried, but found all his efforts wrecked by the Zwinglian Peter Martyr whom the Queen had specially invited to Poissy. The conference met again on 26 September, and once more the Catholic contestants arrived armed with large tomes of the Fathers, marked at the appropriate places. But Lorraine had had enough of argument that led nowhere and only served to increase bitterness. Were the Calvinists prepared to sign the Augsburg article? To this question Beza cleverly retorted by asking whether if they did the Cardinal was prepared to follow their example, and thus equivalently deny Transubstantiation. It was a fair and telling counter-*riposte,* which Lorraine acknowledged by resignedly bidding D'Espence to resume the debate. The argument had not proceeded far when Peter Martyr felt inspired to justify his special invitation to the Colloquy by making a contribution, nor did his ignorance of French in the least deter this bold ex-Augustinian revivalist. They must hear him in Italian, which rather pleased the Italian Queen. After listening to him for half an hour without comprehending anything except his Latin quotations, D'Espence endeavoured to reply, but so fumbled at the task that Laynez, whose temper had been fretted by hearing the most musical of languages turned to the most inharmonious of purposes, could no longer contain himself. He jumped to his feet, dark eyes flashing, and addressed himself directly to the Queen in her own tongue.

"Madama," he began, "though a foreigner has no business to interfere in the concerns of a country not his own, yet as the faith is not national but universal and Catholic I feel entitled to put before Your Majesty my views about this conference in general and about the objections raised by Fra Pietro Martyre and his colleague in particular." Five times over during the discourse the arch-heretic heard himself referred to as "Fra Pietro," to his blushing embarrassment and annoyance, which is exactly what Laynez intended. He went on: "As to the first point, from my reading and constant experience, I am convinced that it is most dangerous to treat with or listen to persons separated from the Church. In the Book of Ecclesiasticus it is asked, Who will pity an enchanter struck by a serpent, or any that come near wild beasts? The Scriptures describe dissidents from the Church as serpents, wolves in sheeps' clothing, and foxes, that we may understand how very necessary it is to be on our guard against the wiles which they invariably employ. . . I venture to recommend two means to this end to you, Madam, the first good, the second less evil than other courses. The first is that Your Majesty should recognize it to be outside your province or that of any temporal prince to deal with matters of the faith. The temporal prince has no authority in such matters, with the subtleties and details of which he is not usually in the habit of occupying his mind, and it is generally agreed that the shoemaker ought to stick to his last. These matters are the business of priests, and it belongs to the Supreme Priest and to the General Council to define them. As the Council is now in operation, it is neither seemly nor legitimate to gather together rival congregations. Indeed, the Fathers of the Council of Basle decreed that no provincial councils may be held while the General Council is in session or during the six months prior to its meeting. Consequently, the best course for Your Majesty will be to direct these gentlemen to Trent where are assembled learned men from all nations to labour under the infallible guidance of the Holy Spirit, which is something we cannot promise ourselves here. His Holiness will not fail to give them a safe-conduct and every other necessary guarantee of security. If, as they say, they desire to be instructed, they will find much better opportunities at Trent. But to tell the truth, I do not believe that they want to be instructed. Rather do they want to instruct and spread their poison, for instead of giving ear to others they hold forth themselves for an hour and a half on end."

That was plain speaking with a vengeance, and so was Laynez's second *remedio non buono ma manco malo,* that if Queen Catherine wished the disputations to continue she should see that they were held in strictest privacy and spare herself and the other illustrious persons now present the boredom and possible danger of any further attendance.[1] Polanco, who was present, told a friend afterwards that

[1] Despite their professed objection to it, more than half (twenty-five, to be precise) of the bishops trooped in to the second Poissy conference. Polanco gives a list of the other notables who came "in spite of the rain" — Queen Catherine; Antoine de Bourbon and his wife, Jeanne d'Albret; Condé and his wife;

while Laynez spoke the Catholic doctors appeared as pleased "as if they were bathing in rose-water." He gave Salmeron his impressions in the following lines: "Your Reverence may like to know how our Father's plain speaking affected his audience. Well, it displeased the heretics mightily, which was a good sign in my opinion. The Catholic doctors near me seemed jubilant at hearing expressed truths which, out of mistaken courtesy, the good men had not themselves had the courage to ventilate. The Queen, I understand, was somewhat annoyed, but I think the animadversions will have done her good, for they say that she is not going to any more of the conferences. In general, I am informed, the speech made a good impression as being sound and necessary, but some people considered its tone too free. Others, on the contrary, thought it inspired by God."[1] Whether too free or inspired it was Laynez to the life, plain and blunt and utterly fearless.

As a consequence of the Jesuit General's speech Lorraine lost his enthusiasm for the discussions, but Queen Catherine managed by much persuasion and cajolery to keep them going a little while longer. Laynez spoke on two other occasions and Polanco also said what seemed good to him, if only in deference to the wishes of the

---

Francis, Duke of Guise; his brother, the Duke of Aumale; the Duke of Nemours; the Constable de Montmorency; Cardinals Lorraine, Bourbon, Armagnac, Châtillon, and Guise, etc. Ferrara and Tournon loyally kept away.

[1] M.H., *Lainii Monumenta,* vi, 58. This same letter of Polanco is one of the chief sources for the description of the conference. The speech itself occupies eight pages of *Lainii Monumenta,* viii. Evennett gives a very good summary of the second part in which Laynez answers Peter Martyr and Beza. His opinion of the speech in general is as follows: "It was obviously sincere, surprisingly moderate, very convincing and astonishingly free from personalities. . . His root-and-branch condemnation of the Colloquy, though quite unforeseen, and occupying no more than about a quarter of an hour of his whole speech, had had important and permanent effect. . . The moment had been skilfully chosen. Beza's escape from the dilemma of the Lutheran articles had finally shattered the whole plan of action to which the Cardinal of Lorraine had pinned his assurance, and the Assembly had just been constrained to sit through a long speech in an Italian dialect from Peter Martyr. . . An atmosphere of restive dissatisfaction prevailed, and the moment was an admirably propitious one in which to drive home the point of view that the whole affair was not only a failure, but a mistake, and a reprehensible mistake at that. The clever Jesuit had timed his blow to a nicety" (*The Cardinal of Lorraine,* pp. 367–72).

Queen. Neither of them had the slightest hope of any useful result coming from the conference, and witnessed its inglorious demise after three further convulsions without the least pang of regret. The Assembly of Poissy itself came to an end on 14 October 1561, with nine little canons to show for all the talk and temper, things good enough in themselves and even approved by Trent, but rendered a dead letter by the disappointed and angry Queen. Net result, nothing. It is to Catherine's credit that she seems to have borne Laynez no grudge for his part in the frustration of her eirenic schemes. At all events, she accorded him two private audiences and accepted from him a great mass of written advice, even if she did not see fit to follow it in every detail. For eight months more he and Polanco remained in Paris, slaving day in and day out for the soul of France and for the interests of the Council of Trent. Not Joan of Arc herself could be said to have had the good of France more at heart than those two aliens who spoke the language with difficulty and had little but their infectious sincerity to recommend them. At home, in that "cambretta molto piccola" with its solitary table and beds on the floor, or in the hardly more comfortable refuge of the ramshackle Hôtel de Clermont, they laboriously drafted a whole series of memoranda and appeals to the Queen, the Prince de Condé, and the bishops of France. One of those addressed to Catherine de Medici runs to four thousand words, and is full of references to ancient councils and ecclesiastical writers, obviously from memory, as Laynez had then no access to his beloved folios. The most interesting of the pieces is his appeal to the restless conspirator Condé, the military leader of the Huguenots.

"Excellency," he says, "it is easy to see the importance of finding some good means of restoring union between the new churches and the ancient Roman Church from which they have separated in our time. It is important not only for the temporal peace and quiet of the Kingdom, but far more for the eternal peace of so many souls. There can be but one true Church, outside of which is no hope of salvation. If the ancient Roman Church is such, then these others are in a state of damnation. If they are right, then she is in a sorry plight. . . First, let us see what were the causes that brought about the disruption of unity. They are principally two, the lives of ecclesiastics from the highest prelate down to the most insignificant cleric, which have given so much scandal and so badly need reform, though that ought not to make us forget Christ's words about the Scribes and Pharisees seated upon the chair of Moses; and secondly, abuses mixed up with the practice of religion, which have crept in through ignorance or avarice or for some other reason, and likewise are an occasion of scandal. Consequently, the remedy for the disunion would be to provide against those two evils, and at the same time to come to doctrinal agreement in a spirit of charity and not of contention. Now the means to achieve this would appear to be the following. The Pope has summoned an œcumenical council and called to it all those with a right to attend, who are not only the bishops, but the abbots and heads of religious orders, and various learned men. . . It would then be expedient to see that a grand array of such persons went from the Kingdom of France . . . and King Philip and the Emperor might also be approached and urged to follow the same course in their dominions. We need not doubt the result, for both monarchs are most anxious for the reformation of the clergy, . . . and the Pope, as his Legate testifies, is ready to make such a reformation one of the principal aims of the Council. It will whet his eagerness if he sees the princes to be enthusiastic. Now the Council being free and having to deal seriously with this question of reformation, the heads of the new churches in France and Germany ought to attend it, in order both to help with the work of reformation and to discuss points of controversy. We may hope that the Holy Spirit, Author of true peace and union, will be present and settle what differences exist, as in past times He came amongst those assembled in His name, and put a peaceful end to great controversies. . . Those of the new churches may rest assured that they will be well treated and shown all courtesy both before and after that union which, if I had a hundred lives, I would give them all to see God bring about." [1]

Alas, Condé preferred to settle controversies by the sword, and at the very time of Laynez's appeal plunged France into the bloodbath of her Religious Wars. But the saddened priest did not surrender his hope. It is recorded of Pope Pius XI that when criticized for treating with Mussolini he declared himself ready "to do a deal with the devil in person," if thereby he could render the Church

---

[1] This and six of the appeals are given in *Lainii Monumenta,* viii, 775–805.

a service or save her from an injury. Such exactly was Laynez's principle. He humbled himself to crave an interview with Beza, and to plead with that proud, intransigent heresiarch. Would he be so kind as to put in writing the conditions on which he might think of honouring Trent with his presence? His petitioner would see to their fulfilment. Suave Polanco, too, was sent on the same fruitless errand, and both he and Laynez went on their knees to the sinister Bishop of Valence, that "loose-living, sceptical and secularized Dominican . . . who had engaged suspected preachers to preach the Lent in his cathedral and who had been denounced as a heretic by the dean of his own Chapter." [1] Polanco even ventured into the presence of the recreant Cardinal Châtillon, so soon to apostatize and find his spiritual home in Elizabethan England. To compensate for that unpleasant interview, it fell to him to attend on his death-bed the saintly old Cardinal de Tournon, who left ten thousand francs in trust for the poor. Laynez could not go because the Paris pulpits, those of St. Augustine's and of the Colleges of Montaigu, Sainte Barbe and La Marche, were absorbing his energies, as were the hospitals, whose almoner he had constituted himself with wealthy Ferrara.[2] So the two men worked and suffered and hoped until the June day of 1562 when they must take the long roundabout road to Trent, where Laynez was expected, not only as Papal theologian, but as a fully accredited Father of the Council.

They had to approach Trent from the north via Germany because France at civil war, as the good Nadal discovered, was no place for wandering, unprotected Jesuits. Polanco gives their itinerary, St. Quentin where was a Huguenot garrison, Cambrai, Valenciennes, Tournai, Brussels, Antwerp, Louvain, Liége, Maastricht, Jülich, Cologne, Trier, Mainz, Frankfurt, Aschaffenburg, Ulm, Augsburg, Ingolstadt, Munich, Innsbruck, Trent. If anyone cares to draw

[1] Evennett, *The Cardinal of Lorraine*, p. 146. Polanco writes: "I spoke with the Bishop of Valence, animating him as I did the others to hope for good results from the Council, and discussing with him the means to secure its freedom and success. He was very candid with me. . . Afterwards I spoke to the Legate, exhorting him to save this Valence for the service of God. . . I went back a second time to the Bishop to stir him up with regard to the Council. . ."

[2] The list of their activities in Paris is given by Polanco in *Lainii Monumenta,* viii, 768–75.

straight lines between those places he will find himself with a diagram very like the chart of a patient in a high and peculiar fever. The reason is that Laynez constantly diverged from the shorter route in order to visit his sons, or to consult with bishops, or to give pleasure to his old friend, Margaret of Austria, ruler of the Netherlands, or to put heart into some despondent prelate of Germany. The journey, which took thirty-three days, was a physical feat in itself for a man so frail and subject to illness, but when we learn that he preached in every place, gave exhortations to his Jesuits, visited the hospitals, heard confessions, and sat down weary in body and soul to a formidable list of banquets arranged in his honour, we wonder that Trent ever knew him at all. For us, much the most interesting of his divagations was that to Louvain, for there, says Polanco, "he was visited by the principal professors of the University, as well as by others, especially Englishmen, of whom there are large numbers in the city, exiles come to practise their religion in peace." Among them was a nephew of St. Thomas More, "still a boy and poor whom he gave orders should be received into the German College out of regard for his martyred uncle; and many other were the steps he took to help that nation." [1] Of the twenty-one places mentioned by Polanco, all but five either had or were soon to have flourishing Jesuit colleges and churches, and this after God and St. Peter Canisius was principally due to the love and esteem in which men held Diego Laynez.

Within the Society of Jesus it is safe to say that no superior was ever better loved than he, and outside its ranks people who could not stomach Jesuits in general made an exception of this Jesuit. Even Melchior Cano wanted to be in his good books. A Spanish priest of noble birth and high attainment named Martin Olave decided, after some experience of courts and camps, that he must be-

[1] "Your well-known goodness of heart and great influence with the Holy Father," wrote the English students to Laynez afterwards, "impel us to fly to you in our trouble. Your singular interest in us, of which we are well aware, emboldens us to beg and pray that you would do what is in your power to relieve our necessities" (*Lainii Monumenta*, viii, 560–1). Polanco's letter to St. Francis Borgia describing the journey is one of the longest he ever wrote, and it was not his habit to spare ink (M.H., *Lainii Monumenta*, vi, 333–55). Among other eminent people visited *en route* were Chancellor Granvelle, George Fugger, the famous banker, and the five daughters of Emperor Ferdinand.

come a religious and if possible sail away to convert the infidel. He had seen some Jesuits in the course of his travels, but being of a gay turn, "natura festivus," liked not their serious preoccupied mien. One regrets to record that he used to indulge in jokes at the expense of the sobersides. Unable to make up his mind which order to join, he begged God daily to indicate His holy will, always, however, with the proviso, "not the Society of Jesus." Then at Trent in 1552 he fell under the spell of Laynez, and we next find him in Rome, an enthusiastic novice whom St. Ignatius on his death-bed appointed jointly with Polanco to govern for a time all the Jesuits in the world. Alas, this delightful acquisition survived the Saint only by a fortnight. More remarkable still was the case of William Postel, that luminary of the Collège de France who saw visions and dreamed dreams. As related on an earlier page, William's attempt to put on the Jesuit harness had not been a great success, and he left, as he said himself, "feeling hostile to Ignatius and all his company with one exception," Laynez, for whose sake he would try to think kindly of the rest. He succeeded very well too. If it is not uncharitable to him to say so, he was a kind of Catholic H. G. Wells bristling with schemes for the unification and education of mankind, theories which did not appeal to the incipient Sacred Congregation of the Index. William therefore led a harassed existence. When Laynez came to France he wrote to him in the following strain: "Lainesi charissime, . . . Seeing you head of the whole order and recognizing in you all of God's gifts except the power of working miracles, I have determined to open my soul to you completely as to an *alter ego,* so that you may decide about my salvation as you would wish our Lord Jesus Christ to decide about your own. . . I speak from my heart. In a letter which I recently addressed to Chancellor de l'Hôpital I chose you alone as the judge of my cause, and will accept your decision as though Christ Himself had made it. . . What I would not trust to the rest of mankind put together I commit to your sole discretion and learning, namely my labours, strivings, and books, undertaken to bring about concord in the human family. . . I am absolutely ready to go on with my work or to retract what I have already written according as you judge best. . . I would like to embrace some form of the religious life and have often thought of becoming a Carthusian, except that I do not like their ban on preaching, or one of the Minims, if my poor stomach would tolerate their diet of fish. But my greatest desire is that, in whatever way you can bring it about, I may live united to you and under your obedience." [1]

The full story of Laynez's third appearance at Trent, with specimens of his oratory and illustrations of the influence which he wielded, would make a book in itself of no mean proportions. Indeed it *has* made such a book and the pages thereof are nearly seven hundred.[2] That is one way the Jesuits had of expanding and progressing, but is not a way with many attractions for the ordinary untheological reader to whom, in affection and esteem, this English book is dedicated. So to round off his portrait let us look for a moment at Laynez the man rather than the theologian as he moves through the pageant of passions and emotions, hopes and disappointments, selfishness and generosity, human frailty and divine power, that was the fascinating, miraculous Council of Trent. In a little biography of Laynez which he composed about twenty years after the close of the Council, Ribadeneira wrote with a flourish that "no sooner was he arrived at Trent than the splendour and effulgence of his learning began as usual to shine forth." One of the three Jesuit censors of the book, Father Manoel Rodrigues whom we salute, scored in the margin opposite the lighthearted sentence: "These words are a gross exaggeration. Let them be removed." The criticism was just, for what in fact shone forth on that occasion was not anybody's learning but everybody's very natural propensity to stand out for his genuine or imaginary rights. "There was strife amongst them which of them should seem to be the greater." The story is best told in an open letter which the four presidents of the Council, Cardinals Gonzaga, Seripando, Hosius and Simonetta, addressed to the "whole Christian world" on 1 November 1562: "We, the Apostolic Legates, have learned with indignation of an idle and unjust rumour spread abroad in various localities and provinces to the effect that Reverend Father James Laynez, General of the Society of Jesus, has intruded himself against their will into the ranks of the prelates in order to voice his opinions

---

[1] M.H., *Lainii Monumenta,* vi, 268–71.

[2] To be exact, 680, a figure arrived at by adding together all the strictly relevant pages of Grisar's two volumes, *Jacobi Lainez Disputationes Tridentinae,* referred to above.

among them, and that he also endeavoured to obtain precedence before the Generals of the monastic orders. . . We, the Presidents and
Moderators of this Sacred Œcumenical Council, have therefore considered it our duty to make known and attest, as we hereby do, to
each and all of the faithful of Christ that the aforesaid Father
General of the Society of Jesus took his place among the prelates
with a definitive vote by their express desire and by the command of
our Holy Father the Pope, according to custom long received in the
Church of God. As, however, this Society is composed of clerks
regular and not of monks, and as it appertains to our Master of Ceremonies to assign to both classes their proper places in the Council, a
doubt arose whether the aforesaid Father General, being a regular
clerk, should take precedence of the monks, or, as the head of an
order founded and approved later than the monastic ones, should be
given a place and the right to speak after the heads of the older orders.
Now, though he affirmed and desired it to be understood that the
institute of his Society was clerical and not monastic, Father Laynez
declared himself ready for the sake of peace and decorum to rank
last among the Generals, and in fact petitioned for the last place.
Having no precedent to guide us, because the Society of Jesus came
into existence and spread far and wide throughout the Christian and
pagan worlds to the utmost profit of souls since the last General
Council of the Lateran, we ordered that its head be given a special
place to himself, apart from the heads of the monastic orders, so
that he might speak and record his vote after them, without prejudice
to his clerical status. In that place the Reverend General has sat with
all modesty and composure ever since he was first admitted to the
Council." [1]

---

[1] M.H., *Lainii Monumenta,* vi, 469–71. The Master of Ceremonies, by name
Firmano, wrote as follows in one of the Council's many Diaries: "On Wednesday, August 21st, a congregation was held at which Reverend Father James
Laynez first appeared. By order of the Legates, to stop controversy with the
other Generals, I assigned him a place after the last Bishop on the left side. The
other Generals sat immediately after the Abbots on the right side, asserting that
they would not give way to the General of the Jesuits because these men were a
new religious order. This controversy was not the fault of the Jesuit General,
for he had no ambition to precede anybody, and would willingly have taken the
last place had not the Legates forbidden it" (Merkle, *Concilium Tridentinum,*
ii, 561–2). The Legates' letter to St. Charles Borromeo requesting him to ob-

That little storm in the teacups of the orders was typical of much that happened at Trent, but it ought not to surprise anyone who has kept even the most perfunctory watch o'er man's mortality. He will feel in his bones that the only corporations which do not indulge in mutual rivalries and bickerings are very probably the nine choirs of angels. What may reasonably surprise us is that historians should be so free and easy, as well as high and mighty, with their judgments. Here is one fairly recent pronouncement on the Council of Trent: "The critical spirit of the Venetian Paolo Sarpi has preserved for us a record of this extraordinary assembly, so unrepresentative of Europe as a whole, so disappointing to the believers in conciliar government, but so true to the tradition of Roman autocracy. The leading figure in the later debates and the man who again carried the papal cause to victory was Laynez, the second General of the Jesuit order. In that scene of subtle intrigue, furious national hatreds, and open profligacy the stern, eloquent, and invincible Jesuit stood out like a giant." [1]   To counteract this exalta-

---

tain a decision from his uncle, the Pope, on the case of Laynez is given in *Lainii Monumenta*, viii, 815.

[1] H. A. L. Fisher, *A History of Europe* (London 1936), i, 557. It is strange that so good and genial a scholar as Mr. Fisher should have gone to the dreary partisan Sarpi for his impressions. Sarpi, a rebellious Servite friar, was only nine years old when Trent entered on its final phase, and his work, first published pseudonymously under Protestant auspices in London, was little else than Venetian propaganda against the Holy See, which had recently put the Republic under an interdict. There is no longer any excuse for depending slavishly on Fra Paolo, now that the carefully selected and one-sided sources which he used have been so magnificently supplemented from all the archives of Europe in the sumptuous folios of the Görresgesellschaft, *Concilium Tridentinum, Diariorum, Actorum, Epistularum, Tractatuum Nova Collectio,* twelve volumes (Freiburg im Breisgau), 1901 sqq. What lover of good learning but would exclaim as he turned those teeming pages, *Il naufragar m'è dolce in questo mare!* Mr. Fisher was a man of much humour, but he seemed to lose all sense of it when Jesuits rambled into his story. Desiring to show that they were not only plotters and persecutors but obscurantists, he told the following tale in the first edition of his famous book: "When, at the beginning of the seventeenth century, Kircher invited a Jesuit professor to look through his telescope at the newly discovered spots on the sun, the Jesuit replied, 'My son, it is useless. I have read Aristotle through twice, and have not found anything about spots on the sun. There are no spots on the sun.' It was therefore heresy to maintain the Copernican theory of the planets. . . Such were the leaden inhibitions which shackled the

tion of Laynez we read in a well-known Catholic *History of Europe*
that the Jesuits at Trent, meaning Laynez, Salmeron and St. Peter
Canisius, "exercised an influence out of proportion to their numbers
or their learning, but not out of proportion to their zeal or enthusiasm." That is a delightful instance of damning with faint praise.
The truth of the matter lies somewhere between those two judgments. It was not Laynez but Cardinal Morone, recently emerged
from five years' imprisonment in the Castle of St. Angelo under
Paul IV, who carried the Papal cause to victory; nor can the Jesuit
General be said to have stood out like a giant in an assembly that
included many of the best intellects and finest characters of that
age. On the other hand, Laynez did not owe his influence merely
to zeal and enthusiasm. The zeal and enthusiasm belonged rather
to the Legates, Archbishops and Bishops who made the life of the
frail and prematurely ageing General [1] a burden by their daily in-
vitations to protracted dinners and interviews, or by their constant
visits to his lodging for information or advice. The pressure became so heavy that Polanco had to appeal to the brethren in Rome
to restrain their epistolary ardour, for greatly though he appreciated
the letters Laynez could not find time to read them, much less answer them.

At the moment of his arrival in the Council discussion turned on
the great subject of the Sacrifice of the Mass, and one point warmly
debated was whether the Last Supper was the first Mass. Cardinal
Seripando, the second Legate and an Augustinian who could be
trusted to take an original line on most theological topics, cham-
pioned the negative opinion, maintaining that, though our Lord at

---

learning of the mediaeval Faculties." It was pointed out to Mr. Fisher that the
Kircher of this anecdote was himself a Jesuit professor, which rather destroyed
its point. But he liked the ridiculous story, as much an invention and not nearly
as *ben trovato* as the *Eppur si muove* attributed to Galileo, liked it so well that
he refused to give it up and merely substituted the words "brother Jesuit" for
"Jesuit professor," to cover up his mistake about Kircher. In that revised form
it still decorates a page of the *History of Europe,* the one Jesuit professor addressing the other Jesuit professor as "My son," to the mild astonishment of all Jesuit
professors.

[1] Though only fifty, he had not much longer to live and knew it, as he told
St. Francis Borgia in a letter of 9 April 1562: "I think my weakness is just a
part of old age, and that is an incurable disease."

the Last Supper had instituted the Holy Sacrifice to be offered by the Apostles and their successors in the priesthood, He had not on that occasion offered Himself to His Eternal Father under the species of bread and wine. When it fell to Laynez to speak in the general congregation held on 27 August, he just as strenuously defended the affirmative view. Only shreds of his discourse have come down, but there remain two interesting comments on it. The first is Seripando's: "Last of all the Fathers to speak was Don Laynez. It cannot be denied that he spoke to the point and eloquently, but I was unable to see anything in his arguments beyond a mere probability and a certain speciousness by which the inexperienced general run of men is most easily swayed." The Archbishop of Zara in Dalmatia considered it a learned and devout speech, but a shade too long, for it "ate up practically the whole morning." [1] The good lay brother, Juan Fernandez, who acted as factotum to the Jesuits at Trent, reported that it lasted two hours and a half and that not a single cardinal, archbishop or bishop was absent from his place when the General rose to speak. That they might not miss a word of his wisdom, a special pulpit was wheeled in for him and set in the centre of the assembly. [2]

Among the Fathers of the Council most often at the Jesuits' house or their host at his own was George Drascovics, Bishop of Fünfkirchen and second ambassador of Emperor Ferdinand I at Trent. He and the first ambassador, Anton Brus, Archbishop of Prague, had shown the Jesuits of their countries the greatest kindness and figured high on the list of the order's most devoted friends. Both men had come to the Council with an urgent mandate from Ferdinand to strive by every means in their power to obtain the privilege of communion under both kinds for German lands, in other words, the concession of the chalice to the laity. The Fathers were divided in their minds as to the wisdom of such a change of discipline, designed as a sop to the Lutherans. The German and Hungarian bishops on the whole favoured it and so did a large number of their Italian brethren, but the powerful and eloquent Spanish party opposed it *en bloc*. Laynez had every human and prudential reason

<hr>

[1] Ehses, *Concilium Tridentinum,* viii, 788, n. 2.
[2] M.H., *Lainii Monumenta,* vi, 383.

to give the petition his warm support, seeing how utterly dependent were the Jesuits of Germany, Austria, Hungary and Bohemia on the goodwill of its prime movers, the Emperor and the Duke of Bavaria, yet he directed Salmeron,[1] Polanco and Peter Canisius to oppose it in the congregation of theologians, and when his turn came to address the Fathers on 6 September he left no doubt as to his sentiments. *Amicus Ferdinandus, amicus Albertus, sed magis amica veritas.* From his long experience of the religious controversy he felt convinced that one concession would only lead to the demand for another, and that the Protestants would not be satisfied with anything short of the abolition of the Papacy.[2] Whether in the sixteenth or twentieth century the Germans of the north could be trusted to run true to form. The Emperor's aggrieved ambassadors wrote that Laynez's speech, "though full of bad arguments," did more than anything else to consolidate the Spanish opposition, rally Italian waverers, and finally wreck all hope of obtaining the grant from the Council. As a mere piece of learning, *pace* the ambassadors, the speech is truly remarkable, but what impresses most is the integrity of mind and heart so patent in its closing words: "I have not come to the conclusion that the chalice ought to be denied from any lack of readiness to meet his Imperial Majesty's wishes in all things according to God and my conscience. All of us who belong to the Society of Jesus know right well our debt to his Majesty. He was the first of Catholic princes to receive our

[1] Salmeron appears to have been the only theologian sent by the Pope on this occasion. Writing to the Legates concerning him, St. Charles Borromeo said: "There is no need for me to expatiate to you on his goodness, learning and experience in the affairs of the Council." He was always called upon to speak first in the congregations of theologians, and he generally spoke the longest, three hours being nothing unusual for him. The Legates did not like this prolixity, but as Papal theologian Alfonso was sacrosanct. His friend, the Dominican, Peter Soto, theologian of the King of Spain, set him a shining example by speaking briefly and cogently, but the expansive Jesuit was not converted. One of the Fathers, Archbishop Bandini, considered his discourse on 10 June, "the best to date and not likely to be bettered" (*Concilium Tridentinum,* viii, 541, n. 2).

[2] Luther himself had said so in a letter to Melanchthon of 26 August 1530: "I utterly disapprove of talk of doctrinal concord. Such a thing is quite impossible unless the Pope is willing to abolish his Papacy."

order into his dominions and to foster its growth, and to him we owe our colleges of Vienna, Prague, Tyrnau, and Innsbruck. His son-in-law, the Duke of Bavaria, following his example, has given us colleges at Ingolstadt and Munich, and is making ready to found others. But the more we are bound by ties of gratitude, the more is it my duty to say out faithfully what I consider to be the more conducive to the glory of God and the salvation of such great princes and their peoples." [1] Defeated in their main endeavour to extort the concession from the Council, the Imperial ambassadors then tried to persuade the Fathers to recommend their case to the Pope, but once more Laynez intervened and what went to Rome was a bare statement of the Emperor's wishes, without comment either favourable or critical. In deference to those wishes Pius IV eventually granted the chalice to the laity in some provinces of the Empire, only to find that the Protestants remained entirely unimpressed, as Laynez had foretold. Various abuses led to the complete and final withdrawal of the privilege by Pope Gregory XIII.

Far more important than the chalice question, and indeed permanently significant, was another controversy which divided the Fathers of the Council during its closing stages. It had to do with the sacrament of Orders, and might be compared to a black storm-cloud long menacing the Council which broke at last in a fearful commotion of tempers, accompanied by torrential eloquence. After the theologians headed by Salmeron had said their say on the subject of Orders, the Legates, at the beginning of October 1562, appointed a committee to draft the usual statement of doctrine and "canons" for submission to the Fathers at the next general congregation. This select body consisted of two archbishops, three bishops, the General of the Servites, and Laynez. The others entrusted to Laynez the task of putting their collective decisions into written form which was then brought to the Legates for revision, and by them handed to Angelo Massarelli, the Secretary of the Council, to

---

[1] Ehses, *Concilium Tridentinum*, viii, 879–98. The twenty folio pages given to the speech in this great collection contrast with the solitary page devoted to all the speeches of the other generals, of whom the Franciscan Observant opposed the concession, while the Franciscan conventual advocated it. The General of the Clerks Regular of the Lateran was silenced by the Legates before he could get properly under way at all.

be multiplied. "The following day," writes Brother Juan Fernandez, "our Father sent me to the Secretary's house with the original copy that I might correct it according to the emendations which had been made. There I found more than a hundred scriptors at work copying, for each bishop had sent his own man, and I saw that they were writing out word for word our Father's text, without changing a single syllable." [1] The seventh canon that was to precipitate the storm ran as follows: "If any one saith that bishops are not superior to priests; or that they have not the power of confirming and ordaining; or that the power which they possess is common to them and to priests; . . . Let him be anathema." Those words were carefully chosen and look innocent enough, yet they contained the explosive potentialities of a colossal bomb because their redactor, with the utmost deliberation, omitted to say on which of two possible bases of law, the ecclesiastical or the divine, episcopal superiority rested.

The Spanish party in the Council, headed by the learned, fiery and truculent Pedro Guerrero, Archbishop of Granada, incidentally a very good friend and patron of the Jesuits,[2] had already endeavoured on numerous occasions to extort from the Fathers a definition that episcopal jurisdiction no less than the spiritual power conferred by episcopal orders derives immediately from God, but the Legates each time succeeded in shelving discussion of a topic so dangerous, designed as it unquestionably was to extend episcopal authority at the expense of that of the Pope. Guerrero was determined that it should be no longer shelved, and when the canons came to be discussed among the Fathers on 13 October immediately proposed an amendment to the seventh embodying his theory of divine right. For ten months afterwards the Council was to know no peace from "this confounded question," as the Jesuits' letters pardonably described it. Though often pinned to his bed by gout or arthritis,

[1] M.H., *Lainii Monumenta,* vi, 455. Polanco says, however, that the committee had "slightly improved the style" of Laynez before passing his work to the Legates, and they must certainly have "improved" his handwriting by the aid of a professional copyist.

[2] "The brethren in Rome," writes Polanco, on 14 September 1562, "are offering prayers for a sister of the Archbishop of Granada, who has died there. To-day, our Father, Salmeron and myself have been to dinner with his Grace to renew our old friendship."

and gravely conscious of the hostility to his order which he was provoking, Laynez fought for the rights of the Holy See during those stormy months as never he had fought before. Pastor adjudges his speech of 20 October "a masterpiece, distinguished alike by its vast learning, its clearness, and its pertinency, which created an impression such as was scarcely made by any other address during the whole course of the Council." [1] However that may have been, and the eulogy is surely somewhat extreme, there is no doubting Laynez's integrity and disinterestedness. He knew very well that he was going to make enemies, but he never hesitated. Shortly after the date of his speech, Charles of Lorraine, with a following of thirteen Gallican stalwarts, including Eustache du Bellay, Bishop of Paris, arrived in Trent, and almost immediately sent up the temperature of the Council to fever pitch. Writing to Father Araoz on 1 January 1563, Laynez said: "Blessed be our Lord, I am reasonably well, though there is no lack of affliction and weariness. A man must obey his conscience and find his consolation in so doing, even if he knows that he cannot, in this wretched world, without offending other people. . . Unless our Lord stretches out His hand, I greatly fear, Father, that once these interminable disputes about the divine right of bishops are bruited in France, the devil may use the occasion to have the French party withdrawn from the Council. They are well-meaning and zealous men, but the consequence of their wrangling may be failure to define matters of faith or to bring about any reform of morals and manners, to the scandal of the whole world. The result might even be schism. . . I have done the little that lay in my power to avert such a disaster by writing to the Pope and entreating him to urge on the definition of dogmas and the passing of such reformation decrees as may be possible, and then to bring the Council to an end. As it is absolutely necessary to complete the work of reformation, I have suggested that, should the Fathers prove unwilling to go on with the little in this matter which they have already achieved, his Holiness, in conjunction with the Catholic princes, might call together a small group of really good, learned, practical bishops from every nation, and with their assistance carry through the great task. Here, there is such diversity of opin-

[1] *History of the Popes,* English ed., 1928, xv, 301. Such also was the opinion of Sarpi and of his antagonist Pallavicini. But Pallavicini was a Jesuit.

ions and inclinations, that I fear it would be morally impossible to achieve it. . ." [1]

Some idea of the feeling aroused by Laynez's speech may be gathered from a letter of the Archbishop of Zara to a cardinal friend immediately afterwards: "I can tell your Lordship that many people have been offended, and some are even saying that the game of Father Laynez and his brethren is to arrogate to themselves the power of bishops by means of their privileges, without the burden of the episcopate. . . Your Lordship knows how I love this Father. I tell you what I hear, and I am much afraid he has not improved the opinion which many excellent people held of him." [2] The pressure to which both Salmeron and Laynez were subjected to make them alter or modify their views, may be estimated from a huge letter of protest which the French theologian, Hervet, addressed to them on 20 March 1563. Here it is possible to give only a few lines of it: "I appeal to you, I implore you, Alfonso Salmeron and James Laynez. . . Have you forgotten the beautiful title which you took to yourselves of Companions of Jesus? . . . You say that you defend the authority of the Vicar of Christ, and all the time, by your opposition to the doctrine that episcopal residence is of divine obligation, you do nothing but bring upon Jesus Himself, so far as lies in your power, ignominy, reproach, and dishonour. . ." [3] That was a cruel thing to have said of one, but Hippocleides didn't care. Far from modifying his unpopular views, Laynez attacked the Gallican theory that general councils are superior to the Pope with all his might in a speech delivered on 13 June 1563. In the heat of the moment he came out with these provocative words: "A crowd always affrights me, even a crowd of bishops!" They gave great offence, as did also his onslaught on the unblushing pluralism of so many of the French hierarchy. Carlo Visconti, the Bishop of Ventimiglia, told his friend Carlo Borromeo that the French and Spanish prelates were sharply criticizing the Legates for their indulgence to the offender, especially for allowing him to address the Fathers seated and for calling emergency congregations to suit his

[1] M.H., *Lainii Monumenta*, vi, 610–11.

[2] M.H., *Lainii Monumenta*, viii, 818.

[3] There are twelve folio pages of this (Le Plat, *Monumentorum ad Historiam Concilii Tridentini Collectio*, Louvain 1785, v, 777–89).

convenience, "that he might have an opportunity of saying whatever he fancies." [1]

Perhaps the critics did not know that he was crippled with arthritis and more than once had missed his turn in the congregations because too cruelly racked with pain to appear. Even at such times when lying in bed he continued to write and write until the room was strewn with memoranda for the Fathers who sought his advice on the various burning questions before the Council.[2] But this chapter threatens to become more long-winded than one of Salmeron's discourses, so let us close remembering that the tired and sick man with the unresting pen and eloquent fearless tongue, had also upon his bowed shoulders the care of the whole Society of Jesus, grown double in numbers and activities since he had taken the helm. From Trent during his sixteen months' stay there no less than 2379 letters went out in his name and by his direction to Jesuits all over the world, an average of about five letters a day. One great reward he had for all this devotion. Like St. Ignatius before him, he felt a little anxious about the attitude of the Council to the Jesuit constitutions when the time approached for the Fathers to discuss the reform of religious orders. He had himself offended both the Spanish and the French parties, and the presence in Trent of Eustache du Bellay and a phalanx of Sorbonne doctors was not reassuring. Humbly he wrote to St. Charles Borromeo begging him to put in a good word with the Legates and Lorraine, which that kind young Cardinal and Secretary of State most willingly did, saying, "These fathers are not only devoted sons of His Holiness and of this Holy See but under my own protection, so that what your Highnesses do for them I shall consider as done to myself." [3] San Carlo had his will, for though the Council legislated that religious must make their profession after a year of noviceship or else retire from the order, the Jesuits, whose constitutions provide otherwise, were specifically excepted in a clause added to the ruling. "By these enactments," it runs, "the Synod does not intend to make any innovation or

---

[1] M.H., *Lainii Monumenta*, viii, 819, 821.

[2] They form a large part of Grisar's *Disputationes Tridentinae*, in fact more than six hundred pages.

[3] M.H., *Lainii Monumenta*, viii, 823-4. San Carlo remained a devoted life-long friend of the Jesuits.

prohibition which would hinder the religious order of Clerks of the Society of Jesus from being able to serve God and His Church in accordance with their pious institute approved of by the Holy Apostolic See." [1] Of 175 archbishops and bishops present only two, both Spaniards, refused their *placets* to this codicil, one of them on the ground that he "knew nothing whatever about the Society of Jesus."

With the words *Andate in pace,* spoken in a breathless silence, Cardinal Morone closed the Council of Trent on 4 December 1563. "The hand of God had turned over a page in the history of His Church." Laynez and his brethren left Trent six days later, returning by Venice, Padua, Ferrara, Bologna, Forli, and Loreto to Rome. He was a month on the road, his last effort as a missioner, and reached home completely exhausted. That summer of 1564 his life was despaired of, but he rallied and when Advent came, though oppressed now with asthma, he once more climbed into a Roman pulpit to preach on the lowliness of Mary the Mother of God. He could not finish the course and died in great suffering on 19 January 1565, a worn-out wraith of a man at the age of fifty-three.

[1] Chapter xvii of the Decree of Reformation of Session XXV, "Concerning Regulars and Religious Women."

CHAPTER IV

THE PEREGRINATIONS OF NADAL

I N THE *Ballad of the White Horse* the Roman legions are finely described as "the walking walls of Rome." Jerome Nadal was a walking providence of the Jesuits. No Jesuit of his period or, it may safely be said, of any period, had such a close acquaintance with all the roads that led to Rome and away from it. The Mediterranean, in the midst of which he was born,[1] was truly his lake and he knew as much about its uncertain temper as any man then living. During his first ten years as a Jesuit St. Ignatius had sent him to traverse Sicily from end to end, to perambulate Italy, Spain and Portugal twice over, and to spy out the land in Germany. Of his own initiative he had gone to spend six baking months on the sands of Tunis as chaplain to the army of Charles V. That time he suffered his second shipwreck. He lived and worked in about thirty-five different European cities, ranging as far north as Regensburg, as far east as Vienna, as far south as Palermo, and as far west as Lisbon. St. Ignatius recalled him from Messina in 1553 and said to him as

---

[1] At Palma, in Majorca, in 1507. He did his arts course at Alcalá and Paris, and then went to Avignon to take a doctorate in theology. So far from sharing the common Spanish antipathy to Jews he sought them out and made himself a good Hebrew scholar with their assistance. But he did feel an antipathy to Jesuits, or to such of them as he had seen at a distance, until he happened on copies of the letters of St. Francis Xavier from India. The vicissitudes of his vocation are described in *The Origin of the Jesuits,* 200–6. St. Ignatius's marvellous gift for reading character is strikingly exemplified in his treatment of this moody and temperamental islander. He trusted Nadal utterly, and, as was his habit with those whom he best loved and admired, showed him the utmost rigour. Nadal, Laynez and Polanco, the flower of his flock, were the Saint's regular whipping-boys. To less stalwart disciples he could be, and generally was, the very soul of kindness. For a time, Nadal went in terror of him and used to tremble when summoned to his room. "On one occasion," he told his friend Ximenes, "he rated me so harshly that I felt as if the world had collapsed on my head. He advanced towards me and again charged me with my fault. I shrugged my shoulders, whereupon what should he do but walk away laughing" (M.H., *Epistolae P. Hieronymi Nadal,* i, 34–5).

soon as he arrived in Rome: "Get ready at once, for you have to go to Spain." To his question whether he should wait for instructions as to what he was to do in Spain, Ignatius answered: "No, you are already sufficiently instructed, and if anything else occurs it will be given to you in writing at the time of your departure, for you to read on the road." As he mounted his horse a document of some sort was put in his hands which he opened at a village near Lake Bacciano. It proved to be a patent signed by Ignatius creating him vicar-general of the whole order. He could hardly believe his eyes, and found a means of returning the document to the Saint with a message that there must have been some strange mistake. But there was no mistake, as appeared the following year on his return from his travels.[1]

In November 1560 he was again jogging along that familiar road to Genoa, now as official visitor of the Society of Jesus throughout Europe, "with plenary powers to arrange all matters of our Society, to appoint or remove superiors, including provincials, in all houses and provinces, to increase or restrict their authority as judged most expedient, to bring all local rules and customs into conformity with the constitutions, and finally to make provision in every other respect as freely as I, James Laynez, General of the Society of Jesus, might do if myself present, in the name of the Father and of the Son and of the Holy Ghost."[2] At Genoa our traveller had to wait a month for a place on one of the galleys which plied between that port and Spain. He was used to such delays and no one knew better how to make the best of them. On this occasion he wrote at the Jesuit house his classic commentary on the constitutions of the order, promising himself leisure to revise it as he sped over the Mediterranean. But the galley and the Mediterranean decided otherwise. The galley was a long, single-decked affair, low in the water, and propelled by both sails and oars, at which slaves and criminals strained. Nadal would find slaves everywhere on his travels through Catholic Europe, mostly Saracens captured in battle or negroes ravished from Africa.[3] His galley eventually accosted the sea in

[1] M.H., *Epistolae P. Nadal,* i, 36–7.

[2] *Loc. cit.,* pp. 358–62.

[3] The Popes unfortunately had sanctioned the seizure of the negroes, thinking thus, if no other way succeeded, to Christianize them. The redeeming feature

company with fourteen others, and this brave fleet, which hugged the coast for dear life, took two days to make Nice, where it lay up for a day and a night.   Every day after that had its adventures, and Christmas Day was spent sheltering from wind and wave in a deserted cove half-way between Nice and Marseilles.   Next, the captains of the fleet set course for Aigues Mortes, but venturing too far from land in order to avoid the shoals of these parts, were caught in a tempest and whirled across the dreaded Gulf of Lions.   Ten of the galleys disappeared into the murk, but the *San Juan* in which Nadal and his companion, Diego Ximenes, lay woefully seasick and half-drowned in bilge-water, fetched up at an anchorage on the Gulf of Rosas, a few miles north of Gerona.   It was Spain, but only just Spain.   Between their paroxysms of sickness the two men had given what material and spiritual attention they could to the galley-slaves, some of whom died on the brief crossing.   The *barahunda,* the din and racket of sailors and soldiers around the little hole amidships in which he was ensconced, made it impossible for Nadal so much as to look at his commentary on the Jesuit constitutions.   "We had our fill of misery," he wrote with brief completeness.   Engaging a slave with whom they had made friends to carry their light packs, the two men climbed out of the penitential galley on Sunday, 29 December, and made their way on foot to the small town of Rosas, which they had been told was only a league distant.   Their hope was to say and to hear Mass, but in this too they were baulked, for, says Nadal, "it was so much of a Catalan league that though we left in the eye of the day we did not arrive at Rosas until Vesper time, realizing then what a stout pair of pilgrims we were." [1]   From Rosas they turned their weary steps towards Gerona where the Bishop received them with fatherly kindness and sent a brace of partridges, a capon, four loaves, and two flasks of wine to the inn for their supper.   "After regaling ourselves on these good things, we no longer felt envious of the people who had remained on the

---

of the story is that the captives were usually well treated, especially in Portugal, where they frequently intermarried with the general populace. Now and then we read of the Jesuits owning negro slaves, but they were given the status of ordinary paid domestic servants. There were several thousand negro slaves in Seville alone (M.H., *Litterae Quadrimestres,* iv, 419).

[1] M.H., *Epistolae P. Nadal,* i, 363–5.

galley." And so they came all booted and spurred to Barcelona, by their own confession "hale and hearty and fighting fit" for the long road to Alcalá, right in the centre of Spain.[1]

Nadal's anxiety to be in Alcalá was caused by the presence there of Father Antonio Araoz, the first of Spanish Jesuits and the provincial of the brethren in Castile. Antonio had done great things for his order during the years of his first fervour when nothing of prayer and work and penance was ever too much for him. He used to consider two hours of sleep at night enough for any man. The rest belonged to God and his neighbour. All through, he showed a great gift for reconciling dissident husbands and wives, which is no mean charism. Alas, the fervour wore off and Antonio became worn out. Among the things which derange judgment and spoil character, Pascal, that unbending realist, reckons "les maladies," and in fairness to Araoz it must be said that he was a very sick man, afflicted physically north, south, east and west. Until 1554 when St. Ignatius had divided the fast-increasing Spanish Jesuits into three provinces with St. Francis Borgia over them all as commissary-general, an office created for the occasion and abolished in 1565, Antonio, hitherto its sole administrator, had shown himself sufficiently amenable to the law. But after that event, when he diminished to being provincial of Castile alone, there was no holding him. He bitterly resented Borgia's special powers, more or less ignored them, suddenly expressed public regret for the insubordination, but was found "even in penance planning sins anew." Laynez could make nothing of him, and Nadal must often have wished him on the top of Chimborazo or a peak in Darien, places then beginning to loom on the

---

[1] Alcalá, the Spanish form of the Moorish words, al kala, the castle, is unfortunately the name of no less than thirteen Spanish towns, all founded by the Moors. But the only one that concerned the Jesuits was the great Alcalá situated on the river Henares, seventeen miles north-east of Madrid, where there had been an old Roman settlement called Complutum. When Cardinal Ximenes brought out his famous polygot Bible at Alcalá in 1517 it accordingly became known as the Complutensian Bible. The university which the Cardinal founded in that city in 1507 was the most splendid and successful of all the Renaissance academies, a fact by itself sufficient to render doubtful the facile and common theory that civilization in Spain disappeared with the Moors. Both St. Ignatius and Nadal had studied at Alcalá, and a flourishing Jesuit college had grown up there.

Jesuit horizon, but he wielded immense influence with the mighty ones of the land, especially King Philip's all-powerful favourite, Rui Gomez de Silva, Prince of Eboli, and so might not have his candlestick removed.   He was a man of fine intelligence, and must also have possessed considerable charm to win his way into the affections of the aloof grandees.   One indignant rector reported that while Father Provincial was in his college it ceased to be a religious house and took on the semblance of a chancellery or a court, so many were the dukes, counts, marquesses, and other nobles who came to consult or dine with the great man.   These dinners used to last for three hours.

Spaniards of that epoch tended to become more than ordinarily sick with self-love, a disease to which all nations are exposed.   Their tremendous history and achievement had gone a little to their heads. They had beaten Islam back to Africa, they had discovered America, they had fought the good fight, they had finished the course, they had kept the faith.   Araoz would have added that they had created the Society of Jesus.   He loved his Society truly, but he thought of it as something peculiarly Spanish, designed to minister to Spanish needs and ambitions.   It grieved him sorely that the General of the order did not see fit to reside in Spain, and it annoyed him intensely that men and money should be removed from Spain to serve other countries and purposes.   He entertained a special dislike for the Roman College, which by its determinedly international composition and outlook was so much of a reproach to his provincialism.   Another great grievance of his burdened heart was the easy-going attitude of Laynez, Borgia, Polanco, Nadal and similar authorities towards the sacred subject of *limpieza de sangre* or racial purity.   It seemed to make little difference to them whether a man was descended from a Jew or a Moor or a heretic, provided that he was himself a good Christian.   Other things being equal, the Society of Jesus welcomed him, and that to Araoz and his many Spanish sympathizers meant absolute contamination.   In 1492 the Jews of Spain had been offered the alternative of exile or baptism.   The majority honourably and bravely chose exile, but large numbers preferred the less heroic course of outward conformity while remaining wedded to their old faith at heart.   A few found Christ our Lord in all sincerity on some private Damascus road, and theirs was the hard lot of being lumped with the pretenders under the designation of *conversos* or New Christians, only a shade less objectionable than the unbaptized *marranos* or swine, of whom Spain had happily ridded herself. *Limpieza de sangre* had become a kind of religion in Spain in those days and Antonio Araoz was one of its high priests. The Spanish-hating Paul IV knew well what he was doing when he taunted the proud subjects of Philip II with being the "spawn of Moors and Jews." [1] No greater insult could he have invented. When, shortly after his succession to the Spanish throne, King Philip required St. Francis Borgia to draw him up a list, with reasons stated, of the secular and ecclesiastical persons whom he considered most suitable to fill the great offices of the realm, St. Francis, knowing his King, put *limpieza* as the first of his candidate's qualifications. Thus, he writes in Spanish which is self-translating: "El Doctor Quiroga es limpio, muy docto, virtuoso y prudente." This Doctor Quiroga went far, for he became Cardinal Primate of Spain, but no matter how virtuous and prudent he would not have advanced a step had he had the misfortune to be descended from the same stock as Christ our Lord.

It is necessary to harp on this matter of anti-Jewish feeling in Spain and Portugal because it is the clue to many a puzzle in the early history of the Jesuits. For instance, the antipathy of the forceful Araoz to Laynez and Polanco was almost certainly due to a belief that they were of Jewish extraction. [2] During the lifetime of St.

[1] Paul was one of the few successors of the Jewish Fisherman who persecuted the children of Israel. The habitual attitude of the Popes towards them is very fairly described in the following words of a modern Jewish scholar: "The Papacy, true to the tradition set by Gregory the Great, figured down to modern times alternately as the protector of the Jews from violence and the repressor of their 'insolence,' departing from this standard most frequently on the side of leniency: and Rome was almost the only city of Europe to preserve its Jewish community undisturbed from remote antiquity down to the present day" (Cecil Roth, in the *Encyclopedia Britannica,* 14th ed., xiii, 56).

[2] Laynez was, but the same cannot be said with any certainty of Polanco, not that he would have minded. The explosion caused among the Spanish Jesuits by the revelation of Laynez's ancestry in the first official history of the order is described in an appendix to this volume. Fairness requires it to be said that the Spaniards had been given the best of reasons for dreading and disliking the Jews, who have ever been their own worst enemies. "Jacob, lame and dreaming, tireless irritant of the world and scapegoat of the world, indispensable to the

Ignatius, Araoz and those Jesuits who felt with him had to restrain their racial ardour because that gloriously broad-hearted hidalgo would not have tolerated their narrowness. Ignatius, besides, was well-known to be sympathetic towards the Jews. Once in converse with a Knight of the Holy Sepulchre named Pedro de Sarate, he said: "Pedro, I would count it a special grace of our Lord were I of Jewish lineage. Just think, to be related by ties of blood to Christ our Lord and to our Lady, the glorious Virgin Mary!" Pedro just thought, ejaculated the one word "Judío?" and spat on the ground with great solemnity. "All right, Señor Pedro de Sarate," resumed the Saint. "Let us thrash this thing out. You listen to me and I shall give you such good reasons for my view that you will yourself begin to wish that you had Jewish blood in your veins." [1]

Just as Ignatius felt a tenderness for the Jews because of their kinship with our Lord, so did his great sons, men such as Polanco, Borgia and Nadal, exercise unlimited patience with Antonio Araoz

---

world and intolerable to the world—so fares the wandering Jew." It is an undisputed historical fact that the conquest of Spain by the Moslems was greatly facilitated by the Jews, who thereafter acquired a wholly disproportionate influence in the management of the country. The Spaniards have long memories, but it is safe to say that the Inquisition was not the right instrument in the hands of a Christian people for dealing with the grave problem presented by the "scapegoat of the world." Israel, as the great Jew, St. Paul, expounded, is first and foremost a providential mystery with which only the charity of Jesus Christ, His "Father, forgive them" on the cross, can hope to make any issue acceptable to God. The best that has been written on this matter is the profound and noble essay entitled, "The Mystery of Israel," in Jacques Maritain's book, *Redeeming the Time* (1943), pp. 123–57.

[1] M.H., *Scripta de Sancto Ignatio de Loyola,* i, 398–9. The writer is Ribadeneira, who gives the story as related to him by Pedro de Sarate, but he mentions that he had himself heard Ignatius utter similar sentiments "with tears in his eyes." The foremost enemy of the Jesuits in the time of Ignatius was Cardinal Siliceo of Toledo, and this prelate's opposition was due primarily to the Saint's acceptance of New Christians. He let it be known that if Ignatius agreed to ban such people he would cease troubling the Jesuits and build them a fine college at Alcalá. Ignatius flatly refused. That is the truth. Here is the legend: "Between Martin Luther and Ignatius Loyola there is commonly supposed to gape a very wide chasm. However that may be, there is one point at which the two apostles meet — hatred of Israel" (Abbott, *Israel in Europe,* 1907, p. 234. Not a single reference of any kind is provided).

because he was the nephew of Ignatius. Antonio liked none of those people on account of their indulgent attitude towards the Jewish question and their definitely lukewarm *españolismo*. His letters are amusing, if only as examples of the art of self-exculpation. He humbles himself to the dust in one sentence, and in the next aims a resounding whack at some offending head, generally Polanco's or Nadal's, though he is careful not to mention Nadal's name for fear of reprisals. Polanco took him very calmly. When he tries to argue his uncle into prohibiting the acceptance of New Christians as Jesuits, Polanco replies: "Our Father is unable to persuade himself that it would be to the service of God to refuse men of Jewish or Moorish extraction. . . If, owing to the attitude of the Court or the King, it seems to you in Spain inadvisable to admit them, then send them here, provided that they are good subjects. I have told you this on other occasions. Here in Rome we are not so particular about a man's genealogy if he possesses the other necessary qualities. Without them, not even a patent of nobility will open the doors of the Society to him." [1]

---

[1] M.H., *Monumenta Ignatiana*, series 1a, v, 335. A little later, Laynez, as general, dismissed his own brother, Christopher, from the order because he lacked the Jesuit spirit. On a previous visit to Spain, Nadal had come up against the problem of the New Christians in Córdoba, where such people abounded. A certain noble lady, the Marchioness de Priego, to whom the Jesuits were heavily indebted, begged him to prohibit the admission of any more *conversos* into their ranks in Córdoba, as it tended to prejudice the local grandees against the Society. Out of deference to her, but against his own inclinations, he issued the required ban. To his relief, St. Ignatius immediately cancelled it, with consequences which profoundly shocked Araoz and his school. Nearly twenty years later one of them complained to St. Francis Borgia that though the college in Córdoba had more than six hundred students, all the sons of noblemen of the purest blood, not one of the boys showed a disposition to become a Jesuit. "Those with vocations all join the Dominicans at the monastery of St. Paul, which, they say, is a monastery of *caballeros,* whereas at our college it is only Jews who become Jesuits. Feeling on the point is such that when some unfortunate joins us he is regarded as practically having donned the *san-benito*" (Astrain, *Historia de la Compañía de Jesús,* iii, 591). The *san-benito* was a penitential garment of yellow cloth, resembling a Benedictine scapular in shape, whence the name. It bore a red St. Andrew's cross before and behind, and was worn by a confessed or penitent heretic. A similar garment of black, ornamented with flames and devils, was put on impenitent heretics before execution.

All things considered, it must have been with some trepidation that Jerome Nadal rode into Alcalá to meet his formidable subject, Antonio Araoz. The fifty brethren at the college there gave him a great welcome, but Araoz showed from the first moment that he intended to be unco-operative if not definitely obstructive, though the visitor took him completely into his confidence. They were both much concerned about St. Francis Borgia, who had fallen foul of the Inquisition and gone into Portugal under a threatening cloud. There are many indications that Francis entertained no great enthusiasm for the Inquisition, and that all-knowing and all-powerful body was not in the habit of tolerating such coldness.[1] When about the year 1557 Lutheranism raised its head in Spain a rumour was put about that the Jesuits had started the mischief. "I am reported to have been laid by the heels," wrote Borgia to Ribadeneira from Valladolid, "another of us is supposed to have hanged himself, and yet others to have been garrotted. Elsewhere they are committing us to the flames. . . *Et ecce vivimus!*"[2] Two years later the Saint was obliged to witness a solemn *auto-da-fé* at Valladolid, when fourteen out of thirty condemned persons were burnt at the stake in presence of royalty, though all but one of them had recanted. Francis wept many tears that day. Among the sixteen prisoners subjected to infamy almost as bad as death was the sister-in-law of his daughter, Juana of Aragon, and it fell to him to visit this poor lady in prison and tell her her sentence. One of the noblest born in the land, a friend of St. Teresa of Jesus, and the spiritual child of Teresa's holy director, the Jesuit Balthasar Alvarez, she was to be paraded before the mob, candle in hand and garbed in the shameful *san-benito*. "She would sooner have died," wrote Francis, "and she looked like death when she left the prison for her public exhibition. With God's help, and God knows I needed it, I gave her courage to regard the loss of honour, dignity and good name as a price paid for knowledge of the truth and as a satisfaction for her sins." Another count against Francis was his unconcealed sympathy with the Inquisition's victim, Archbishop Carranza of

---

[1] In Spain, Portugal and Italy the Jesuits were often invited, and even pressed to serve as theologians to the Holy Office, but they invariably showed reluctance and managed to evade the equivocal honour.

[2] M.H., *Sanctus Franciscus Borgia,* iii, 323.

Toledo. Carranza had been arrested on account of a book, and a book also nearly led to Borgia's undoing. Ten years earlier a little spiritual work of his had been a great success, which prompted an enterprising publisher of Alcalá to re-issue it together with other lucubrations by anonymous authors. This much larger volume he craftily entitled: *Obras del Christiano compuestas por D. Francisco de Borja, Duque de Gandía*. At once the Inquisition pounced, and in its first Index or "Catalogue of Books forbidden by order of the Most Reverend Lord Ferdinand de Valdes, Inquisitor General of Spain," which appeared in 1559, Francis found himself condemned as a heretical writer. At first he seemed inclined to let the matter be, for he was never one to care much what the world thought of him, but a bad mark from the Inquisition meant a bad mark from the King and that censure brought the courtly Araoz to his feet, with sword drawn and trumpet to lips. Under pressure from Araoz, Francis permitted a case to be stated on oath before the chief magistrate of Alcalá in proof, and there could not have been clearer proof, that he was in no way responsible for nine-tenths of the offending book. This evidence was several times laid before Archbishop Valdes without having the slightest effect on his peculiar Lordship.[1]

Chief among those who sought the advice and direction of Francis was Princess Juana, sometime regent of Spain on behalf of her brother, King Philip. His influence with this great lady bred jealousy at court and the jealous ones concocted a story of immoral relations between priest and princess. So much for his spiritual writings and his reputed sanctity! The cynical Philip knew right well that the story was a base invention but he did not lift a finger to scotch it, nor was Antonio Araoz much concerned to find redress from his following of dukes and marquesses. In the same black year, 1560, the Saint's well-loved sister and daughter died to complete his desolation. Sick and sad, he went on with his work of visiting the Jesuit houses and encouraging the anxious brethren to give of their best to God. He had himself given God everything, including his honour of a Spanish nobleman and a priest, but there remained a final sacrifice. Towards the end of the preceding year Laynez had

[1] M.H., *Sanctus Franciscus Borgia,* iii, 553–76. "Inquisitor Generalis (Valdes) peculiari affectu charitatis ac devotionis Patrem Araoz prosequebatur" (M.H., Polanco, *Chronicon,* v, 460).

asked superiors for details about any of their subjects who showed a special inclination and aptitude for the foreign missions or for "the great work and charity of teaching little boys in the lowest classes." St. Francis took this as applying to himself and answered in the following terms: "Your Paternity has bidden us to tell you our inclinations with regard to the Indies and to the teaching of the *minimos*. As for me, Father, I have not health enough for the first nor talent enough for the second, and so I can tell you only of a longing which has possessed me here for some months. It is to shed my blood for the truth of the Catholic and Roman Church. How this is to come about I do not know, . . . but I do know that though the desire is strong in me I have not the courage to suffer the bite of a mosquito without a great grace of our Lord. Will your Paternity of your charity offer my desire to Him and beg Him to realize it, if it would be to His service. At least may He grant that it be to me another death to have to die without shedding my blood for His sake. *Ecce adsum!* if, as He has given me the will, He would also show me the way." [1] God led him by a way harder even than the road of martyrdom. Shortly before Nadal's arrival in Spain, Cardinal Henry, the Regent of Portugal for his little grand-nephew, King Sebastian, had invited Francis to Lisbon to discuss with him the transfer of his new university of Evora to the control of the Jesuits. When he crossed the frontier which King Philip was even then plotting to erase a cry immediately went up in Spain that he had fled in order to avoid the fate of his friend Carranza, or perhaps even that of the poor wretches whom he had seen cremated at Valladolid. The indignation of Antonio Araoz knew no bounds and, sad to say, even Nadal, misled by that propagandist, went over for a time to the camp of the critics. Nadal was in a most difficult position. He hardly knew whom to believe in the maelstrom of passions that swirled around him, and he had to exercise consummate caution lest it suck in and drown his beloved Society of Jesus. The first thing to be done was to meet Borgia, so he wrote to Francis, then at Oporto, suggesting a rendezvous in Castile, which of itself would give the lie to those who regarded him as a fugitive. While waiting for an answer, he made an expedition to the picturesque old Moorish town of Cuenca, a hundred miles from Alcalá, to see how his brethren

[1] M.H., *Sanctus Franciscus Borgia*, iii, 512–13.

there were faring. He did not know then that Laynez, who loved and reverenced Borgia, had procured a brief from friendly Pope Pius IV inviting Francis to shake the dust of grudging turbulent Spain from his feet and come to generous peaceful Rome.

The Jesuits of Cuenca had had a painful struggle for existence but were saved from collapse by a gallant preacher named Pedro Martinez whom they imported from Toledo. Pedro was one of those obstinate heroes who never know when they are beaten. He prepared his first sermon with the greatest care and preached it to a few devout old ladies with as much verve as if empresses sat in serried ranks before him. The effort won him an extra pewful the following week, when he delivered an even more powerful discourse, and so week by week and pew by pew he built up his audience, until at last the whole of Cuenca was streaming to the church and struggling to get in.[1] One consequence of Pedro's persevering eloquence was that a canon of the town named Marquina decided to put the Jesuits on their feet by endowing their college. But there was a canker in this proffered rose, as Nadal discovered when he had smelt it, for Marquina had attached to his gift conditions which warred with the Jesuit constitutions. It required all Nadal's extensive powers of persuasion to get the conditions removed, but he grew to like the good canon so well during the battle that he earnestly begged Laynez to defer to his wishes in every way possible. Much of his busy life was taken up with similar wearisome negotiations which often came to nothing in spite of his tact and patience. For instance, there was the case of Dr. Vergara, another canon and benefactor of the Jesuits at Alcalá. By permission of St. Francis Borgia, who was too kind to refuse, he had taken up his abode in the college of Cuenca, and Father Araoz had subsequently made over to him a brother of that community to be his cook and valet. The brother did not appreciate this species of helotry in the least. "I argued with the Doctor," says Nadal, "and endeavoured to abstract our Michael from his clutches, but it was very difficult." The

---

[1] Sacchini, *Historia Societatis Jesu* (Antwerp 1620), p. 165. Martinez had been a soldier before he "stormed his way into the Society of Jesus" at Valencia in 1553. He is an attractive figure and will appear again in these pages. An account of his unconventional method of entrance into the order is given in *The Origin of the Jesuits*, p. 212.

canon threatened to renounce his stall and bury himself in the desert as a hermit if not left in peaceful possession of his apartments and his man, for both of which privileges he contributed only a crown a month to the college's depleted exchequer. Nadal patiently explained that nobody wanted to turn him out and that his only concern was for the oppressed Michael, whose vocation was being jeopardized. As he made no impression he gave up the fight and put his trust in the other canon's imminent building operations, which with luck might be expected to uproot the obstinate but comfort-loving doctor. This excellent man was an affliction to the Jesuits in Alcalá also, for on the strength of his benefactions he claimed a right of interference in their domestic arrangements. No changes in the staff might be made without his approval nor could the fathers put up so much as a hen-coop until he had passed the plans. Afflicted though he was with his inveterate enemy, chronic catarrh, Nadal worked all his wiles on the aggressive doctor without obtaining the slightest concession. Before he died Jerome could have written a folio volume on what the Jesuits of his time had suffered from their benefactors.

On his return to Alcalá he learned that Borgia lay seriously ill at Oporto. He had had a stroke but passed it off, as was his way, with a smile: "If only the old Adam in me would become and remain paralysed, all my troubles would be over!" To the exceeding joy of the Portuguese brethren who had their own big bundle of tangles for him to unravel, Jerome announced that he was coming to see Francis as soon as he had paid his devoir to the King of Spain at Toledo. Araoz the expert was commissioned to arrange this audience. "Nothing on earth could he have arranged worse," wrote Jerome in his journal afterwards. He was admitted to the presence for a moment as Philip passed along a corridor to Mass, fell on his knees in confusion, and forgot the little set speech which he had memorized. But he managed to gasp a few words of humble duty and to present the grandly worded letters of credence which had been given him by the Pope and Laynez. It was a picture for El Greco's brush, that meeting of the two most opposite characters in the whole great empire of Spain. "You are welcome," said the King, "address yourself to Rui Gomez," and then moved on to his devotions. When Nadal addressed himself to Rui Gomez that

Joseph to the Spanish Pharaoh lectured him on the importance of excluding persons of Jewish descent from the Society of Jesus. He wasted his distinguished breath, for Jerome replied respectfully but firmly that it was surely a matter of which the Jesuits themselves might be considered the best judges. Another whom he visited at Toledo was Valdes the Grand Inquisitor: "He began to speak to me about Archbishop Carranza and said that it was not only his Catechism but the Cardinal himself who had been condemned as heretical. As he seemed to me to be derogating from the dignity and authority of cardinals, in general, I reminded him without caring how he took it that such men were princes of the universal Church. . . . I left Toledo on 20 March, very weary of the company of those courtiers." [1]

Jerome had many things besides his catarrh to keep him awake at night: what to do with Araoz, how to obtain funds for the support of the two hundred young Jesuits of all nations at the "collegio universal" in Rome,[2] where to find the right fathers and brothers, to man the ever-expanding missions of Brazil, Peru, New Spain, India and Japan. Three very suitable Spanish fathers had expressed a desire to work in India, but, alas, that was Portugal's sphere of influence, and what might not the suspicious Araoz say or do were Nadal to draft the three volunteers to the wrong side of the globe? It would have been about this time that Jerome made a plan to circumvent Araoz, as he did also to outwit the usurers who took a heavy toll of his collections for the Roman College. When he had finished the visitation of the three Spanish provinces he would suddenly divide that of Castile into two, summon the principal fathers to Burgos, appoint two new provincials, and whisk the deposed Araoz away to France before the King or Rui Gomez had time to interfere. It was a grand plan, but Araoz had a grander, and in the end it was not he but Nadal who found himself suddenly on the other side of the Pyrenees. Very difficult, too, for the visitor

[1] M.H., *Epistolae P. Nadal,* ii, 69. The reference is to his *Ephemerides,* to which he committed his inmost thoughts about people and affairs. His letters on the same topics are usually more reticent and diplomatic, as was natural. In his sympathy for Carranza, he created him a cardinal without historical warrant.

[2] At this time, in the space of six months, twenty Italians, eight Germans, five Irishmen and thirteen Frenchmen joined the Society of Jesus in Rome.

was the affair of St. Francis. He admitted that the long round to Oporto via Medina del Campo and Salamanca — more than 350 miles as the crow flies, and possibly twice that as the mule trots — had tested his endurance, and after the weary journey dear Francis tested his patience. He knew from Araoz and Rui Gomez that King Philip and the Inquisition would feel affronted if the Saint departed to Rome, and for that reason he was opposed to the move. As for Francis himself, he desired nothing now but to be left in peace in some private and lowly office of Portugal, but he had received a second invitation from the Pope, and the two briefs had begun to trouble his sensitive conscience. In vain did Nadal wrestle with that conscience, pointing out that the briefs, far from expressing an order or even a wish, were merely an act of courtesy, a little diplomatic dust for the suspicious eyes of King Philip, such as they were experts in mixing at the Vatican. Francis clung to his scruple, and eventually the two men, so different in character and yet so united in heart, decided on a diplomatic ruse of their own whereby each would exculpate the other. They drew up two documents, in the first of which Nadal affirmed that he did not think Borgia ought to go to Rome, but that the decision must rest with himself owing to the Papal invitation. This document was signed by Francis as well as Jerome. In the second one Borgia quoted the Jesuit constitutions to show that, as a professed father, he was under a duty to obey the slightest behest of the Holy See, that he had determined to do so, and that Nadal disapproved of and was in no way responsible for his decision. This document was signed by Jerome as well as Francis.[1]

Eventually the Saint attempted to reach Bayonne from Portugal by sea, but became so ill that he had to be put ashore almost immediately. He then ventured the long land journey through Spain, to the consternation of Nadal who feared his arrest at any moment. It was in these circumstances that Jerome addressed a long memorial to the Grand Inquisitor, declaring his opposition to Borgia's departure and requesting to be informed of the precise charges which the Holy Office had laid against him: "I guarantee to your Lordship that if Father Francis is shown to be culpable in any important respect,

---

[1] M.H., *Epistolae P. Nadal,* i, 485-7. Though planned at Oporto, the documents were not written until two months later at Coimbra.

I shall be the first to move for his expulsion from the Society." [1]
Those hard words were intended as a sop to the inscrutable Valdes
who might easily have visited his wrath on the Spanish Jesuits at
large, and Nadal found it possible to write them because he knew
well that the Pope and the whole college of cardinals would as soon
be convicted of heresy as St. Francis Borgia. Shortly after the
dispatch of the memorial he learned a circumstance of Borgia's so-
called flight which changed his view of it completely. It was that
Francis had fallen gravely ill on his journey at a place almost under
the hand of the Grand Inquisitor, and yet not a finger of that hand
had been raised to hinder his further progress. "When I heard this,"
wrote Nadal, "I was filled with wonder and began to look upon the
affair of Father Francis in a new light. It was as though I could
sense the divine power in operation and see the hand of God guiding
his departure. Where will all this lead? I thought, for it seemed
to me that Francis would never have gone to Rome had not those
events happened to compel him." [2] Jerome had his answer four
years later when the suspect of the Inquisition was elected general
of the Jesuits. Meantime, King Philip fumed and Araoz wrung his
hands, while Jerome thanked God fervently that his friend was safe
for good from their contrivances. Araoz thought to reach him in
Rome by requesting Laynez not to give him any other post of
authority in the order for fear of wounding Spanish susceptibilities,
but Laynez replied by appointing him its vicar-general when Salmeron, the holder of the office, was summoned to the Council of
Trent. [3]

Nadal's work in Portugal and Spain was so strenuous, so continuous and so various that even such a monument of assiduity as Polanco marvelled. "It amazes me," he wrote, "that in the midst of
all your whirl of affairs you can still find time to devote to your
commentary on the constitutions. It will be welcome indeed when

[1] M.H., *Epistolae P. Nadal,* iv, 764–70. The memorial was written at Alcalá
in June 1561, when Nadal himself was in King Philip's bad books.

[2] M.H., *Epistolae P. Nadal,* ii, 79.

[3] In fairness it must be said that Nadal also recommended caution about giving Francis a new appointment, lest King Philip should imagine it an affront to
his dignity.

it reaches us, but for the love of God do not kill yourself.   The body is not made of iron, you know, though the will may never weary." [1] At Oporto he began the long series of exhortations on the Jesuit rule and way of life which contributed more than any other single influence to foster a corporate spirit in the order and to shape its tradition.   How necessary his labours were becomes apparent from the case of Father Bustamante whom Nadal took with him to his next halting-place, the grand old city of Braga, where the Jesuits had been installed by its saintly Dominican archbishop, Venerable Bartholomew of the Martyrs.   Bustamante, an able and ascetic man who fancied himself as an architect,[2] was provincial of the brethren in Andalusia and had nearly driven them to revolt by his high-handed methods of government.   Believing strongly in the good old medieval ways of doing things, he had introduced into the houses under his obedience prisons, stocks and even stripes for offenders against rule.   He imposed a new style of recreation also, requiring the brethren to sit around in silence until each in turn was called upon to analyse some virtue or vice propounded by the superior. Nadal handled the situation in such a way that Bustamante, who at fifty-eight considered himself the Methuselah of Spanish Jesuits with a consequent claim to veneration, was not offended, while the down-trodden Andalusians rejoiced in their delivery from oppression.

Across the frontier at Monterey a lively colony of Spanish fathers had established themselves in a very poor and poky house to which every day four hundred boys of isolated Galicia, the Connemara of Spain, came to wrestle with Latin and Greek.   Nadal's visit, a flying one, was made a great occasion for declamations and syllogistic fire-works, Jerome himself in the true spirit of the thing taking on all the local doctors of divinity.   After seeing the influential men of the neighbourhood and doing all in his power to assure the future of the struggling college, he returned to Braga and Oporto for more exhortations, interviews and business.   Then he rode away to Coimbra, where the Jesuits had two colleges, both great nurseries

---

[1] M.H., *Epistolae P. Nadal,* i, 438.

[2] He tended to boast of the fact that King Philip had asked his opinion on the plans for the Escorial, in which he found many mistakes.   He also indulged in blueprints himself and built places without consulting anybody (M.H., *S. Franciscus Borgia,* v, 392–8, 459).

of missionaries and martyrs. Here he was in his element and gave no less than twenty-two of his exhortations. One who listened to him reported that he spoke as a man inspired, all the passionate love and devotion which he bore to the Society of Jesus pouring into his words. "Cast your eyes over the Society throughout the world," he said, "and what shall you see but an exuberant vigour and fervour, afire for the great hard tasks of a strenuous charity, a Society never idle, never crying halt, never defeated. Wherever there is a soul in need, there is a Jesuit's appointment. To visit the prisons, to console the sick in hospitals, to gather children and the uninstructed about him and teach them their faith, these are no less his ministries than to convert heretics or to cross the seas and preach the Gospel to the Indians of Brazil and the warlike natives of Japan. The wide world is his parish, and his work in it is not merely to cure men of their vices but, so far as in him lies, to make them a perfect people for God."[1]

Nadal interviewed his one hundred and seventy Jesuits at Coimbra by inviting them in twos and threes to dine with him until he had seen and taken the measure of them all. The meals were pleasant informal functions, set in a parlour apart, and enlivened by Jerome's reminiscences of the interesting men he had known, particularly St. Ignatius, about whom he never tired of talking. To help the brethren spiritually he saw each one in private also and heard the general confessions of the whole house before he departed. He had brought them a quantity of little keepsakes in the shape of holy pictures and other pious objects, and these he distributed by means of a community draw. If any earnest-minded reader considers such proceedings childish and unworthy of stern hatchet-faced Jesuits dedicated to world-conquest, he is entirely welcome to his opinion. Nadal was a strong believer in the use of pictures as a prop to the imagination and caused paintings or engravings of the Last Supper and other Gospel scenes to be hung in Jesuit refectories and corridors wherever he went. In his old age he produced a quarto volume of considerations on the Sunday Gospels illustrated by some four hundred full-page engravings of fine workmanship which cost him,

[1] Sacchini, *Historia Societatis Jesu,* pars 2a (Antwerp 1620), 167; M.H., *Epistolae P. Nadal,* i, 804. The exhortations were lengthy affairs, excerpts from one of them filling seventeen pages of the *Monumenta.*

or rather his friends, more than a thousand *scudi*. Among the subscribers was Pope Clement VIII. While composing the book he had chiefly in mind the neophytes of his brethren on the foreign missions, at whose lowly doors truth embodied in a picture would enter in more readily than by any other aperture.[1] Studies he promoted with all his might, and it was owing to his encouragement that the brilliant but singularly modest Coimbra professor, Father Pedro de Fonseca, later dubbed the "Aristotle of Portugal," set his hand to a vast commentary on the Metaphysics of the Stagyrite in which the famous theory of *scientia media* made its first innocent and trustful appearance. Fonseca, who cared nothing whatever for the credit of a great name on earth, was not aggrieved when his illustrious Spanish pupil and brother, Luis de Molina, took over the theory, developed it, and delivered it to the theological world as his own in an epoch-making book entitled, *The Concordance of Free Will with the Gifts of Grace*. That *Concordance* has caused more discord among theologians than probably anything else published since the days of Arius.[2] Finally, at Coimbra, as at the other Jesuit houses, Nadal did not forget the servants and slaves employed by the fathers, nor the carpenters and stonemasons engaged on their buildings. He was so particular to see that everyone was being treated well and spiritually assisted that a father of the house who liked a quiet life felt rather inclined to wonder why he omitted to interview the dog and the cat!

While visiting the two Jesuit houses at Lisbon Nadal took occasion to pay his respects to the regents of Portugal, Cardinal Prince Henry, brother of the late King John, and John's widow, Queen Catherine, sister of Emperor Charles V. The new King, Sebastian, aged seven, was the grandson of John and Catherine. Having learned that the

---

[1] M.H., *Epistolae P. Nadal*, iv, 726–8. The work was produced by Plantin of Antwerp, one of the most eminent printers of his age.

[2] A very interesting account of Molina and his *Concordantia*, based largely on hitherto unpublished material, is given in Rodrigues, *História da Companhia de Jesus na Assistência de Portugal*, tômo segundo (Porto 1939), ii, 137–70. From this it appears that Padre Luis, a somewhat truculent metaphysician, was distinctly the aggressor in the great fight which followed, but when it came to hard knocks he met his match in Friar Bañes, of the Order of Preachers. There is a brief account of the controversy in the English Life of St. Robert Bellarmine (1928), ii, 1–66.

visitor was a very powerful Jesuit, this enterprising young man ran up to him and demanded a holiday from the lessons of his Jesuit tutor, Father Luis Gonçalves da Câmara, which Jerome delightedly granted. "Placuit mihi vehementer puer rex," he wrote, and indeed Sebastian was then a charming little fellow, full of spirit and a dreamer of wonderful dreams. Father Gonçalves did his best to cope with those dreams, but he might as well have tried to harness a sunset or a rainbow. Sebastian worshipped him and went on dreaming. He saw himself as the last and greatest crusader, the peerless Affonso Henriques born again, and again heading glorious charges against the infidel. The motto which he chose for himself when he came of age was a presage of his tragic destiny: "Un bel morir tutta la vita honora." Everybody knows the melancholy story, but the true part which Luis Gonçalves played in it has only lately been revealed. The legend is that he encouraged Sebastian's quixotic ideas, that he dissuaded him from marriage, and, altogether, that he bore no small responsibility for the disaster of Alcacer Quibir and the downfall of Portugal. The truth is that this man of noble lineage and noble character detested what he described as his "imprisonment" at court. He had been elected one of the four assistants to Laynez in 1558 but was torn soon afterwards from the busy peaceful avocations of Rome to be a sort of general scapegoat of intriguers in Lisbon. From the first the Dowager Queen Catherine honoured him with her Spanish suspicions and endeavoured by every means in her power to make impossible his already difficult task of putting some sense into the romantic head of young Sebastian. Catherine did not want Sebastian to become a successful king. She wanted to deliver over Portugal to her scheming nephew, Philip, who was one of five pretenders to that uncertain throne. For Sebastian to marry and produce an heir would have been fatal to Philip's chances, so the lady plotted to keep him celibate, an easy task with one whose only ambition was for martial glory. But she must not let her hand be seen and therefore spread the lying tale that Gonçalves was the real obstacle to Sebastian's wooing. Her letters to the Pope and to King Philip are full of this wail, but Gonçalves wrote letters also, and they have now at last been published to prove his absolute innocence. He did his best, poor man, to enmesh the reluctant feet of his dreamer in sweet family toils, but for Sebastian a dead Moor continued to be a greater attraction than any live lady. With all his might Luis strove to exorcise those perfectly inoffensive Moroccan Moors from his pupil's imagination. He had no success, and his only comfort was to die [1] before that fatal summer's day of 1578, when at the end of the lost battle Sebastian charged the Moorish cavalry single-handed and was cut to pieces.[2]

[1] His successor as Sebastian's confessor, Father Gaspar Serpe, tried equally hard to deter the King from his course. So far from prevailing, he was compelled to accompany the rash expedition. The Moors captured and beheaded him in hatred of the faith (Beccari, *Rerum Aethiopicarum Scriptores Occidentales,* Rome, 1910, x, 435 and note). Here also, pp. 429–48, is the evidence of Father Gonçalves's assistant-tutor, Father Rebello, as to his attitude.

[2] The new evidence for the whole sad story is given in Rodrigues, *op. cit.,* ii, livro segundo, "Na Côrte de Lisboa," 253–445. The most joyous piece published here for the first time is the sermon preached in the cathedral of Evora on the eve of King Philip's invasion by the Jesuit, Luis Alvares. It has the gallant and rallying ring of Winston Churchill's speeches in 1940. Portugal has no arms, no cavalry, no ammunition, no artillery to defend herself. Must the glorious, the feared, the famed, the royal Kingdom of Portugal then have the crown torn from her head and the sceptre from her hands? A thousand times no, for her sons united and dedicated, cheered on and led from Heaven by their immortal heroes, by Affonso Henriques, John the Great, Manuel, Nuno Alvares Pereira, the holy Constable, will constitute an invincible army. Union of hearts will be their best artillery. "Courage, ye men of Portugal! An enterprise consecrated and supported by the tears and blood of so many servants of God cannot fail of a fair and glorious issue. . ." Alas, the brave words went for nothing, and King Philip, with the best army in Europe at his command, prevailed. It must be said to his honour that he treated his captive very handsomely, but his wretched successors did not, and after sixty years of the Spanish yoke little Portugal regained her independence. It is worth noting that doughty Father Alvares was not reprimanded by his Jesuit superiors for the stand he made, but that the Spanish Father Deza, one of the many theologians of all orders consulted by Philip to obtain comfort for his uneasy conscience, received a stern admonition from the Jesuit General, Everard Mercurian, when he pronounced the King justified in his aggressive policy (Rodrigues, *op. cit.,* 422, 438–9). On the other hand, Pedro Ribadeneira, a much more important and representative Spanish Jesuit, tried to dissuade Philip from his enterprise. In his book, *The Golden Century of Spain* (1937), Mr. Trevor Davies asserts (p. 189) that "there was one powerful influence turning popular opinion in Philip's favour, viz. the Jesuit order." No evidence is supplied for the statement which is merely one of those airy things that even good historians, like Mr. Davies, are given to saying in their unguarded moments. In his excellent work, *From Virgil to Milton*

Father Gonçalves so much appreciated the good work Nadal was doing for his Portuguese brethren that he earnestly entreated him to prolong his stay in the country indefinitely, urging above all the claims of those mission-fields afar, white now to the harvest, which depended almost entirely on Portugal for reapers. That was an argument to make Jerome's heart beat faster, but he was committed in a hundred directions and found himself obliged to scrawl across the foot of Luis's appeal, "No por agora." Lisbon, where he spent forty hectic days, was a place to stir any man's imagination. Still the commercial capital of the world, though near the end of its epical glory, up its famed river came the ships of the rest of Europe to fetch "the muslins of Bengal, the brocades of Gujarat, the calicoes of Calicut, the spices of the Spice Islands, the pepper of the Malabar Coast and the teas and silks of China," that China which disputed in Nadal's soul the primacy of missionary affection with Germany. The Tagus for Nadal was indeed a Pactolus of golden dreams, for down it to the sea sailed the best and bravest of his brethren, bound for the ends of the world, with little prospect of ever sighting again the marvellous towers of Belem. Though Queen Catherine detested Father Gonçalves, she became quite an admirer of Father Nadal and presented him at his departure from Lisbon with what he considered to be the finest mule in Portugal until, much bruised and shaken, he discovered that it was too fine to allow a mere plebeian on its back. The Queen also gave him five hundred ducats to meet his travelling expenses, but of these he kept only fifty and sent the remainder to Laynez for the Roman College. During this period the College practically lived by his devoted exertions which brought it an average of eight hundred or a thousand ducats a month.[1]

After Lisbon there remained only Evora to be visited where the Jesuits had charge of Cardinal Henry's new university. The Car-

---

(London 1945), Dr. C. M. Bowra advances the charge that the Jesuits encouraged the natural fanaticism of Sebastian (p. 131). The opposite is the truth.

[1] It was not only money that he sent but also large quantities of books. Thus from Lisbon he dispatched two cases filled with tomes which might not easily have been procured in Rome. His letter to Laynez introducing the good ship's captain who undertook the transport is charming: "Give him the best welcome in your power, because to his kindness and faithfulness everything is owing" (M.H., *Epistolae P. Nadal,* i, 515–16).

dinal, who became King of Portugal after Sebastian's death in 1578,[1] was the deadly enemy of his co-regent, Catherine, but Nadal somehow achieved the feat of getting on well with both of them. Jerome's appearance in Evora provided an example of what an admirer described as his "craftiness." He found his brethren much troubled and distracted by the attentions of certain young noblemen whose habit it was to saunter into their garden and waylay the fathers for purposes of gossip. A trap was promptly baited for those time-wasters, the bait being, says the historian, "a father of proved virtue and notable severity." Him Jerome commanded to patrol the garden and when the noblemen came to accost them smilingly and at once plunge into a brisk account of the pains of Hell, the terrors of the Last Judgment, death, and other such sobering topics. A brief course of this treatment administered by a keen expert purged the college for good of the unwanted hidalgos, who avoided the garden thereafter as though' rattlesnakes lay concealed in its flower-beds.[2]

After Evora, rumour of mounting trouble compelled Nadal to hurry back to Spain. "I depart," he wrote to Laynez in September 1561, "full of contentment and consolation at seeing the eager good-will of the superiors of this province, and the fervour and alacrity with which they and their subjects strive along the way of perfection." The men thus eulogized say for their part that the new spirit evident in their midst was chiefly the creation of Nadal himself: "To see and consider his profound humility and simplicity of heart, to experience his affability and admirable cheerfulness in the midst of continuous and back-breaking labours, and with all that to think of his charity and of his zeal for the honour of God and for the progress and increase of the Society, these have left us in a state of

---

[1] He was sixty-six at the time, and sought a dispensation from Pope Gregory XIII to marry, but Philip of Spain deceived and browbeat the Holy Father into refusing it.

[2] Sacchini, *Historia Societatis Jesu*, pars 2a (1620), 169. Evora University already had 66 Jesuits within its walls and 750 students, "not counting crowds of little boys who came to learn reading and writing." The community testified that they felt "a new fervour of charity, a new love of obedience and the other virtues, a new eagerness to help the neighbour, and a new desire for mortification," as a consequence of Nadal's month among them (M.H., *Litterae Quadrimestres*, vii, 716).

permanent wonder." [1] Jerome's cheerfulness was now to be put to the test, for there came hurrying to him on his way back as many messengers of woe as had once rushed along the camel-paths of Hus. One warned him against proceeding to Madrid because King and Court there held him for an enemy. Another, in Plasencia, directed him to the mayor of the place, who read him in the presence of witnesses an order from the King putting a stop to his visitation until he had shown and proved his credentials. A third came in hot haste with a decree from the Council of State sternly prohibiting the dispatch of money or men out of Spain for the advantage of other Jesuit provinces. Nadal noticed with a wry smile that the grandees described him in their decree as a "foreigner," as though Majorca belonged to the King of France or the Grand Turk. Apparently to have lived abroad and to have worked for a wider cause than Spanish nationalism deprived a man of his Spanish nationality. He had to wrestle with himself awhile in order to prevent a suspicion taking root in his mind that Antonio Araoz was responsible for those catastrophic measures. "Many have thought so," he wrote in his diary, "but I vigorously resisted the idea, and could now swear to my belief in that Father's innocence. I could not bear to think that such an atrocious deed, such a piece of black treachery, proceeded from him or from anybody calling himself a Jesuit." Rui Gomez, he decided, the King's favourite and the bosom friend and patron of Araoz, must have spontaneously set the machinery in motion against him, under the mistaken impression that his coming to Spain was somehow meant for Araoz's discomfiture. But why did Araoz, who hobnobbed with Gomez daily, allow the impression to remain? There was the mystery from which Nadal steadfastly averted his mind. He hastened to Alcalá, where he learned of another charge against him, that he had plotted and promoted the so-called flight of St. Francis Borgia to Rome. It was then that he wrote his memorial to Archbishop Valdes, the Inquisitor General. "I badly wanted to meet the Archbishop face to face," he says, "as I felt perfectly confident of being able to defend Father Francis, . . . and I wanted to see the King too, to deliver him from his suspicions of me, but the fathers urgently entreated me to keep away." He sent Araoz instead, and that inscrutable soul returned a few days later with a rose

---

[1] M.H., *Litterae Quadrimestres*, vii, 435.

and a thistle for his superior. Nothing further was to be feared from
the Archbishop. As for the King, he graciously permitted the visitation of Castile, but Nadal must not go near the Jesuits of Aragon
and Andalusia. This restriction on his movements galled him
sorely, for he guessed it to mean that Philip and his Council were
determined to keep him under observation. His surmise was confirmed by a visit from the great Rui Gomez in person, bringing a
letter from Laynez to Nadal which had been intercepted in the post.
In this the General had charged his lieutenant with the task of getting Araoz away from the Spanish Court by any means possible,
even by sending him to the Council of Trent. The prince angrily
demanded an explanation of this injustice to his *protégé*. "Es mi
amigo, Padre," he kept repeating, and declared that he would defend
his Antonio against the envy of the Jewish-born Laynez who had
thought nothing of travelling into France with Cardinal d'Este, a
notorious enemy of Spain. Nadal tried to soothe his ruffled feelings by an assurance that the last word rested with himself, that he
would not in any way interfere with Araoz, that, in fact, he had
already offered him the post of commissary-general for Spain left
vacant by the departure of Francis Borgia. Yes, retorted Gomez,
you offered him that post because you already knew that it was
about to be abolished in your order. Afterwards Nadal wondered
how in the world this grandee had come to know so much about the
inner counsels of the Jesuit curia. He still refused to believe that
Araoz was playing traitor behind his back, and he did everything
in his power to reconcile that spoilt darling of the hidalgos with his
two *bêtes noires,* Laynez and Polanco. But he merely wasted his
breath, as Araoz was now thoroughly immersed in Spanish politics
and had ceased to recognize Laynez as his superior after the expiry
of his third year of office some months earlier. Pope Paul IV might
have been an enemy of Spain, but one must admire and respect his
orders when they curtailed the rule of a man descended from Jews.[1]

In spite of all the bad omens on his skyline, Nadal at this period
felt happier and more confident than ever before in his Jesuit life.
The fathers and brothers of Alcalá, sixty in number, declared that
the mere sight of him acted like a tonic on their spirits, filling them
with a new zest for the service of God: "He addressed to us many

[1] M.H., *Epistolae P. Nadal,* ii, 83–6; Sacchini, *Historia,* pars 2a, 170–3.

inspiring exhortations on the Society's rules and customs, at once enlightening our minds and kindling our hearts to fresh fervour. . . . Infinite thanks to the Divine Majesty for the blessing. . ." [1] Barred as he was from Aragon and Andalusia, Jerome appointed a new provincial of the latter region in place of the erratic Bustamante, and summoned him and the provincial of Aragon to Alcalá for consultation. While awaiting their arrival he made hasty visits to Jesuit centres at New Castile, Cuenca, Villarejo de Fuentes, Toledo, Belmonte, Ocaña, in all of which houses he gave himself heart and soul to the service of his brethren.[2] But he had constantly to be looking over his shoulder, for fear of what those "satraps" of the Court, as he called them, might be up to. Back in Alcalá, he busied himself visiting the forbidden provinces of Aragon and Andalusia through the post, writing to the brethren there what he was precluded from saying orally. Then he hurried on into Old Castile, always fearful of some new embargo on his progress. He nearly lost his life in the snows of the Sierra de Guadarrania near Segovia. It was then January 1562 and the fierce Spanish winter had the country in its paralysing grip, but he defied it to keep his appointed tryst with the Jesuits of Avila,[3] Salamanca and Medina del Campo.

Meantime Laynez, encouraged and coached by Nadal, had written to Philip II from Paris: "JHS. Maria. Your Sacred Catholic Royal Majesty, Though unworthy in my lowliness to address you, I am emboldened to do so by hearing of certain enactments which you have made concerning our Society with whose care I am charged. I am given courage especially by my sincere desire that our Lord may direct Your Majesty in all things to act for His greater glory, your own eternal happiness, and the temporal welfare of your realm and of the Church. I do not write because I have any doubt of Your Majesty's good intentions in making those enactments, nor because I consider the enactments other than very just, granted the truth of

[1] M.H., *Litterae Quadrimestres,* vii, 642.

[2] "Dici non potest," wrote the rector of Belmonte, "quantum ejus praesentia solamen, quantamque in Domino laetitiam nobis omnibus attulerit." Nearly all the reports mentioned joy as a result of Nadal's sojourns with his brethren.

[3] The college in Avila was kept going on the fortune of Father Luis Medina, who had been a soldier "in Italy, in the galleys, in Peru, and all over the world." Luis was a great character and could turn his hand to anything, nursing, cooking, cobbling, as well as preaching or lecturing.

what you have been told. . . As for the first of them, your restriction on Father Nadal's movements, I would humbly represent to Your Majesty that no one, I think, knows that Father more intimately than I, and I call our Lord to witness that this your vassal is a very good, a very learned, and a very prudent man. Wherever he has been he has done great good, leaving behind him a cherished memory in every house of our Society which he has visited. So with much humility and yet confidently I beg Your Majesty to permit him to complete his work, which will prove no disservice to you but rather result in creating for you better and more devoted subjects. . .

"As for Your Majesty's second enactment prohibiting the removal of members of our Society from Spain, I know that it has been occasioned by the circumstances of the present age combined with your holy zeal to preserve your dominions untainted in the faith, but I would ask you with all deference to take into account the following considerations. . . By the grace of our Lord zeal and discipline are flourishing in our Society, and its members are so solidly grounded and orthodox in their faith that, though we have colleges all over Germany and some in France, not a single man has fallen away. Rather have they drawn great numbers of heretics to the Church. If this is true of the rest, there is even better reason to trust the Spanish members of our Society, who by tradition and education under Catholic princes are more attached to our holy Catholic religion than any others. Another point worthy of consideration is the injury that would be done to our Society, as indeed to any family, by a restriction on the free intercourse of its members for mutual assistance. To hinder religious of one province from going to the help of their brethren in another would be to injure them all because they are living members of an organism, and, as St. Paul writes, no member of such can say to another: I have no need of thee. Your Majesty might use the words of our Lord in the Gospel of St. Luke: O man, who hath appointed me a judge and divider between thee and thy brother? Finally, we ought to take into account the succour and spiritual assistance of which Christians in other lands, and pagans also, would be deprived by Your Majesty's restriction. I am sure that by the grace of our Lord the Society has done much good in Italy since its establishment there, and in Germany it is the hope of the Catholics and the dread of the Protestants that by its means heresy will be extirpated from the country. As for this poor land of France from which I write, it is the saddest thing in the world to see it go daily faster to ruin, even though as yet there is but one heretic to two hundred or three hundred Catholics. It breaks one's heart to witness how dispirited the Catholics are. We have now in Paris a college staffed with some promising men of our Society who teach the sciences and letters and do other good work. The colleges which we hope gradually to establish in other places will be able to draw on this one for professors, and so we may look for excellent results in time, as the two or three colleges already functioning elsewhere in France give us good reason to do. To help with all this work we have taken out of Spain only a very few of Your Majesty's vassals, and these certainly are not suffering any harm, but rather rendering great service to our Lord, and bringing Your Majesty great merit and glory by the help they afford to so many souls in peril. . . As I am speaking of the spiritual succour of this kingdom, which would redound to the universal advantage of Christendom, I cannot forbear to represent to Your Majesty that, as far as I can judge here on the spot and as others better qualified judge also, the most efficacious means of helping will be found in the General Council, . . . and so I venture humbly to beseech Your Majesty to send many prelates of your realm to Trent. We are trying our best to procure that the rulers of this country do the same.

"To come, finally, to the third enactment, prohibiting the transfer of money in cash from Spain, I would only say that my brethren have not accepted a penny piece in contravention of any law. They have not taken coin out of the Kingdom except with the express permission of the authorities, and where this was withheld they have transferred sums by cheque, as it is lawful for anybody to do. I entreat Your Majesty not to deny to us a right which all other Spaniards are free to exercise. I promise you before our Lord that the students of the Roman College for whose support the alms are intended are true servants of our Lord, diligently preparing to be of great assistance to their neighbour and promoters of the public good. I can also assure you that they are given nothing but the barest necessities of poor religious. How to support them is my heaviest anxiety. As the Holy See has not been moved so far to grant the College a permanent endowment, it has occurred to me that our Lord is reserving this charity for Your Majesty, since He has made you so great a monarch. From your childhood you have known the founder of the College,[1] and he and many of its most eminent men are Your Majesty's subjects. Were you to apply to the College the revenues of a vacant abbey in the Kingdom of Naples, as the Emperor your father applied those of an abbey in Sicily to the college of Palermo, then its future would be assured. . . I humbly beg Your Majesty to give the matter consideration, and if our Lord inspires you to embrace the project not to refuse Him. . . . I also beg you to pardon my temerity and prolixity. I have not the gift of words, but my good intention and my whole-hearted and faithful desire to serve Your Majesty will plead for your gracious forbearance. . ." [2]

Meantime Nadal felt as if he were perched on the summit of a muttering volcano. The eruption came in the shape of an urgent summons back to Alcalá which he guessed to mean serious trouble. Accordingly he rushed to Valladolid and made a whirlwind visitation of the college there before obeying it. The snows and blizzards of the sierras through which he struggled home were hardly colder than the words of Rui Gomez as he informed the half-frozen priest that the King's ministers would no longer tolerate his presence in Spain and desired him to be gone without further delay. This Jerome knew to be the end and bowed his head to the orders. Joseph de Acosta, famous afterwards for his books about the New World and for his championship of the Indian natives against Spanish exploitation, was at Alcalá at this time and has left a brief record of the scene at Nadal's departure: "On his knees this best of fathers embraced each one of us tenderly, and his tears were mingled with ours as he said good-bye." [3] Jerome had thought of making his

---

[1] St. Francis Borgia.

[2] M.H., *Lainii Monumenta*, vi, 137–41. The letter achieved nothing with King Philip. It is possible that it was not allowed to come into his hands, but in any case it is unlikely that he would have been swayed by considerations for the welfare of France or by childhood recollections of the quondam Duke of Gandia.

[3] M.H., *Epistolae P. Nadal*, i, 185.

way out of the country along the coastal road from San Sebastian to Bayonne but, in deference to the views of Araoz who was opposed to that route, he headed his mule towards Jaca and the formidable Pic du Midi instead. There was nothing short of sin which he seemed unwilling to do to conciliate Araoz. From three posts offered to him Antonio had chosen that of commissary-general, vacant owing to the disappearance of St. Francis Borgia, and Nadal's last endeavour in Spain was to make everything as smooth as possible for him in the exercise of his extended authority. While visiting the Jesuits of Saragossa on his way to the Pyrenees, he wrote twice to Salmeron, then vicar-general in Rome, praising Araoz and pleading for confidence in him: "He has been my principal and practically my only go-between in all those negotiations, and he has given me great consolation and satisfaction throughout. Our Father General and the Society have in him a great servant. . . Your Reverence must believe that he is a true and faithful brother of ours, . . . and not only have confidence in him but show your confidence, never letting anything appear in your letters which might give a different impression. . . Write to him, Father, with all trust and love, and see that others do the same. . ."[1]

At Jaca Nadal and his faithful companion Ximenes had the luck to fall in with a mule caravan guarded by soldiers, which was taking Spanish gold to Lyons. In that company they crossed the mountains and so came to Oloron, where they parted from the leisurely and hard-drinking muleteers and struck out on their own for Pau, Tarbes and Toulouse. "Our journey," wrote Ximenes, "was made very difficult by three things, heresy, pestilence and war." It was April 1562 and their route lay through country patrolled by armed and inquisitive Huguenots. Every day brought its quota of adventures and each night presented the problem of finding a place to lay their heads. "None of the inns would admit us," Ximenes reported. Nadal made a detour from Tarbes to visit the college of Pamiers eighty miles away, only to find that his brethren had been expelled months earlier by the Huguenots. He discovered the refugees at Toulouse, guests of the ever-hospitable Benedictines, and spent six days negotiating with leading citizens for the permanent establishment of the Jesuits in their midst. Out of those negotia-

[1] M.H., *Epistolae P. Nadal*, i, 674-8.

tions there blossomed not only colleges and residences but an entire separate province of the order. Referring to his first night in Toulouse, Jerome noted in his diary: "Periculum a calvinista impetuoso." From then on till he reached Paris, impetuous Calvinists caused him to miss an increasing number of heart-beats. The archbishop of Toulouse, Cardinal Armagnac, resided at Rodez, seventy miles north-east, and there too the untirable Jerome plodded his dangerous way because the great man wanted to see him about opening a college in the town.

On this journey, near the small town of Rabestens, in what is now the department of Tarn, he, Ximenes and a Bearnese novice ran into a roving band of Huguenot soldiery, who debated for three hours whether to hang, shoot, drown or cast them from a convenient tower that stood in the vicinity. The youthful Ximenes was so excited by the adventure that he has bequeathed us twelve solid pages about it. Nadal has left two lines: "We were closely questioned, threatened, insulted. We were in deadly danger." The captain of the band ordered them to dismount: "Father Nadal asked him why, and for answer found a number of muskets levelled at his breast. He then dismounted and so did we his companions, to be immediately surrounded by the soldiers, who gave us very rough treatment and announced that they were going to hang us. But the captain and a minister with him wanted to have a religious argument first. Father Nadal refused to argue, that not being the time for it, and still with those muskets pressed against his heart answered all their questions in one sentence: I am a priest of the Catholic Church. It amazed me that they did not shoot him." Whether it was that the captain admired his sangfroid, or because he feared the reaction of the local Catholics if he hanged his prisoners, he decided to observe the forms of law and to charge them before a magistrate with being spies of King Philip of Spain. After examining them, the judge, who was an upright man, declared that he had no power to sentence anyone to death for religion and dismissed the case. How they got away, much battered and knocked about, is not stated, except that it was "per la divina protettione." Another day and a half of riding brought them to Rodez, where Cardinal Armagnac, who was going to Paris, urged Nadal to join his own well-armed cavalcade for the rest of the journey. But

Huguenots or no Huguenots, Jerome was determined to visit his brethren at Tournon and Billom, and so declined the tempting invitation. After another twenty-four hours in the saddle, on the main road to Lyons, he was about to turn off towards Tournon when a chance Benedictine monk informed him that it would be much easier to go to Billom first. The Society of Jesus owes that unknown monk a great debt, for it is almost certain that had Nadal proceeded to Tournon, then in the hands of the savage Baron des Adrets, he would have been hanged without ceremony. He never dreamt of wearing any disguise and travelled with a large rosary suspended from his girdle. The little party reached Billom on 29 April and had the great joy of meeting there Father Paschase Broet, whom St. Ignatius used to call his angel. Though well on the wrong side of fifty, which was regarded as old age in those days, Broet had walked the whole three hundred miles from Paris, and returned in similar style to die of the plague at his post a few months later.[1] At Billom also Nadal found the refugees from Tournon and so was able to carry out a combined visitation of the two communities. He spent twenty strenuous days over this and then was off again with Paris for his goal and Broet and Ximenes for companions, all three now on foot. At Moulins, soon to be a busy Jesuit centre, they were warned to turn back as the Huguenots had taken possession of the entire country through which ran the direct road to Paris. But they were not the kind of people who turn back and continued their journey by an alternative route through Burgundy until they reached their destination on 28 May. It was hard going the whole long way, for, says Nadal, "all the cities, towns and villages were in arms, and not a bridge was left over any river." [2]

He was just in time to catch Laynez whom, with Polanco, he found "about to put his feet in the stirrups" for the long ride to the Council of Trent. It was a delightful reunion, as Laynez had almost given up hope of ever seeing his great and dearly loved lieutenant again. Together they journeyed into Flanders, which Jerome

[1] See above, pp. 62–3.

[2] The details given are all from Ximenes's accounts, except where Nadal himself is mentioned as the source (M.H., *Epistolae P. Nadal,* i, 38–46, 722–48). The second reference is a huge letter written by Ximenes at Nadal's direction to Antonio Araoz.

regarded as a peaceful paradise after the tumults and perils of France. At Tournai they parted, Laynez going on to Trent and Nadal remaining to do for the Belgian and German Jesuits what he had done for those of Spain and Portugal. At the college in Tournai there were several English students of noble birth, and among the Jesuit postulants the interesting Father Thomas Darbyshire, nephew of Bishop Bonner and chancellor of the diocese of London in the time of Mary Tudor.[1] From Tournai Nadal made an expedition to Antwerp to hunt for books, both Catholic and Protestant, which might be useful at the Council of Trent. He and his brother Jesuit, St. Peter Canisius, constituted themselves, as it were, unofficial librarians to the Council, and earned the warm gratitude of the Presidents and Fathers for their service in this respect. At Antwerp Jerome spent money very freely, for he says that he bought "fere

[1] Ximenes makes Bonner an archbishop, but then he says of himself very disarmingly: "I haven't much of a memory and I do not think that I am particularly bright." Father Darbyshire, who came from Nottingham, was a wealthy man, but sacrificed all his property for the sake of his faith. He was received in Rome the following year (1563) by St. Francis Borgia and lived as a Jesuit to the fine old age of eighty-six. He was preceded into the Society by a number of other Englishmen, of whom the pioneer seems to have been Father Simon Belost, a Lincolnshire man of fifty-five. He had spent six years at Oxford, and was received among the Jesuits, apparently at Louvain, in 1559. Dr. Oliver, in his *Collections,* and Foley, in his *Records,* know him not, nor have they heard of Alexander Belseyr (so he signs himself), an old Etonian who, after his Oxford course, had been a master for two years at Winchester. Yet he was only nineteen years of age when he joined the Jesuits at Mainz. The second up as an English Jesuit would appear to have been Father Richard King, who came from Wells in Somerset. King was received into the order at Cologne on Easter Sunday, 1561, by Father Everard Mercurian and then sent to Rome to study metaphysics under the great Toledo. Whether it was the metaphysics or the Roman climate, his health broke down completely, and Laynez, hoping that his native air might help, sent him back to work quietly among the persecuted Catholics of England, but he did not last long, dying in 1565 at the early age of thirty-one. The same premature fate seems to have befallen Robert Cox, of Winchester, a young priest from Louvain who was received into the order by Laynez at Trent on 2 November 1562. These and other unfamiliar details about the first English Jesuits are to be found in the "Examina Patrum ac Fratrum e Societate Jesu a Patre Hieronymo Nadal collecta" (M.H., *Epistolae P. Nadal,* ii, 530, 583, 585–6, 587–8). The first Welshman to become a Jesuit was Vincent Powell, who joined, already a priest, at the same period as those others, the decade 1559–69 (*ibid.,* 589).

omnes doctores theologos antiquos," as well as all the new Protestant volumes on the market. When he had arranged for their transmission to Trent, he set his face towards Louvain, the great university city, where, as in Paris, the few Jesuit settlers were long regarded by the academic body with anything but friendly eyes. "The state of affairs here fairly disgusted me," says our forthright Jerome. And the rector of the Louvain brethren, an adherent of the Bobadilla faction in 1558, disgusted him too. There is frequent uncomplimentary mention of this professed father in the correspondence of the period. He was a kind of Flemish Araoz with the additional demerit of being an oppressor of his subjects. When Nadal arrived he refused to recognize his authority and declared that he would prefer "to go off to the Turks rather than to be ordered about by him." He would render no account of himself or of his college, and maintained that, as the constitutions did not bind under sin, he had a right to adapt them to his own particular needs and circumstances. With typical generosity Nadal attributed his unfriendliness to ill health. For the community's sake he recommended Laynez to appoint a new rector, but in such a way as not to hurt the other man's feelings. Polanco's letter from Trent announcing the change is a masterpiece of charitable diplomacy and tact. The deposed superior is told that an eminent professed father like himself, who incidentally must have had some undisclosed qualifications, is worthy of higher things than merely ruling a small and undistinguished house, so the General has handed over the drudgery to Father Schipman, while elevating himself to the high and leisured office of superintendent, "with the new rector as your Reverence's son and subject to your obedience." [1]

The relationship between superior and subject was one of Nadal's principal concerns and forms a large part of the myriad written instructions which he left behind at each Jesuit house in the course of his travels. With that difficult Louvain rector in mind it will not be irrelevant to give here some extracts from a little "Compendium of Instruction for Superiors" which he wrote as a sort of *vade-mecum* for all rectors and provincials: "The superior bears the person of Christ and is His representative. The fathers and brothers obey Christ in obeying him. They are Christ's servants,

[1] M.H., *Epistolae P. Nadal,* i, 96, 608–9; *Lainii Monumenta,* vi, 563–6.

not his. Let him sustain the weaknesses of his subjects, distrusting himself and counting them his betters in every respect. In governing it ought to be his aim to imitate the charity, meekness and bounty of Jesus Christ and of the Apostles Peter and Paul.[1] His government ought to be at once firm and sweetly kind. If he is by nature severe, let him tone down his severity; but if naturally indulgent he should try by a graver mien to redress the balance. . . When he speaks, it ought to be courteously and sweetly, with a serene and cheerful countenance making manifest the charity that is in him. He must not betray that he remembers the fault of fathers or brothers when dealing with them, but, if he can, rather excuse it and make light of it. On the other hand, let him show that he has not forgotten such things as may be praised in their conduct. He should not give them orders in an imperious way, but in a kindly tranquil manner, yet clearly and plainly, saying, for example, 'Would you do this; it would be good of you to do this; for your love to God I would ask you to do this.' He will not say, 'I order or command you'; much less, 'I order or command you in virtue of holy obedience or in the name of the Lord.' That formula can be used only when there is no other way of averting some serious danger or injury. . . The superior's way of acting ought to be easy, open, cheerful, friendly, . . . and accommodated to the disposition and character of him with whom he deals. In everyone there is some good, and he ought to concentrate on the good in the person before him and so speak as to show his appreciation of it. Let him not show distrust of anyone, but rather by referring to praiseworthy things which they have done put heart into all and cure their faults. . . Severity will sometimes be necessary, but it must plainly proceed from a desire of the subject's perfection and from zeal for God, and be always less than the fault deserves. . .[2] Even in the

[1] Nadal was well known for his tender devotion to those two Apostles, which very probably he derived from St. Ignatius. St. Ignatius was never out of his memory, and he says that he used to weep "many sweet, spontaneous tears" when thinking of that beloved Father.

[2] Here Nadal devotes an entire page to the precautions which must be used before proceeding to the extreme penalty of expulsion even against the most inveterate offender. The superior is not easily to credit what he hears about such a one, and "if any hope remains of helping the unquiet soul, he must bring all care and diligence to this task."

case of grave offenders, there will be pity, and pity plain to read, in the rector's heart. He will offer an amnesty for all repented faults, refrain from embittering the culprit by harsh words, and, should sternness be sometimes necessary, take pains at the end to smooth down ruffled feelings. . . He must try every remedy at all likely to help the troubled man, taking careful account of his character, . . . and if nothing else avails, the superior might see whether exemption for a time from all studies and duties would not work a change. . . Should this happen, he is to receive the penitent in the pleasantest and most joyful fashion, letting bygones be bygones." [1]

After the work of Flanders was done, Nadal gave his bridle-reins a shake, bound for his favourite Canaan, Germany. But we may leave him for the present at Spa, to which place he turned aside in hopes of deriving some benefit from its famous and horrible waters. "I drank them for ten days," he notes in his diary, "until heavy rains made them undrinkable. Even this short course caused me to feel better, so ever afterwards I hankered to return and resume my potations, if given an opportunity." [2] It says something for the fullness of his laborious vagabond existence that five years passed before he found an opportunity.

[1] M.H., *Epistolae P. Nadal*, iv, 435–40. Being only human, rectors and provincials, as we have seen, did not always come up to this ideal of government, but on the whole they made a very good effort.

[2] M.H., *Epistolae P. Nadal*, ii, 97.

CHAPTER V

SAINTS ASCENDANT

NADAL'S eagerness to reach Germany is not a feeling which a writer about him can be expected to share. Germany was then the land of the Great Confusion, the Witches' Cauldron of Christendom already simmering for the terrible ebullition of the Thirty Years' War. The first Jesuit to labour there had been Pierre Favre, the first steadfast disciple of St. Ignatius and one of the sweetest souls that have ever been beatified. Pierre used to beg God daily to show His mercy to Henry VIII, Luther, Melanchthon, Bucer, and the Sultan of all the Turks. His German experiences nearly broke his brave heart, but he was given a wonderful compensation three years before he died, when there came to him at Mainz, in 1543, a young graduate of the drowsy University of Cologne, Peter Kanis, the future St. Peter Canisius. The meeting of those two Peters was like one recorded at the beginning of history: "The soul of Jonathan was knit with the soul of David, and Jonathan loved him as his own soul. . . Then Jonathan and David made a covenant, . . . and Jonathan stripped himself of the robe that was upon him and gave it to David, and his garments, even to his sword, and to his bow, and to his girdle."

After being guided with deep affection and insight by Favre on the long uphill soul's pilgrimage of *The Spiritual Exercises,* Peter Canisius returned to Cologne, feeling, as he said, newly born, and quickly organized the first small Jesuit community on Germany's soil, not a member of which was a German. Peter himself at this time could not even speak German. He came from Nijmegen and was as Dutch as an interior by Vermeer or one of Albert Cuyp's old brown windmills. One might describe him as the Church's most eminent *polder-man,* who reclaimed from the Protestant sea by his personal exertions or his influence with bishops and princes great tracts of Southern Germany, Austria, Hungary, Bohemia and Poland. Naturally, in a book such as this it will not be possible to do more than glance at his incessant draining and dike-building operations.[1] They began in Cologne even before he was a priest. Cologne's Archbishop and Elector, Hermann von Wied, declared like Cranmer, whom he influenced, for the Reformation and made determined efforts over several years to Lutheranize his dominions. In this he enjoyed the active co-operation of Melanchthon and Bucer, both experts at persuasion, who came to Bonn and Deutz to preach for him. But happily for the faith of the Rhineland, the Catholic cause did not lack defenders, and when the Archbishop published his *Book of Reformation* in 1543, an elaborate answer to it by his own Chancellor, Dr. Johann Gropper, followed within three weeks. Never before or since in the history of printing was so big and learned a book produced in so short a time. With Gropper, Billick, Stempel and the other leaders of the Catholic resistance Peter Canisius became closely associated. Gropper concludes a letter to him with the words, *Tibi addictissimus.* He put himself completely at their disposal and undertook arduous and dangerous missions to the Emperor at Antwerp, to the Prince-Bishop of Liége, and to other great personages, all before he was twenty-six. At home in Cologne he mobilized the students for battle, particularly by the promotion of frequent Communion, brought Favre from Mainz to inspire them, and himself, when made a deacon, began at once to wield that Sword of the Spirit, the Word of God, which would never after sleep in his hand until he died. He was not a natural orator like Luther, and he had painfully to learn the complicated German language, but faith, hope and charity went into the pulpit with him and laid a spell upon his listeners.

Peter was the first Jesuit in history to write a book, the pioneer of an enormous and highly diversified army of scribes. At the age of twenty-five he astonished the dull doctors of Cologne by presenting them with editions in three folio volumes of the works of St. Cyril of Alexandria and St. Leo the Great. Untrained and without a guide, he entered the kingdom of scholarship as it were by storm and

[1] His correspondence alone, edited by Otto Braunsberger, S.J., fills eight large octavo volumes of 7550 pages (*Beati Petri Canisii Societatis Jesu Epistulae et Acta,* Freiburg im Breisgau 1896–1923). This colossal work, completed just two years before St. Peter's canonization and declaration as a Doctor of the Church in 1925, involved research in upwards of 260 libraries of eleven countries, including England.

bore off his trophies in a fashion reminiscent of Samson and the gates of Gaza. Doubtless the editing was faulty enough to make Erasmus turn in his ten-year-old grave, but the unexacting Catholics delighted in the volumes and nothing else mattered to Peter. The surprising thing, as Dr. Johnson said of the dog walking on its hind-legs, is not that he did his feat awkwardly but that he was able to do it at all. He admitted that it cost him "Herculean labours," and the few tools available to him were mostly of the Old Stone Age.[1] But he carried on, daring to hope that some bishops might be inspired by the example and counsel of his Cyril and Leo, those perfect pastors, and that students for the priesthood might be stimulated, those hungry lambs who looked up and were not fed in the bleak winter-age of scholasticism.[2] To the end of his days bishops and students would always have first claim on the devoted heart of St. Peter Canisius.

[1] The few Cologne Jesuits at this time were much too poor to be able to afford the luxury of books. Their private library, catalogued by Canisius himself, consisted of the following eight volumes: Erasmus's *Paraphrase of the New Testament,* an anonymous *Moralization on the Bible,* St. Bridget's *Revelations,* the *Soliloquies* of St. Bonaventure, *The Golden Legend,* a work entitled *Opus trivium notabilium Praedicabilium,* another called *The Properties of Things,* and an *Annotated Book of Notable Sayings.*

[2] The decline in intellectual vigour since the Middle Ages may be illustrated by a comparison, in their respective approaches to problems of natural history, between St. Peter himself and St. Albert the Great, who also lectured in Cologne and died there in 1280. In one of his books St. Albert, a German interested in everything, gives a perfectly accurate description of the appearance and habits of the Libyan ostrich, derived from his own study of the creature in a Cologne zoo. He then continues: "It is said of this bird that it swallows and digests iron; but I have not found this myself, because several ostriches refused to eat the iron which I threw them. However, they eagerly devoured large bones cut into small pieces, as well as gravel" (H. Wilms, O.P., *Albert the Great,* translated from the German, London 1933, p. 59). Plainly Mr. H. A. L. Fisher knew nothing about St. Albert and his ostriches when he wrote of the "leaden inhibitions which shackled the learning of the medieval Faculties." Now let us turn to St. Peter Canisius, three hundred years later. Peter once preached an entire sermon on the honeybee as a model of industry and the community spirit. Bees are not nearly so scarce as ostriches. The world has always been full of bees and our preacher could have gone to watch them at work whenever he liked. But he went to the library instead and took down the elder Pliny's *Natural History,* first published about the year A.D. 77. All the bee-lore of his sermon is lifted bodily from this famous old farrago of portents and marvels.

Peter's own ordination took place in June 1546, just a month before Favre, the light of his youth, laid down his earthly burden in Rome. He wept when he heard the news, and re-echoed in humble prose the bitter-sweet distich of the Greek Anthology:

In life like morning star thy shining head,
And now my star of eve among the dead.

Inheritor of Favre's mantle, he soon found favour with a good and lovable but extravagant German prelate, Cardinal Truchsess, Bishop of the Protestant stronghold of Augsburg, and was by him induced to betake himself to the Council of Trent. Peter entered the Council as the Cardinal's representative within nine months of his ordination and he must certainly have been the youngest member of the congregation of minor theologians who prepared the material for the bishops' discussions. It needed some courage for a mere fledgling to shake his wings in the presence of the many golden eagles such as the future Archbishop Carranza in the assembly, but Peter rose to the occasion, though it cannot be said that he gave his learned auditors any new lights on theology. He spoke several times, and well enough to earn inclusion in Massarelli's complicated *Diary,* the Hansard of the Council. Much more important, he spent his days in company with Le Jay, Laynez and Salmeron, three of the original nine patriarchs of the Society of Jesus. And Trent took hold of him completely. For the next fifteen years, until its close in 1562, the Council will be flesh of his flesh and bone of his bone. Nothing that he can do to promote its interests will ever be esteemed by him enough. Soon he will have all Catholic Germany praying for it. He will canvass for it incessantly, travel on its business thousands of miles, buy all its wanted books, be its unofficial handyman, its undecorated factotum, with a heart that would have been grateful to God for the privilege of polishing the Fathers' shoes.

After the transfer of the Council to Bologna and its prorogation there owing to the hostile attitude of Charles V, bent as always on appeasing his unruly Protestants, Canisius was called to Rome, where he completed his Jesuit training under the immediate direction of St. Ignatius. Then, early in 1548, he was dispatched as one of a band of ten, captained by Jerome Nadal, to open at Messina the first Jesuit school and seminary known to history. On the eve of departure and again when Naples was reached, Peter wrote to his Cologne brethren: "Commend me to the prayers of all our friends, and remember me at the shrines of the holy Magi and St. Gereon and the Theban Martyrs and St. Maurice and all the virginal company of St. Ursula. If I dare ask so much, would you say a weekly Mass for me? I beg Father Prior of the Carthusians, my dearest friend, to get each priest to say one Mass for his Canisius. . . Goodbye always in the tender love of Jesus crucified for us, and never forget the confident hopes and desires formed for his Cologne people by Father Peter Favre of sweet memory." Those words weigh on the heart to-day when Colonia Sancta is in ruins. Nadal succeeded in retaining the services of his invaluable Dutchman for little more than a year, a busy inglorious year which he passed expounding to an audience of mercurial youth the uncongenial mysteries of Quintilian or more happily preaching in uneasy Italian to crowded congregations of their elders. Peter tried very earnestly to be the complete schoolmaster but Germany would keep breaking in. He had even to be admonished gently from Rome for "brooding upon Germany." Meantime, in that distressful country, the Duke of Bavaria, whose good Catholicism was somewhat complicated by a detestation for the House of Habsburg, had become anxious about the fate of his solitary university at Ingolstadt. The universities were key-points in the Reformation struggle, and Ingolstadt meant to the Catholics what its raw but vigorous and enterprising rival, Wittenberg, did to the Protestants. Until his death in 1543 Ingolstadt had been the stronghold of the doughty and formidable Johann Eck, the David of the Catholics and the only one of them capable of making the Goliath of Wittenberg wince. His death was a catastrophe for the Catholic cause. Ingolstadt began at once to decline and within a few years it seemed that Protestantism could not be prevented from triumphing in Bavaria. The crisis impelled Duke William to appeal to St. Ignatius for help, and that led to the recall of Peter Canisius from Sicily, much against the will of Nadal. In Rome again, Peter repaired to the Castle of St. Angelo for the Pope's blessing on the new venture, which was to be shared by Le Jay and Salmeron. He then visited the tomb of the Apostles to pray, and has himself recorded very simply what went on in his soul: "There I felt, O Holy Father and Eternal High Priest, Thy great consolation and present grace, sweetly dispensed to me by those Thy intercessors. They gave me their blessing and strengthened me for my mission to Germany, and they seemed to guarantee their assistance to me as to an apostle of Germany. Thou knowest, O Lord, how much and how often Thou didst on that day commend Germany unto me. From that day forth Germany would occupy more and more of my anxious thoughts, and I would long, like Father Favre, to spend myself utterly in life and death for her salvation. Thus would I be a fellow-worker with St. Michael, the Angel of Germany. For a little while Thou didst hide from me the vast mountain of my unworthiness, showing me that in Thee and through Thee there was nothing too great to be achieved." [1]

As the chief duty of Peter and his companions at Ingolstadt would be to teach theology and to carry on the good fight against heresy which Eck had so long and so valiantly maintained, St. Ignatius desired them on their way north to stand for a doctor's degree at the University of Bologna. The examination was reputed to be "arduum, rigorosum ac tremendum," a circumstance that intimidated the youngest member of the trio and drove him on visits to the shrines of the saints, especially the shrine of St. Dominic, whose great son, Bishop Ambrose Catharinus, one of the most brilliant and independent thinkers of that age, headed the board of examiners. With St. Dominic's help Peter won his biretta, and so did Le Jay and Salmeron, a result which the Secretary of the Council of Trent was gracious enough to say caused nobody the least surprise. Their arrival at Ingolstadt on 13 November 1549 was heralded by a modern Protestant scholar as "a day momentous in the history of Germany." But the gay students of the place did not notice any portents in the sky on the occasion, and the largest number of them which the Bologna doctors succeeded in attracting to their lectures was fourteen, including ten blockheads unwanted by the other professors. After eight months of frustration Le Jay and Salmeron packed up with pleasure and betook themselves, on an order from Rome, to more promising pastures, leaving Peter to plough the

[1] Braunsberger, *Epistulae et Acta,* i, 53–4. When Germany was first converted St. Michael displaced the pagan god Odin, or Wotan, and became patron of the Holy Roman Empire. St. Peter was born on 8 May, feast of the Apparition of St. Michael.

Bavarian sands alone. Never did he show himself greater than during the following three years of heartbreak, plodding disconsolately up and down those stubborn unyielding furrows.. "Dear God," he exclaimed in a moment of utter weariness, "what a task it is to keep the Catholics in the ancient Faith!" At Ingolstadt the commandments of the Church were completely disregarded, the few priests of the place had long since given up saying Office, and both professors and students eagerly perused the latest productions of the Protestant press, brought to them by zealous hawkers from Wittenberg. As for the practice of their religion, Peter sadly told Polanco that were he to bribe them with gold he did not think that he could persuade any of these men to come to Mass. Ingolstadt had a seminary of sorts, presided over by a layman who made a hobby of collecting Lutheran books for his library. Peter decided to concentrate all his guns on this Laodicean and so bombarded him with prayers, entreaties and acts of charity that the good, easy man capitulated after a brief resistance, burnt his Protestant books, became a priest and set about the reform of his seminary. That was a victory for *The Spiritual Exercises* and typical of St. Peter's methods. In other and happier places it might be possible, if we may change the metaphor, to achieve impressive results with a net, but he, like St. Francis Xavier in Japan, must always do his fishing with a line. It was a slow laborious process, well suited, however, to a man who had not the least objection to drudgery. Peter Canisius might indeed be described as the Great Drudge of the Counter-Reformation.

The love of God which inspired him and which is so evident in the prologue to his unfinished *Dictionary of Theology,* written at this time, with its fifty different titles of our Lord neatly arranged in a heart-shaped pattern,[1] slowly wore away the apathy of students and professors alike. They elected him their rector and vice-chancellor successively, and took to visiting him in his room and to patronizing his sermons. He is never an easy subject for the biographer or historian, this plodding unromantic composer who gives so few chances to the drums and trumpets. He flits evasively before us, on the way to preach at sunrise, coming home from the sick at midnight, visiting the town gaol, his favourite outing, at any

[1] There is a photograph of this prologue in the English *Life of St. Peter,* facing p. 822. It reveals his spirit better than almost anything else in the book.

and every hour. Then there were the children to be gathered together and instructed, and many poor folk in those bad times who needed a word of encouragement and whatever food and clothing he could buy or beg to bring them. There are no high lights in the story. It is a sort of "Passing of the Third Floor Back" in a different and entirely unsentimental idiom.

Early in 1552 St. Peter received orders from the Pope to proceed to Vienna, where King Ferdinand had need of his services. Then did Ingolstadt mourn. His farewell sermon at the church in which Eck is buried was accompanied by "much weeping and sobbing," and when he climbed aboard a Danubian ship for the four days' voyage the quayside was black with people waving him a sad farewell. But Ingolstadt had not seen the last of him. He left his heart among its gabled houses and returned three years later to plant beside them one of the greatest of Jesuit colleges, which would profoundly influence the course of the Counter-Reformation. At Vienna he became a community man again, joining a highly international team of his brethren composed of men from France, Flanders, Spain, Italy, Brabant, Germany, Austria, Holland and Hungary. They lived like evacuees in cramped quarters shared by other people, lectured at the moribund University, evangelized the Italian engineers engaged in fortifying Vienna against the Turks, and pored daily with despair in their hearts over grammars of the German language. At the head of the mixed company, most of them scholastics or Jesuits in the making, presided the great and lovable Father Claude Le Jay, whose French larynx had for years been wrestling in vain with the gutturals of the Empire. Father Claude was mainly responsible for the withdrawal of Peter Canisius from Ingolstadt. He needed a German-speaking preacher, professor, missioner and jack-of-all-trades, especially of the hard, unhappy writer's trade. A year before, King Ferdinand, distressed by the rapid progress of Protestantism in Austria and Hungary, had imposed on Le Jay the task of producing a new compendium of Christian doctrine for priests and people that might help to stay the invading gospel. The Father ruined his health trying to satisfy the King, but nothing came of his efforts except a vast chaos of notes which he could not reduce to order. In his perplexity he remembered that at Ingolstadt Father Canisius had proved himself an excellent catechist and was always talking about the need of a new *Catechism* to match Luther's famous and ubiquitous productions. Well, let Father Canisius come and write the unmanageable masterpiece himself! No sooner was Peter in Vienna than Claude joyfully made over to him his mountain of notes and shortly afterwards lay down and died. "He showed us the straight way to Christ both in life and in death," wrote his literary heir to Polanco. "Wherever he had been he left behind the sweetest memory. He was a true apostle of Germany."

Peter's own apostolate in Austria lacked nothing of variety. He took Le Jay's place at the University and, discarding scholastic tradition, blossomed out as the first of the long line of Jesuit controversial theologians whose chief glory is St. Robert Bellarmine. He preached in season and out of season, sometimes to almost empty pews, sometimes to thousands, whether in the grandest churches of Vienna, or before the King and his Court, or at country crossroads, or in derelict village chapels far up in the mountains, until a people not easy to impress became "lost in astonishment at the burning eagerness of Father Canisius for the salvation of souls." [1] Within a month of his arrival in Vienna he is telling his Cologne brethren, his lifelong confidants, that he has "found a way to get in touch with prisoners in the gaols" and intends "to supply the place of parish priest" to those excommunicates of the social order. The state of religion in Austria may be guessed from the fact that in twenty years not a single priest had been ordained in its capital, and that in the diocese of Passau adjoining Vienna 254 parishes were without Mass and sacraments. To such places St. Peter hastened whenever he could steal a day from his other occupations, toiling to them though snow and rain and expending on their needs the charity that had become a proverb in the slums of Vienna. At home with his brethren he acted as a sort of combined master of novices and prefect of studies, built up a good library, and stone by stone laid the foundations of the best Catholic school for boys that Habsburg lands had ever known. But no one place or emergency could monopolize this man's illimitable sympathies. In less than two years he had dispatched twenty-three students to the German College in Rome, recruits gained with infinite difficulty but willingly surrendered for the

---

[1] M.H., Polanco, *Chronicon*, ii, 574; *Litterae Quadrimestres*, ii, 114.

long-term strategy of the Popes, whose victories he would not be there to witness and acclaim. At this period of intolerable strain he entered on active negotiations with various princes and prelates for the establishment of the Society of Jesus in Holland, Bohemia, Tirol, Prussia and Hungary. A Polish envoy to Turkistan had spoken to him about conditions in that wild, mysterious back of beyond, whereupon he immediately writes to St. Ignatius: "May our Eternal Lord open for us a way to Tartary, for I hear that its people have never been Christians and are of a most cruel and barbarous disposition. The Polish envoy tells me that their country is larger than Spain, Italy and Germany put together. May Almighty God who is helping barbarous India by our brethren also deign to enlighten the darkness of Tartary, so that there may be one fold and one shepherd."

In 1554 Vienna stood in need of a local shepherd. The see had been vacant for nearly two years owing to the difficulty of finding a suitable man to fill it. Good bishops were hard to come by and King Ferdinand had had enough of bad ones. Suddenly the name of Canisius was suggested to him and the excellent King felt much as did the perplexed people of Milan when the child in their midst cried out "Ambrose! Ambrose!" The Jesuit seemed a candidate sent from Heaven until he pointed out that he had taken a solemn vow to Heaven to refuse ecclesiastical dignities unless commanded to accept them by the Pope. Then began a battle royal in Rome, with St. Ignatius and his friends on one side and the King's agents on the other. The issue, a serious one for the Jesuits, remained long in doubt and caused Peter Canisius many a sleepless night. Apart from his vow and the wound his elevation, as the first of its kind and so a dangerous precedent, would inflict on his order's constitutions, he felt a natural shrinking from what he considered would be for him a "yoke of all unhappiness." Referring to the manœuvres of the King's party in a letter to Polanco, he says: "I promise your Reverence seven Masses in honour of the Holy Ghost the minute you give me news that their efforts have come to nothing. If it falls out otherwise I shall know for certain that God is angry with me for my sins, and all my life I shall have real cause to be afraid." In the end, St. Ignatius, an old campaigner in this country of the diplomats, so far prevailed that Peter was appointed, by a brief of Julius III, merely administrator of the diocese, with a bishop's authority but without his title or revenues. The new office made not the slightest difference to his usual routine of sermons, lectures and big and little charities. He had the joy of publishing the Jubilee Indulgence granted by the Pope at the accession of Mary Tudor, and at court seized the occasion to deliver a whole series of sermons expounding and defending the doctrine of merit and good works which had been so much travestied by the reformers. To his friend, Martin Cromer, private secretary of the King of Poland, he sent a little book about recent events in England as an encouragement of hope, assured him that he was ready at a nod from the Pope to plunge into the dark waters of Prussia, Poland's Protestant neighbour, and promised to keep always looking out "for a chance of labouring and suffering among the Poles themselves, in the service of their crucified Master, their afflicted brethren, and their little ones with nobody to instruct them." [1] The width and depth and sincerity of St. Peter's zeal for the faith is revealed in his incessant cry for prayers on behalf of countries a prey to or threatened by heresy. Every letter he writes, and he is everlastingly writing, contains such petitions. He literally pestered all the good people whom he knew to join in his apostleship of prayer, and it was entirely his contriving that every Jesuit priest in the world since his day has been obliged by rule to say Mass once a month for the return to the Catholic fold of the nations which left it at the Reformation, particularly England and Germany.[2]

But the great work of the Saint during that crowded Viennese period was his *Summary of Christian Doctrine* or Catechism, the most famous book of the entire Counter-Reformation. Many others, and especially his friend, Gropper, had preceded him in the field, but they lacked his pedagogic flair and his infinite capacity for taking pains. Their slipshod and ill-arranged productions were a poor match for Luther's little manual of genius which carried the new evangel into a hundred thousand homes and engraved it on the hearts

---

[1] Braunsberger, *Epistulae et Acta,* i, 514.

[2] Braunsberger, *Epistulae et Acta,* i, 429. The prescription of St. Ignatius, issued in direct answer to St. Peter's appeal, applied to non-priest members of the Society of Jesus also, who are required to say certain prayers every month "for the northern nations and the reduction of heresy" (*Monumenta Ignatiana,* series prima, v, 220–1).

of Germany's children. While at Ingolstadt, Peter Canisius bemoaned the unsuitableness of those Catholic catechisms and implored Laynez to employ his great gifts in the writing of a better one, adapted to the capacity of children and to the needs of Germany. Laynez must have smiled wanly on receiving this appeal on behalf of the Church's nurseries, as he was just then being deluged with petitions to write a new textbook of theology for her universities and seminaries. At Vienna Peter found himself committed to the production of a work which, according to King Ferdinand's lordly specifications, must apparently be milk and meat at the same time, a horn-book for abecedarians and a textbook for seminarians. Only allegories or fairy-stories full of hidden symbolism written by imaginative geniuses could satisfy both parties, and the Jesuit from Nijmegen, being neither a Bunyan nor a Swift and wanting something totally different, solved his problem by excluding the adult party altogether. Let Laynez look to them; he would concentrate on youth in its various growing stages. In the event he produced three Catechisms, a short, a shorter, and a shortest, each adapted to the ability of a particular class of young readers. The first of these, his *Summa Doctrinae Christianae,* written in easy Latin and intended for boys in the upper forms of schools who might be expected to have acquired some command of that language, was sufficiently far advanced at the beginning of the year 1554 for him to submit part of his manuscript to the judgment of King Ferdinand and of the Jesuit authorities in Rome. The King replied in the following terms: "Honorable, religious, devout and beloved Son, We have seen and examined the first part of your Catechism which you sent for our inspection. Our opinion and expectation of it is that, God helping, it will when published greatly promote the salvation of our faithful subjects. Accordingly, it is our gracious request that you finish the remainder without delay and transmit to Us the Catechism whole and complete as soon as possible, for We have resolved and determined that this your Catechism shall be translated also into our German tongue and taught publicly to youth in all the Latin and German schools of our five Lower Austrian provinces and of our County of Görz, to the exclusion of any other catechism, under the severest penalty and the threat of our indignation. We return you herewith the first part, charging you before everything to note throughout in the margins thereof the books and chapters where are to be found the contexts of the passages from Scripture, the Fathers and Doctors of the Church, and canon law, cited by you learnedly appositely and devoutly in that Catechism. . ." Ferdinand wanted the references given in hope that great numbers of his subjects who had lapsed from the faith might be tempted to look them up and so "be brought back to the bosom and saving embrace of our holy mother, the Catholic Church." Peter not only supplied the references to the number of more than three thousand, but later on in furtherance of the good King's hope persuaded and actively assisted one of his Cologne brethren to collect and publish in full all the passages which he had used. They needed four bulky tomes of 2271 pages for their accommodation and inspired an eminent modern authority on catechetics to say that "no one studying them could fail to be amazed by the erudition of Canisius or to be filled with admiration for the skill with which he works on his abundant stores of knowledge, reducing them to the compass of a little book that appears as if it had been cast from a mould and yet contains not a sentence nor hardly even a word other than those of Scripture or the Doctors of the Church." [1] That perfection of form was not attained without struggle and pain. "My sensations," wrote St. Peter to Polanco, "are like those of a woman in labour. It is impossible for me not to be anxious while the child remains unborn that it may be such as can be offered and consecrated to God." The birth took place in the spring of the year 1555, and Ferdinand, brother of the Emperor, gave the baby for a present exclusive rights in the kingdom of the young: ". . . We therefore charge you herein addressed, particularly those who govern and administer justice as our representatives in our provinces of Lower Austria and County of Görz, to see to it most diligently that this Catechism alone and no other is propounded, explained and taught to schoolchildren, whether publicly or privately, by schoolmasters, tutors and instructors, in so far as you and they desire to avoid our severe anger and other penalties, reserved according to our judg-

---

[1] Dr. Fr. Knecht in Wetzer und Welte's *Kirchenlexikon,* vol. vii, col. 303. Dr. Knecht sums up his opinion of the Catechism as follows: "It is not the genius of a particular man that speaks to us here; it is the spirit and the voice of the Church."

ment for delinquents and contemners of this our Edict. . ." The
little book appeared without any name on its modest title-page, but
the Protestants quickly divined the secret and within a few months
of publication Melanchthon at Wittenberg publicly denounced "the
impudent and odious author of the Austrian Catechism, whose
name is derived from the Latin for a dog." [1] Shortly afterwards,
Johann Wigand, the Lutheran superintendent of Magdeburg, came
out with a *Scriptural Refutation of the Catechism of the Jesuits,* full
of such bouquets for St. Peter as "dog of a monk, fearful blasphemer
of God, gross blockhead, idolater, wolf, ass of the Pope, swindling
trickster, shameless and miserable devil." For the rest of his days
these flowers of the Reformation garden would constantly bestrew
his path. But time brings great changes, and when a modern Protestant scholar had occasion to speak of the same *Summa,* this is what
he said: "The Catechism of Canisius has taken his name through
the world and down the centuries. Hardly any other book has circulated so widely, running as it did into close on four hundred editions a century and thirty years from the date of its first publication.
The whole plan and construction of the book is skilful in the highest
degree, and the writing a model of lucidity and exact statement
unmatched among Catholic productions of the period. All the moral
doctrines and commandments of the medieval Church here come to
life again, and the strong emphasis laid on them makes it plain that
the age of the Counter-Reformation has dawned." [2]

Having made provision with the *Summa* for youth on the threshold
of manhood, St. Peter went on to write his "Shortest Catechism"
for little boys and girls just emerging from childhood. One of his
last actions on earth, as an old man of seventy-five, was to prepare
a new edition of this tiny book with the words divided into syllables,
to enable, he said, his "dear little children to learn it more easily."
Finally, in 1558, he brought out at Ingolstadt his third or "Shorter
Catechism," which in course of time he fashioned into a combined
catechism and prayer-book, the most popular of all his works. It

[1] Breitschneider, *Corpus Reformatorum,* vii (1844), 107 *sq.*
[2] Dr. Paulus Drews in an essay on Canisius contributed to the proceedings of
the *Verein für Reformationsgeschichte* (Halle 1892), pp. 45–6. Drews labours
to paint St. Peter, whom he admires, as more of an "episcopalian" than a proper
Papist.

was illustrated with little pictures in the margins and 105 larger woodcuts representing our Lord, our Lady, and various saints and ceremonies of the Church. So much tenderness and love for children went to its making that, as an eminent authority has said, "one might think one was reading Tauler, Suso, or St. Gertrude, and name the little book a later flowering of medieval mysticism." In order to associate the saints in the children's minds with the changes of the seasons, Peter cited verses from the charming old *Bauernregeln* or Shepherd's Calendar of Catholic Germany,[1] and used similar devices to lodge the words and deeds of our Lord securely in their memories. Those Catechisms cost him an immense amount of labour, for he never stopped trying to improve them, as new editions were called for, while he had energy enough to hold a pen. Thus, to the 1566 edition of the *Summa,* the first to bear his name, he added a long appendix of twenty sections on the Fall and Justification of mankind, according to the teaching of the Council of Trent. It went forth with magnificent sponsoring, prefaced by decrees of Philip II and of his Imperial Majesty Ferdinand I, making its use compulsory in all the Catholic schools of their vast dominions. Before St. Peter died thirty years later the Catechisms were circulating in fifteen different languages, including English, Lowland Scots, Hindustani and Japanese, and had been re-edited or reprinted more than two hundred times. In the opinion of the distinguished modern authority on Lutheran literature, Gustav Kawerau, "they certainly had as much significance for the Counter-Reformation as the Catechisms of Luther had for the Reformation." [2]

The only way possible to give some faint indication of Peter's activities during the middle years of his life is to do it statistically, by means of a list of the places where he preached, lectured, hammered out his big books, and transacted the Church's and the Jesuits' business. (*See table opposite.*)

This journeying went on without intermission for another thirty

---

[1] Such as this:

> St. Clement's Feast doth winter bring,
> St. Peter's Chair will urge the spring.
> The summer's here with St. Urban
> And autumn with Symphorian.

[2] *Theologische Literaturzeitung,* xix (1894), 84.

Year	Miles travelled as the crow flies	Places visited and revisited
1555	1372	Augsburg, Vienna, Prague, Augsburg, Vienna, Prague, Munich, Ingolstadt.
1556	1562	Augsburg, Vienna, Prague, Oybin, Prague, Oybin, Prague, Regensburg, Ingolstadt, Regensburg, Ingolstadt, Eichstätt, Regensburg, Ingolstadt, Passau, Padua, Innsbruck, Augsburg, Dillingen, Ingolstadt, Regensburg.
1557	1630	Padua, Venice, Florence, Rome, Perugia, Florence, Bologna, Ferrara, Padua, Venice, Padua, Trent, Innsbruck, Munich, Ingolstadt, Munich, Ingolstadt, Ellwangen, Worms, Cologne, Bonn, Worms, Zabern (Saverne).
1558	1467	Strasbourg, Schlettstadt (Selestat), Colmar, Ruffach, Breisach, Freiburg im Breisgau, Strasbourg, Dillingen, Ingolstadt, Nuremberg, Munich, Ingolstadt, Dillingen, Straubing, Ingolstadt, Dillingen, Augsburg, Ettal, Loreto, Rome, Pesaro, Rimini, Vienna, Cracow, Lowicz, Piotrków.

years, during which the Church's courier covered not less than twenty thousand miles of Germany, Austria, Bohemia, Switzerland and Italy. It may be seen in the list given above that he visited and revisited Prague five times in the years 1555–6. The explanation is that he had begun there one of his great "poldering" operations, the foundation of a Jesuit college which was to be one of the principal instruments of Divine Providence in reclaiming Bohemia from Hussitism and Lutheranism and making it into a permanently Catholic country. He thought nothing of undertaking a nine days' journey on horseback, from Prague to Augsburg, to consult with King

Ferdinand on some detail of business connected with the new college, and at Augsburg had the melancholy experience of witnessing the conclusion of the so-called Religious Peace, which brought not peace but in the whirligig of time all the tears and blood and bitterness of the Thirty Years' War. However, his influence with the helpless and unhappy King who "loved him as a brother" contributed to save from the wreck of Catholic hopes at least the "Ecclesiastical Reservation," as an obstacle to the further spoliation of the Church's properties. From Augsburg he made a dash to Vienna to help the incipient college there and to fight another round of a long and painful contest with the popular Lutheran apostle, Johann Phauser, preacher and *protégé* of the vacillating Prince Maximilian, eldest son of Ferdinand and heir to the crown of Charlemagne. The prospect in Vienna looked so black that the Jesuits anticipated martyrdom, not that that unduly depressed them. To his friend, Cromer, in Poland, where things were even worse, St. Peter wrote: "In these great storms let us watch for a better wind. Christ sleeps, the ship is buffeted, and all seems lost. But He shall neither slumber nor sleep that keepeth Israel. To Him, therefore, let us with perfect confidence entrust ourselves and all the Church's affairs, for He hath a care of us. To Him be praise and glory for ever."

From Vienna he returned to the drudgery of Prague, where his chief occupation apart from teaching and preaching was the famous one of trying to make ends meet, to scrape together enough money for the purchase of twelve very plain beds for the weary limbs of his brethren and enough very plain food to keep them from starvation. They had at least the satisfaction of knowing that the members of the family who had sailed away to pagan lands could not be much worse off, and one of them exclaimed with some lightheartedness, "Ecce in Aquilone, India!" Ingolstadt also, as the list makes plain, claimed a great deal of Peter's attention. It was typical of him that while engaged in complicated and exasperating negotiations with the officials of the Duke of Bavaria about the foundation of a college he must also produce a book *in usum scholarum,* a handy edition of the Epistles and Gospels from the Vulgate, each preceded by a clear summary and explanation of its contents. For many a year to come the colleges of Vienna, Prague and Ingolstadt were to be the torment and joy of his life. He watched with loving solicitude over every step of their progress and almost, one might say, mixed his blood with the mortar that kept their stones together, until institutions of insignificant and precarious beginnings grew under his nurturing into powerful forces for the regeneration of Germany. Ingolstadt rapidly regained its fame as a great centre of intellectual life, and from the printing-presses of the town, as in the brave old times of Eck, huge, learned tomes of polemics, history and theology began to pour, including the most famous books of that kind ever published anywhere, the *Controversies* of St. Peter's brother-Jesuit and brother-Doctor, St. Robert Bellarmine. Catholic theology, which Le Jay had once mourned as dead and buried, *per tutto sepolto,* arose from the tomb in more comely robes than she had worn since the palmy days of St. Albert and St. Thomas, and a new race of priests and laymen, born of St. Peter's college, girded themselves like happy warriors for the battles of the Counter-Reformation. There too, towards the century's close, Jesuit masters educated the future emperor, Ferdinand II, and Bavaria's first Elector, Maximilian, who in alliance won for the Catholic cause some of its most famous victories. The colleges in Vienna and Prague had equally prosperous histories to come, and contributed more than perhaps any other single cause to the ultimate defeat of heresy in the lands to which they belonged.

In June 1556 Father Canisius, to his sudden wonder and consternation, had been appointed superior of the newly constituted "Upper German" province of the Jesuits, comprising Austria, Bohemia, Bavaria and Tirol. Asked for a report on his behaviour at this period in all matters trivial as well as important, one of the Prague pioneers replied that if he had "a hundred tongues and a hundred mouths" he could not adequately celebrate his praises: "I think his match is not to be found on earth. He is the pride and ornament of all Germany. Day and night he sweats and toils to propagate and promote true religion. He is a great man, a man whose heart overflows with the love of God. Among Catholics he is universally venerated and loved. This is what I have to report about our Father Canisius." [1] In the early part of 1557 Peter attended the Diet of Regensburg as theological adviser of King Ferdinand, and spent four laborious and perilous months there preaching Catholicism

---

[1] M.H., *Epistolae Mixtae,* v, 371 *sq.*

might and main. Many great prelates came to the Diet, and seeing
them he felt inspired to compose a little treatise, *De Officio et Re-
formatione Episcopi,* into which went the whole of his heart. In
the summer of the same year he is in Rome, and a few months later
we find him confronting Melanchthon and other Lutheran leaders at
the Religious Conference of Worms, the sixth of those futile attempts
to marry the old and the new, the true and the untrue, which so
much appealed to the hopeful hearts but untheological heads of the
Habsburg brothers, Charles and Ferdinand. He did not like this
commission at all, but accepted it to please the brave, well-meaning,
unhappy King who, while fighting to save Europe from the Turks,
had always to be looking over his shoulder in anticipation of a stab
in the back from the Protestants. A little later he had an interview
with Ferdinand at Nuremberg, of which he spoke in a letter to Laynez: "His Majesty confided to me the most intimate secrets of his
heart. I was moved to great pity, and consider it my bounden
duty to help him, especially with the prayers and Sacrifices of your
Reverence and the whole Society. For the love of God I implore
you to have special Masses said by our priests for him, that he may
persevere manfully on his cross and be able to fulfil his Christian
duty at this time when he is in grave peril." The Saint's attitude
to the Worms Conference is made clear in an earlier letter to the
same superior and friend: "I am utterly unsuited and useless for
this business, and I dislike the prospect of it intensely. The King
has assembled for it two bishops and five theologians, among which
latter men I am assigned the foremost place. From this alone your
Reverence can guess the quality of the others! May God have
mercy on us all."

Peter worked very hard at Worms, so hard that sometimes he had
difficulty in finding a spare half-hour for his Mass. The bishops
present and the other Catholic delegates turned to him daily for information and advice, and the local canons joyfully hoisted him into
the pulpit of their ancient cathedral. The Conference itself, as he
had anticipated, went up in smoke, very acrid smoke, due principally to dissension in the Lutheran ranks. Melanchthon, the dis-
illusioned and world-weary inheritor of Luther's mantle, tried
bravely to maintain the fiction of Protestant unity, of a "dulcis con-
cordia" in anti-Catholic belief, but was crossed and thwarted and

most vilely traduced by the disciples of his rival, the fantastic, half-crazy fanatic, Flacius Illyricus. The squabbles of those Girondists and Jacobins of the religious revolution supplied Peter Canisius with all the powder and shot which he needed for some effective skirmishing. He could not help a feeling of grim satisfaction as he watched the Conference drift to its inglorious close, which, as the historian Ranke reluctantly admitted, was brought about, "not by disputes between the two great parties; it never even got so far — the divisions among the Protestants themselves put an end to it altogether." [1] Peter prayed that the spectacle of those divisions might turn men's hearts in the direction where his own always lay, towards the Council of Trent, for whose resumption he tirelessly plotted and pleaded.

Having done all that he could at Worms he sailed down the Rhine to Cologne to visit his brethren and his friends, Dr. Gropper and the Carthusians. One of several sermons which he preached during his week in the city was at the Dom on the feast of All Saints. As he left the great church afterwards, people, we are told, "rushed to look at him exactly as though he were some king or emperor." [2] He then returned to Worms to be present at the obsequies of the ill-fated Conference, which done he went off campaigning in Alsace in the depths of winter to satisfy the good desires of the Bishop of Strasbourg. He left an ineffaceable impression, and each place which heard his voice and observed his charity, Strasbourg itself, Saverne, Selestat, Ruffach and Colmar, afterwards boasted its Jesuit mission or school. On his way back to Ingolstadt he visited Freiburg in Baden, which also became a Jesuit centre, and then went to Dillingen to receive from Cardinal Truchsess the gift of his newly founded university in that city. It was not a gift to sing about and it took Peter five laborious years to get it into any sort of scholastic shape, but it became in time second only to Ingolstadt as a power-house of German Catholicism. The good Cardinal, who was a prince of the Empire as well as of the Church, had so much veneration for his guest that on this occasion he greatly embarrassed him by insisting on washing his feet. Peter truly loved this man, whom he used to call "our Abraham," but he was not blind to his faults, especially his tendency to amass provostships and other benefices, and his fondness

[1] *Ferdinand I and Maximilian II,* Eng. tr., p. 80.
[2] Braunsberger, *Epistulae et Acta,* ii, 804–6.

for display. Writing to him shortly afterwards from Straubing, whither he had gone at the request of the Duke of Bavaria to fight it out, even in the law courts when necessary, with pugnacious Lutheran evangelists, he unburdened his heart in the following fashion: "Sara complains that Abraham introduces handmaidens. She sorrows to find herself vilely used and neglected while her lord devotes himself to those strangers. But yet more hardly does she take it when besides the handmaidens there are strumpets on the scene who sway her husband's mind this way and that and permit him no leisure to be quiet at home, to care for his household or to preserve and increase his estate. By Sara I mean the Church of Augsburg which is, as it were, the spouse of our Abraham and might, according to her just deserts, be much better cared for if the hand-maidens, that is the provostships, were excluded and the strumpets put away, namely those new splendours on which money is squandered. . . We are given only a short course in this life during which it behooves us to fight unencumbered, steadfastly, and like brave men. Let us not sit down on three chairs [1] when one is enough. . . Let us go about our business in the Church of God as far as possible utterly strangers to the cares and concerns of the secular world, daily subtracting something from our vanities or pleasures or desires so that we may ever more nearly approach to the ideal of the Perfect Pastor. . ." The new and excellent bishop of Vienna, Anton Brus, was another of Peter's devoted clients who turned to him, certain of assistance, in every emergency, and so was Stanislaus Hosius, the saintly Polish bishop of Ermland in East Prussia. For Hosius, later cardinal and president of the Council of Trent, he undertook in 1558, when burdened with a hundred cares a task the most tedious to which a writer could address himself. The Bishop had written a fine book of apologetics in answer to an attack by the learned Protestant divine, Johann Brenz. Though in style and matter one of the most effective polemical works of the sixteenth century, it was badly produced, without a table of contents or chapter divisions or index, and so almost useless for purposes of consultation. But in 1558 a new edition of the great tome appeared at Cologne in a

---

[1] An allusion to the Cardinal's three benefices. At the time he had set his heart on acquiring a fourth, but by the low standards of the age he was a relatively mild pluralist.

form to satisfy the most hurried or the most fastidious students. To index even a small book is a task requiring patience and hard concentration, as may be judged by the number of authors who shirk it; to index in detail and provide paragraph headings and marginal summaries of the argument all the way through such a forest of erudition as this folio of Hosius must have required heroism. None but Hosius himself and a few friends knew that the hero had been Peter Canisius.

In March 1558 King Ferdinand became Emperor, an event which Peter celebrated by having each of the priests in his province say seven Masses to obtain the seven gifts of the Holy Ghost for His Majesty. The summer of that year saw the Saint in Rome again, and its winter in Poland, trying like a weary giant to prop there the tottering fabric of Catholicism. The faith seemed doomed to extinction, but he never despaired. "The more afflicted and even desperate things are in the world's opinion," he wrote to Laynez, "the more will it be our part to come to the rescue of forlorn hopes, because we belong to the Society of Jesus." By the time of his death forty years later, nearly five hundred of his brethren of the new Polish province sprung from the mission established by him on the shores of the Baltic had rallied to that trumpet-call to help bring about one of the most remarkable revivals and victories of a forlorn hope in religious history. The same thing happened on a smaller scale at Augsburg, then the most important city in Germany and one dear to Lutheran hearts because it had given its name to their famous Confession. But it is not the statue of Melanchthon, the author of the Confession, which may be seen in front of Augsburg Cathedral to-day, if the bombs have spared it; it is the statue of St. Peter Canisius. He was summoned by the Emperor to attend the Diet held in the city early in 1559, and he remained several years to become its apostle. That Augsburg is to-day three-fourths Catholic, approximately 130,000 out of a total population of 170,000, is due almost entirely to his labours. He made the pulpit of its cathedral the chief platform of German Catholicism, preaching from it in eighteen months 225 enormous sermons. But that was only a fraction of his activities, which resulted in so many conversions among the Protestants and so much fervour among the Catholics that the new Pope, Pius IV, wrote to congratulate and encourage him: "It has come to our ears through our beloved son, Otto, Cardinal of Augsburg, with what zeal, diligence and charity you labour in that city to bring back to the way of salvation the multitudes who have strayed therefrom, deceived by the frauds of the heretics, and how well you are succeeding, with the aid of divine grace. . . We thank Almighty God who in His mercy has already recalled so many to the Catholic Church by means of your preaching. Press on, Son, as you have begun, and continue to strive that the greatest gain of souls may be yours. He whom you serve will requite your diligence, . . . and if there is any favour you desire from Us for the good of souls, We shall gladly accede to your petition." [1]

The favour lying nearest to St. Peter's heart was that the long-suspended sessions of the Council of Trent might be resumed. Several months before this happened in January 1562, he caused special litanies to be sung by the Jesuits and their pupils in the colleges for a change in the attitude of Protestants towards the Council, to which they had been very courteously invited by the Pope. His sermons in Augsburg, preached daily during Advent and Lent, were always preceded by public prayer for it and frequently devoted to explaining what it meant, or to refuting Lutheran libels against it. When it reassembled, it became at once the biggest interest, the biggest hope, and, at critical stages, the biggest anxiety of his daily life. His letters are so full of Trent and its concerns that one could hardly guess he was establishing at this time in Innsbruck the fifth of his colleges, editing the letters of St. Jerome for the convenience of students in a volume of nearly eight hundred pages, and helping the best scholar of his province, Father Theodore Peltan, to produce a complete Latin translation and explication of the Acts of the Council of Ephesus from a Greek codex discovered in the Ducal Library at Munich. [2] Often enough, too often for the good of his

[1] Braunsberger, *Epistulae et Acta,* iii, 64–5.

[2] St. John Berchmans (+ 1621, *aet.* 22) was led to become a Jesuit by reading St. Peter's edition of St. Jerome, just as at an earlier time St. Aloysius Gonzaga (+ 1591, *aet.* 23) had been helped to the same decision by his addiction to the *Shorter Catechism* with the prayers and meditations added to it by Peter during his years at Augsburg. It was Peter himself who sent the third of the young Jesuit saints, Stanislaus Kostka (+ 1568, *aet.* 18), a student of the college in Vienna, to the novitiate in Rome. The other work referred to above, Peltan's pioneer Ephesian achievement, ran to six quarto volumes, not one of which

health, he used to spend the whole day and part of the night hearing confessions; he gave innumerable retreats; and week by week this man whom George and Mark Fugger, heads of the greatest banking house on earth, declared to be "the outstanding glory of Germany and a pillar of the universal Church," [1] might be found at his happiest employment, teaching a group of Augsburg boys their catechism. Peter's spells of relaxation consisted in packing with his own hands and dispatching to the Legates at Trent scores of new Protestant works which he had purchased at the book-fair in Frankfurt, including the seven forbidding and ponderous tomes (they weigh as much as a stone apiece!) of the famous *Centuries of Magdeburg*.[2]

And now we must take leave of St. Peter in these cramped and crowded pages, without having said more than a word here and there about the best part of his story, his uninterrupted intercourse with God, the source of all his greatness. He is among the dearest of saints, so little in his own eyes, so much attached to his swarms of friends, so sweetly human, so generous, so near to us in his world-ranging compassion and sympathies. *Cor Petri cor mundi,* we might truly say of him. To picture him as a great commanding figure, a Bismarck of religion, would be to misunderstand him completely. He was a very simple man who believed in God and

---

would have seen the light but for the tireless enthusiasm and active assistance throughout of Canisius.

[1] Braunsberger, *Epistulae et Acta,* iv, 901. The Fugger brothers, both ardent Catholics, had reason to admire St. Peter, for it was he who converted their straying wives, Ursula and Sybil, from Lutheranism. He took upon himself the spiritual charge of the Fuggerei, the famous self-contained village of almshouses which the family had built in the midst of Augsburg.

[2] Ten years later, those same *Centuries,* the first and worst of all Protestant church histories, provided Peter with a very fair substitute for the Purgatory which they derided, as he was required by the Pope to write some kind of answer to them, after several other men had been worsted by their intolerable confusion and prolixity. Peter produced two big folios, *De Verbi Dei Corruptelis* and *De Maria Virgine incomparabili,* great repertories of patristic learning, which stirred that good judge of controversial writing, Cardinal Hosius, to enthusiasm, and served as valuable forerunners to the *Annales Ecclesiastici* of Cardinal Baronius. The volume on our Lady was reprinted by Migne in 1866. Of it an eminent modern scholar has said: "Il est peu d'ouvrages qui fassent mieux connaître les luttes doctrinales du XVIe siècle" (Émile Mâle, *L'Art religieux après le Concile de Trente,* 1932, p. 20).

the Church of God with all his heart and acted accordingly.

In the summer of 1562 Jerome Nadal, whom we left taking the waters at Spa, appeared in Germany. To Peter Canisius he came like an angel of deliverance. Ever since their pioneering days together in Sicily, Peter had put Jerome on a pedestal that reached to heaven. "Ah, how different things would be if Father Nadal were here," he had exclaimed before he took the road to Worms for the abortive Conference. "You are our protector and father of fathers," he wrote to the man himself a little later, and indeed it was so, for during the subsequent decade Germany and its desperate needs filled almost the whole of this Spanish apostle's horizon. He worked as it were underground and in the dark, and yet you could track him all over Europe by the colleges which bloomed afresh at his touch and the dying embers of religion in cities and towns which flamed up again because the wind of his passage had fanned them. The college in Cologne begun by St. Peter with one companion in 1543 numbered fifty-seven Jesuits in 1562, when Nadal made his first visitation. "So great a change did he bring about," reported one of the community to Rome, "that it might be called a new college altogether. I have never known it in so flourishing a state, blessed be God." The Rector, the admirable Leonard Kessel, who had been there ever since St. Peter's time, had a similar tale to tell: "He remained with us three weeks and helped and heartened us enormously by his counsels and daily addresses on the constitutions. He spoke to our boarders also warm words of encouragement. He was so well while here that he said he had never felt better since he left you in Rome for his travels, and this happy state of affairs he attributed to our Cologne beer. Indeed, the great charity wherewith he is consumed for the conversion of Germany makes him now in his old age take on the nature of the Germans." [1] The same story came from all the colleges and missions which he visited, Trier, Mainz, Vienna, Tyrnau in Hungary, Prague, Munich, Ingolstadt, Dillingen, Innsbruck. To their number he and St. Peter prepared to add another at Würzburg, which, like Dillingen and Innsbruck, became transformed into a university and boasted more than a thousand students by the end of the century. At Vienna Nadal found the brethren somewhat depressed owing to the plague, the Turks,

[1] M.H., *Epistolae P. Nadal*, ii, 610, 613.

the unpleasant wind called the *Föhn,* and their own excessive austerities. He was just the physician they needed, as may be judged from the adjectives which they gratefully applied to him, *suavis, jucundus, hilaris, laetus ac facilis.* "With great art," said they, "he knew how to console the sad amongst us, to encourage the downhearted, very sweetly to stir up the slow-coaches, and to restrain the eager spirits lest they outrun their strength." Once when counselling them to moderate their austerities, Father Jerome incautiously added that because they were Germans he did not want to burden them with such things as disciplines and hair-shirts, which came natural to Spaniards and Italians. "They were all agitated by his words," we learn, "thinking it an indignity to be so indulged, for they would not allow that they were less stalwart than any others in the Society."

To keep his patience from growing rusty through disuse, Nadal discovered in his Utopia the double of the unforgettable, unforgotten Araoz in the person of Father Juan Vitoria, the energetic Basque who for years had been absent-mindedly sanctifying the soul of St. Peter Canisius. Never did Peter show himself more magnanimous than in his handling of this Pyrenean Don Quixote, who abounded in grandiose schemes for the glory of the Jesuits, ate up work of all kinds with insatiable relish, and rode roughshod over the susceptibilities of his northern brethren. Like Araoz, he had the ear of royal persons who enjoyed his fiery sermons,[1] and he invited an emperor, a king and a cardinal to grace the ceremony of his last vows. When they excused themselves he found a couple of bishops ready to oblige and rewarded them with a fine banquet and pageant. For Peter Canisius and his plodding Dutch methods he had no use in the world. One must deal in thunders and lightnings in order to impress those easy-going Germans and Austrians. One must bring the bravura of Italy and Spain to bear on their dull imaginations. It came to a point when the cook of the college in Vienna where Juan ruled was compelled to Latinize even his methods of dealing with an egg or a cabbage. "Another thing he has done," wrote the distressed father in charge of domestic arrangements, "is to spoil the

---

[1] He became confessor to Marcantonio Colonna, the hero of the Papal fleet at Lepanto, and sailed under his flag with six other Jesuits in a preliminary expedition against the Turks in 1570.

wine by an order that it is to be mixed half and half with water.
Now, these German wines, unlike the heavier Italian ones, will not
stand such treatment, and the Hungarian wine in the house has
already been ruined by it. . . He is constantly giving out that the
rules for rectors require him to demand hard service from the brethren." That was Vitoria's own private gloss on the rules, which, in
Nadal's words, required rather that "superiors should studiously beware of burdening anyone with too many orders or too much work,
especially the willing horses, lest, as might easily happen, they be
tested beyond their strength and worn out by such injudicious treatment." [1] The slave-driving Juan had been receiving similar warn-
ings, couched in the most tactful terms, from Peter Canisius for
many years. "We must ever bear in mind," he would write, "the
claims of charity which come first, and always remember the great
importance of dealing gently rather than imperiously with the Teu-
tonic soul. May our Lord Jesus who alone is perfect order all things
sweetly as well as mightily through you and me, dear Father." It
was of no avail, and nothing remained but for Nadal to solve the
problem of Vitoria much as he had partially solved the problem of
Araoz, by appointing him to a post in which his industry and business ability would have full scope without detriment to the wits or
the wine of his brethren. After giving a long list of the new and
highly flattering powers conferred upon the dethroned rector, Nadal
concluded his charter with the words: "Father Vitoria will have
no jurisdiction in any college or over any of our men." [2]

Perhaps the most notable joint activity of Canisius and Nadal at
this period was their determined stand against certain Erastian reform schemes of their friend and patron, the Emperor, which must
undoubtedly have compromised the authority of the Holy See. The
ship of Trent might have foundered in the great storm that arose
but for the presence at Ferdinand's court in Innsbruck of those two
Fabian and halcyon heroes who managed by their learning, their
eloquence and their goodness to stave off dangerous decisions until
Cardinal Morone came with his diplomatic genius to steer the la-

---

[1] M.H., *Epistolae P. Nadal*, iv, 409.
[2] M.H., *Epistolae P. Nadal*, iv, 283. The rift between Vitoria and Canisius is
described at length in the English biography of St. Peter, pp. 307–33.

bouring Council safely into harbour.[1] Immediately after the Council's close Nadal returned to Rome, where he made it his first business to write a colossal letter (twenty-two printed pages) to Antonio Araoz giving him an account of all his German experiences. It is a letter that one would like to be able to cite in full, so well does it mirror the heart of him who composed it. He begins by an assurance that throughout the whole time of his *peregrinación* he has never forgotten Antonio and all his Spanish, Portuguese, French and German brethren in his "pobres sacrificios y pobres oraciones." They too, he knows, will have remembered him, and so they make a great united family which, though dispersed and separated in this world of exile, will by God's grace be brought together "para siempre in la patria eterna." Peter Canisius he declares to be "the pillar and support of the Catholic cause, a man of great authority throughout Germany, so much detested by the heretics that they fasten on him such epithets as hateful dog, bird of prey, patriarch of all hypocrites." Nadal dilates on the good being done by the college in Vienna which has many boys of noble birth, especially Poles, and makes provision for those too poor to pay for their board out of alms obtained by the staff from Spain and Italy. At the university two of the fathers lecture on the *Summa* of St. Thomas Aquinas, then an almost revolutionary proceeding. The Hungarian college of Tyrnau delights the good Jerome because it is situated "á la frontera de los Turcos." In Prague he is astonished to learn that the Hussites and other heretics send their sons to the college, though they are required to conform to all Catholic customs and practices. At Ingolstadt the Duke of Bavaria tells him of a remark made by the princely Archbishop of Salzburg: "Were it not for the Jesuits, it would be a bad look-out for your Grace's dominions." So one by one Jerome recalls the incidents of his long itinerary for Antonio's benefit and then concludes the whole story with the following words: "Each province and each college that I stayed in seemed to me at the time the one I loved best of all. But I can say now that Germany comes first with me because its need is so great. I find myself moved with pity for that noble nation, so miserably deceived

[1] There is a detailed account of the Innsbruck negotiations in the book mentioned in the preceding note, pp. 522–65.

by pestilent and infernal impostors. Other nations in which the Society exists have alternative means of spiritual assistance, but in Germany we are practically the only ones to help, and, if we fail, there is, humanly speaking, no remedy left. It is not only the Catholics who say this. The heretics say it too in their own fashion by atrocious libels against us and threats of our extermination. . . For the love of God our Lord I beg all of you in Spain to help the reviled and persecuted Church in Germany with your holy desires and prayers and sacrifices; and I entreat superiors by their regard for the constitutions of the Society which bind us to render most assistance where the need is greatest, to use every means in their power for the succour of Germany. So will the good God help us and the whole Society, increasing in it His holy gifts unto the greater service and glory of His Divine Majesty." [1]   Many a Spanish father left his bones in Germany in consequence of that appeal. Sixty years after it was made there were 2283 Jesuits of various nationalities working in 120 colleges, seminaries and missions within the confines of the Holy Roman Empire.

On 2 July 1565 — *dies meae crucis,* as he called it in his diary — St. Francis Borgia succeeded Laynez as third general of the Society of Jesus. The *patres conscripti* who elected him by a majority of thirty-one votes out of thirty-nine considered that the order was growing too fast, at least in Europe, and so, knowing his large-hearted and enterprising ways, gave Francis for his watchword consolidation rather than expansion. They showed him what they meant by themselves refusing with grave thanks the most honorific offer so far made to the Jesuits as an educational body, control of the University of Valencia. One of the many decrees issued by the fathers abolished for good the office of commissary which Antonio Araoz had inherited, but they elected him in compensation "assistant" to the General, a curial post of the highest importance. St. Francis, the magnanimous and handsome-hearted, was delighted at the prospect of having this critic, this gainsayer, this almost enemy by his side, and wrote without a moment's delay to welcome him to Rome: "Your Reverence must not be surprised that no letters have come from me recently, since with my new cross the burden of my work

[1] M.H., *Epistolae P. Nadal,* ii, 488-510.

increases. But now that this morning the general congregation
elected you assistant by a majority of all except one or two votes,
Joseph is unable to restrain himself any longer from congratulating
his dearest brother.[1] He entertains a good hope that your arrival
here will mean great service to God through your advice and aid in
the affairs of His new plant, the Society of Jesus, of which you were
among the first members after the original ten fathers. All the
greater, then, is your obligation to share the solicitude of government,
and I have no doubt that you will take advantage of the good travelling month of September so as to arrive here in October before the
rainy season begins. Rest assured that I shall be counting the days
and finding them very long until you come, both for my own consolation and for that of the fathers who elected you with so great
unanimity. I repeat that I hope for great fruit from your coming,
and you will be able to serve your friends just as well here as in
Spain. . . Your Reverence knows my unfailing love for you, and
that many waters cannot extinguish it. Come, then, Father, in
that same spirit of affection with which you are desired, so that it
will be possible to say truly of us two in our measure, *sicut in vita
se dilexerunt ita in morte non sunt separati*. . . Pater carissime, pray
for me and let me know the day of your departure." [2]

[1] "And Joseph made haste for his heart did yearn upon his brother" (Genesis
xliii. 30).
[2] M.H., *Sanctus Franciscus Borgia*, iv, 28–30. Francis told him also as an
encouragement that they were engaged just then drawing up decrees on various
subjects which he would find very much to his taste. In his earlier period of
fervour Araoz had greatly desired an extension of the time allotted by rule for
prayer in the order and himself used to devote three hours a day to meditation
until St. Ignatius let him know that he must be satisfied with one hour. Ignatius prescribed no particular time for priests and professed, leaving it to their
devotion but warning them not to let their devotion interfere with their pastoral
duties. For others, the general rule was one hour of set prayer a day, the first
half vocal or mental as each one found suited him best, and the other half divided between the two examinations of conscience. The Little Office of the
Blessed Virgin was the vocal prayer usually adopted. As time went on the
inadequacy of this spiritual provision for the day seems to have been widely
felt. The first general congregation discussed the matter but made no change.
The second, which elected Borgia, empowered him by its twenty-ninth decree to
settle the question as he judged most expedient. St. Francis doubled the time

On receipt of that letter Araoz made an elaborate pretence of setting out, but, if not by his contrivance certainly with his connivance,
was intercepted in the process by a king's messenger bearing written
orders from Majesty itself forbidding the journey. Almost we can
see him shrugging his shoulders and throwing wide his arms, palms
upwards, as he breaks the bad news to the Valladolid brethren. Of
course, the King's interference and his subsequent peremptory letter to Borgia were procured by Antonio's devoted crony, the omnipo-
tent Rui Gomez, Prince of Eboli. Rui Gomez addressed himself to
Francis also, saying in so many words that he suspected the motives
of the Roman fathers in their election of his friend as assistant for
Spain. And Antonio wrote, reams and reams, telling of the "tears
of blood" which he felt like shedding when he heard that his beloved superior was grieved with him. He appealed to the Saint's
son, Carlo Borgia, Duke of Gandia, to put him right with his father,
to explain to him the purity of his motives and how he was ready to
go not only to Rome but to the farthest Indies if the good of the
Society of Jesus required it. Oh, what martyrdoms of heart and
afflictions of body he had suffered for that same Society! As for
what touches the person and affairs of Borgia, he could do him more
service in Spain in a month than would be possible over many years
in Rome. "To imagine that there ever had been or could be in the
Society a man more truly and sincerely devoted to our Father's very
shadow than I, Antonio Araoz, would be to lay hands on the *sancta
sanctorum,* the apple of my eye, the fibres of my heart. *Retro vaya
tal blasfemia, tal imaginaçion, y tal juizio. . ."* He makes it plain
that, like Rui Gomez, he believes he was elected assistant purely
"with the design of removing from Spain a terrible person, feared
by some as a plotter and by others as an obstacle to the despoiling of
the country of money for Rome and of men for Italy," though in
fact he had "never held up so much as a peseta." There are fourteen more large pages in this vein, concluding with a blushing avowal
that many of his brethren had expected him to be elected general

---

set by St. Ignatius for those in their training and made an hour of vocal or
mental prayer daily obligatory on all Jesuits. Before very long the vocal element disappeared and the custom of "morning meditation" became firmly established throughout the order, though there has never been any explicit ruling
that the prayer must be mental.

of the order. "However, I would not have accepted the office, it being perpetual, and I made my mind known to that effect several times." [1]

Though his conduct grieved and dejected him, St. Francis took Antonio's palaver in good part and bore him not a trace of ill-will. "It is not only because I am your father in God," he wrote, "that I would shed my blood for you. I would shed it even more gladly for old friendship's sake, if thereby God might be served. Padre charisimo, let the pair of us cast into the fire of the charity of Christ our Lord all the papers and arguments and ideas which imagination is wont to produce in times of trouble. Be sure that I hold you for my friend and comrade, my son and my dearest Father, who will console me and be my support and helper always, acting, to use your own words, as an angel of peace. Let that suffice to silence those questions, so alien to two hearts which love each other in our Lord." The little spiritual diary which Francis kept to remind himself of God's past and present mercies and of all the intentions to be recommended in his prayers contains many references to Araoz. Thus, on 11 June 1565, he writes: "After Mass great consolation. Prayers for King Philip, Rui Gomez and Araoz. For Francis that he may always belong to Jesus. Amen. Sorrow for my failure to appreciate the medicines which our Lord has administered to this heart, for my little gratitude for them, for my hurt feelings and tears over a matter that should have made me praise and glorify Him." Next day the entry runs: "Sorrow for my failure to improve, for feelings of resentment that should have been feelings of gratitude and joy. Item, supplication and the offering of my life for Philip, Gomez, Araoz." On 30 November of the same year he writes: "Began prayer for the King, Rui Gomez, Araoz, etc., that God may make them saints." [2]

[1] M.H., *Sanctus Franciscus Borgia*, iv, 81–2, 95–6, 100–3, 186–93, 194–208. Of course, there was never the slightest question of Araoz being elected general. If his name was mentioned at all in the congregation from which he had loftily absented himself, it was with sadness, perplexity or regret.

[2] M.H., *Sanctus Franciscus Borgia*, iv, 226; v, 788, 805, 813, 818, 821. Though it consists for the most part of mere headings and clue words, usually abbreviated and written in a deliberately obscure scrawl, the Diary reveals the heart of the Saint better than any biography could. We see him striving all the year round to creep closer to Christ in His mysteries, especially the mystery of the Passion.

In February 1566 Nadal set out on his travels again in answer to urgent petitions from Germany. He was so ill at the time that St. Francis let him go only because he wanted to go, because the call of Germany was in his blood. For six months he roamed the country, revisiting his old haunts with his message of encouragement and peace. While at the Diet of Augsburg in March, he learned that an expedition was being organized against the aggressive Turks in Hungary. "As for me, Padre," he wrote to Borgia, "my feet are dancing to be away on that enterprise, and I think I shall offer my services to the Emperor as an army chaplain." *Mi saltano li piedi* — and he was fifty-nine and a martyr to chronic catarrh! Only the dissuasions of the two saints, Canisius and Borgia, prevented him from going. Knowing that St. Francis had much influence with the new Pope, St. Pius V, he wrote many times begging him to impress upon his Holiness, so long Inquisitor General of Italy, the necessity of using "gran moderatione et longanimità, grande charità et mansuetudine," in his dealings with the distracted northern nations, "remembering the affliction, travail and extreme need which they endure." The full rigour of the law ought to be tempered for those shorn lambs who "are deserving of the greatest compassion because they are so sick and weak." Another thing which he urged most earnestly was that, when dealing with such nations as Germany and England, the Pope should take advice, not from stay-at-home Roman officials, mere arm-chair strategists, but from men who had lived in those countries, "who knew from practical experience the dispositions of their rulers and peoples, and who bore a special love to them."[1] After Germany, he traversed Austria, Hungary and Bohemia again, and then passed into Flanders, where he spent an entire year coaxing the future Belgian Jesuit provinces into existence. Louvain, Brussels, Liége, Antwerp, Courtrai, Tournai, Cam-

---

Each saint's feast as it occurs has some special message, comfort or reproach for him. And we gain some idea of the largeness of his heart by the multiplicity of the intentions for which he constantly prays, offers penances and says Mass. He remembers every country in the world, every form of human suffering, and every creed and class, Jews, Moors, heretics, sinners (*ibid.*, pp. 736, 184–5, etc.).

[1] M.H., *Epistolae P. Nadal,* iii, 139, 146, 147. Seven years earlier this Father and St. Peter Canisius had between them secured a valuable modification of the drastic Index laws of Paul IV (Hilgers, *Der Index der verbotenen Bucher,* 1904, pp. 197–8; Braunsberger, *Epistulae et Acta,* ii, 377, 425–6, 500, 533).

brai, Saint-Omer, he laboured and suffered in them all, and only at the end turned wearily towards Spa to find some relief for his crushing infirmities. Sixty years later the Belgian Jesuits numbered 1574 in charge of thirty-two boys' colleges and fourteen other establishments. Finally, after two years and a half of almost continuous travel, the exhausted Jerome rode into France to help as best he could in the midst of civil war his brethren of Paris, Verdun, Chambéry, Lyons and other places, until at length St. Francis Borgia decided that it was high time to summon him, or what was left of him, home.

How busy Francis himself had been in his work of consolidation may be appreciated from these few bald facts. He produced and promulgated universally in 1567 the first edition of the Jesuit rules as they are known to-day; he saw to the establishment of separate houses for the training of novices in all the provinces, beginning with that of St. Andrea in Rome, to which came in its first year St. Stanislaus Kostka and the greatest of the Jesuit generals, Claudius Aquaviva; he purchased with money scraped together from all quarters the site of the Gesù, witnessed the laying of the foundation-stone of that great fane by Cardinals Farnese and Truchsess on 26 June 1568, and so may be said to have inaugurated the era of Baroque architecture;[1] above all, he fostered and controlled the growth of

[1] "Baroque architecture first appeared in 1568, when the foundation-stone of the Gesù was laid; the date of the first Baroque sculpture may be approximately fixed in the very last years of the sixteenth century; and the first Baroque painting was executed about 1602. . . Renaissance churches are designed as perfectly harmonious buildings, the interiors of which may be used incidentally for religious purposes, whereas early Baroque churches (above all the Gesù) are so planned as to provide interiors which focus the attention as intensely as possible on one single spot, the altar, and on the sacred mysteries there enacted" (Fokker, *Roman Baroque Art,* 1938, pp. 3–4, 26). Baroque art in general, the art of the Counter-Reformation, was a natural development of Renaissance art, but it became in many respects a form of controversy. St. Peter Canisius wrote: "The innovators accuse us of prodigality in the ornamentation of our churches; they resemble Judas reproaching Mary Magdalen for pouring the precious ointment on the head of Christ" (*De Maria Virgine,* p. 712). The Protestants whitewashed their churches in order to veil the images of the saints and the Catholic mysteries. "The Jesuits replied by multiplying in their churches frescoes, paintings, statues, and ornamentation in lapis-lazuli, bronze and gold. The richness of the Gesù is then, an argument, a chapter of the religious controversy" (Mâle, *L'Art religieux après le Concile de Trente,* p. 22).

Jesuit missionary activity, and did more from his narrow room in Rome to spread and strengthen the Church in pagan lands than any man since St. Francis Xavier. He it was who first conceived the idea of the Congregation *De Propaganda Fide,* which in its primitive form of a committee of four cardinals came into existence in 1568 as the direct result of his intercession with St. Pius V.[1]

[1] M.H., *Epistolae P. Nadal,* iii, 625–6 and n. 2.

CHAPTER VI

A WOMAN WHO WAS A SINNER

DURING a sojourn at Mainz while on his German travels, Nadel met an interesting and very likable Dutch Jesuit named Nicholas Floris. From this Nicholas, whom his brethren commonly called Goudanus or De Gouda, after his native town, the home of good cheeses and churchwarden pipes, Jerome learned a curious story, now to be told. Goudanus and Canisius were bosom friends. Together those two Dutchmen had gone campaigning ten years earlier in Germany. Together they built up the Jesuit strong points at Ingolstadt and Vienna. Together they faced the Lutheran champions, Melanchthon, Brenz and Pistorius at the Conference of Worms in 1557. But Nicholas's health, never good, failed completely under the strain of his labours, and he was obliged to quit the battlefield. St. Peter missed him sorely and addressed to him some of his most affectionate letters, a consolation which the sick man needed, for he had been sent to recuperate under the jurisdiction of Nadal's critic, the gloomy rector of Louvain. In 1561 this Father was responsible, quite innocently, as will be seen, for the appointment of his ailing guest, Nicholas, to the intimidating post of Papal envoy to Scotland. At that time Scotland was the most dangerous country in the world for a Jesuit to enter. Calvinism had completely triumphed there the previous year, and Mary Stuart, recently returned and believing herself to be at nineteen "the most afflicted poor woman under heaven," could afford visiting nuncios little protection. Even to have Mass said in the privacy of her own chapel at Holyrood was to invite upon her head the thunders and lightnings of the portentous John Knox, Scotland's Flacius Illyricus. The sudden collapse of the ancient faith in Scotland is no inscrutable mystery. John Knox undoubtedly had a case. Immorality was rife in convents and monasteries; the three bastard sons of Mary's father, James V, held three of the richest benefices in the Kingdom, and the clergy in general had "Mammon" plainly written on their phylacteries. During her eight years of regency, the young Queen's mother, Mary of Guise, innocently paved the way for John Knox by her well-meaning endeavours to turn the unruly and clannish Scots into polished and law-abiding Frenchmen. When we read that she sent her Scottish soldiers abroad to fight the battles of France and imported French soldiers to fight the battles of Scotland, we can guess, if we know Scots at all, that there will be an explosion. And explosion there was, the sharpest heard anywhere during the whole of that noisy century. It even reverberated among the Seven Hills and startled the Pope and his Curia. Scotland had been long and sadly neglected by Rome, partly because it was so remote and partly for less defensible reasons, such as the pique of Paul IV over France's desertion of him during the Spanish war. Paul's successor, Pius IV, was the first of the sixteenth-century Popes to busy himself seriously with Scottish affairs, but this wise and far-sighted man came on the scene too late, when the two splendid assets of Catholicism in the northern Kingdom, the addiction of the people to traditional ways of life and their age-old antipathy to heretical England, had already been squandered by the blunders of French policy and the cold indifference of Rome. Reports reaching the Pope from Scotland after the return of Mary Stuart were so contradictory that in December 1561 his Holiness determined to send a messenger of his own to investigate the true state of the country, to confirm the Queen in her opposition to heresy, and to persuade her to send bishops and ambassadors to the re-convoked Council of Trent. His choice fell upon the Jesuits, who were so far from being delighted with the honour that they did everything in their power to escape it.

Like John Knox, they had a case. In fact, they had a hundred cases, in the shape of their ever-increasing colleges and missions. Most of them were doing the normal work of two men under the satisfied, wary eyes of bishops prepared to fight the Pope himself for their retention. Even their General and their "key-man," Polanco, the holder of all the threads, had been taken from their letter-strewn desks and packed off to France on Papal business. Now, the Pope summons Alfonso Salmeron and demands an envoy for Scotland. Salmeron, vicar-general in the absence of Laynez, had been to Scotland himself on a similar mission in the year of Mary Stuart's birth and knew the perils and hardships of such undertakings. He would not willingly condemn another man to the purgatory he had been through, even if he knew of one who was, in the modern jargon, expendable. He explained his difficulty to the Pope, and the Pope remained adamant. The vicar must search his lists again and find a man. In this emergency there arrived a letter from the rector of the Louvain Jesuits announcing that Father Nicholas Goudanus had gone to preach some sermons in Holland. Those sermons were Nicholas's undoing, for Salmeron snatched at them as proof that he had recovered and forthwith wrote to him in the following terms: "His Holiness Pope Pius, hearing that the Queen of Scotland is a very estimable lady and an excellent Catholic, and wishing to send some religious and learned person to visit her in his name and strengthen her to persevere in our religion, has been pleased to avail himself of our Society rather than of others. He has therefore caused much pressure to be brought to bear upon us in order that we might at once choose a fit person for so holy and important a work. Thus forced to provide somebody with the requisite qualifications, we could think of no such man who was free owing to the great dearth of labourers in the Society at present, until we heard from Father Adrian that your Reverence had recovered from your indisposition. The fact that you are preaching in Holland is the proof. I have therefore resolved in agreement with my consultors to designate your Reverence for this enterprise. You must accept the hard mission with a brave heart for the honour of God our Lord, for the general good of the Church, and particularly for the good of the Kingdom of Scotland. Plainly, we could not fail the Pope and there was nobody but yourself available. Had there been, your Reverence may rest assured that we would not have burdened you with this toilsome duty. Be it known to you that it was of little use to tell his Holiness we had nobody to his purpose, and that your Reverence, who alone occurred to us as a possibility, was gravely ill. Make ready therefore; provide yourself with seemly and dignified apparel and all other things necessary, that you may go well appointed and have such comforts as may lighten in part the fatigues of the journey and the discomfort of leaving home. . ."

Salmeron sent the provincial of Flanders, Father Everard Mercurian, a bill of exchange for two hundred gold *scudi*, to be made over to the astonished Nicholas for the purchase of his wardrobe.

Other sums needed he could obtain by borrowing on the Pope's security or however he liked, "so long as no disedification is given to
the neighbour." He was advised, too, that he might choose for himself some Herculean lay brother of Flanders to be his companion,
bodyguard and nurse. Various briefs from the Pope were being sent
to him, some without superscriptions, so that he might address them
to such persons as he considered suitable. "This has been done,"
writes the candid Alfonso, "because nobody here in Rome has knowledge of the entire nobility of that Kingdom, nor of those who can
help the cause of religion." [1] When Laynez learned in Paris of
Nicholas's appointment, he permitted himself to marvel at the ways
of vicars-general in a tight corner. "I can understand," he wrote to
Salmeron on 31 December 1561, "your reluctance to despoil the colleges of a useful man for this mission, but I fail to see how the mission is going to profit from the choice you have made. Why, Dr.
Goudanus knows no French and is besides a sick man, so much
so that I doubt whether he will return from Scotland alive. Surely
it would be better to send Master Ponce Cogordan who is an adept
at all languages? . . . If this advice reaches you too late, God will
protect and direct Dr. Goudanus." [2] It was too late, as the Papal
brief had already been made out in Nicholas's name and dispatched
to Louvain.

Salmeron was so urgent about the affair that he wrote separately
the same day to Mercurian at Mainz, instructing him to return
immediately to Louvain or Brussels and to send a special messenger
in search of Goudanus in Holland. Then some mysterious inertia
seemed to come over the brethren in the Low Countries. Salmeron
waited impatiently for news of Nicholas's departure, but weeks and
months went by without a word reaching him. At long last, on 2
May 1562, a letter from Mercurian was put in his hands which caused
him a thrill of overdue satisfaction, until he opened it and found
that Goudanus had not yet stirred from Belgium. The indignant

---

[1] Pollen, *Papal Negotiations with Mary Queen of Scots* (Edinburgh 1901), pp.
75–8. Father Pollen in this admirable volume, edited for the Scottish History
Society, gives the texts in their original languages with an English translation.
In the *Monumenta Historica S.J.* Salmeron's letter is erroneously attributed to
Laynez.

[2] M.H., *Lainii Monumenta*, vi, 188.

and alarmed vicar thereupon bade his secretary, Francis Petrarch, tell Everard Mercurian, a future general of the Jesuits, exactly what he thought of his conduct. Petrarch's letter was in the following terms: "For a long time now we have been waiting with great eagerness to hear of the progress of Father Goudanus's embassy to Scotland, hoping to receive by the first post some good news wherewith we might satisfy his Holiness and Cardinal de Amulio, who greatly desired it. But instead of this we have received a letter of yours written on 3 April which has caused us no little vexation and astonishment at the negligence shown in the execution of this mission up to the present. We have been even more astonished by your statement that you wrote about the difficulties of the mission on 24 January and then waited until 3 April for an answer, without having taken the precaution of sending many copies so that we might be sure to know of those difficulties. You are well aware that letters constantly get lost. Besides, after receiving orders both from his Holiness and from us that immediately on reading them you should summon Father Goudanus and send him to Scotland, what object was there in writing to Rome and waiting for an answer, especially when no such urgent cause was evident as to justify delaying the orders given with such insistence? We have spoken to Cardinal Commendone here in Rome and he denies that he advised the postponement of the mission. All he did was to give you some advice as to how it might be better executed. Anyhow, now that the damage is done, send the said Father Goudanus to Scotland without further delay. . . Inform us whether you have drawn the two hundred *scudi* from the merchant; if not, send back the bill to Rome." [1]

It says something for the character of Mercurian that he made not the slightest attempt to exculpate himself, though he might have done so with ease, as the following letter of Commendone, the Apostolic nuncio in Germany, to Carlo Borromeo, the Pope's nephew and secretary of state, sufficiently indicates: "At Ehrenbreitstein today, 21 January 1562, I met Father Everard, Provincial of the Jesuits of Lower Germany, at the house of the Archbishop of Trier. From him I learned with great joy of the commission on behalf of the Queen of Scotland which our lord the Pope has given to Father

[1] M.H., *Lainii Monumenta*, vi, 294–5; Pollen, *Papal Negotiations*, pp. 101–2.

Goudanus. Really, no better way could have been found of com-
municating with that Queen, or of assisting that realm, than by
making use of one of these fathers, among whom the said Goudanus
is noted for his goodness and learning. He is also a most amiable
and unassuming man. I gave the Provincial some particulars of
that country which I had heard, and urged him to send with Goudanus another Jesuit well versed in French to be his interpreter with
the Queen, one capable also of making further investigations. . .
This I did because Father Goudanus impressed me after a few days
of his company at Brussels as a man wholly wrapped up in spiritual
things, and so not a person likely to understand and investigate
the true state of that Kingdom. But though the Provincial has
assured me that the most diligent search would be made for such a
one, I greatly doubt whether they will find him, unless Father
Everard, who is an excellent man, prudent, assiduous, and a fluent
speaker of French, goes himself. . . But I do not see much hope of
this, except on orders from the Pope, which incidentally would
arrive in time, as there is not much chance of obtaining a passage
on a ship before Easter, owing to the necessity of avoiding England." [1]

Commendone had monopolized Father Lambert Auer, Rector
of the Jesuit college of Mainz and one of the most important of
Mercurian's subjects, as the companion of his travels, and now we see
him plainly hinting to Borromeo that an order from his uncle to
Mercurian himself might be a good idea. Had such a policy been
extended a little further, it must have spelt honourable death to the
Society of Jesus. Commendone's last sentence is undoubtedly the
explanation of Mercurian's apparent dilatoriness. No ship was
available before Easter, which that year fell on 29 March, just five
days before the Provincial wrote his explanatory letter. Unless
Salmeron expected Goudanus to emulate St. Raymond of Penafort
and sail to Scotland on his cloak, he had no cause to be so indignant.
Besides, the fact that Nicholas had a bit of preaching still left in him
proved nothing except his zeal, and did not justify Salmeron in
jumping to the conclusion that he had recovered his shattered health.
If Mercurian endeavoured to shield his broken soldier from the
rigours and dangers of a long sea journey and the misery of a Mid-

[1] Pollen, *Papal Negotiations with Mary Queen of Scots,* pp. 91-3.

lothian winter, who will blame Mercurian? In any case, the real
villains of the story were the postal officials of the sixteenth century,
as plainly appears in a letter of Goudanus to Salmeron from Louvain,
6 June 1562:

"Reverend Father in Christ. *Pax Christi.* I have received two
letters, the one a duplicate of the other and both dated the same day,
2 May. . . I answered them immediately, telling you that Father
Everard was hourly expected here from Tournai. He hastened
hither at once on receipt of your Reverence's letter, and is wholly
employed in making preparations with all possible speed for my
journey. Otherwise he too would have written to you to-day. And
now practically everything is ready. Two priests will go with me,
a Frenchman of the Society named John Rivat, and a Scot of good
family who has resolved to become a Jesuit and volunteered his
services to Father Provincial. . . We shall take all possible pains
with the help of Christ to carry through the business committed to
us most carefully, and shall inform your Reverence of every particular at the first possible moment. We have but one petition and
entreaty to make, that an undertaking so momentous, arduous,
perilous, and far beyond my powers, should be assiduously and
ardently commended to God in the Holy Sacrifices and prayers of
your Reverence and the other fathers and brothers. I should have
embarked on it long ago if a more speedy answer had come from
Rome to the many letters about this business which Father Everard
sent thither at various times. He would not have had the slightest
hesitation in the matter but for the sound objections put to him by
a third party.[1] As it was, he wrote to me several times while I was
in Holland, bidding me to return at once. From the letter which I
addressed to you a month ago you will easily see how it was that
none of those missives ever came into my hands. Three days hence,
with the help of God, we shall start for Zeeland, accompanied by
Father Everard as far as Antwerp. . . When he has bidden us good-
bye, he will let you know all the details. . . The two hundred *scudi*
were not obtained from the merchant and herewith I send you back
the bill. Father Leonard Kessel of Cologne provided us with the
necessary sum. *Postscript.* In my native town of Gouda there are
two aged women who when young made a vow to become nuns.

[1] Cardinal Commendone, the Apostolic Nuncio in Germany.

They are too old now to be received and therefore humbly beg from the Apostolic See absolution *in foro conscientiae,* as the matter is secret. I entreat your Reverence to obtain this favour for them." [1]

The Scot of good family mentioned in that letter was Father Edmund Hay, a graduate of Louvain University aged twenty-eight, on his way home to settle his affairs before joining the Society of Jesus. Hay's cousin and fellow-student at Louvain, Father William Crichton, had gone ahead of him to Scotland with the same determination. But for those two resolute and fearless scions of Scottish nobility [2] whom we find only three years later rectors of the Jesuit colleges of Paris and Lyons respectively, Nicholas Goudanus would almost certainly have met a violent death in Edinburgh. Nicholas set off from Louvain in the highest spirits, both because he experienced at the last moment "by the singular favour of God a wonderful increase of strength, beyond all expectation," and because he was "guided by Edmund as by the Angel Raphael." He needed this sudden access of energy, for when he reached Antwerp on 10 June, he beheld his ship slowly receding down the Scheldt to join a little fleet bound for the Firth of Forth, and had to scramble hastily and breakfastless into a boat to overtake it. "Christ thus leading us onward," he wrote to Laynez afterwards, "we got aboard and put to sea with a favourable wind that same tenth of June. Next day, however, so great a storm arose that we were nearly swamped, but Jesus our Lord, moved by the prayers of your Reverence and of the Society, in His goodness delivered us and brought us safe and sound to Scotland in the space of nine days. The day before we disembarked, the heretical Scots, of whom there were many on board, began to grow very suspicious and curiously to question Master Edmund who we were and on what business we had come. He answered roughly, 'What have I got to do with them? They are of age; let them speak for themselves.' And so we passed undiscovered."

On landing at Leith, Father Hay took the Nuncio and Father

---

[1] Pollen, *Papal Negotiations with Mary Queen of Scots,* pp. 103-5.

[2] Father Hay belonged to a junior branch of the family whose head was the Earl of Errol, hereditary High Constable of Scotland since the days of King Robert the Bruce. Edmund's eldest brother, Peter, held the dignity of "bailie" or chief magistrate of Errol, as his father and grandfather had done before him.

Rivat to the house of a relative in that seaport, where he was promptly visited by Father Crichton and a friend named Stephen Wilson, one of Queen Mary's courtiers. Through this man Goudanus notified her Majesty of his arrival and begged for an audience. Unfortunately, Wilson was a talkative person, so the news quickly spread in Edinburgh that the Pope had sent a messenger to the Queen, with such lively consequences as the following, described in a memoir of the mission written by William Crichton: "Almost on the first day the heretical ministers knew about it and clamoured in their pulpits that the Papal Antichrist had dispatched an ambassador to corrupt the Queen with his bribes and to destroy the Gospel. Wherefore, let all true gospellers search for, capture and slaughter that enemy of Christ and His Gospel. It would be, they said, a noble sacrifice to God to wash their hands in his blood. If the Pope had sent the devil with his horns, he would have found a Scotsman to be his guide, as this emissary found Master Edmund Hay. . . This was the reason why Father Edmund speedily retired to his home, entrusting Father Goudanus to Father Crichton, . . . who soon clad him in court finery, with top-boots, a plumed hat and a sword swinging at his girdle. Thus adorned, he led him about everywhere."

According to the English envoy and spy, Thomas Randolph, in a report to Sir William Cecil, it was only the intervention of Queen Mary's heretical and despicable half-brother, James Stuart, at the time Earl of Mar,[1] which saved Goudanus from prompt execution by the enraged ministers. But though Mar deprecated shedding the envoy's blood, he did everything in his power to thwart his mission, and it was by his advice that Mary delayed for over a month to answer the plumed and sworded Nicholas. That gallant soul regarded the delay as providential, for it enabled him to recover the use of his legs, which had been badly injured in the storm at sea. Meantime, Edmund Hay had spirited him out of danger to his family's mansion at Megginch in Perthshire, where he lay concealed

---

[1] "He was cold and supple as a snake, stealthy and silent as a snake, merciless as a snake, and like a snake he bit with poisoned fangs the sister who had warmed him against her heart" (Mackenzie, *Catholicism and Scotland*, London, 1936, p. 87). If he spared the life of Goudanus it was merely to make things more difficult for the Queen.

and comfortable for nearly two months. Edmund, who was known at court, then went to see the Queen and settled with her to bring Nicholas very secretly to Holyrood at an hour when the Protestant zealots, including the Earl of Mar, would be in kirk under the spell of John Knox's blazing eloquence. At the time appointed, the Pope's ambassador in all his fine feathers mounted a horse and set off for Edinburgh, escorted by Hay and three heavily armed cavaliers. "When we had reached the city and dismissed our guard," he reported to Laynez, "we proceeded under Stephen Wilson's guidance, but not without risk, across the fields and along the town walls to the residence of the Queen's almoner. A short time before, this man had declined to receive us out of fear of the heretics, but now he admitted us out of regard for the Queen and the Pope, and at once announced our arrival to her Majesty. In order to keep a veil of secrecy over the proceedings, she sent us word to come to the palace next day, 24 July, the vigil of St. James, in the almoner's company, to a private chamber, at an hour when her Protestant courtiers would be attending the sermon, so that none of them might know of our interview. I was admitted first by myself, and, having respectfully saluted the Queen in the Pope's name, I briefly stated the purpose of my mission and delivered his Holiness's letter. She said that she understood my Latin, but could not so easily reply to everything in that language. I accordingly asked if I might call in my colleague, Master Jean Rivat, the Frenchman, and Master Edmund Hay, who were waiting in readiness outside the door and would faithfully interpret all her proposals. She agreed, and when they had come in she turned at once to Master Edmund, her subject, whom she had met before, and began her answer in the Scottish language." [1]

Mary's first remark was a little queenly apology for not receiving the Pope's envoy in a more open and honourable fashion, owing to the disturbed state of the Kingdom. She hoped that his Holiness would have regard to her ready good-will rather than to anything which she had actually achieved since her return, and expressed a wish that he were more alive to the troubles in which she found herself. To save the remnant of Catholicism in the country, she had been obliged most unwillingly to tolerate many things that she

[1] *Scotice.* Not Gaelic, but Lowlands English, in which dialect Mary wrote many of her letters.

would not otherwise have borne, and she appears to have resented somewhat the Pope's exhortation to her to emulate the example of Mary Tudor, whose position and chances, she said, had been very different from her own. That was perfectly true, but Mary Stuart on her side had advantages denied to the other tragic queen, her beauty, her womanly charm, her gay and justified confidence in her power over the hearts of men, whether friends or foes. Also, she could be extremely energetic when she liked, as in her expedition against the great Catholic Earl of Huntly, which resulted in his death on the field of Corrichie and in the execution of his son, Sir John Gordon.[1] On the other hand, Mary made no attempt to shelter her Catholic subjects from the rigours of the penal laws launched against them. For all her personal loyalty to the Church, she was a true *politique,* faithful to the principles of appeasement which she had imbibed at the court of Catherine de Medici. Jesuits, who are relatively simple and unsophisticated people, were never born to deal with *politiques,* and the honest Goudanus could obtain from clever Mary nothing but evasive answers. As for sending delegates to the Council of Trent, she would try, of course, but "under present circumstances with little hope of success." Questioned whether she would prefer to deliver the Pope's letters to the Scottish bishops herself or to let Goudanus do it, she equivalently answered that neither course appealed to her: "She said that my delivering them was out of the question, adding after a moment that it could not be done without causing disturbance or even revolution. I replied that my orders were to deliver them, but she repeated that it was impossible, except perhaps in the case of the Bishop of Ross, who was then in the town." Poor Nicholas thereupon proposed a visit to her brother, the Earl of Mar, in order to disabuse him of any suspicions he might entertain about the purpose of the Papal mission, which was entirely unpolitical. Mary said that she would consult the Lord James, and that was the last he heard of the matter. Next, the baffled envoy petitioned for a safe-conduct to cover his stay in

---

[1] Mary was persuaded into making the expedition by her brother, "the Bastard of Scotland," on the ground that the Earl, to whom the Scottish bishops had entrusted the national relics at the time of the religious collapse, threatened her by being too powerful. Did the inscrutable Lady want her Catholic nobility weak while the Protestants went from strength to strength?

Scotland: "She answered that she thought no one would do me any injury in public, while as for the secret attempts of miscreants, she could not hinder them even by the law. If I did give you one, she added, I should rather betray you and greater danger would threaten when you were known. You are safer unknown, so do not walk abroad but keep to some hidden chamber." By this time Mary had become restive, and Nicholas, noticing her anxiety lest the courtiers should return from their sermon and find them together, made his final appeal: "I said in brief that the easiest and most suitable way of succouring her people was to follow the example of the Emperor and many Catholic princes, secular and ecclesiastical, including her uncle, the Cardinal of Lorraine, and to establish a college where she could always have devout and learned men at hand for the instruction in faith and piety of adults and of children, the future hope of the country. She replied to the effect that this might come in time but was impracticable just then, and so dismissed us."

Goudanus did not see the Queen again, but later that same day she sent her secretary to ask him what were the other points he had wished to set before her. The answer is rather touching. "I said that there were two principal ones," he reported to Laynez, "which I then told the secretary verbally, afterwards writing them more fully in a letter to Her Majesty. One was that before I came to Scotland I had meant to strengthen her adhesion to the true and orthodox religion by various reasonings, examples and testimonies taken from the Scriptures, but since my arrival in the country I had heard so many things on such good authority of her exceptional piety and constancy in the faith that I thought the exhortation superfluous. Instead of this I prayed her to reflect on the great benefits (and these I set down in writing) which her perseverance in the faith would occasion, and to rejoice at so singular a grace given her by God and to remain steadfast therein. Secondly, I said that I should have liked to explain at greater length the benevolent feelings of Pope Pius towards her, his goodwill and singular affection both for her and for the whole Kingdom of Scotland, as well as his very loving endeavours to promote its peace, tranquillity and good estate, as he did that of all Christendom and the whole Catholic Church, whose faith, unity, peace and safety he strove to preserve and promote, as became a true pastor of the Church who is also the supreme vicar of Christ on earth."

The tribute here paid to the Pope was well deserved, for his Holiness spared no pains to restore the shattered unity of Christendom, even condescending to plead with her haughty and contemptuous Majesty of England, whose rights to her throne, as against Mary Stuart's determined claim, he would willingly have acknowledged in return for the courtesy of a few English representatives at the Council of Trent. Queen Mary did try half-heartedly to persuade one bishop, Henry Sinclair of Ross, to treat with Goudanus. Father Nicholas reported his answer to Laynez: "At whatever time or place, or in whatever disguise, the Pope's nuncio should come to me and I should deal with him, I am certain that my house would be sacked within twenty-four hours, and I would expose myself and all my household to the greatest peril." The contrast in courage between the sick Dutch Jesuit and the lordly Scottish prelate, president of the Court of Session, is sufficiently indicated in those words. By the intermediary of a brave Carthusian monk, Nicholas then wrote personally to the timid Bishop, who said on receiving the letter, "I do not thank you at all." When the Carthusian urged him at least to answer the letter, or better still to write to the Pope, he said that he dared do neither for fear of the document being intercepted and read by the Protestants. "He therefore desired the Carthusian," writes Goudanus, "to offer his excuses, alleging that the administration of justice and some other business prevented him from writing to me. So much for him."

The next move of the undaunted Nicholas was to make the day's journey to Dunblane in hopes of contriving an interview with the bishop of that see, of whom he had heard good reports.[1] "When I got there," he writes, "I completely changed my dress, disguising myself as one of the Bishop's own servants, so that no one could have suspected me of being the Pope's nuncio, and yet he dared not admit

---

[1] He was William Chisholm the First, so called to distinguish him from his coadjutor and successor, William Chisholm the Second, a person much more important in Scottish history. William the Second later wanted to retire and become a Jesuit but was dissuaded from that course by Laynez, in view of Scotland's crying need for good bishops.

me to a conference for the same reasons which had made the Bishop of Ross refuse." The persevering man then wrote to the remaining bishops, except such as had turned Protestant, and received answers from two, St. Andrew's and Dunkeld. Robert Crichton of Dunkeld, who resided on an island in a lake, alone had the courage to give Nicholas a hearing. "This he did," writes that hero, "only on condition that I should pass myself off as a certain banker's clerk, come to request payment of a debt, so that not even his servants might discover who I was. . . He entertained me at dinner, stipulating, however, that we talk of nothing except money matters all through the meal." The Bishop's namesake, Father William Crichton, adds a pathetic detail to this sad story of frustrated effort: "When Father Goudanus gave him the Pope's brief in his chamber, the poor Bishop shed so many tears, and Goudanus no less, at the thought of the miserable state of religion in the Kingdom of Scotland that for a while they could not say a word to one another." It seems to have been on this occasion that a French merchant from Aberdeen was waylaid and nearly beaten to death by the minions of the Kirk, who believed him to be the Papal nuncio. They carried the unfortunate man to Edinburgh to hang him publicly, but he was there recognized not to be the elusive Jesuit, and so escaped with his life.[1]

Three of the Catholic nobles were particularly recommended to Goudanus as worthy of his attention, and to each he sent a Papal brief with a covering letter of his own. Among these the Earl of Huntly was his chief hope, but the Queen and her abominable brother quenched the little gleam shortly afterwards at Corrichie. For Mary, the good Father, who was incapable of thinking evil, had nothing but admiration and compassion. After giving Laynez a lurid account of the religious condition of the country, he goes on to exculpate the Queen: "The leading men in the government[2] acknowledge her title but do not let her use her rights. They have many ways of acting in opposition to her, and they set themselves to draw her over to their way of thinking. They often impose upon

---

[1] Father Crichton reports the incident (Pollen, *Papal Negotiations*, p. 148).

[2] Her brother, the Lord James, soon to be Earl of Moray, and the chameleon Maitland, Laird of Lethington, the most crafty and double-faced of men, to whom she gave her complete confidence.

her with falsehoods, and sometimes influence her with threats of an English invasion, especially when she would attempt to execute any measure in support of her faith, reminding her that the English did in fact invade Scotland three years ago, at the time when her mother, of pious memory, tried to expel the heretics by means of the French, whom she had called in. What, I would here ask, can a devout young lady do who was nurtured in princely luxury, is scarce twenty years of age, and stands absolutely alone, without a single protector or adviser? Even her confessor had left her before I returned to Flanders. . ."

Nicholas concludes his long letter with some suggestions for the relief of Catholicism in Scotland which must have appeared sadly unpractical to the lady chiefly concerned. What was the use of urging Mary to marry "a strong Catholic prince, one powerful enough to restrain the enemies of the faith," when the young Queen's whole heart was set on the English succession, from which such a marriage would have finally barred her? And how could she who was obliged to hear Mass as furtively as the meanest of her subjects establish a college, that great Jesuit remedy for all evils, "where good and learned men would be ready to give pious and Catholic instruction to the people and to the young"? But though the good priest brought no light into the darkness of Scotland, he shines in his own right and gives the dignity of one faithful selfless heart to a story wherein all else is folly, treachery, black bigotry and meanness.

Nicholas had almost as much difficulty in getting out of Scotland as in getting into it. "As for the threats uttered against me," he writes, "it would take too long to recount them. I shall only mention that almost all the ports were watched to prevent me escaping in safety with my letters. I succeeded only by the great skill and industry of Master Edmund and his kinsman, Master William. They dressed me as a sailor and bargained with the seamen that we should be taken on board from a boat some miles out from the port. Master Edmund, the guide of our voyage, remained behind for a while to ensure our getting off safely, and to gather together and bring with him a band of young men whom he had enlisted to be educated as Catholics overseas, — no contemptible result of our foray into Scotland. . ."[1] As far as the Jesuits were concerned it proved

---

[1] Pollen, *Papal Negotiations with Mary Queen of Scots*, pp. 138–9.

a very splendid result, for among the recruits won to the order by Edmund Hay and William Crichton were James Tyrie, John Hay, Robert Abercromby, William Murdoch and James Gordon, each of whom subsequently earned his modest niche in the temple of Catholic fame.[1]

To his dying day, which came within three years of his return from Scotland, Father Goudanus cherished that country with a love as great as if it had given him birth. He enfolded it in his prayers and obtained for it the Masses and intercessions of his countless Jesuit friends. Young Catholic Scots arriving in Flanders for the education denied them at home could always be certain of the help of this dear old Dutchman, who had so cheerfully staked his life in the interest of their people. He was extremely sensitive on the point of obedience. Though full of aches and pains from the dismal crossing to Antwerp, he hurried on the same day to Louvain to report to his provincial, Father Mercurian, and not finding him there followed his trail to Cologne, only to be told that his Reverence had departed for Mainz. To Mainz went Nicholas without a moment's delay, and there, as he says, "to our great contentment we ran to earth Father Nadal and Father Provincial." Nadal, who loved him dearly, bade him rest at Mainz until further notice, but shortly after that father's departure Scotland took a delayed revenge on the Pope's envoy and laid him low with a deadly fever. The doctors of those days were great believers in the virtues of native air and ordered his immediate return to Flanders. His rector, Father Lambert Auer, endorsed the order, and so Nicholas made his painful way homewards, but not before writing to explain to Laynez why he was doing so. Hardly had he posted the letter when he regretted it, thinking that he had been unfaithful to divine providence, and sent off another the next morning. In this he said: "I submit myself completely and without the slightest reserve to holy obedience. Deal with me entirely according to your pleasure and tell me what I am

---

[1] Tyrie's eminence as a theologian in France has already been referred to. After a long period as a missioner in East Prussia, where he eventually died an octogenarian, Father Abercromby returned to work among the persecuted Catholics of his native land, and had the supreme joy of receiving into the Church Queen Anne of Denmark, the wife of Mary Stuart's son, King James VI. The others also risked their lives a hundred times to bring succour to Scotland.

to do and where I am to do it. One thing only I pray that in this brief unhappy life, in death, and in the life to come I may ever be reckoned among the true and living members of the Society of Jesus." Two months later this candid childlike man is still seriously troubled in conscience because he had left Mainz before receiving an *exeat* from Nadal. Again he addresses Laynez: "I beseech your Reverence to write me a few words on this point, for if I have done amiss I desire by God's grace to make amends and to obey in all things whatsoever you may enjoin. I am also very anxious to know what has been achieved in the business of Scotland, which with all my heart I commend to your Reverence that once and for all both the good Queen and many Catholics with her may be delivered from the tyranny of those heretics. . ."[1]

It cannot be said that Pope Pius IV or his successor, St. Pius V, were of much assistance to Mary in her difficult position. In June 1563, the former Pius nonchalantly suggested to the Legates at Trent that the Council might well excommunicate Elizabeth of England and transfer her title to the Scottish Queen. The English exiles at Louvain strongly advocated this course and addressed a memorial to the assembled Fathers assuring them that "the number of their countrymen, both nobles and commoners, is infinite who resent the miserable slavery of their souls under the tyranny of Nicholas Bacon and William Cecil more than the Israelites ever hated the yoke of Pharaoh." The matter was ventilated at the Council in the same casual fashion in which it had been proposed, but when news of the proceedings reached the Catholic monarchs on whom rested the responsibility for the peace of Europe, a stop was soon put to the dangerous game. According to the Nuncio Delfino, Emperor Ferdinand, who had no partiality for Queen Elizabeth or Protestantism, was more angry than he had ever seen him before and peremptorily demanded that the memorial on Mary's claim to the English throne should be absolutely suppressed. A letter milder in terms but identical in view was soon after received from King Philip II, whereupon the Pope gracefully bowed to the unexpected storm, and Queen Elizabeth's slumbers were not just then disturbed by an anathema from Trent.

After that serio-comic interlude, the great preoccupation of the

[1] Pollen, *Papal Negotiations,* pp. 151, 155.

Catholic crowned heads became Queen Mary's marriage, but they vacillated to such an extent in their choice of a candidate that the lady at length lost patience and threw herself into the arms of her cousin Darnley, with consequences "the tragedy of which has hardly been surpassed in the history of the world." [1]   It was a midsummer-night's horrible dream, the queen of the fairies enamoured of an ass. As the Jesuits only touched the edge of the tragedy we are happily spared the necessity of going into its details, which can be found in a hundred books.   From his watch-tower in Paris Father Edmund Hay followed with anxious foreboding the developments in his native land.   Referring to the Darnley marriage, into which impetuous Mary entered without waiting for the Papal dispensation from the impediment of consanguinity, he wrote as follows to Polanco on 12 June 1565: "At first we shall hear of nothing but disturbance, nor, as far as human conjecture can tell, will the new king-consort be able to pacify the affairs of the kingdom without much blood and slaughter.   Afterwards, we may hope that a time will follow more adapted to our ministrations.   During the past, silence has been our safest course, but we shall now write more diligently and frequently.   To-day we have received news by a dependable messenger that our Queen's marriage is soon to be accomplished, and that a very solemn embassy has been sent from England to honour it. [2]   Also, that the Queen had spoken very sharply to her illegitimate brother, the Lord James, who afterwards departed in anger from the court.   God grant that all may tend to His glory, and that all princes may become friends one with another and with Him."

In September of the same year Father Edmund wrote again, this time to St. Francis Borgia: "In Scotland all tends to war, for the Queen's bastard brother, together with some other Protestant nobles, have been declared enemies of their Majesties, and against them the King is preparing an army.   The Queen of England will furnish aid to the rebels, and so, as always, continue to fill up the measure of her sins.   The King of the Scots [Darnley] has restored

---

[1] Pollen, *Papal Negotiations,* pp. lxviii–lxix.

[2] The purpose of the embassy was not to honour the wedding of the two grandchildren of Margaret Tudor, Queen Elizabeth's most dangerous rivals, but to frustrate it, or, that failing, to encourage the Protestant nobles to take up arms.

to liberty all those whom the Bastard, while he was in power, had
exiled or shut up in prison.   First amongst these is the eldest brother
of our Master James Gordon, to whom all that had been taken from
his father will be restored.[1]   This your Reverence might communi-
cate to Master James, if it seems good to you in the Lord, so that
he may pray for his brother.   I entreat you by Christ our Lord and
Saviour to commend the affairs of Scotland to the prayers, the pious
aspirations, and the Holy Sacrifices of all.   The crisis has now been
reached.   If the King is victorious, the controversy about religion
will entirely cease.   If, which God forbid, our adversaries gain the
upper hand, much good will be prevented and much postponed, to
say the least.   Of these things I write, though such is not our Society's
custom, for no other reason than to get your Reverence to commend
them to the prayers of all."

The Masses and prayers did not fail, for the Jesuits in Rome took
almost as deep an interest in the fate of the northern Kingdom as
Father Hay himself.   Polanco constantly wrote to him or to Father
Crichton at Lyons for news of Mary's activities.   They were both
under the delusion that Darnley possessed soldierly qualities, whereas
it was Mary herself who was the soldier and who had sent her
enemies flying over the Border in the Chaseabout Raid.   The
Catholics on the Continent were thrilled by the news of her victory,
but to no one did it give greater delight than to the new Pope,
St. Pius V, who strongly believed in the employment of temporal
weapons for the achievement of spiritual ends.   In a letter of Polanco
to Nadal of 17 June 1566, we are afforded a glimpse of what the
holy old man was prepared to do in order to help the Scottish Queen.
She had sent him the Bishop of Dunblane, William Chisholm the
Second, who was a Jesuit at heart and always stayed at Jesuit houses
on his travels, to obtain a dispensation for her marriage to Darnley
and a subsidy for the maintenance of an army.   "A little while
before the said Bishop left," writes Polanco, "he was present at
the Pope's supper, which, as a rule, is a very small one, at which
he drinks only once.   After supper, he called the Bishop and said to
him: 'You see, Monsignor, the expense of my table.   Know that I

[1] His father was Sir John Gordon, second son of the Earl of Huntly, Chancellor of the Kingdom of Scotland.   The Earl lost his life at the battle of Corrichie and Sir John was tried and executed at Aberdeen the next day.

restrict myself in order to have the more wherewith to aid your
Queen.' Then in the Bishop's presence he summoned his majordomo and ordered him to dismiss a good part of his household.
After that, he said again to the Bishop: 'This also I do for the greater
aid of your Queen,' in order that he might understand his Holiness's
readiness to take the food from his mouth and the goods from his
house to succour her Majesty." [1]

Alas, that so much goodwill should have been so sadly mis-
directed. Sanctity seems never to be enough in the conduct of this
world's affairs and Pius might have done the Church better service
if he had been less of a saint and more of a diplomatist. The best
remedy he could think of was to send an Italian bishop, a man of
his own somewhat narrow outlook,[2] to counsel Queen Mary to
make an example of those rebel lords, her most powerful subjects
and the *protégés* of England, who had been responsible for the
murder of her secretary, the "merry fellow and good musician,"
David Rizzio. "Off with their heads!" was the Papal policy for
Mary, and this bloodthirsty advice, which if carried out would certainly have been the signal for an English invasion, poor Edmund
Hay was dispatched in advance to urge upon her indulgent Majesty.[3]
The provincial of the French Jesuits, Oliver Manare, strongly disapproved of the project of sending an Italian bishop to Scotland
and expressed himself very candidly to St. Francis Borgia on the
subject: "We shall beg Almighty God to direct everything according to the devout intentions of the Pope and submit our intellect
to the judgment of his Holiness and of your Reverence. But I,
who am only dust and ashes, have one more word to say, namely
that the Queen of Scotland has great need of advice and consequently
of grave, prudent and God-fearing men about her, men of the
country rather than foreigners, least of all foreigners sent by that
See which the heretical Scots hate more than the Devil. It therefore seems that it would much promote the service of God if his

---

[1] Spanish text published in the *Analecta Bollandiana*, vii (1888), 54; Pollen,
Papal Negotiations, p. 239.

[2] Vincenzo Laureo, Bishop of Mondovì, in Piedmont, afterwards cardinal.

[3] The Pope did not know, of course, that Mary's husband, the jealous and
vicious youth, Darnley, had been a ringleader in the plot against Rizzio.

Holiness were to command the Archbishop of Glasgow,[1] a person of high integrity, prudence and authority, who resides here as ambassador to the French court, to return to Scotland for this purpose. . . With him our rector, Father Hay, and others, either seculars or priests of our Society, might go as members of his household to aid him with their advice, until the Lord shall have opened a greater door. So much for the opinion of your humble servant." [2]

Those wise counsels found no echo in Rome, so Father Hay was compelled to carry to Queen Mary the proposals of the head-hunting Bishop of Mondovì. Manare felt very sorry for him and wished to have him professed before he set out as a sort of substitute for Extreme Unction: "He has to go into a very difficult country, more so than the Indies, . . . and he goes as it were to martyrdom." The good man himself took it all as part of the day's work. "To tell the truth," he wrote to Polanco, "I feel less inclined to my country than is perhaps becoming of me. I fancy that this body of mine has a presentiment of the delights that there await it. However, may the Lord's will be done, whatever it be, and may His name be every way glorified in us." Edmund was a very discreet and reticent man, very little helpful to perplexed historians. All we know is that, after a month's delay due to the solemn baptism with Catholic rites of the future Solomon of England, Hay was given an audience by Mary at Holyrood on 14 January 1567, repeated to her the lesson drilled into him by the Bishop of Mondovì, and received her reluctant refusal of the Pope's terms. She could not be responsible, she said, for the blood of her subjects, though it was traitors' blood and richly deserved to flow. No doubt, she was quite right in the circumstances. Father Hay remained hidden in Edinburgh for a month after the failure of his mission, affording what consolation he could to the harassed Catholics. He was there on the night of 10 February, when the sleeping city was shaken by the tremendous explosion which signalled the murder of Darnley. How far Mary was involved in that famous crime has been a source of controversy ever since. But there is no controversy about Bothwell's part in it, and

[1] James Beaton.
[2] Pollen, *Papal Negotiations with Mary Queen of Scots*, p. 499.

Mary married that engaging ruffian [1] before a Protestant minister only three months later. A year earlier, Father Crichton had styled her "la santissima Regina" in an Italian letter to Borgia. Now, Father Hay writes sadly to the same man, with the echoes of the Kirk o' Field explosion still ringing in his ears: "I shall only beg of you of your wonted charity towards the Queen to be sure that she is remembered in the Sacrifices and prayers of the Society. It may be that some day all things will co-operate for the good of that sinful woman, and that she will become the doer of great deeds who formerly would not consent to sound counsel." [2] There was prophecy in Father Edmund's lines which was fulfilled on the scaffold at Fotheringhay. Mary had only "to exchange the altar at Holyrood for the preachings at St. Giles," and she would have been freed of all her troubles. But she never for a moment contemplated such a solution and many sins will be forgiven her because she loved Holy Church so much.

[1] He has found an accomplished champion in our time in Mr. Gore-Browne, who, however, is not justified in stating that Edmund Hay had helped the Bishop of Mondovì to formulate his "expeditious remedy" (*Lord Bothwell*, London 1937, p. 278).

[2] Pollen, *Papal Negotiations with Mary Queen of Scots*, p. 508.

CHAPTER VII

THE TESTIMONY OF BLOOD

FIVE years before he died St. Francis Borgia, who was ill of a wrongly diagnosed and incurable disease, had more than once expressed an ardent desire and hope of ending his days as a missionary in India. That was thoroughly in the Jesuit tradition, for had not St. Ignatius, after his experiences at Manresa, when he conceived the great missionary manifestoes of the "Kingdom of Christ" and the "Two Standards," sailed forthwith from Venice, not only to satisfy his devotion at the Holy Places of Jerusalem, but also very definitely to convert the Moslems of Palestine? And when he and his first six companions made their vows subsequently at Montmartre, was not "the most powerful motive which united them the hope of preaching the Gospel to infidels and of dying for the faith"? [1] Nearly all the novel features of the Jesuit constitutions had their origin in the missionary propensities of the man who wrote them and of the disciples who took them for their law. The fourth solemn vow of the order's professed members gives the note: "I promise special obedience to the Pope regarding the missions." It was with the same idea of freeing his men for a wider apostolate that St. Ignatius debarred them from ordinary parochial duties in Catholic countries, from the regular spiritual direction of nuns, and from the acceptance of ecclesiastical dignities, all of which would have had the effect of tying them to a particular place. Similarly, the traditional choral duties and privileges of the monastic orders were given up, and to toughen the spiritual fibres of his new "commandos" Ignatius not only doubled the usual length of the novitiate but deferred ordination and final profession to such an extent that they came to be regarded whimsically by the men most concerned as the reward of a long life of hidden service in the order. [2]

[1] M.H., Polanco, *Chronicon*, i, 51.
[2] Like the Theatine Paul IV, the Dominican St. Pius V, though otherwise a good friend of the Jesuits, could not reconcile himself to the absence of choir among them and imposed it in a modified form during his pontificate. He also

India, as a missionary land, was the first love of the Jesuits, and has continued ever since St. Francis Xavier arrived there four centuries ago to be their chief love. At the centenary of his coming, in 1941, there were 1201 of them maintaining the tradition in India alone and another 98 in Ceylon. The *Litterae Indicae* which St. Francis himself inaugurated at the desire of his "Padre mio unico," Ignatius, brought to Europe the first authentic news of the fabled East since the days of Marco Polo. The volumes of the *Monumenta Historica* are full of the excitement created by those Letters. They made the young men of the order see visions and the old men dream dreams. They won the anchoretic Jerome Nadal from his Majorcan retreat and sent him hurrying in the footsteps of his beloved Ramon Lull to convert the Moors of Barbary, or to die in the attempt as Ramon had done, which latter part of the programme he very nearly achieved.[1] They kindled or reinforced in many hearts that desire of martyrdom which was so marked a feature of the ardent and passionate piety of the age, especially in Spain and Portugal. The seven-year-old Teresa slipping away from her Avila home in 1522 to seek the coveted crown at the hands of the Moors was a symbolic figure. Her junior by eleven years, the Jesuit, Gonçalo da Silveira, scion of two of the noblest families in Portugal, is the type of the martyr dedicated, a man who yearned for the last sacrifice with a

---

required all religious, the Jesuits included, to be professed before ordination, which made a sad havoc of the Ignatian plan. Thus was the grade of "spiritual coadjutor," which had enabled Ignatius to embark on his educational enterprises and to branch out in other directions not at first contemplated, abolished at a stroke. But the restriction lasted only five years, during which time it was most loyally observed by St. Francis Borgia. St. Francis and St. Pius both died in 1572, whereupon the new Pope, Gregory XIII, promptly restored the *status quo* (Suau, *Histoire de S. François de Borgia,* 1910, pp. 403-6).

[1] "He was a great enthusiast — *muy entusiasta* — for the writings of Ramon Lull, to which he dedicated himself with much eagerness during his brief periods of leisure at his farm in the country" (M.H., *Epistolae P. Nadal,* i, 28, n. 2). Like Nadal, Blessed Ramon Lull, O.F.M., was born at Palma in Majorca. When young he led a gay life as Grand Seneschal at the Court of King James the Conqueror. Converted by a vision, he spent the rest of his heroic and picturesque days on earth trying to bring the faith to the Moors of Tunisia. By them he was stoned on 29 June 1315, and died of his wounds. He was one of the most attractive personalities of the Middle Ages, philosopher, poet, theologian, scientist, orientalist and saint.

longing so uncontrollable that it broke out in his sermons and gave a tinge as of sunset fire to all his actions and prayers. It is significant that for Jerome Nadal Gonçalo's love and reverence barely stopped short this side idolatry. "I know but one thing to say about our *unissimo Padre,*" he tells St. Ignatius, "and it is that I can only describe him in terms of the constancy and unchangeableness of our God. When I look upon this sweetest Father and Master, Jerónymo Nadal, I see him always the selfsame, fixed and immovable in the composure of holiness, in wise charity, in prudent activity, in purest kindness, in humblest liberty of heart, in devoted and provident longanimity, in heroic and simple sanctity." [1] Those words equally well describe Gonçalo himself, a genuine aristocrat of the next world as of this. He pronounced his last vows before Nadal at Lisbon in 1553 and a few years later sailed away happily round the Cape of Good Hope to his rendezvous with death on the night of 15 March 1561, among the Kaffir tribes of Mashonaland. He spoke of himself as a merchant-trader, and such indeed he was, "a merchant seeking good pearls who, when he had found one pearl of great price, went his way and sold all that he had and bought it." He was thirty-four when the negroes strangled him, and had crowded into five years of labour under the Indian and African sun the substance of a dozen martyrdoms.[2]

When in Portugal in 1560 St. Francis Borgia, ever a sanguine soul, came to the conclusion on very slight grounds indeed that the time was ripe for a Christian assault on the entrenched and hoary paganism of the Celestial Empire.[3] Unfounded though it was and little

[1] M.H., *Epistolae P. Nadal,* iii, 829.

[2] An excellent brief sketch of Gonçalo's apostolate, based on much careful research, was published by H. Chadwick, S.J., in 1910, with the sub-title, *Pioneer-Missionary and Proto-martyr of South Africa.* The Martyr's letters from Africa were published earlier by George MacCall Theal in his extensive *Records of South-Eastern Africa.* "Es increíble la edificación que ha causado en todos estos reynos su muerte," wrote the Portuguese provincial to Laynez on 25 August 1562, and Laynez on hearing the first news of the "glorioso martirio," wrote joyfully to tell the Jesuits in France, so that they might be encouraged in their own tribulations. "By the grace of God," said he, "things are going from good to better with us" (M.H., *Lainii Monumenta,* vi, 369, 531).

[3] In reward for their services against a local pirate who had made himself a nuisance to the Chinese authorities, the Portuguese were permitted to open a trading station at Macao on the doorstep of China in 1517, but the door itself

more than an aspiration to do something to realize the dying wishes of St. Francis Xavier, this proposal of the other St. Francis caused a mighty commotion in the Jesuit dovecots. Three letters, two to Laynez and one to Nadal, will show how men felt about it. The first was written in hot haste from Toledo in May 1560 by Father Pedro Martinez, whose sermons to empty benches were shortly after-wards to save the Jesuits of Cuenca from having to abandon their mission: [1] "My Father in Christ. As I am preparing a sermon for to-morrow morning and the bearer of this letter is on the point of departure, I shall be brief. I merely want to unveil my heart to you, Father, and to beg you prostrate at your feet to send me of your charity and by the blood of Jesus Christ to China with those who, I believe, are going. Though I am a nobody and it must appear sheer impudence for me to ask such a thing, yet I do ask it, trusting in the grace of our God who made great persecutors of His name into vessels of election and poor fishermen into great preachers. If your Reverence still thinks it an audacious request, please attribute it to the overwhelming desire which has possessed me for this enter-prise many a year now. I do not think it can be from the devil, and if it is from God His Divine Majesty will not have given it to me purposelessly. I have great strength and health, blessed be God, and I want to spend them both in His divine service, even to the shedding of my blood and the giving of my life. I was sent with the expedition to Oran,[2] and our sufferings on that occasion, which

---

remained bolted and barred except for carefully supervised periodical visits of the merchants to Canton through a wicket in the wall built across the peninsula. Even then the merchants were not allowed to land but must do their business with the Canton traders on board their ships. The Jesuits did not succeed in getting to Macao until 1562, and seventeen more years went by before the wicket opened to the adventurous Father Ruggieri. In 1555, however, Father Melchior Nunez Barreto, on his way to Japan, had made two journeys with the merchants to Canton. He appears to have been the first Christian missionary to set foot on Chinese soil since the Middle Ages. His visit had no significance, as he merely acted chaplain to the Portuguese.

[1] *Supra,* pp. 122–3.

[2] In 1558. There were three Jesuits with the Spanish fleet in the capacity of chaplains and infirmarians. The expedition met with disaster and Martinez spent most of his time tending the wounded and burying the dead (M.H., *Lainii Monumenta,* iv, 28 *sq.*).

were heavy, have put heart into me for even worse trials. This is what emboldens me to ask you for China. By the blood of Jesus Christ, I beg you again not to deny me this favour, and Him I pray by His most holy Passion and Death to put it into your Reverence's heart to concede me this so great mercy and charity for my soul. Your Reverence's unprofitable servant, Martinez." [1]

The second letter came to Laynez from the same place, Toledo, three months later, and was written by a priest aged thirty-two named Juan Rogel: "Very Reverend our Father in Christ . . . I write to tell you what I have in my heart for the sake of my heart's peace. Unless I am deceived and self-seeking in the matter, I think that what moves me to want the Indies, as I have done since I entered the Society, is a desire of suffering our Lord has sent me. God knows I have little natural ability for such an enterprise, but I get much consolation from the thought that He chooses the base and contemptible things of the world to confound the strong. My work in the Society so far has been to hear confessions and to teach Christian doctrine. I am no good as a preacher because I stammer and have very little learning. I studied medicine before I entered the Society and since then have acquired the merest smattering of theology. If after giving your Reverence that account of myself you still think I might go, *Ecce ego!* Another particular I ought to tell you is that I have good health, glory be to God, and find it no great hardship to spend the entire day in the confessional, often for days on end. Indeed, I practically live in it. I want to beg another charity and alms from your Paternity for myself and for another father in this house named Juan Segura, who also used to be a student of medicine. It is the privilege you sometimes grant to our fathers of being able by each Mass they say to release a soul from Purgatory, even though the Mass is not applied for that soul. I know well that I do not deserve such a great favour, but my confidence in your

---

[1] M.H., *Lainii Monumenta,* v, 44–5. Laynez held out some hope that Pedro might be sent to Ethiopia, if not to China, whereupon he wrote again: "On my knees I beg your Reverence a thousand and one times — *una y mil vezes torno a pidir de rodillas* — not to forget me, but to put me down for one or other of those expeditions. I do not want to rest, but to suffer for Christ." The dear enthusiast mentions naïvely that he has been making "extracts from all the Councils and scholastic theologians" as a means of bringing conviction to the Chinese or the Ethiopians (*loc. cit.,* pp. 272–3).

Paternity's charity and kindness emboldens me to ask it. . . The least of your sons and servants, Juan Rogel." [1]

The third letter was addressed to Nadal from Salamanca on 25 January 1563, by a young professor of theology named Fernando de Alcaraz, who a few years earlier had brilliantly won the competition for the chair of classical studies at the University of Alcalá, only to renounce it and to join the Society of Jesus the very day of his triumph. He was teaching at Salamanca when Nadal came there in 1562, and on being asked by that Father whether he had any preferences among the foreign missions, should he be chosen for such work, replied: "Beyond all comparison with other missions, I feel drawn to the East Indies or China, and for no other reason than that I imagine there will be more hardship and suffering in those countries. I think if I heard of a country that provided a still larger share of the cross, I would transfer my affections to it immediately." The rumour of a possible chance of getting to China or at least to India inspired Fernando's letter to Nadal in 1563. It was in the following terms: "My Father, I am unable to contain my desire any longer. As you are well aware of its intensity, I shall not need to give you many explanations. I must tell you, though, that it waxes stronger every day and I can find no way of halting its growth. Our Lord presses and urges me with it to such a pitch that often I weep and sigh and moan to Him, imploring Him to satisfy it. And yet this fire is not a burden to me nor a weariness, but rather gives me an indescribable comfort. The more it burns me up the more diligent and fervent I feel, and the happier in the tasks which obedience sets me. How little this labour would seem if our Lord were to give me in exchange for it my portion of India or China. Such as it is I offer it to His Divine Majesty, begging Him to grant me that Rachel of my heart for which I would count many years of suffering as nothing. . . Padre mio, it is not possible that our God should allow the wind to carry away such hopes. This soul of mine, Father, I place wholly in your hands that of very pity you may grant its desire. You know well it is yours. I ask now for the fulfilment of the prom-

---

[1] M.H., *Lainii Monumenta*, v, 192–4. The privilege mentioned in the text is not the same as that associated with a "privileged altar." The latter requires that the plenary indulgence gained be applied to the particular soul for whom the Mass is offered.

ise which you made in your letter. It binds you *in foro conscientiae,* and would to God that I had it in my power to bind you even more! I would not let you off for anything in the world, for from that promise I hope to become no less than the great friend and the true servant in labour, suffering and death of my India or China. Your Reverence will say, 'Alcaraz, you play the bachelor too much.'[1] I admit it, Father of my soul, and God grant that it may be of some avail to me who by His grace might be of some use to those abandoned pagan souls. As you have a great deal to do and may have forgotten what you wrote to me, I shall now transcribe word for word your promise. Your letter is open before me as I write, but I know every word of it by heart. You said: 'It is too late to do anything about the voyage this year, but you can rest assured, Father, that when I come with Father General I shall do all in my power to arrange for your sailing next time.' Well, Father, the next time has come and Father Ramirez has received his sailing orders, but for me there is nothing. I do not deserve such a great blessing and it has not been granted to me. But I am determined to wait one, two, ten, twenty years, if I must, and at the end of that time and of my life itself I shall still be begging it from God. You can be sure, Father, that even if you receive no more appeals from me my eager longing will remain always the same. I hear from Rome that Father Francis[2] is not very enthusiastic about my going because he thinks me too delicate. But that long illness I had when he was here is quite departed. Our Lord has turned over a new leaf for me, and I have been as strong as a horse during the last four years, except for one brief bout of fever. In fact, there is not a healthier man in this house, and if I become dejected and exhausted with lecturing and studying, I have only to turn confessor and preacher to recover my spirits. Another thing that I believe might hinder my chances is my supposed learning, which would not be necessary in the Indies. Father, that learning is purely imaginary, as I have explained to Father General. My memory is as bad as could be and writing makes me ill. By your love for the Immaculate Conception of our Lady, by the wounds and cross of our Lord, by the Holy Trinity, by St. Joseph and the other saint of your predilection, do not let

[1] He had recently become a bachelor of theology.
[2] Borgia, then vicar-general of the order.

this poor good-for-nothing be deprived for the sake of a few old lectures, which others could handle much better, of the fruit he might bear with God's grace among the Gentiles. . . From Salamanca, the feast of the Conversion of St. Paul, 1563." [1] Such was Fernando's letter, which, perhaps, might be censured for a certain lack of Ignatian *indiferencia*, were it not that Ignatius had made an exception of such cases. A man may be as biased and undetached as he likes, provided that it is the cross of Christ he is seeking. The rest of Fernando's story can be told in a few lines. Given his heart's desire in 1566, he sailed like a conqueror into the sunrise and was never seen again, for his ship foundered in a typhoon within sight of that Chinese coast which had been the background of all his dreams. He was only thirty-four when he died, the same age as Gonçalo da Silveira.[2]

The way in which Pedro Martinez and Juan Rogel found the suffering they desired was a little more complicated and needs a few words of explanation. Until the year 1565 the Jesuits had not been invited to share in the evangelization of Spain's vast dominions

---

[1] M.H., *Epistolae P. Nadal,* ii, 205–9, 556.

[2] Knowing nothing of the tragedy until the following year, St. Francis Borgia wrote to Nadal in October 1567: "Father Alcaraz has gone from Goa to the door of China to obtain entrance with some companions into that vast country. The more the Gentiles resist our entrance, the more must we hope that God our Lord will have mercy on their poor souls." This letter was addressed to Nadal "in Anversa o dove si trova" — "at Antwerp or wherever he may be." The first news of Fernando's fate was sent to Europe from Goa by one of the greatest of the Jesuit missionaries, the Italian Father, Soldi-Gnechi, commonly known in his order for some reason or other as Father Organtino. He mentioned that another Spanish Jesuit, Father Pedro Ramirez, went down with Alcaraz. They were not, as Borgia thought, making for China but for Japan. Organtino's letter is simply a long catalogue of the perils and hardships awaiting the young men at home who entertained thoughts of China or Japan. "I think now," he concludes, "that you will understand what coming out to these parts means. It means nothing else than to offer oneself gladly to suffering and death for the sake of Christ our Lord" (Maffei, *Historiarum Indicarum Libri XVI: selectarum item ex India Epistolarum Libri IV,* Cologne 1589, pp. 429–34). A considerable number of Jesuits perished in typhoons in those long-ago times, which was one of the reasons that led the order to specialize in meteorology and to establish a chain of meteorological stations along the Chinese coast. Whatever the rest of the world may think about the sons of St. Ignatius, they have long been in high favour with those who go down to the China Sea in ships!

overseas. Franciscans, Dominicans and Augustinians were the pioneer heroes of the missions in the New World, but the fame of St. Francis Xavier's exploits in Portugal's empire made one of the Spanish *conquistadores* eager to have some Jesuits also out west. This man, Pedro Menéndez de Avilés, the Drake of Spain, was commissioned by King Philip in 1565 to reconquer Florida where French Huguenots had had the audacity to install themselves the previous year. Pedro thereupon wrote in haste from Madrid to St. Francis Borgia at Rome in the following interesting terms: "Very Reverend Lord. The Father Provincial and his companions will write to you about the expedition I am making to the land of Florida by order of His Majesty. Florida is a land bordering on New Spain. To the north and west it is very nigh to Tartary, China and the Moluccas, being either joined to those countries or only separated from them by an arm of the sea, so that a journey to and fro between them and Florida is quite feasible.[1] It is a vast land and its climate is very healthy, but its native peoples are without the light of the faith. . . Now, thinking of the great fruit that might be gained if I could take with me some fathers of the Society, I begged His Majesty's permission to do so, and seeing how eager I was, he granted it. I then spoke about the matter with the Provincial and other fathers in Madrid, but they told me that, owing to the death of Father General,[2] they could not come to a decision until the congregation met within three months from now. As I must sail with God's help towards the end of May and cannot delay longer, I begged them to write to you for a dispensation, so that some fathers might be ready to take ship with me at Seville. . . Since my desire is so much for the service of our Lord and the increase of our holy Catholic faith, I now beg you myself graciously to permit some fathers to come with me. . . If Father Avellaneda[3] happened to be one of them I would be doubly grateful and more

---

[1] This was generally believed by Spaniards at the time, for they had not yet been able to explore Florida northwards. But Pedro Menéndez mentioned the matter as a bait for the Jesuits whom he knew to be very anxious to find a shorter and safer route to China and Japan than by going round the Cape.

[2] Laynez, who died 19 January 1565.

[3] Provincial of Andalusia at this time and one of the main props of the Society of Jesus in Spain.

than ever consoled. . . I kiss your Reverence's hands. Pedro Menéndez." [1]

Busy from morning to night with the affairs of the forthcoming congregation, St. Francis found it impossible to have his men ready in time for the sailing of the armada, and perhaps it was just as well, for they might not have liked Pedro's first exhibition of zeal on the coasts of Florida. He at once captured the Huguenot stronghold of Fort Caroline and then massacred in cold blood every man of its garrison, as well as every boy over the age of fifteen. Immediately after that base inhuman deed he founded the oldest city in what is now the United States of America and piously named it St. Augustine because he had arrived in Florida on 28 August, the great Doctor's feast. We have to take *conquistadores* as we find them, but we are not obliged to like them, however zealous they may have been.[2] Pedro's zeal was genuine enough, and even disinterested. He wanted the Indians converted not merely for Spain's glory but for God's glory also. He now wrote to King Philip asking for no less than twenty-four Jesuits, and the King passed on this request, adding an appeal of his own, to the embarrassed Francis Borgia, who had just received a similar appeal from an old friend of St. Ignatius and a great friend of the Society of Jesus, the provincial of the Augustinians in New Spain. This man, Fray Augustín de Coruña, had recently been appointed bishop of Popayan in the South American province of New Granada, a region where there were no priests of any kind. So he came home to seek for some helpers. "On my being ordered to accept the bishopric," he wrote to Borgia, "I at once determined in my heart to strive with all my might to have men of the Society of our Jesus with me, because what I had heard of them out there in Mexico drew me to them and now what I have seen of them since my return to Spain makes me love them. When I was a novice in Salamanca the holy Ignatius and his companions stayed in our house, so my love dates a long way back." [3]   That was a very

---

[1] M.H., *Sanctus Franciscus Borgia,* iii, 762-3.

[2] It is small justification for him to plead, as does the well-known American Catholic historian, John Gilmary Shea, that he only treated the French Huguenots as they and the English Protestants regularly treated Spanish captives (*The Catholic Church in Colonial Days,* New York 1886, pp. 135-6). That is simply the *lex talionis* of the pagans and Jews, which was abolished by our Lord.

[3] M.H., *Sanctus Franciscus Borgia,* iii, 785-7.

winning plea, but, alas, he too wanted at least twenty-four men —
"á lo menos dos docenas" — including Father Sanchez, a former rector
and famous professor of the University of Salamanca. Sad to say,
the good Bishop — *el obispo santo* everybody called him — did not
get his Jesuits, for the simple reason that there were not enough of
them to meet half the demands then being made on their General.[1]
First come first served was a fair rule, and so Menéndez in Florida
must at once be given at least a token trio of the people he wanted.
That was how Pedro Martinez and Juan Rogel attained their ambition.

Together with a brother named Villarreal — "a man," wrote Martinez, "after my own heart and I think after the heart of God also"
— they sailed on a Flemish hooker in a fleet bringing reinforcements to Menéndez, at the end of June 1566. All went well until
they reached the island of Santo Domingo (alias Hispaniola or
Haiti), when the hooker left the fleet to discharge some cargo at
Havana in Cuba. That done, the Flemish captain innocently looked
round for a local steersman who knew the course to St. Augustine,
only to find to his consternation that nobody knew it. He had
consequently to trust to a nautical map which he found, and that,
being based on the geographical theories of Pedro Menéndez, was
no great assistance. For an entire month the little ship groped in
vain over the sea, though it is only about two hundred miles from
Havana to the tip of Florida. At length it made a landfall and the
captain determined to send some men ashore to reconnoitre. But
they refused to face the perils of the unknown unless a priest accompanied them, hearing which Father Martinez immediately jumped
into the skiff and so earned the distinction among his brethren of
being the first Jesuit to set foot on North American soil. The six
thousand Jesuits of the United States to-day certainly could not have
wished for a more lovable and inspiring pioneer. With him went
three Spanish and six Flemish sailors. Hardly had the skiff reached
the wild and desolate shore when the heavens darkened and a sudden
storm arose which drove the hooker far out to sea. After floundering

---

[1] Shortly after this time, Borgia had to provide twenty men for Peru and fifteen for Mexico, the latter headed by Pedro Sanchez. It may have given Fray
Augustín a grain of comfort to know that his admired Sanchez was going to the
land where he had himself laboured for thirty years.

about for some days at the mercy of the winds, the captain managed to bring it to anchor at Cape Canaveral, about a hundred miles south of St. Augustine. The sufferings of Father Rogel and Brother Villarreal, who had never been on the sea before, can be imagined. Food, water, everything gave out, except the courage of the sailors and their two passengers. To stay at Cape Canaveral meant to starve or be killed by the very hostile Indians, so the captain put to sea again and fetched up after many adventures at the port of Monte Christi in Santo Domingo, without having any such intention. From there he took his battered ship and exhausted men back to Havana. The two Jesuits were gravely ill for a long time afterwards.

Meanwhile on the mosquito-infested coast of Florida Father Martinez and his nine companions searched vainly for any trace of Spanish settlement, keeping alive as best they could on herbs and roots. Alone in a lost or undiscovered world, they took to their frail boat again and rowed north along the shore in hopes of meeting some living thing, even an Indian. At one point they saw three young braves fishing who seemed friendly fellows. Encouraged by their grins, the whole party went ashore, headed by Father Martinez carrying his crucifix tied to an oar. They gave the Indians a necklace of glass beads and received from them half of a large fish. That put new heart into the starving castaways, who rowed on feeling that Florida was not such a bad place. They encountered several other parties of Indians and traded articles of their clothing with them for some maize or a few fish. When nothing else was left to barter, Father Martinez with a little scissors he had and some blank pages torn from his breviary, cut out figures of men and beasts, which the Indians delightedly accepted as payment. So the dreary autumn days went by, a misery of rowing, of gnawing hunger, of always searching that lonely desolate coast and never finding a trace of Spain. On 6 October 1566, while some of the party were ashore, twelve Indians suddenly attacked the boat, dragged Father Martinez to the beach and beat him with their clubs. He flung them off for a moment and dropped on his knees to offer his life to God for their salvation. In that posture one of his assailants killed him by smashing in his head. He was thirty-three years of age when he died.[1]

[1] Three others of the party were killed, but six escaped and eventually made

Meantime, at Havana, Father Rogel made friends with some Indians from Florida whom he found there, and tried to learn their language and to teach them Christianity. Another class for whom his heart bled were the negro slaves so numerous already in the West Indies. It was estimated, he said, that there were three hundred thousand of those unfortunate Africans on Santo Domingo alone. He constituted himself their apostle and thus became the forerunner of St. Peter Claver. But Florida had first claim on Father Juan's services, so thither he returned with Menéndez de Avilés in the spring of 1567, only to find the few thousand Spanish colonists almost at the end of their resources. Juan and Brother Villarreal established themselves at one of the settlements called Fort Tequesta, and there, half-starved, ragged, in constant danger from the arrows of the Indians, they laboured for a whole year to bring the light and love of our Blessed Lord to the poor savages who sought their lives, without making a single convert. It was very like St. Francis Xavier at Kagoshima, only that in twelve months he made a hundred converts. Back in Spain, whither Menéndez had gone for supplies, the news of Father Martinez's death kindled excitement among his brethren, and six of them returned with the Governor to replace him, including Rogel's friend and fellow-student of medicine, Father Juan Baptista Segura, and the great pioneer of Jesuit enterprise, Father Antonio Sedeño. They came, they saw, they were appalled. The soldiers and colonists of St. Augustine who turned out with such pathetic enthusiasm to meet the ships looked like an army of skeletons, poor starved creatures with hardly a stitch on their backs. Father Rogel was there too, and from him Father Segura, the superior of the mission, learned the truth about Florida, that it was not the Promised Land of Menéndez's propaganda, not a place of flowers and abundance, but a forbidding green desert inhabited by treacherous Indians to whom the story of Christ made far less appeal than a handful of maize or a piece of fish. The Governor, who now also had Cuba under his sway, seems for once to have been subdued by the situation. At all events, he made no objection when Father

contact with the soldiers of Governor Menéndez. It was from them that the story of Father Martinez's death reached Europe (Sacchini, *Historia Societatis Jesu*, pars tertia, Rome 1649, pp. 88–90; Astrain, *Historia de la Compañia de Jesús en la Asistencia de España*, ii, 284–9).

Segura proposed to take his whole company to Havana in order to think out the best way of tackling the grave problem of the Indians. A college for this purpose and for the evangelization of the negroes was then set up in Havana, under the direction of Father Rogel. What men could do those brave men certainly did, and in circumstances of poverty as dire as the Indians' or negroes' own.

By the year 1570 all were back again in Florida, with three other Jesuits recently arrived from Spain. They expended prodigies of charity on the Indians, nursed them in a pestilence, shared with them their own scanty food, protected them from the marauding and demoralized Spanish soldiery, but all to no purpose. As the soldiers with their vices and cruelties seemed to be the principal obstacle to the conversion of the savages, Father Segura at length determined to withdraw into the far interior of the country where no white man's foot had ever trodden, leaving only Fathers Rogel, Sedeño, and two brothers to wear out their hearts in the barren vineyard along the coast. A letter of St. Francis Borgia to Rogel at this time is touching in its sympathy and hopefulness: "The more your Reverence has toiled and suffered in these beginnings which to the eyes of men seem all in vain, the greater confidence does our Lord give us that the middle and the end of the course will be full of spiritual flowers and fruit. . . It is winter now. The snows and the winds have their way with the newly planted vine. The plough hides the seed in the ground. But spring will show that these agencies were not the enemies they seemed. The verdure of hope will appear, and then the summer's sun will warm and mature the grapes and the grain, so that they can be gathered and served at the table of the King of Heaven. Florida is its name, so we must hope for flowers. It is the vine of the Lord, so we must look for fruit. . ." [1]

Father Segura and his seven companions disappeared into the unknown in September 1570, putting five hundred miles between themselves and the Spanish colonists. A convert Indian chief of whom Menéndez thought the world [2] acted as guide to the party,

[1] M.H., *Sanctus Franciscus Borgia,* iv, 688–9.

[2] He had even taken the handsome warrior, whom the Jesuits called Don Luis, to Spain and proudly presented him at court as a specimen of King Philip's new subjects. He was more of a specimen than Menéndez imagined.

professing great zeal for the evangelization of his people. But no sooner was he well back in the wilds and safe, as he flattered himself, from Spanish vengeance, than he turned Judas and sold his eight friends to death for the poor clothes they wore and the little chalice with which the priests among them said Mass. Three were killed by the Indians on 4 February 1571, and the remaining five four days later. The traitor himself split open Father Segura's head with his tomahawk.[1] Several months before this tragedy was enacted, St. Francis Borgia had begun to entertain doubts about the wisdom of the Floridan mission. In August 1570 he wrote as follows to Father Luis Mendoza, an outstanding Spanish Jesuit at Madrid: "Señor Pedro Menéndez, the governor of Florida, is insistently demanding several fathers of the Society for that country. He maintains that their presence there would be of great usefulness. But from what I hear it would be of no use at all, owing to the impossibility of converting those Indians. The life of the fathers already in Florida is hard in the extreme. They live separately among the savages without any hope of winning them to the faith, and the daily ration of food allotted to them by the Governor is half a pound of Indian corn, that and nothing else. Some have died from this diet and the stomachs of others have been so gravely affected that they will go the same way if they remain much longer on the regimen. Father Segura, the vice-provincial, tells me that on one occasion he wanted to send an ailing brother out of the country, but the captain of the settlement where the brother was stationed showed his Reverence a written order from the Governor to the effect that he would hang the captain from a yard-arm if he permitted any 'Theatine' to go." This was too much for even the humble and patient Francis to endure, so he requested Mendoza to protest to the Cardinal President of the Royal Council. "It ought to be enough," he continued, "for our men to give their labour and their lives in the service of God without being deprived altogether of

[1] The details are given in a letter to St. Francis Borgia from Father Rogel, who made a personal investigation into his brethren's fate. The letter was published by Astrain, *Historia de la Compañía de Jesús,* ii, 640–4. Menéndez captured and executed the Indians responsible for the massacre, including the dignified miscreant whom he had presented with such a flourish to Philip II.

their liberty. . . Perhaps they would be better employed in the Indies of Peru." [1]

How barren the missionary soil was may be estimated from the fact that the labours and sufferings of Fathers Segura, Sedeño, Alamo, and Brother Villarreal during an entire year at the station of Santa Elena had resulted in the baptism of seven persons, four children and three adults at the point of death. Of the sixteen Jesuits who had come out to Florida since 1566 only six remained alive in 1572. Even the two experts in hardship, Juan Rogel and Antonio Sedeño,[2] realized that the position was hopeless, and advised St. Francis Borgia to send his men elsewhere. Just at that time Philip II asked Borgia for Jesuit help in the part of the world now called Mexico but then known as New Spain. It abounded in colonists from Old Spain and those people needed schools for their children. St. Francis sent Sedeño ahead to reconnoitre, so he was the first Jesuit into Mexico as he was afterwards the first into the Philippines. Juan Rogel followed, and after him came Father Pedro Sanchez with fifteen of the brethren from Spain. They rode into Mexico City on 28 September 1572, just three days before St. Francis Borgia died, and lodged at the hospice founded by Hernando Cortés. Shortly afterwards, a wealthy gruff old caballero named Villaseca offered them some dilapidated property which he owned in the town, consisting of a number of adobe huts thatched with straw. The place was a wilderness but the new-comers set to work with such vigour to clear it and render it habitable that they won the admiration of a native Indian chief, the governor of the town of Tacuba, who offered to build them a church and supplied three thousand labourers for the purpose. It was dedicated in April 1573. The fathers themselves built modest schoolrooms and had six hundred Spanish boys in their charge the following year. Meantime, a college had been started at Pátzcuaro in the province of Michoacán,

---

[1] M.H., *Sanctus Franciscus Borgia*, v, 466-7.

[2] Another Jesuit who knew him well said of Sedeño that he "had never heard of a man who ate less, nor of one cleverer in concealing his fasting." He was such a martyr to asthma that for many months in the year he had to find his sleep standing or sitting because lying down brought on suffocating attacks (Colin, *Labor Evangelica de los Obreros de la Compañia de Jesús en las Islas Filipinas*, Madrid 1663, p. 340). Sedeño was in England during Mary Tudor's reign as a page to the Duke of Feria.

under a rector described by one who knew him as the "humble, happy, charitable Juan Curiel." Juan had the joy and honour of receiving into the Society of Jesus no less a person than Pedro Caltzonzín, the ninth and last Aztec King of Michoacán. His Majesty and his Reverence both died martyrs of charity in 1576, attending the plague-stricken.

At Oaxaca, the capital of the province so named, Juan Rogel received a splendid civic welcome from both priests and people when he arrived there in 1574 to open a college. A canon of the town gave him a residence and a plot of land on which to build, but, alas, this property was much too near the Dominican monastery and trouble ensued. The three older orders, Franciscans, Dominicans and Augustinians, had enjoyed from time immemorial a Papal privilege which prohibited other orders from making a foundation within a certain radius of any building belonging to them. The distance varied between three hundred and four hundred *cannae,* a *canna,* or reed's length (from which the English word cane), being 2.23 metres. Now, in 1571 the Jesuits received a privilege from Pope Pius IV authorizing them to build or to accept buildings as close as 140 *cannae* (roughly 340 yards) to a convent of the older orders.[1] The reason for this dispensation was the great multitude of such religious houses, which rendered it almost impossible for the Jesuits to find a spot *extra cannas* in many cities and towns. But the Dominicans of Oaxaca, who had borne the burden and heat of Mexico since the days of Cortés, knew nothing of Rogel's privilege and very naturally resented his intrusion. They complained to their Bishop, who was himself a Dominican, and that good man excommunicated the offending Juan without more ado. However, the story had a happy ending. Looking from the windows of his palace one day, the Bishop, who was a holy if hasty man, almost wept to see the disgraced Jesuit down in the hot, dusty street in the midst of a group of little Indian children, teaching them their catechism. It was the only office left to him, since he had been deprived of all other priestly faculties. The Bishop sent for him immediately and having heard his explanations, not only removed the censures, but gave him a much better property of his own in another and safer

[1] Jacobsen, *Educational Foundations of the Jesuits in Sixteenth-century New Spain,* University of California Press (1938), p. 262.

part of the town. That made three colleges in a very few years. Before the century closed, the Jesuits had opened eight more in various parts of Mexico.

In South America the fathers had been labouring with very in-different success since 1549, when St. Ignatius confidently raised their few mission stations on the coast of Brazil to the high dignity of a province. It was one of his numerous risky investments in the market of hope, and it yielded good dividends after his death, largely owing to the spiritual greatness of another Ignatius, fashioned in his likeness and in that of the original bearer of the name from Antioch. Born of a noble family at Oporto in 1528, Blessed Ignatius Azevedo joined the Jesuits at Coimbra in 1548. Though charming always to others, he treated his own poor body with so much rigour that he soon became as thin as a rake. "Get fat, Ignatius, get fat," the genial Simon Rodriguez used to say to him. At twenty-five he found him-self, to his intense unhappiness, rector of the College of St. Anthony in Lisbon, his only consolation being that his friend, Father Gonçalo da Silveira, must rule the other Lisbon house of St. Roch at exactly the same tender age. Under him at St. Anthony's, as a constant provocation to missionary thoughts, there studied a Japanese convert of St. Francis Xavier named Bernard, who had come to Europe to equip himself for the evangelization of his native land. But it fell out otherwise, says the record, because Bernard "made so much progress in spirit that he ceased to care about his patrimony or his *patria* or any created thing *sed tantum Creatoris sui obsequium.*" [1] He died like a saint at Coimbra shortly afterwards, but not before having gravely infected his rector with the fever of Japan or some good alternative to Japan.

As Eusebius of Caesarea fortunately thought and said long ago, "there is nothing like quoting passages." In May 1558 Azevedo opened his heart as follows to Laynez: "Coming to myself in par-ticular, I have to manifest to your Reverence the desires which God our Lord has always given me to serve Him among the pagans and unknown peoples now being converted to Him. By labour and prayer I might be able to help them, as the learning which I lack would not be so necessary in their countries as it is here at home." The only consequence of that appeal was that Ignatius found himself

[1] M.H., Polanco, *Chronicon*, iii, 409.

charged with the government of all the Portuguese Jesuits in the temporary absence of Miguel Torres, the provincial. Five months later he wrote again to Laynez: "This charge has been to me like the armour of Saul to David. It has taught me a great deal about myself but I am not anxious to learn more on that subject. The province has suffered badly, too. I tell your Paternity this that, as the deputy of our Lord, you may remedy it. I have also to tell you that our Lord has long filled my heart with a desire to be sent to the Indies or Brazil. It would give me the profoundest consolation if this desire could be fulfilled without any intervention on my part, but solely through our Lord putting it into the mind of my superior. If my own representations or petition were the cause of my being sent, I would not be happy." [1]

After his brief and anxious spell as vice-provincial, when in fact he endeared himself to all his subjects, Ignatius was required to resume the office of rector for another eight years. Besides the duties common to all the priests of his community, such as teaching, preaching and hearing confessions, he took upon himself the spiritual care of Lisbon's two largest hospitals and of an unspecified number of prisons. He felt a peculiar attraction to the denizens of those sad places, and the more sick or sinful they were the better he seemed to like them. One day as he was about to sit down to dinner after a hard morning's work, he heard by chance that a criminal was then on the way to execution. Leaving his dinner untouched, he hurried off to await the unfortunate at the scaffold, climbed the steps with him, heard his confession, and stood by praying with and encouraging him to the end. Another time he was told that three men suffering from diseases too loathsome for admission to the hospitals lay abandoned in some open place. "He flew to them as to some treasure," says his biographer. The disease seems to have been leprosy, for one of the poor wretches cried out to him to keep his distance. With the help of some friends he got all three under a roof, and then with his own hands removed their filthy rags, washed them, clipped their hair, and with more than womanly tenderness bound up their disgusting sores. At one point in the proceedings Father Leo Henriques, Rector of the new Jesuit university of Evora, came in to watch Ignatius doing his surgery and promptly fainted away!

[1] M.H., *Lainii Monumenta*, iii, 282, 577-8.

"These for your pleasure," writes the old and excellent biographer, "are specimens of Ignatius's daily activities." [1]

Father Azevedo begged his superiors again and again to relieve him of his office of rector, for which he felt utterly unsuited, but they merely transferred him in the same capacity to the new college of Braga, founded by the saintly Dominican archbishop, Bartholomew of the Martyrs. At Braga, owing to a shortage of men for the huge amount of work, Ignatius was obliged to be not only rector but "minister, sub-minister, procurator, Sunday preacher, ordinary confessor, guest-master, and director of building operations." He could not find time even to make his solemn profession, which was urged on him by Rome. "I badly need to look after my own soul," he told Laynez, "and I have no talent at all for promoting other people's souls in obedience and devotion. For their consolation and my own, it is very necessary that I should quit this post of rector. . . I have always wanted to be sent to the Indies, as your Reverence knows. During the fifteen years I have been in the Society this desire has never left me. And I have been such a useless person at home that it would be a great mercy to let me go and see if I could not bear a little fruit at the ends of the earth. The greatest joy that could be given me would be an order from your Reverence to set out for Japan. . ." [2] Laynez answered that his India must for the present remain Braga, and so he carried on heroically in prison and hospital, in pulpit and confessional, another three years, always longing, like the great lover of Christ that he was, "to be an imitator of the Passion of my God," in the spirit of his patron saint who wooed death more eagerly than men do their sweethearts. [3]

At long last, in 1566, Father Azevedo was appointed visitor or

[1] Alegambe, *Mortes Illustres et Gesta eorum de Societate Jesu qui in odium Fidei, occasione Missionum, aut Virtutis propugnatae . . . confecti sunt* (Rome 1657), p. 50.

[2] M.H., *Lainii Monumenta*, vii, 485–6, 538.

[3] The Epistle of St. Ignatius of Antioch to the Romans, which has been well described as "a sort of Martyrs' Manual," was familiar to the early Jesuits. The founder of the order changed his baptismal name of Eneco or Iñigo, given him in honour of an eleventh-century Spanish Benedictine, to that of Ignatius out of his devotion to the saint of Antioch. It was the saint's passionate love of our Lord which so greatly attracted him, for he felt the same way himself, and so did Ignatius Azevedo.

official inspector of the Jesuit missions in Brazil, where a small band of his brethren had been labouring for seventeen years to Christianize the cannibalistic natives and to moderate the rapacity and cruelty of the white colonists and half-breeds, who saw in the Indians only subhuman creatures to be slaughtered or enslaved. Writing from Bahia on 28 March 1550, Father Juan de Azpilcueta mentioned a visit he had recently paid to a native village: "At the time of my arrival they were cooking in a pot the legs, arms and heads of ene-mies captured in battle, and six or seven old women were dancing round the fire like demons out of Hell." He says that he found it almost impossible to cure even his best converts of their craving for human flesh, which they would ask for as they lay dying. Another disconcerting habit of those primitive nomads was to go completely naked, both men and women, a fashion made possible by the mild climate of the country. But the colonists, reported the Father with a sigh, were no better than the savages whom they persecuted, and sometimes even worse: "We have suffered heavy tribulation of body and soul from both parties. May God our Lord who has taught us patience by His words and deeds accept our sufferings and give us grace to fulfil in all things His holy will." [1] From their first coming to Brazil and right down to the time of their expulsion from the country by the Portuguese dictator, Pombal, in 1759, the Jesuits sturdily defended the human rights of the Indians, whether pagan or Christian, and opposed by every means in their power, including appeals to the Portuguese court, the exploitation of those children of nature at the greedy hands of the children of mammon. One beneficent result of this policy, for which the missionaries had to pay a heavy price of misrepresentation and obstruction, was that "the great domain of Portugal in South America was saved much of the terrible warfare with savages which marks the history of the Eng-lish settlers in North America." [2]

The gravest problem of the Brazilian Jesuits continued for long to be a shortage of labourers in their enormous vineyard. Their

[1] *Nuovi Avisi dell' Indie di Portogallo, terza parte, dell' India de Brassil* (Venice 1562), pp. 9–12.

[2] Morse Stephens, *Portugal* (Story of the Nations series), 1899, p. 231. Four of the Jesuits were killed by the Indians within six years of the start of the mission.

brethren in Portugal could do little to help, for they had India, the Moluccas, Japan, China and large tracts of Africa already as their responsibility and only a few hundred men on whom to call. It need not surprise us, then, that they tended, like the King and his councillors, to regard Brazil as the Cinderella of the colonial family and, the climate being healthy, to send thither their invalids, men such as the deformed, half-dying youth from Tenerife, José de Anchieta, who turned the tables on them in a very heavenly fashion by labouring for forty-four years among the Indians and becoming the most famous apostle Brazil has ever known.[1] In his first

----

[1] Anchieta came to Brazil in 1553 and died there at an Indian encampment in 1597. To those who knew him and wrote about him he seemed to be a new St. Francis of Assisi and a new St. Francis Xavier combined in one. Alas, they have piled upon his memory such a mountain of miracles that it is difficult to distinguish the features of the living, breathing man. Even Astrain confessed himself baffled. However, José plainly could not have come by his amazing reputation as a thaumaturge without there being some foundation for it, or at least without his having been the sort of person to whom miracles would naturally be attributed. The same thing happened in the cases of his two junior South American contemporaries, St. Francis Solano and St. Rose of Lima, but the Spaniards seem to be more efficient in getting their holy ones through to canonization than the Portuguese. Father Anchieta still remains only a venerable. There is another side to this question of miracles in the mission-field which may easily be overlooked. In Anchieta's lifetime a brother-Jesuit in Spain wrote a remarkable book, translated into English and published by the Hakluyt Society in 1880, entitled, *De Natura Novi Orbis et de Promulgatione Evangelii apud Barbaros* (Cologne 1596), of which one long chapter bears the significant heading, "Cur miracula in conversione gentium non fiant nunc, ut olim, a Christi praedicatoribus?" To point the difficulty, the author, José Acosta, refers, on the authority of St. Gregory the Great, to the many miracles worked by St. Augustine and his monks in the conversion of England, and then asks, "Why are our times so denuded of miracles when such great geographical discoveries have been made that, compared with them, England is but as a small house in a vast city?" He answers by quoting St. Paul to the Corinthians: *The signs of my apostleship have been wrought upon you in all patience: in signs and wonders and mighty deeds.* "Observe, I beg you," Acosta continues, "that among the signs of his apostleship Paul accords the first place to patience." In all ages, he maintains, holiness of life in the preacher rather than miraculous power has been the great converter of souls. His theory was certainly right with regard to Father Anchieta. That wonderful man was a living miracle of patience, as we may read between the lines of a fully authentic letter, forty-four pages long, which he addressed to Laynez in May 1560, describing the boa-constrictors, rattlesnakes, alligators, jaguars, scorpions, poisonous spiders, and tormenting

extant Brazilian letter to St. Francis Borgia, written from Bahia or San Salvador, on 19 November 1566, Father Azevedo came at once to the problem of man-power, for which he could see no solution except to obtain more recruits from Europe. He had fifty-two Jesuits under him, but what were these among the thousand miles of coast that separated him at San Salvador from the great pioneer of the mission, Father Manoel de Nobrega, at San Vicente? He explained the way the country was loosely organized in "captaincies" and how difficult it was to keep the settlers and Indians from one another's throats. Law being in its infancy, he continued, and ministers of justice few, "the Indians have no defenders except ourselves who teach them." That teaching meant first learning the difficult native languages, and not all the Jesuits were as quick to acquire them as José de Anchieta, who published in Portugal, not only the first grammar and dictionary of the principal Indian dialect (Tupi), but a book of sacred poems written in it for the pleasure and instruction of his neophytes.[1] The missionaries in those parts, Azevedo hinted, needed to be versatile people capable of turning their hands and hearts to a little carpentry, doctoring and church-building, as well as to preaching and teaching, in fact, men like José de Anchieta. He suggested to Borgia that the best plan might be for him to return to Europe in search of such paragons, but though he wrote six times in a few months none of his letters reached the General for nearly a year. Such was the South American post in that dilatory age.

flies encountered by him on his missionary journeys (*Nuovi Avisi . . . dell' India del Brassil*, 1562, pp. 150–72, pages numbered on one side only). He seems to have had a genuine Franciscan power over wild things and wild people. He was a lifelong sufferer from maladies brought on in youth by his terrible austerities, but pain could never keep this great-hearted little hunchback of God long away from the primeval, danger-haunted forests where his beloved Indians lurked in their filthy wigwams. He wooed them, as did St. Francis Solano afterwards in Peru, with music and song, and when, as frequently happened, they threatened to make a meal of him, he merely smiled, knowing what a tough, unsatisfactory meal it would be. Anyhow, by him and his like, the vast land of Brazil, sixty-five times the size of England, was completely Christianized. That ought to be miracle enough for anybody. The letters of Anchieta were edited and translated at Rio in 1933 by two Brazilian scholars, so an authentic biography may now be forthcoming.

[1] Alegambe, *Bibliotheca Scriptorum Societatis Jesu* (Antwerp 1643), p. 284.

We next find Ignatius at Rio de Janeiro, and writing, 20 February 1567, to tell Borgia of the recent foundation of that city, after the expulsion of the French Huguenots who had bravely attempted to set up a new Geneva on the Tropic of Capricorn. Those same Huguenots were to come vividly into his own story three years later. From Rio he sailed on to San Vicente, then the limit of Portuguese conquest, to visit Father de Nobrega at his lonely outpost, afterwards returning on his tracks to Porto Seguro, about midway up that interminable coastline. From there he wrote once more to Borgia, and apparently received a letter shortly afterwards at his headquarters in Bahia telling him to stay or to come home as he judged best for his health and for the good of the mission. He was back in Lisbon by the end of October 1568.[1]

In Rome, whither he journeyed after his recovery from the buffeting of the Atlantic gales, Ignatius received the most affectionate welcome, Pope and General vying to do him honour. St. Pius gave him a unique present, the first copy ever permitted to be made of the famous picture of the Blessed Virgin in Santa Maria Maggiore which was supposed to have been painted by St. Luke, while St. Francis appealed personally to the four Jesuit provincials of Spain for a contribution of twenty men between them for Brazil, including an expert tailor named Hernandez, on whom Father Azevedo had cast a covetous eye. But the Spaniards could spare only nine, and not their precious lay-brother tailor. The Portuguese province rallied to the call in a much more generous fashion. Twenty of its 100 priests had recently died in Lisbon, victims of charity in the terrible plague of 1569, yet forty volunteers, three priests, twenty-six priests in the making and eleven brothers offered themselves gladly to Ignatius. Holiness and heroism are infectious. He had only to paint the rigours of the missionary life in that new unknown world, its grinding poverty, its hard incessant toil, its unpredictable dangers, its loneliness, and then to say "Come!" and they came. Some of them were mere boys of fourteen or fifteen; the oldest, Father Pedro Diaz, aged forty-four. Besides his forty-nine Jesuits, Ignatius attracted also about twenty lay helpers who desired to put their various crafts at the service of so great a man and so noble a cause.

---

[1] The relevant letters are in M.H., *Sanctus Franciscus Borgia*, iv, 341 *sq.*, 411 *sq.*, 591 *sq.*; Borgia's answer, 523 *sq.*

Together they constituted probably the largest band of missionaries that ever sailed from Europe as a unit under one leader.

Meantime, across the Atlantic, José de Anchieta was pining for Azevedo's return. "Here in this captaincy of San Vicente," he wrote to St. Francis Borgia, "we live in daily hopes of seeing Father Ignatius again, desirous to profit in spirit from his example and counsel. . . I think that if anywhere in the world your Paternity has sons needing your holy prayers it is here, and especially myself, your unworthy son, Joseph." [1] But the plague still raged throughout Portugal and prevented Ignatius from sailing, though, at the risk of his life, he had secured passages on three ships for his entire company. While awaiting the longed-for day of embarcation, he invited them in the early spring of 1570 to come apart with him into a secluded place on the outskirts of Lisbon called the "Valley of Roses." There, during five months, he put his recruits through an intensive course of spiritual training, a sort of "commando" course of prayer and self-denial, which kindled in their young hearts so great a flame of divine love that many waters, even all the waters of the Atlantic, could not quench it. They sailed on 5 June 1570 in a little fleet of seven ships, Ignatius and forty-two of his brethren being on one with the Spanish name of *Santiago,* and Father Diaz heading another group on the man-o'-war that carried the new governor of Brazil, Dom Luis de Vasconcelos. The weather or some unspecified contingency decided Dom Luis to lie up for a while at Funchal in the Madeira Islands, whereupon the captain of the *Santiago* remembered that he had some business to transact at Palma in the Canaries, three hundred miles south. Ignatius was not very happy at the prospect of being thus separated, however briefly, from the rest of the fleet, as a rumour of pirates had come to his ears, but he was too kind a man to deny the good captain his chances of trade. He even obtained for him the necessary sanction of Vasconcelos, and at the same time invited any of his young men who felt uneasy about the pirates to transfer to another ship. Three faint-hearts then left him. On the eve of departure, 28 June, he heard the confessions of the remaining thirty-nine and gave them Holy Communion. The *Santiago,* a merchantman with little armament, made a prosperous voyage until within nine miles of her destination, when the wind

[1] M.H., *Sanctus Franciscus Borgia,* v, 440.

failed completely. At that critical moment five French privateers manned by Huguenots from La Rochelle swooped down upon her, and after a brief fight, in which they lost their pilot and two of their crew, boarded the helpless vessel. Father Azevedo and Father Andrada, who had come on deck to minister to the Portuguese sailors, were cut down immediately and their bodies, clasped in a last loving embrace, thrown into the sea. Then their young companions, who made no secret of their profession, were dragged on deck in threes and, by order of the brutal Calvinist commander, Jacques Soury, stripped of their soutanes, pierced through the stomach and cast overboard in that dying condition. The sturdier among them had their arms cut off to prevent escape by swimming. Thus perished those forty hopes of Brazil on Saturday, 15 July 1570. All were beatified by Pius XI on 11 May 1854.[1]

That, however, is not the end of the tragic and glorious story. The hapless *Santiago's* six consorts at Funchal set sail for Brazil immediately after the news of her fate had come through to Dom Luis de Vasconcelos. They were not long at sea when a violent Atlantic gale sent some of them to the bottom and drove the Governor's ship, on which travelled Father Diaz and eleven of his brethren, so much off her course that she fetched up in a sinking condition at a small port on the western tip of Cuba. There she had to be abandoned, and, as no other ship could be found to take them, her passengers and crew, headed by the brave Dom Luis, attempted to reach Havana, five hundred miles away, by a land journey. But three days of the Cuban jungle reduced them to such an

---

[1] The above account is from a letter of Father Pedro Diaz at Funchal to Father Leo Henriques, the Portuguese provincial, dated 18 August 1570 (Maffei, *Historiarum Indicarum, Libri XVI*, pp. 448–50). Diaz received the details of the massacre from two Portuguese seamen who witnessed it. They mentioned that Father Azevedo clung so tightly to the picture of the Blessed Virgin given him by the Pope that the Huguenots could not wrest it from his grasp and it went overboard in his arms. Father Diaz concludes his letter with words of profound regret that he had not been himself on the *Santiago*, but, as may be seen below, he need not have mourned. About one at least of the young martyrs, Blessed Francisco Perez Godoy, a cousin of St. Teresa of Jesus, something is known, as he figures prominently, with his long black mustachios which it cost him so much to surrender, in Luis de la Puente's famous *Life of Father Balthasar Alvarez* (English trans., 1868), i, 218 *sqq.* Francisco was blind of one eye, otherwise the Spanish Jesuits would not have parted with him so easily.

extremity that they were glad to take to the sea in open boats and so reached Havana, starving, barefooted, and with their clothes hanging in rags on their backs. There the Governor chartered a new ship, with the intention of returning to Portugal to refit and start his expedition all over again. But once more the Canary Islands proved a death-trap. Off Gomera the ship was sighted and chased by four Huguenot privateers and one English marauder, whereupon followed an episode of valour quite as magnificent and worthy of song as that which twenty years later immortalized the *Revenge*. Vasconcelos, the Governor, an elderly man worn out by his recent fearful experiences, was its central hero. Having made his confession and received Holy Communion from Father de Castro, he turned at dawn of 13 September 1571 to face his pursuers, answering their summons to surrender with a salvo which brought down the mast and killed twenty of the men of the leading Huguenot galleon, a ship twice the size of his own. The other ships then closed in and raked his decks with cannon-balls, until only ten of his fighting men, all like himself badly wounded, were left to meet the swarming enemy. Among them moved Father Diaz, Father de Castro and some of their young companions, administering the last rites to the dying, tending the wounded, and bringing food and drink to the forlorn little band at the prow, who kept on their shattered legs by holding on to a rope with one hand, while in the other they clutched a cutlass and waited for the boarding party. They died to a man at their post, Dom Luis himself being the last to fall and not before having wrought terrible execution on his foes. Father de Castro was hacked to pieces almost immediately, and a little later Father Diaz fell under many blows, the happiest man in the world. With him died two young novices and a scholastic who had all along clung to his company. On the following day the remaining nine Jesuits, after being submitted to every kind of torture and indignity, were thrown naked into the sea. Two of them, strong swimmers, kept afloat so long that the Huguenots relented and pulled them into one of their ships. They escaped on reaching land and made their way back to Portugal to tell their superior there, Father Leo Henriques, the story of their twelve companions' martyrdom.[1] But the

---

[1] Letter of Henriques to the Roman Jesuits, 9 December 1571, in Maffei, *Historiarum Indicarum*, liber xvi, pp. 450–3.

blood of martyrs is proverbially seed and each of the slaughtered Jesuits was soon replaced by two of his brethren on the Brazilian mission. In 1584 there were nearly 150 of them at work there and they had made a hundred thousand converts among the Indians. An English and an Irish Jesuit, John Yate and Thomas Filde, joined the mission in 1575, straight from their novitiate. They were a wonderful pair of men, and their courage and devotion evoked a tribute from the not very generous pen of Robert Southey in his *History of Brazil*. Father Filde had the honour of sharing for ten years all the adventures and sufferings of Venerable José de Anchieta, whom he accompanied on his ceaseless wanderings. His, also, and Ireland's, is the distinction of being one of the five pioneers who started the famous Reductions of Paraguay.[1]

The first Jesuit to give his life for the faith on European soil was Edmund Daniel, like Filde, a native of Limerick, who joined the order at Rome while still in his teens, and is frequently mentioned in the correspondence of Polanco under the sobriquet of "Edmund the Irishman." Polanco specifies that he was delicate in health and suffered from "aquel ayre sutil" of Northern Italy. He needed, the Secretary opined, the "ayre gruesso," the good, strong, moisture-laden breezes of his native land, and so, in 1564, he was sent to labour among his fellow-countrymen, in company with Richard Creagh, the new archbishop of Armagh, and Father William Good, an English Jesuit.[2] The programme set for Edmund was to "instruct the youth of Limerick in the rudiments of the Catholic faith and in the rules of Ciceronian eloquence." For years he laboured

---

[1] A very interesting sketch of Father Filde's career is given in Hogan's *Distinguished Irishmen of the Sixteenth Century* (London 1894), pp. 128–62.

[2] Archbishop Creagh, a notable confessor of the faith who died a prisoner in the Tower of London, owed his appointment to the see of Armagh to the recommendation of the Jesuit, David Wolfe, for many years Papal nuncio in Ireland. Alas, Wolfe, who did excellent service for the Catholic cause and suffered five years' imprisonment in a filthy dungeon of Dublin Castle, did not stay the course, but fell into moral delinquencies, and had to be dismissed from the Society of Jesus. Previous to that sad ending, he had caused what a Flemish Jesuit described to Polanco as "gran escandalo de todos" by his escape from bondage in 1572, for apparently he broke his parole (M.H., *Polanci Complementa*, ii, 301). Richard Creagh's heroic life was all compounded of adventures, some of which he described in a huge letter addressed to St. Francis Borgia from Antwerp on 23 May 1564 (M.H., *Sanctus Franciscus Borgia*, iii, 703–14).

undisturbed at that humble hidden task, but at length he was betrayed by the Catholic mayor of Limerick, a miserable opportunist, and taken in fetters to Cork, where he underwent the usual third-degree methods favoured by the Elizabethans. He was not yet a priest but that fact did not save him from rack and rope. Condemned for his Catholic profession and for refusing to take the oath of Royal Supremacy, he was hanged, drawn and quartered at Cork on 25 October 1572, thus anticipating by eight months the first Jesuit martyr in England, Blessed Thomas Woodhouse, who suffered in the same way at Tyburn on 19 June 1573.[1]

Telling of his first experience of the amenities of the Tower, he said that his dungeon had "not more light in it than Jonah had in the belly of the whale." But the gaoler afterwards kindly gave him a candle to enable him to say his office. His escape on that first occasion very much resembled St. Peter's from the prison of Herod. Though he suffered so much at the hands of the English, Creagh always preached friendship with them, even in the presence of their greatest enemy, Shane O'Neill, the Bothwell of Ulster. Shane retaliated by burning down Richard's cathedral. Of Father William Good it has to be said that he tended to malign his Irish brethren. He spent six years labouring on the Irish mission, always on the move, always in danger. Once when passing through a forest he was despoiled of his pack by some robbers who, opening it, discovered from its contents that their victim was a disguised priest. The poor fellows immediately rushed after him and fell on their knees with arms outstretched, begging absolution in Irish. He could not make out what they wanted till one of them seized his hand and made with it a large Sign of the Cross over his repentant companions. And so he came by his pack again, with its little battered chalice and few threadbare vestments (Hogan, *Ibernia Ignatiana*, Dublin 1888, pp. 15–16). The chief commission given by Pope Pius IV to Archbishop Creagh and Father Good on their expedition to Ireland was to found in that country out of the revenues of various vacant benefices a university "ad instar Universitatum studiorum generalium Parisiensium et Lovaniensium." Of course, the project came to nothing, and the only university permitted to Ireland for more than three hundred years was Trinity College, Dublin, founded expressly by Queen Elizabeth's government to spread English and Protestant culture among the benighted Catholic natives.

[1] All the older authorities gave 1575 or 1580 as the year of Edmund Daniel's martyrdom, but in recent times Father John MacErlean, S.J., an expert on the religious history of the period, discovered the true date, given above, in a letter of David Wolfe. One of the charges against Daniel was that he had been an agent on the continent of the gallant and saintly James Fitzmaurice, the moving spirit of the Irish Confederacy of 1569, but that political fact ought not to stand against Edmund's beatification, as the Confederacy had the wholehearted support and blessing of Pope Pius V, and was not a rebellion but a true crusade.

CHAPTER VIII

PRESTER JOHN'S BUSINESS

LONG before the Jesuits thought of sailing to the lands of Aztecs and Incas, they had become deeply involved in what Nadal called "las cosas del Prete Joan." That famous and fabulous Melchizedek of medieval dreams was presumed to rule a great undiscovered Christian empire in the Orient until at long last in 1491 he was tracked down by the hardy Portuguese traveller, Peres de Covilham, and identified with the Negus of Abyssinia. At least, Covilham succeeded in fastening the name and some of the fame of the mythical Priest-King on to the dusky descendant of Solomon and the Queen of Sheba. Here, at any rate, was a Christian ruler of a moderately Christian country, and better, men thought, an African Prester John in the hand, however much he fell short of the traditional specifications, than any number of undiscoverable ones in the Asiatic bush.[1] The Negus himself was, of course, blissfully unaware of the commotion which the new rôle assigned to him had caused in Europe. He and his people did not particularly want to have anything to do with Europe. After they had been cut off from contact with the civilized world by the Mohammedans in the Dark Ages, the Ethiopians, in Gibbon's sonorous words, "slept for near a thousand years, forgetful of the world by whom they were forgotten." They desired to continue their millennial slumber, and accordingly interned Covilham for the rest of his life. It is said that he found sixty earlier European internees, all pining for Portugal, at the Negus's court. They seem to have been fairly well treated, and we read that poor Covilham was given a wife and an income as some compensation for his enforced sojourn.[2]

---

[1] There are at least nine alternative forms of the word Prester. Pope Julius III spoke of the Emperor of Abyssinia as "Precious John." How the word originated and became associated with the name John has never been determined. Marco Polo identified the Prester with Un-khan, an historical Tartar prince defeated and slain by Jengiz-khan.

[2] Beccari, *Rerum Aethiopicarum Scriptores Occidentales*, v, 249; viii, 82 (Rome, 1907, 1908). This great collection of sixteenth- and seventeenth-century

One object of Vasco da Gama's famous voyage in 1597 was to
discover Prester John, but he discovered the sea-route to India instead.[1] News of this feat penetrated into Abyssinia and made an
impression on the haughty Negus. A few years later, the conqueror, Albuquerque, came with a powerful fleet in pursuit of Arab
marauders and discovered Prester John on his own account. The
fleet made a distinct impression, for these same Arabs were the perennial terror of all good Ethiopians. So, gradually and very cautiously,
a succession of Prester Johns and Johannas put out feelers towards
Portugal. The Portuguese by this time knew that, though Christians, they were heretics and schismatics, owing allegiance to the
Monophysite Patriarch of Alexandria. The Ethiopians hinted that
the allegiance might possibly be transferred elsewhere, if sufficient

---

documents on the history and antiquities of Abyssinia was completed in fifteen
volumes in 1917. It contains the three histories of the country written in Portuguese or Latin by the Jesuit missionaries, Manoel de Almeida, Pedro Paez and
Affonso Mendez. A fourth Jesuit missionary, Jerome Lobo, wrote an account
of his experiences which had the distinction of being abridged and translated
into English, from a French version, by Dr. Johnson in 1735. It was the Doctor's first book and consequently a subject of much interest to Boswell, who
quotes the following tribute to Father Lobo from the preface as an example of
his hero's style at twenty-six: "The Portuguese traveller, contrary to the general
vein of his countrymen, has amused his reader with no romantic absurdities or
incredible fictions. . . He appears by his modest and unaffected narration to
have described things as he saw them, to have copied nature from the life, and
to have consulted his senses, not his imagination. He meets with no basilisks
that destroy with their eyes, his crocodiles devour their prey without tears, and
his cataracts fall from the rocks without deafening the neighbouring inhab-
itants." The same could be said for Lobo's brethren mentioned above. Indeed,
they go out of their way to pour some cold water on the pyre of the phœnix and
other such figments still believed in at that time (*loc. cit.,* v, 328–32, 257–8).

[1] While sailing north from Mozambique, Vasco heard rumours of the Prester's
empire, but failed to locate it, probably because he confused it with the fabulous
empire of Monomotapa, supposed to lie between the Zambesi and Limpopo
rivers. It was to seek and to convert this fairyland's "Golden Emperor," as the
romantic geographers of the time named him, that Gonçalo da Silveira went
from India to the country now called Rhodesia. The Golden Emperor turned
out to be a Kaffir chief living in a very ordinary kraal. The geographers had
this much justification for their flights of fancy that gold certainly abounded in
the country and there were also the colossal ruins of Zimbabwe, long accredited
to the Phœnicians but now believed to be the work of Bantu tribes in the fourteenth or fifteenth century A.D.

military assistance against the Moslems were forthcoming. We hear of three envoys whom they sent to Lisbon, an Armenian named Matthew, one of themselves called Zagâ Za Ab, and John Bermudez, a Portuguese internee, all three gifted with great powers of imagination. In 1520, his last year on the throne, the excited and delighted King of Portugal, Manoel the Fortunate, dispatched an impressive embassy to Abyssinia, one member of which, the priest, Francisco Alvarez, published afterwards a *True Account of the Lands of Prester John*.[1] This book, whose title is rather kind to its contents, enormously stimulated Portuguese interest in the newly discovered country, but the Abyssinians were very slow to return the compliment. Their interest waxed or waned in strict proportion to the activity or passivity of the Moslems.

About the year 1527, one Moslem in particular, a local sultan named Ahmed Granh, speeded up the negotiations by invading Abyssinia with a large and ferocious army, which carried fire and slaughter throughout the land and reduced its unhappy Negus, Lebna Denghel (David to the Portuguese), to the last extremity of appealing in the humblest terms for Portuguese help. In return, he guaranteed to bring his people into the Catholic fold, and, as an earnest of that reward, had his envoy, John Bermudez, consecrated Patriarch of Ethiopia by the Abuna Marcos. Bermudez was to go first to the Pope to obtain confirmation of his new dignity, and then hasten to Lisbon with the Negus's letters for the new Portuguese monarch, John III. Though the King seems to have doubted the genuineness of Bermudez's Patriarchal claims,[2] he accepted him as

---

[1] *Verdadeira informaçam das terras do Preste Joam* (Lisbon 1540).

[2] All the historians, with the exception of Almeida, who confesses himself puzzled, believed that Bermudez had been duly appointed by Pope Paul III in 1539. But St. Ignatius did not share the general conviction. Seven years later, he asked Father Salmeron at Trent to investigate the story. Salmeron consulted Cardinal Cervini, who had been one of those appointed by the Pope to deal with Bermudez's case. Cervini assured him that there had been no confirmation or consecration, that the Pope in fact had not given Bermudez any answer at all (M.H., *Salmeronis Epistolae,* i, 33; Beccari, *Rerum Aethiopicarum Scriptores Occidentales,* v, lii–lix). There, to this day, the mystery rests. Beccari believes Bermudez to have been an impostor but his brethren, the editors of the *Monumenta Historica Societatis Jesu,* do not agree.

an ambassador and dispatched him to his viceroy in India with orders that military assistance was to be sent immediately to Prester John.

One of the most thrilling pages in the history of Portugal's heroic age was then written. The viceroy, a son of Vasco da Gama, had few soldiers to spare, but he gave 450 of his best and put his own gallant brother Christopher at the head of them. Helped by some native levies of doubtful military quality, this tiny force engaged thousands of well-armed Moslems, beat them back, captured their strongholds by storm, and reduced them to such straits that they had to appeal to the Turk of Turks himself to rescue the cause of the Prophet. Reinforcements poured in but still Christopher fought on, fought until he was overwhelmed by sheer weight of numbers. Captured and covered with wounds, he was taken before the Sultan who offered him his life if he would embrace Mohammedanism. "Moor," he answered, "if you knew the Portuguese you would not waste your breath making me such a proposal," whereupon the unchivalrous Granh immediately killed him with his own hands. It is said that the Turks were so disgusted by this action that they withdrew their regiments. The Portuguese who had escaped, two hundred in number, joined the new Negus, Asnâf Sâgad I, alias Claudius, in his mountain fastness, and persuaded him to continue the fight. Continue it he did under that valiant inspiration until Granh Ahmed was slain by a Portuguese bullet and his disheartened forces retreated precipitately out of the country.[1]

But the Abyssinians in victory were not a gracious people. They resented having been saved by the Portuguese, to whom Claudius no less than his father, David, had promised a third of his kingdom and its entire submission to the Pope. With the smoke of the last battle both promises faded into the blue. However, the Moslems rallied and soon showed a disposition to resume the contest, which menace resulted once more in appeals from the Negus to King John. This time, to attest his good intentions, the wily Claudius asked for a patriarch of the Pope's own choosing, as well as a band of missionaries to instruct his people in their new allegiance. King John, who knew nothing of the scurvy treatment meted out to the remnant of

[1] Beccari, *Rerum Aethiopicarum Scriptores Occidentales,* v, 271–316; viii, 84–6.

his heroes, believed the protestations to be sincere and instructed his
agent in Rome, Balthasar de Faria,[1] to urge the matter with the
Holy See. At the same time the King wrote requesting the support
of St. Ignatius, and that is how the Jesuits became involved in Prester
John's Business. The reply of Ignatius, written in Ocober 1546, was
typical: "I have thought it well in our Lord to write this with my
own hand. If my companions in this profession to which we believe His Divine Majesty has called us do not forbid me, and in
case none of them wishes to go, I offer myself to you most gladly
for the enterprise of Ethiopia, should I be chosen. I cannot show
myself a rebel to all my brethren, but I do not think that that issue
will arise."[2] From the moment of penning those lines to the day
eight years later when thirteen of his sons set out for Abyssinia, Ignatius always had Prester John's business at the back or front of his
mind. Few things in his life preoccupied him more, and he gave
his time and attention to it with prodigal enthusiasm. Owing to the
dilatoriness of Prester John himself, whose interest as before depended entirely on his danger, the negotiations were constantly in-
terrupted or hung fire for long periods, but the hopes of St. Ignatius
never waned.

From merely being asked to forward the business in Rome, the
Saint was very soon requested by King John to supply the necessary
men. His Majesty insisted "con todas fuerças possibles" that the new
patriarch should be a Jesuit, and that proposal gave Ignatius a scruple,
for the constitutions of his order which he had then begun to draft
forbade the acceptance of ecclesiastical dignities. However, as he

---

[1] He was not the regular ambassador but a special envoy appointed, in succession to many others, for the purpose of obtaining the Pope's consent to the establishment of the Inquisition in Portugal.   Contrary to what is usually thought,
the Holy See was strongly opposed to the idea, and it required all the great influence of the Portuguese and Spanish crowns, exerted vigorously for twenty-six
years (1521–47), to break down the Pope's opposition.   Nor did Paul III give
way without having exacted stringent guarantees that the "New Christians,"
against whom the measure was chiefly directed, should have fair treatment.
For instance, they were to be allowed to quit Portugal if they chose and to take
all their possessions with them. St. Ignatius, who was not a modern liberal,
favoured King John's design, on the strength of what Simon Rodriguez told
him about crypto-Jewish power and propaganda in Portugal.

[2] M.H., *Monumenta Ignatiana*, series prima, i, 429.

pointed out to Simon Rodriguez, the Portuguese provincial, there would be very little of the usual sort of dignity in being Patriarch of Ethiopia. The first choice of King John for the post was Pierre Favre, Ignatius's oldest disciple, but Pierre escaped to Heaven before anything could be done. Broet, Le Jay, Laynez, Araoz and Rodriguez himself, all were mentioned and all found to be indispensable where they were. In India, the Flemish Jesuit, Father Gaspard Berze, St. Francis Xavier's finest lieutenant, interested himself wholeheartedly in the project, in which he longed to have a part. He made diligent inquiry about the state of religion in Abyssinia, and reported his findings, not all of them accurate, in a long letter to Rome. Then, in October 1552, he addressed himself to Prester John personally, a very touching letter telling of his "vehement desire" to come to Ethiopia to do His Majesty "algum pequeno serviço." This kind man did not forget the relics of Christopher da Gama's little army, stranded in Ethiopia. Let them be of good heart, he was coming along himself to help them. But he died, aged thirty-eight, two months later, worn out prematurely by a long apostolate at Ormuz on the Persian Gulf.[1] His successor as superior of the Jesuits in India was Father Melchior Nunez Barreto, one of the giants of the eastern missions who traversed Japan as well as India and even found his way to Canton. But his business in this context is merely to tell us about his brother John, who on 24 January 1554 was designated first Catholic Patriarch of Ethiopia by Pope Julius III. Melchior had good reason to be proud of John, for it was he who lured him from a hermitage into the Society of Jesus and filled him with the same holy longings that consumed his own ardent soul. A younger brother, Affonso, followed the lead too, and the four girls of the family, not to be outdone, all became nuns. The seven of them belonged to the Portuguese nobility and renounced great possessions. John had indulged his contemplative soul with five or six hours of prayer daily before he became a Jesuit, but Pierre Favre to whom Melchior introduced him, said that he knew an even better way of serving God than that, the renunciation of his own sweet will in the matter of prayer as of everything else. John saw the point and surrendered.

In the summer of 1548, when the enthusiasm of King John for the

[1] Beccari, *Rerum Aethiopicarum Scriptores Occidentales*, x, 23–39.

business of Prester John had decidedly cooled.[1] Affonso de Noronha, the governor of Ceuta, then a Portuguese stronghold in Morocco, asked that some Jesuits should be sent to evangelize his highly un-evangelical garrison and to minister to the Christian slaves in the adjacent Moslem stronghold of Tetuan. For this dangerous mission Simon Rodriguez chose Fathers Gonçalves da Câmara and Nunez Barreto, and gave them as their general helper a splendid brother named Ignatius Bogado. "I can testify," wrote the delighted Governor to Rodriguez shortly afterwards from Ceuta, "that my rascals here whom I used to think worse than the Moors are now, after a bare fortnight's work of those fathers, behaving themselves like monks. God grant it may last!" He went on to say that he had arranged for the fathers to enter Tetuan as official envoys coming to bargain with the Moslems about the ransom of some of their captives. In that capacity Christians were not only tolerated but welcomed by the followers of the Prophet. But he had one great anxiety. Could the brave pair, and especially John Nunez Barreto, be trusted to refrain from telling the Moslems what they thought about them and where exactly they were bound for if they did not renounce their Prophet? Would Father Rodriguez, then, please send them "an express order not to preach to the Moslems, but to confine their attentions to the Christian captives, consoling them, hearing their confessions, and seeing what could be done about their ransom?"[2] Otherwise martyrdom certainly impended, and that was too great a temptation to put in the way of a man like John Nunez Barreto.

Life in Tetuan had a nightmare quality. "Gangs of Christian

---

[1] "Quanto ao que toca ao Preste," wrote Father Simon Rodriguez, the Jesuit provincial of Portugal, to one of his men in Rome, "folgara de ter mais que vos escrever, porque el-rey se tornou a esfriar, de maneira que que nenhuma lembrança nem instância o move." This apathy was brought on by the Negus's shifty attitude. It distressed Father Rodriguez greatly, for no one after St. Ignatius had the Abyssinian project more at heart than he. He earnestly begged several times to be sent there himself, but St. Ignatius knew that King John would never agree.

[2] M.H., *Epistolae PP. Paschasii Broeti . . . et Simonis Rodericii*, pp. 594, 602-3, 607-11, 803-4. Noronha was among the finest of the Portuguese colonial administrators. Shortly after this time he was appointed Viceroy of India and performed an exploit which even the great Albuquerque had attempted in vain, the capture of the key to the Red Sea, Aden.

slaves loaded with chains, poor emaciated deformed creatures, half-dead with hunger and ill-treatment, were always to be seen in the crowded streets. From dawn to dark they sweated turning mill-stones, drawing ploughs, or carrying heavy burdens. They seemed to be not men, but rather walking corpses." [1] At night they were herded into foul underground caves, so many to each that they could hardly move hand or foot. To those caves which were "a living image of Hell," the two priests and Brother Ignatius repaired every night, for in no other way could they make contact with all the unfortunates. On the first night among them, Father Barreto found the words of the Psalmist persistently running through his head: *Posuerunt me in lacu inferiori, in tenebris et in umbra mortis.* He administered what consolation he could in the hideous circumstances, brought food and medicine for the body and then supplied with unwearying patience and love the more necessary food and medicine of the soul. He was strong and could stand up to unlimited hardship, but the more delicate Father Gonçalves quickly succumbed to the fever that was rampant among the slaves and had to be hurried away to Ceuta. Then for six years, with never a break, Barreto and Bogado remained together at their post. As his brother said of John very truly, "era captivo, por amor de Jesu Christo, dos captivos" — he made himself the slave of the slaves. During the day, while the poor wretches were at their tasks, he would sweep out the dungeons, wash away the accumulated filth, and prepare warm meals for his charges at their return. All the time, too, he bargained and interceded with their owners to secure the release of this one and that, especially children and the sick. When a slave died, as happened every day, it was this good man and his faithful adjutant, Ignatius Bogado, who dug his grave and laid him to rest. "I remember," his brother recorded, "that he wrote from Tetuan to the Father Provincial of Portugal begging to be allowed to spend the remainder of his life in the service of those captives, if our Lord had no other use for him." There were two hundred captives whom he particularly desired to ransom and for that purpose decided to seek alms in Portugal, leaving Bogado to hold the fort. He brought home with him thirty-four European boys and girls, nearly all of

[1] Godhino, *De Abassinorum Rebus deque Aethiopiae Patriarchis Joanne Nonio Barreto et Andrea Oviedo* (Lyons 1615), p. 268.

whom had lost whatever Christian faith they once possessed. They would make a good advertisement for Tetuan. In a short time he was able to send the stout-hearted Bogado over two thousand *cruzados* for more ransoms. He pleaded with the King and the nobility, he appealed incessantly from the pulpits of Portugal, he enlisted charitable confraternities in the good cause. Not since another John's time, St. John of Matha, had the Christian slaves of Africa found such an advocate. But his very zeal and charity barred his return to them. King John wanted a patriarch for Ethiopia, and what better patriarch could be found than this saintly apostle? The news of his election came as a terrible disappointment, for his heart was in Tetuan.[1]

On 6 April 1554 Barreto confided his trouble to St. Ignatius: "Father Miron tells me that I am not to return. It is enough for me to be told, for whether your Reverence or any superior speaking in your name directs me to Greece or Africa or Turkey or Prester John, I humbly hope by the goodness of God rather to die than to deflect in the slightest particular from your wishes. . . One thing only I beg your Reverence by the five wounds of Christ crucified that you will not require me to accept any dignity, especially that of patriarch. I know in my heart of hearts that I have not the qualifications necessary for so responsible a charge. . . God has given me but the one soul to save, which cost Christ our Lord so dearly, and I do not want to jeopardize it trying to fulfil duties beyond my powers. But still, I submit myself soul and body into the hands of your Reverence, to be disposed of as you think best for the service of God. . ." Ignatius replied in a letter full of tenderness and encouragement: "If you have any scruple, Father, in this case, let me bear the consequences before God, and also the Pope who, speaking in the name of Christ, has given you this responsibility."[2] Six months later, Barreto fell so gravely ill at Coimbra that his life was despaired of. But even in the extremity of his fever when, as he said, he felt he was being burned alive, his solicitude for Ethiopia gave him strength to write a most touching letter to the Portuguese

---

[1] Beccari, *Rerum Aethiopicarum Scriptores Occidentales,* x, 180; M.H., Polanco, *Chronicon,* iv, 567–71.

[2] M.H., *Epistolae Mixtae,* iv, 136–7; *Monumenta Ignatiana,* series prima, vii, 313.

Provincial, Father Miron: "What with blood-lettings, haemorrhages and vomitings, I am very much exhausted. May our Lord be praised for everything. . . I try hard to be 'indifferent,' but the flesh, being weak, struggles against it, and even the spirit is afraid of death, with all my sins upon it and my little amendment. Still, I put my trust in the infinite mercy of our Jesus. . . What a blunt instrument I am for use in the service of God! But I am determined as always to go wherever I am sent, sick or well no matter. I think it would be a good service to God if your Reverence were to inform Father Ignatius of my condition, so that he may provide for Ethiopia in case I die now, or on the sea or in India. . ." [1]

King John's interest in the Ethiopian enterprise appears to have revived during the summer of 1553 and was further stimulated by the receipt of two letters from the Negus Asnâf Sâgad or Claudius early in the following year.[2] "The King of Portugal," wrote Polanco on 22 December 1553, "has this month urgently requested our Father Ignatius to nominate twelve of the Society, including a patriarch, for the lands of Prester John, which, we understand, are much larger than Italy, France and Spain put together. As there is great hope of these peoples returning to the bosom of Holy Church from which they are separated, and to the purity of the Catholic faith from which they have seriously diverged, corrupting it with the errors of Judaism and paganism, our Father cannot fail them, though we have had many deaths among priests this year and are so straitened for men that we are unable to accept various excellent and well-endowed colleges offered to us. But even from his small resources our Father wants to seek out those twelve." [3] Ignatius had hundreds of Masses said to obtain the guidance of God in his quest, and he consulted a whole array of cardinals and prelates, as well as every prominent Jesuit in Europe. The upshot of it all was that he found himself obliged to provide two bishops in addition to the patriarch, in fact, a miniature hierarchy of those sons of his

---

[1] M.H., *Monumenta Ignatiana,* series prima, viii, 708–9.

[2] They made a stir in the land because nobody in Portugal could interpret them, until a Daniel, in the shape of an Abyssinian hermit, was found and produced.

[3] M.H., *Monumenta Ignatiana,* series prima, vi, 74. Altogether, there are sixty-two letters during the one year 1554 dealing entirely or partially with Prester John's Business.

who by their own law were precluded from accepting any ecclesiastical dignity. Nothing shows better the eagerness of Ignatius to help Ethiopia than the meek way in which he bowed his head to this first heavy assault on his constitutions. All parties agreed that John Nunez Barreto was the best man for patriarch because of "his well-known goodness, learning and prudence," but the choice of the bishops gave rise to a certain amount of discussion. Eventually a Portuguese, Melchior Carneiro, and a Spaniard, Andrew Oviedo, were nominated. Carneiro never saw Ethiopia but died at Macao long afterwards as the first bishop of Japan. Oviedo's fortunes will occupy us presently. He was one of the most attractive of the early Jesuits, a shy, brilliant, original character, with a passionate addiction to solitude and contemplation.

Andrew joined the Society of Jesus, already a priest, in 1541, and two years later fell among thieves on the road between Louvain and Cologne. They stripped him of everything except his shirt and left him for dead. But he came to, and seeing himself to have five wounds was so much comforted by the number that he found strength to crawl to his destination. Another two years, and this man with the soul of an anchorite was appointed by St. Ignatius and the Pope first rector of the first Jesuit adventure in lay education, the College and University of Gandia. There, he set his penitent and feudal lord, Francis Borgia, on the road to canonization. He detested being a superior but showed a real gift for government, except that he could not conquer in himself a great hunger to be alone with God and so would frequently disappear into woods and solitary places to give himself up entirely to contemplation. Sometimes he would be absent for as much as a fortnight. He even entreated St. Ignatius to let him be a hermit good and proper for seven years, but Ignatius answered by bidding him go to Naples and make that his desert. The Saint knew what he was about, for the strangely practical contemplative built up from nothing in Naples one of the most flourishing colleges and missions that his order possessed. One who watched Andrew closely during those years has recorded his impressions: "I was a novice in Rome when this Father came there on his way to Naples. It astonished and edified me greatly to see him every day and all day long helping the novices to draw water from a well and bring it to the house, which was very

hard work. He did not carry himself at all like the doctor and professed father of the Society that he was, but like the least and last of
the novices. I knew nothing at the time about him, but I said to
myself, 'Here is a great servant of God.' He slept in a room near
the sacristy where I had a cubicle, and after the others had retired
would kneel bolt upright like a statue on the floor for the space of an
hour. I saw this night after night with my own eyes, and sometimes
I know that he spent the whole night in the same posture. . . At
Naples, where I was with him, he chose for himself the saddest room
in the house, a little, dark, stuffy, unfurnished hole, with not so much
as a chair or a towel in it. . . So too, he always wore the worst
clothes, shirts and shoes, other people's cast-off things, and would
never have anything new for himself. Once, the soles of his shoes
came right off, but he tied them on again with string. . . In these
beginnings in Naples when everything was so difficult, he was given
much provocation both by us, his brethren, and by lay persons. But
he was never known to show the slightest sign of impatience or to
utter a single sharp word. . . He would never let us be without
anything if he could possibly help it. But we were very poor, and I
remember once when the wine gave out and the good Father had
no money to buy more, what should he do but exchange our only
copy of the Bible for a supply. . . Whenever we showed signs of
wear and tear, he would take the whole ten of us for a picnic in the
country. But it was when any of us fell ill that he showed the full
extent of his charity. He would wait on the invalid hand and foot,
cook and serve his meals, make his bed, wash him, and give him
every other loving attention. . . And if any of us fell sick in soul,
he received the same preferential treatment, as I know from the way
he yearned over me, helping, consoling and animating me during a
long period of spiritual troubles. . . As a superior, he did not need
to give us any orders at all. His example was enough. Every day
he took his share of sweeping the house, helping in the kitchen,
washing-up after meals, and all the other duties. When I came
down in the morning before the others to light the lamps, I would
often find the good Father already busy at some household task. . .
He was a very simple humble man. The very day I was ordained,
by Papal dispensation under the canonical age, he came to my room
to make his confession to me. He was very hard on himself but

the soul of generosity to us. I never knew him to eat anything except bread and salt. If he were offered some herbs he would take them, but he would not ask for them. And his only drink was water. We, on the other hand, were given the best of everything that his small means or his ingenuity could provide. . ." [1]   On being informed in 1554 that he was to go to Abyssinia as coadjutor to the new patriarch, Father Oviedo made the following protestation: "I accept the mission to Ethiopia with all my heart, and I desire to serve our Lord in it till death with all my might. . . I also accept the office of coadjutor to the Patriarch in so far as it means giving him my labour and service. But as for being a bishop, designated to succeed the Patriarch, should he die, I have a difficulty. . . In that capacity I would be exempted from obedience to the Society, and I do not want to be so exempted. . . Whether here or in Ethiopia I want to be a Jesuit under Jesuit obedience." [2]   This little exhibition of recalcitrance pleased St. Ignatius, but the King of Portugal, all-powerful at the Vatican, found an easy way of countering it, and it was not long before the three Jesuits received a command from the Pope to accept their dignities without further argument.[3]   They knew where they stood then, but the Portuguese ambassador in Rome, a man bearing the half-English name of Alphonsus of Lancaster, does not seem to have known where he stood. At any rate, he did not show himself diligent enough about Prester John's business to suit St. Ignatius. "Because he was so slow in expediting the affair," wrote Father Gonçalves da Câmara, who was then in Rome, "Father Ignatius ordered me to go to his house every second day for three whole months to remind him to get on with it." [4]

[1] Beccari, *Rerum Aethiopicarum Scriptores Occidentales*, x, 411–28. The writer of the reminiscences, Father Giovanni Araldo, was sent to Father Oviedo by St. Ignatius to be cured of the melancholy and scruples from which he suffered. The cure by his own testimony was a complete success. Among other things which it involved was permission to come to the Rector's room at any hour of the day or night. He says that he often carried his fears and scruples to Father Andrew in the small hours of the night and never once found him asleep. He was either lying on the bed reading some book of theology or else on his knees beside the bed.

[2] M.H., *Epistolae Mixtae*, iv, 233–4.

[3] *Cartas de San Ignacio*, v, 100–1.

[4] M.H., *Monumenta Ignatiana*, series quarta, i, 211.

Early in 1555, the Jesuits for Abyssinia, thirteen all told, had fore-gathered in Lisbon to await the sailing of their ship on 1 April. But Pope Julius died on 23 March, and that event delayed the arrival of the bull required for the canonical institution of the Patriarch and his two coadjutors. King John was in a ferment, but winds and tide wait for neither monarch nor Pope, and the ships must sail on the appointed day. He was therefore obliged to retain Fathers Barreto and Oviedo while the other missionaries went ahead of them to Goa, their appointed springboard for Ethiopia. The voyage had a tragic ending. Four of the ships reached their destination after many adventures, but the fifth, the *Conception,* with 250 souls on board, including three of the Jesuits, was dashed to pieces off a tiny Maldive island, a thousand stormy miles from Goa. The sailors managed to salvage a longboat from the wreck and in this the passengers were all rowed to the sandy strip to perish slowly of exposure and starvation. Forty brave fellows made a bid for Goa in the longboat and by a miracle of seamanship reached it, but when rescuing ships found the microscopic island four months later not one of the castaways was alive to greet them. So ended a quarter of the expedition to Ethiopia.

Meantime in Portugal the death of Pope Julius raised new hopes in the minds of John Nunez Barreto and Andrew Oviedo that they might yet escape their dignities and go to Prester John as Jesuits unadorned. But the bull eventually arrived and they were consecrated with great solemnity at Lisbon on 5 May. Andrew in particular found his ring and rochet a great trial, and begged without success to be dispensed from wearing them. His title, Bishop of Hierapolis, also gave him a scruple, as he contended that bishops were bound by canon law to reside in their dioceses. Hierapolis, a handful of grey classical ruins near a drab and lonely Turkish village in Asia Minor, would have suited him admirably as a place of residence. Throughout the year that intervened before the next sailing to India, Pope Paul IV, King John of Portugal and St. Ignatius laboured strenuously to make the Ethiopian expedition as impressive as possible. Father Azevedo, who was then in Lisbon, estimated that King John disbursed 100,000 *cruzados* on vestments, altar plate, crucifixes, statuary, books and pictures for the Patriarch and his companions; the Pope addressed a fine and friendly letter to Emperor Claudius; and Ignatius, though suffering torments from the liver disease of which he died eighteen months later, drew up a long list of instructions for the guidance of his men. These came straight from the Saint's heart and would of themselves be enough to disprove the legend of his coldness and despotism. The Patriarch and his coadjutors must not, he says, consider themselves in any way bound by the instructions, which are purely directive, but in all circumstances use their own discretion. "Though their aim and purpose is to bring the Abyssinians into uniformity with the Catholic Church, they will go about the business *con dolcezza,* taking care to do no violence to those souls habituated by long custom to another way of living." The expression, *con dolcezza,* sweetly, gently, occurs again and again. It is an Ignatian slogan. He would tolerate even the rite of circumcision which the Abyssinians had borrowed from the numerous Jews in their midst, if it could not be uprooted without troubling the native conscience. The practices to which he showed himself most opposed were the excessive fastings and other debilitating forms of austerity, derived also from Jewish sources and from the tradition of the Egyptian desert. The Jesuits should try to moderate those rigorous tendencies by emphasizing the greater importance of spiritual mortification and of the practice of Christian charity, for which purpose it would be well to establish hostels and hospitals, orphanages, and confraternities devoted to the ransom of slaves. In this way the Abyssinians would gradually come to see that there was something better than their long fasts, though these must by no means be decried if not carried to excess. At the same time, February 1555, that he penned his instructions, Ignatius addressed himself directly to the Emperor of Abyssinia, inspired, he says, "by the particular desire which God our Lord has given me and our whole Society to serve your Highness as one labouring to preserve the faith and glory of Christ in the midst of so many infidels." The letter is a little treatise *De Unitate Ecclesiae,* not very learned but glowing with humility, charity and zeal for souls. It must be said that Ignatius, like King John and his brother, Cardinal Affonso, who also wrote a long letter to the Negus, had much too high a conception of that monarch's power and sincerity. Led astray by the fairy-tales of such optimists as Bermudez and Alvarez, dazzled by the appearance in Europe of the glib Abyssinian envoy, Zagâ Za

Ab, they seemed to be witnessing the fulfilment of the Psalmist's prophecy, "Ambassadors shall come out of Egypt, Ethiopia shall soon stretch forth her hands to God." They did not know, how could they? that Prester John was half a barbarian, of little more consequence than the Kaffir chief of Monomotapa, that he had practically no control over the swarm of tribal chiefs who were the effective rulers of Abyssinia, that the people were sunk in superstition, and that their religion appertained much more to the Old Testament than to the New.[1]

When the day for sailing arrived, 30 March 1556, half of Lisbon turned out to escort Barreto and Oviedo to their ships. Andrew, we are told, was received on board his vessel "con mucha salva de artilleria." Patriarch John went on a different one, named romantically the "Flower of the Sea," the idea being that he and his coadjutor might not both perish in case of trouble. And trouble there was in abundance. Barreto had always hated the thought of the sea. He told St. Ignatius that before he became a Jesuit he used to be fond of a song with the refrain, "O Wild North Wind, my sails you'll never fill." But Aquilo had its way with him before he was a day on the waves, and he suffered grievously. So did Oviedo, who was too sea-sick to officiate even on Easter Sunday. As usual, the four ships lost one another in fog and gale, were driven right across the South Atlantic, and nearly fetched up in Brazil instead of India. They came together again by what everybody considered a plain miracle, and as they approached the Cape dear Miss Deborah Jenkyns "misnomered Cape of Good Hope," passengers and crews, as a matter of course, prepared themselves carefully and devoutly for sudden death. Indeed, Father Gonçalo da Silveira, who was on one of the ships, compared the whole voyage to death, about which we hear so much but never really know anything until we come to die ourselves. Even the captains and steersmen admitted, he said, that it was God alone who took the ships to India and back, though they tried to help Him to the best of their ability. What the Patriarch thought of his "Flower of the Sea" as it lumbered with tattered sails and broken spars into harbour is not recorded. Yet this was regarded

[1] Beccari, *Rerum Aethiopicarum Scriptores Occidentales,* i, 237–54 (the instructions of St. Ignatius in Spanish and Italian); M.H., *Monumenta Ignatiana,* series prima, viii, 460–7 (the letter of the Saint to Claudius).

by old salts as the best voyage in twenty years, the fleet making Goa in the record time of five months and seven days.[1]

At Goa bad news awaited the weary travellers. The situation there was pretty desperate for many reasons. The evil climate of this "Rome of the East" took a heavy toll of the missionaries, who mostly died in the prime of life. Only ten priests remained in 1555 to run the ever-expanding college of St. Paul, founded by St. Francis Xavier, which then numbered 450 Christian and pagan pupils. The same conditions prevailed in the other missions dependent on the Jesuits of Goa, at burning, fever-ridden Ormuz, at Bassein and Chaul north and south of Bombay, at Cochin, at São Thomé near Madras, in Malacca and the Spice Islands on the Equator. The cry that ever went up from those places was "More men, more men!" But the Portuguese authorities in India could not see the difficulty. They pestered the fathers to spread themselves in every direction until one good provincial was goaded into saying to the Viceroy, Dom Pero Mascarenhas, "Sir, we cannot take on the whole world." It was precisely what tiny indomitable Portugal ambitioned to do, and thereby her far-flung empire came to irretrievable disaster at the hands of the more patient and prosaic Dutch and English. Dom Pero made the mission to Ethiopia his own concern, and early in 1555 conceived the idea of sending out scouts to investigate the religious situation of the country before the arrival of the Patriarch from Lisbon. The Jesuits protested that they had nobody to spare for such an enterprise, but he forced his will on them and detached two of their best missionaries, Father Gonçalo Rodrigues and Brother Fulgencio Freire, to accompany his own ambassador, Diogo Diaz, to the Negus's court.

The three adventurers embarked in February on a merchantman escorted by seven warships and spent a week among the isolated and neglected Nestorian Christians of Sokotra, whom St. Francis Xavier had wanted to evangelize. Father Rodrigues reported that only the ghost of Christianity remained, a couple of Alleluias in their strange semi-pagan rites, a devotion to the memory of St. Thomas

---

[1] M.H., Polanco, *Chronicon*, vi, 770–5. Polanco, a confirmed lover of dry land, took much interest in sea voyages and describes them with considerable skill. Even members of the Hakluyt Society might find something to repay them in his pages.

the Apostle, and a great fondness for the name of Mary. He pleaded
with all his might that help be sent to them, but no help came and
Islam long ago gathered all the islanders into her fold. "If Sokotra
had mines of gold and silver, it would not lack soldiers and missionaries, but since there are only souls more precious than gold, not a
good Christian is to be found who will come and instruct them."[1]
From Sokotra the fleet sailed through the Strait of Bab-el-Mandeb,
the Gate of Tears, and very nearly came to battle with a Turkish
fleet in the process. Our heroes were put ashore at a small port near
Massawa, which a daring survivor of Christopher da Gama's army
had seized from the Turks, and then began a journey overland as
picturesque and painful as any in the history of travel. The men
had nothing to eat but hard tack, for Dom Pero Mascarenhas was a
stingy viceroy. At night they camped in the open, lighting many
fires to keep at bay the lions and tigers whose roaring was their
lullaby. Their route is difficult to trace owing to the changes and
confusion of Abyssinian place-names, but the general direction of
it seems to have been via Aduwa towards Lake Tsana, the source
of the Blue Nile, which Father Rodrigues was undoubtedly the first
European to visit and describe, though he had no inkling of its importance. Near Aduwa they fell in with a score of Da Gama's
soldiers, and great was the rejoicing on both sides. For fifteen
years those poor fellows had not seen a priest, and the wild life they
led rendered confession extremely necessary. In return, they provided the little party with mules and guides, and even made a contribution to their expenses out of the miserable pittance which their
gaoler, the Negus, allowed them. That potentate was on one of his
royal peregrinations and took a great deal of finding. But on 17
May they came upon his camp pitched in one of the rare level places
of that mountainous land. Nothing so far in their experience had
accorded with the rosy tales of Bermudez and Alvarez. The grand
churches of their story turned out to be thatched huts, quite bare of
ornaments, and the people, for all their boasted connection with
Solomon, lived like savages, with only the most primitive ideas of
tillage, sanitation, or anything else. There were no roads worthy
of the name and not a bridge to be seen over any river. When people wished to cross rivers they made use of a primitive kind of raft

[1] Beccari, *Rerum Aethiopicarum Scriptores Occidentales*, x, 49.

built on the inflated hides of cattle. The Jesuits thought it a very dangerous contraption and it gave them many a soaking.[1]

After two days' parleying, the envoys from India were admitted to the royal pavilion, where they gazed with awe upon Prester John reclining in barbaric splendour amid a profusion of tiger-skin rugs and rich silk tapestries from the looms of Ormuz and Cairo. As instructed by their Portuguese friends who knew the etiquette and the language, they approached on their knees to kiss the mahogany hand languidly outstretched to them. Diogo Diaz then presented the letters of his master, the Viceroy, asking permission for the entrance to Ethiopia of Barreto, Oviedo and their companions. Those documents signed by a Pope and King the Negus commanded a Portuguese interpreter to read aloud, but at the end he dismissed his visitors without a single word to indicate what impression they had made on him. They retired to the tent of a Portuguese soldier, perplexed and disappointed, and there they remained cooling their heels for an entire month while His Majesty continued his progress oblivious of their existence. It was a strange way to be treated after coming so far, but that was how they did things in Abyssinia. A survivor of Da Gama's army, who had been many years in the Emperor's entourage and knew him well, told Father Rodrigues that Claudius had no intention whatever of admitting Catholic missionaries or of submitting to the Pope. Even had he so wished he could not bring it about because his vassals, the *Ras,* would prefer "to come under the yoke of their inveterate foes the Saracens rather than change their religious customs and rites for ours." That seems to have been the true state of affairs. Had Claudius been complete master in his own house, he might very well have come to some understanding with the Pope, seeing that he was so genuinely anxious to retain Portuguese friendship as an insurance against Moslem aggression. But he was very far from being in practice the King of Kings, which his title of Negus implied, and he could hardly have exchanged the age-old allegiance of his people to Alexandria without danger of a social revolution. Dioscorus, the Monophysite

---

[1] St. Ignatius seems to have been aware of the lack of bridges and the general backwardness of civilization in Abyssinia, for he recommended his men to take with them some engineers to teach the natives bridge-building, as well as a few agricultural experts and a doctor of medicine.

Patriarch of Alexandria and president of the famous "Robber Council" of Ephesus in A.D. 449, was still very much of a national hero in Abyssinia, and Pope St. Leo the Great with his famous Tome very much the national villain. Sentiments such as these, bred in Ethiopian bones, were not to be reversed in a day by a stroke of anybody's pen. Against them, poor Father Rodrigues's eloquence and learning, embodied in a treatise which he composed for the Emperor's enlightenment, beat in vain. Claudius read the book on his return and expressed some satisfaction with it, to the great annoyance of the Alexandrian Abuna, who threatened excommunication against anyone found listening to the Jesuit or studying his arguments. Nevertheless, many monks and others came to visit the Father secretly, and the Negus even attended his Mass. But the thing that chiefly impressed his Majesty was the effect produced by the Sacrament of Penance on the Portuguese soldiers. Those bold fellows came to the encampment from all quarters to be absolved, accompanied hopefully by groups of native peasants whom they had robbed or defrauded. After the confessions followed the restitutions, to the passing wonder of the Abyssinian gentry who were not themselves in the habit of repenting in so thorough a fashion. Nor did the absentees escape, for Rodrigues pursued them even unto Lake Tsana, where he encountered and disliked very much his first hippopotamus. The good man's zeal was not satisfied until he had absolved more than half of the two hundred soldiers scattered in parties of ten or a dozen throughout the country.

To the end the Negus continued to hedge, maintaining that he had asked for the missionaries simply and solely for the sake of the Portuguese soldiers and their families. For himself, he believed in the "Branch Theory" of the Church, which made it unnecessary that he should submit to the Pope, and he urged Rodrigues to transfer his attentions to the Moslems and pagans around, leaving the Abyssinians in their Alexandrian peace. The Father would gladly have done so, for he was tired of Abyssinian diplomacy which, after a whole year, still hesitated to commit itself one way or the other. The Roman Curia might have helped Claudius to a decision had its cardinals been a little wiser in their generation and plainly stated that there was no intention of superseding the venerable Coptic liturgy of Abyssinia. But this they neglected or were reluctant to do, uniformity of rite as well as of belief being then the inclination, though not the express policy, of the Vatican. It is impossible to avoid a feeling that good men on both sides were "moving about in worlds not realized," that the muse of history was left standing in the cold while the two parties talked at cross purposes to no purpose at all. This was the sad story which the worn-out Rodrigues carried back with him to Goa, after being involved in a naval battle, a shipwreck, and a few other alarms incidental to voyaging at that period in the Arabian Sea.[1]

On hearing the report, the new viceroy of India, Francisco Barreto, who was primarily a soldier, meditated sending a thousand musketeers with his namesake the Patriarch to teach the shifty Ethiopians the faith of Chalcedon. But the Patriarch protested so strongly to the King of Portugal against any such show of force that he dropped his truculent plan for more pacific counsels. He even addressed a very long friendly theological letter to Claudius, full of echoes of the ancient Monophysite wars.[2] One thing, however, he was determined to prevent, that a high ecclesiastic sponsored by Portugal should be slighted or rejected by a mere blackamoor calling himself the Lion of the Tribe of Judah. That would mean a punitive expedition to avenge the insult to his King, and he did not want adventures in Africa while he had his hands so full in India. He accordingly decreed that Oviedo with five other Jesuits should go ahead to prepare the way for the Patriarch, who, poor man, was allowed no say in the business at all, though he professed himself perfectly willing to face the hardships and risks involved. Oviedo sailed on 13 February 1557 and reached Debaroâ[3] in the province of Tigré six weeks later, without more than the usual share of escapes from death and other diversions. Five days after he had landed at Massawa the Turks seized that port and closed the Eritrean coast to European shipping for several years. Thus were the Jesuits completely cut off from their base and indeed isolated from the

[1] Beccari, *Rerum Aethiopicarum Scriptores Occidentales*, iii, 27–33; v, 358–65; M.H., Polanco, *Chronicon*, v, 685–707.

[2] Beccari, *loc. cit.*, x, 68–78, 81–90.

[3] It is useless to look for this place on a modern map, or for most of the places mentioned by the Jesuits. They were mere kraals and disappeared long ago. Even today there are hardly any towns in the European sense of the word in Abyssinia.

whole civilized world, which event, however, had its compensations, for it frightened Prester John and his vassal princes into an attitude of much greater friendliness to the representatives of Portugal. In that country's naval and military might they recognized their only hope of temporal salvation, whatever reservations they might have about the eternal side of the question. So Oviedo was well received at court and Claudius arranged for disputations in his presence between the Catholic bishop and the leading theologians of Abyssinia. They were not as orderly as the disputations in which Andrew had participated at Paris, Louvain and Coimbra. The fierce warriors of the Negus's bodyguard banged their shields and yelled encouragement to their man much in the spirit of a modern football crowd. Oviedo they overwhelmed with abuse, while Claudius on his throne smilingly listened to the hubbub and congratulated himself on having discovered this harmless way of satisfying the argumentative Portuguese. But Oviedo, who had not braved a thousand dangers to provide the Abyssinians with a free entertainment, was far from satisfied, and disconcerted the Emperor by writing and presenting to His Majesty a book in the native language entitled, *The Primacy of the Roman Church and the Errors of the Abyssinians.* That was something not to be shouted down by lusty retainers, and Claudius, who appears to have regarded books as an unfair method of arguing, did not like it. A coldness developed between him and Oviedo, which grew into anger when he discovered that the Bishop was actively and successfully proselytizing among the simple people of the villages. He summoned the offender to his presence and sternly forbade him under heavy penalties to speak a word about religion in future to anybody except the Portuguese soldiers. Andrew, who was a fearless person, answered quietly in the words of the Apostle, "We must obey God rather than men." Claudius and his father, David, had expressly invited him to Abyssinia to preach the faith of the Roman Church to his people and preach it he would while breath remained in his body. Then was war declared on the missionaries, but the Saracens immediately afterwards declared war on Claudius and slew him in battle, together with eighteen Portuguese soldiers fighting gallantly under his standard.[1]

[1] All from a letter of Oviedo's three Jesuit companions, Fathers Manoel Fernandes, Gonçalo Cardoso and Francisco Lopez, addressed to Laynez *ex Aethi-*

For the Jesuits it was a case of from the smoke into the smother. The new Emperor, a younger brother of Claudius named Minâs, proved himself such a tyrant that in a short time he had set the country ablaze with rebellion and civil war. A proud and vicious man imbued with the ideas of the Turks among whom he had spent his youth, he could not brook to see any of his subjects come under Western influences. The increasing number of converts made by Oviedo enraged him to such a pitch that he attacked the Bishop with his royal fists, tore off and trampled upon his habit and threatened him with a hideous death if he dared to open his lips again on the subject of religion. Black and blue from the pummelling he had received, Andrew was then banished with his companion, Father Lopez, to a wild and desert place among the mountains infested by lions and bandits, who might be expected to settle in their own fashion the controversy between Alexandria and Rome. The beauty of the scheme was that the Portuguese in India could hardly declare war because one of their people had been eaten by a lion. There was no international convention making a monarch responsible for the good behaviour of his lions.

According to several accounts that have come down, the two exiles lived for eight months in a mountain cave, subsisting on whatever roots or berries the desolate land provided. Oviedo had certainly found the hermitage of his dreams, but it was spoilt for him by the fact that he could not say Mass because Prester John had stolen his chalice and supply of wine. So great was his devotion to the Holy Sacrifice that in the old days in Spain he had worried St. Ignatius by his yearning to say three Masses a day. In the end, he was rescued from starvation and the lions through the intercession of an Abyssinian princess, whose kind heart had been touched by his courage and goodness. But the incorrigible evangelist was no sooner back among the haunts of men than he started his campaign for souls once again and so was banished a second and a third time. Plainly, nothing but death would stop him, and to that extreme the Negus, fearful of his own skin, hesitated to go. But he soothed

---

opia, 29 July 1562 (Beccari, *Rerum Aethiopicarum Scriptores Occidentales*, x, 146–51). Apart from what they call his perfidy, the Jesuits all praise Claudius in the highest terms.

his wounded pride by killing several of Andrew's converts.[1]

For three years the fathers in India waited anxiously for some sign from the darkness into which their brethren had disappeared. Having tried several times in vain to get letters and supplies through the Turkish blockade of the Abyssinian coast, the Patriarch at Goa determined in 1560 to see whether the gallant Brother Fulgencio Freire might not be able to penetrate it. Fulgencio set off in high spirits. He had been a commissioner of taxes in Ormuz, Bassein and other dangerous places before he became a Jesuit, and was familiar with hardship and the ways of the world. The Portuguese captain, Christopher Pereira, with whom he sailed in a small ship, used all his skill to elude the Turkish galleons, but he was discovered, brought to battle and captured, after most of his men had been killed. Fulgencio, crucifix in hand, remained in the thick of the fight, though bleeding from eight wounds. In that state the Turks hustled him into one of their galleys and chained him to an oar. He was taken first to Mocha in Arabia, where the coffee comes from, and then sold into slavery in Cairo. An ingenious man, he succeeded in getting several letters through to the Jesuits in India, to Laynez in Rome, and even to Father Fernandes in the wilds of Abyssinia. In none of these did he ask a single thing for himself but only that everything possible might be done to ransom his Portuguese companions in slavery, "lest their consciences be put to too great a test." One letter describes their progress through the entire length of the Red Sea to Cairo: "I was loaded with a chain of thirteen heavy links, blessed be our Lord. We were eighteen slaves at the beginning of the voyage, but some died at their oars before the three months of rowing was over. We were constantly lashed by the captain of the galley, and we were always very hungry, because they gave us only two small cakes of millet a day. I felt terribly weak and collapsed often over my oar because I had lost so much blood from those eight wounds made by the Turkish arrows. I often thought I was going to die. May our Lord be greatly glorified for all His goodness to me who have so little deserved it." [2]

In November 1561, when Fulgencio had been more than a year in captivity, two of his brethren, Father Christopher Rodriguez and

[1] Beccari, *Rerum Aethiopicarum Scriptores Occidentales*, v, 392–403.
[2] Beccari, *Rerum Aethiopicarum Scriptores Occidentales*, x, 113–15.

Father Gian Battista Eliani, an interesting convert Jew skilled in eastern languages,[1] arrived in Cairo on one of the queerest wild-goose chases to be found in the pages of church history. The affair began in the pontificate of Paul IV with the appearance in Rome of a genial Syrian named Abraham, who claimed to represent the Coptic Patriarch of Alexandria, Gabriel VII, and to have been commissioned by him to negotiate the reunion of his Jacobite flock with the Holy See. He presented letters in Arabic supposed to have been written by the Patriarch, but as none of the cardinals could read that language they were not at first much impressed. Indeed, they suspected him of being a fraud. However, as he persisted, the next Pope, Pius IV, who was interested in the eastern churches and wished them to be represented at the newly convened Council of Trent, gave orders that the story was to be investigated. Cardinal Ghislieri accordingly wrote to the Venetian consul in Cairo with a request for information. To the astonishment and delight of the Vatican, the consul replied that the claims were perfectly genuine and enclosed another letter which he had himself received from the Patriarch, asking for a nuncio to settle the details of the reunion. Abraham became a hero overnight and was fêted and banqueted to his heart's content. The Pope turned to Laynez for advice, and in this way Father Rodriguez, who had already distinguished himself on Papal missions, was appointed to treat with the Patriarch. But Laynez did not share the general enthusiasm for the expedition. Even after the Venetian consul's report, he remained deeply suspicious of Abraham. "Lo tiene per bugiardo," wrote Polanco — he considers the man a liar. However, the Pope wanted the matter to go through, so there was no more to be said.

Laynez drew up instructions for his men under twenty-four heads, some of which throw an interesting light on their writer's mind and character: "They will esteem the good example of their lives as the most necessary and efficacious means to the success of their mission, for charity, integrity, modesty and the other virtues have more power to persuade than mere arguments from reason. . .

---

[1] He was converted at Venice in 1551 by the superior of the Jesuit college there, André des Freux from Chartres, a truly devout humanist whose Greek and Hebrew learning, good though they were, contributed less than his charming character to making John Baptist a Christian. Des Freux died in 1556.

They will entirely avoid meddling in secular matters or the affairs of princes, seeking only the salvation of souls redeemed at the dear cost of the blood of Christ our Lord. . . While showing respect and true deference to the Most Reverend Patriarch, they will endeavour to discover his real intention in sending that envoy to the Pope with an offer of submission, being careful not to betray any suspicion that his motives were bad or insincere. The aim will be dexterously to test whether his intentions are in fact those stated by his envoy or whether he has some other design. In treating with the Copts about dogmas of faith, they ought to start off from the ground which is common between them and us, avoiding all contention and division. . . In conferring and arguing with them they must always remember to speak in a spirit of meekness and patience, so as not to annoy or alienate anybody. Though they must themselves say Mass according to the Roman rite, they will not show dislike of other rites not condemned by the Apostolic See, for the Eastern Churches have many rites different from those of the West but all good and used by the saints. . . With Christians of the Latin Church, whether merchants, slaves, or persons of any other quality, they will endeavour to do some good by teaching them the Christian doctrine, by preaching, by administering the holy sacraments, and also by consoling and helping them in sickness or poverty, to the best of their ability. It would be a very good thing if they could learn the Arabic tongue, because honest and intelligent interpreters of that language are not easy to find. As touching our Society, they might see whether any door is open for us in Cairo to start a college or mission there for the help of souls, in accordance with our vocation." [1]

The rest of the story is tragedy or comedy as one chooses to consider it. Armed with a Papal brief, a commendatory letter from the Doge of Venice, and a splendid set of vestments as a gift for the Patriarch from the Holy Father, the two Jesuits set off across the pirate-infested sea, accompanied by the famous Abraham. The Patriarch, a simple, kindly, austere old man of eighty-five, received his visitors from the West very courteously and said many nice things about the Pope. But after one or two meetings Rodriguez noticed in him a distinct reluctance to come to business. He was going, he said, to the "Desert of St. Anthony" for Lent in two

[1] M.H., *Lainii Monumenta*, v, 576–81.

months' time. Would they not wait until then when he would be happy to explain everything? The explanation when it came was sufficiently startling. The embassy to the Pope and the letters proffering submission were entirely of Abraham's contriving. He wanted to see Rome, and in what better and pleasanter way could that be done than by going there in an official capacity bearing a friendly greeting to the Patriarch of the West from a Patriarch of the East? Naturally, his Beatitude, who esteemed the would-be tourist very highly, fell in with his plan. But the words of his letter to the Pope implying subjection and obedience had been interpreted too literally. They were merely a form of Eastern courtesy, such as he would have addressed to any prelate. He had never had the slightest intention of submitting to the Pope, for he was the Pope's equal in power and dignity, being the successor of St. Mark as he was of St. Peter. As for his second letter sent through the Venetian envoy, he had written it out of compassion for Abraham, who did not seem to be doing very well in Rome.[1]

The two Jesuits mounted their camels for the desert journey back to Cairo sadder and wiser men. But they did not give up hope of yet winning the Patriarch over, and remained in Egypt a whole year more, tirelessly arguing, contending, pleading with the Coptic theologians. Their efforts were of no avail whatever, so, hearing that the plague raged in Alexandria, they resorted thither to minister to the sick and dying, and very nearly died themselves.[2] In Cairo they came upon poor Brother Fulgencio, worn out with his sufferings but always cheerful and ready for more. Seeing their interest in him, his crafty owner put up the price of his ransom at each approach until it stood at a thousand ducats. At first, Fulgencio would not hear of so large a sum being spent on him. The Turk

---

[1] M.H., *Lainii Monumenta*, vi, 245–55. This volume contains no less than ten long letters from Rodriguez in Cairo or Alexandria to Laynez. There is this to be said for the Patriarch that Abraham hoodwinked him no less than the Roman cardinals. He smuggled a letter out to Cairo, saying that he was in prison and would probably be executed unless the Patriarch wrote authenticating his claims.

[2] Father Eliano was subsequently sent by Gregory XIII as nuncio to the Maronites of Syria, and in 1582 a second time to the Copts of Egypt, at whose hands and those of the Jews he suffered much persecution. He has left a very interesting account of his life and labours, published for the first time by José C. Sola in *Archivum Historicum Societatis Jesu*, iv (1935), 291–321.

then offered a bargain. For 1500 ducats the fathers could have him and eight other sick and aged slaves. They jumped at it, and by stinting themselves in every possible way raised the sum and carried off their men in triumph. From Fulgencio they learned of the tragic situation of their brethren in Ethiopia, so little understood in Rome that Pope Pius IV addressed a letter to Oviedo instructing him to exhort the barbarous persecutor Minâs to send legates to the Council of Trent.[1] The Brother would have shown them letters he had received from Oviedo and Fernandes in which they entreated him to forgive their inability to ransom him, as they had not a single ducat to their names, their only property being five mules and a mare, still unpaid for. They were in the direst straits, blessed be God, for civil war raged around them and the Turks had invaded Tigré.[2]

At this point we may listen for a moment to young Samuel Johnson booming from his bed in Birmingham, with Legrand's French translation of Father Lobo's *Voyage to Abyssinia,* borrowed from the library of Pembroke College, Cambridge, propped up in front of him: "This learned dissertator [Legrand], however valuable for his industry and erudition, is yet more to be esteemed for having dared so freely in the midst of France to declare his disapprobation of the Patriarch Oviedo's sanguinary zeal, who was continually importuning the Portuguese to beat up their drums for missionaries who might preach the Gospel with swords in their hands, and propagate by desolation and slaughter the true worship of the God of peace. It is not easy to forbear reflecting with how little reason these men profess themselves the followers of Jesus, who left this great characteristic to His disciples that they should be known by loving one another, by universal and unbounded charity and benevolence."[3] Such is the story to be found in most English books which treat of Abyssinia, and it is completely unfair. The only truth in it is that Oviedo, who became Patriarch after the death of Barreto at Goa in 1562, did constantly solicit Portuguese inter-

---

[1] Beccari, *Rerum Aethiopicarum Scriptores Occidentales,* x, 130–1. This letter and a longer one addressed by the Pope to Minâs himself never reached their destination.

[2] *Loc. cit.,* pp. 141–6.

[3] *A Voyage to Abyssinia.* By Father Jerome Lobo, a Portuguese Jesuit. London (*vere* Birmingham) 1735. Preface, p. ix. Cf. Boswell's *Life of Johnson,* chapter iv.

vention, but purely to save the country from chaos and to prevent its being overrun by the Turks. Neither he nor any of his brethren dreamed of suggesting that the Catholic faith should be forced on the Abyssinians or that their country should become an apanage of Portugal. They wanted the Portuguese to intervene for very much the same reasons that inspired English intervention in Greece in 1944, to save the country from an unchristian tyranny and to secure for the common people freedom from fear and freedom to follow their consciences, even into the Church of Rome if they so desired. In 1566, Father Fernandes summed up the preceding seven years of Ethiopian history with the phrase, "wars without end," and this internecine strife, abetted by the Turks, took on a new ferocity after the death of Minâs and the succession of his young son, Sarza Denghel. This Emperor and his principal enemy, the powerful Ras Isaac Barnagaes of Tigré, both appealed for Portuguese assistance to deliver the country from the anarchy into which it had fallen. With all respect to the Great Cham reclining on his pillows in Birmingham, Oviedo's appeals had no other or more sinister purpose.[1] One of his principal reasons for wanting the Portuguese to come was that they might put a stop to the abominable traffic in slaves which the Abyssinians carried on with the Turks.

In 1567, the Patriarch received instructions from Pope Pius V and the Portuguese Crown that he and his remaining companions were to abandon Abyssinia and betake themselves to Japan. His answer to the Pope, written in very bad Latin, is a moving document. "There are now," he says, "four or five hundred Catholics, perhaps more,[2] scattered throughout the land. Here in Tigré, not far from the sea, I have gathered together 230 of them in two little villages which I caused to be built. To these we preach and administer the sacraments. Holy Father, it would be inhuman to desert them, even were they fewer, and were our villages not sanctuaries for other Catholics, as for any who desire to become such. The Good Shep-

---

[1] Practically all the 140 letters in Beccari's tenth volume contain appeals for Portuguese intervention. Oviedo wrote twenty-six of them, the remainder being from Fernandes, the Portuguese soldiers left from Da Gama's expedition, and various Abyssinian worthies.

[2] Fernandes reckoned that there were upwards of a thousand. These were not all converts of the Jesuits, except indirectly. The Portuguese soldiers had married Abyssinian wives and brought up Catholic families.

herd, Christ our Lord, who laid down His life for His sheep, did not abandon the one stray member of the flock. . . Suppose we were to go and leave behind even one or two succourless, what would Christ say who, to strengthen the faith of a single man, showed him the print of the nails and bade him put his finger into His wounds? . . . If the decision rested with me, I tell your Holiness frankly that I would never permit Ethiopia to be abandoned. But if it is otherwise determined and if the King of Portugal will not deign to send us the help we need, then I most earnestly beg your Holiness to write and ask His Majesty to send a strong fleet to take us all away together. A small fleet would be no use whatever on account of the power of the Turks at the coast. As for myself, Holy Father, I am by the grace of God completely at your disposal, either to remain here in Ethiopia, or to go to Japan or among the Turks, or to put away this patriarchal dignity and serve my brethren of the Society of Jesus in the kitchen." [1]

Though often rumoured to be coming, the rescuing fleet for which Oviedo asked never came, because the degenerate Portuguese authorities in India were too busy feathering their own nests to have time for adventures in charity.[2] Andrew remained at his post in vanished Fremona, two and a half miles north-west of Aduwa, to the end. It cannot be said that he made an ideal bishop or accomplished diplomat. He was too rough-hewn a character for such delicate rôles. He did not keep the peace to perfection even with his own brethren. They understandably resented his indiscriminate charities, as when he slaughtered their only bullock to feed some hungry natives or gave his only alb to a ragged visitor. He disposed of the costly mitre presented to him by the King of Portugal to help other cases of poverty, and when there was nothing left in his thatched hut would walk eight or ten miles with a sack on his back to beg food for the many needy folk who depended on him. As was his custom in Europe, he fasted all the year round himself, never touching meat or anything but herbs and a sort of porridge made from the bitter-tasting native *tef*. This belated Desert Father, so ruthless to himself, had the tenderest heart for the sufferings of others.

[1] Beccari, *Rerum Aethiopicarum Scriptores Occidentales,* x, 215-20.
[2] Always excepting the generous and gallant Dom Constantino da Braganza who did everything in his power to help the Ethiopian mission.

Hearing that an Abyssinian chief known for his hatred of the Catholic Church had fallen victim to a loathsome and contagious disease which exhaled so nauseating a smell that his own relatives had abandoned him, Andrew at once repaired to the man's cabin and took complete charge. He washed the poor fellow, dressed his sores, fed him with a spoon, swept and tidied the room, laundered the filthy bedclothes, and performed daily every other necessary service until the patient had completely recovered.[1]

The kind heart of Francis Borgia bled for Andrew and his companions in their sufferings and isolation. Writing to the Patriarch on 11 January 1570, he said: "Your Paternity's eagerly awaited letter dispatched from Tigré in June 1568, has reached me and given me the greatest joy. I see from it that our Lord in giving you to drink of His chalice of tribulation mingles with the bitter draught spiritual refreshment and consolation. He is so good a Master who, for one drop apportioned to us, drinks Himself the overflowing cup of sufferings. Oh, most Reverend Father, how I envy you your exile, your loneliness, your poverty, as also the patience and joy which our Lord communicates to you in the midst of so much tribulation. But even though you rejoice in your sorrows, I hope that our merciful Redeemer will deliver you from them soon. . . You ask me for news of our brethren in Rome, Naples, Valencia and Gandia. They are flourishing by the goodness of God our Lord. In Rome now we have passed the 300 mark, and all are as busy as bees. Father Salmeron, to whom I have sent your greetings, is in his old age provincial of Naples with seventy subjects under him. The college in Valencia has fifty of us within its walls, and Gandia also is doing well, the Pope recently having given the University a benefice which brings in six hundred ducats a year in income. As for the scruple which your Paternity mentions concerning the vow of poverty, I would say first that your dignity and office entirely dispense you from the obligation of the vow. . . For the rest, I feel very sure that not many poor religious in their monasteries are so poor as you out there, and it consoles me to see you who are in want of all things still having a scruple about poverty. Secondly, I would point out that neither our constitutions nor any other part of our institute bind

[1] Beccari, *Rerum Aethiopicarum Scriptores Occidentales,* iii, 94-6; v, 453-5; Godinho, *De Abassinorum Rebus,* 394-400.

under sin, and on that ground alone the little gifts you make to others are perfectly innocent. Again, it is no infringement of the vow of poverty for a professed father to have a mule to carry him about on his necessary journeys. As for land to till, it is true that one of the professed cannot own it or bequeath it, but he is quite free to work it for food in such extreme necessity as you labour under in Ethiopia. Why, the House of the Professed itself here in Rome has a garden and an orchard wherein the good brethren labour and eat of the fruit of their toil. . ."[1] That letter is doubly precious as revealing the thoughts of two holy hearts fast bound to each other in sympathy and love.

Twenty years Andrew spent tending with sacrificial charity the unrewarding vineyard of Prester John, and then died in great agony from the stone, but blessing God to his last breath, at Fremona on 9 July 1577. Some years earlier, Father Cardoso had been murdered by robbers while journeying through the mountains to bring the consolations of their religion to an isolated group of Portuguese. Father Gualdamez was martyred by the Turks of Massawa in 1562, and the remaining three props of the forlorn hope died, like Oviedo, in great poverty at Fremona, the last to go being the simple-hearted, lovable Father Francisco Lopez in 1597, after forty years' toil and suffering in the wilderness. So ended for a time in absolute failure the Jesuits' concern with Prester John's Business. But they came back, as they have a habit of doing, to the scene of their defeat, headed by the smiling athletic figure of Pedro Paez, who endured seven black years of Moslem servitude, explored and described the source of the Blue Nile half a century before Bruce, and by his sanctity, learning and impeccable tact shepherded two successive Prester Johns into the one true Christian fold.[2]

[1] M.H., *Sanctus Franciscus Borgia*, v, 270–2. Three days after the dispatch of his letter to Oviedo, Francis was writing to console another unfortunate, Father Gerardini, who had been captured by the Barbary Pirates. "As your Reverence knows," he said, "we are terribly poor but we shall ransom you, even if it means taking the bread out of our mouths."

[2] Father Paez came to Abyssinia in 1603 and died there in 1622, so his story, one of the most absorbing in all missionary history, falls outside the limits of the present volume. But there may be another occasion of telling it. The Father is noticed under his name by the *Encyclopedia Britannica* but ignored by the *Catholic Encyclopedia*. His work on the Nile was translated into English and published by the Royal Society in 1669.

CHAPTER IX

SILHOUETTES

IT WAS not only in Abyssinia that the Turks made the lives of Christian men a burden. They remained a perennial threat to Europe. Smarting from their repulse before Malta in 1565, they girded themselves once again for the conquest of the Mediterranean and, under Sultan Selim II, a savage hater of Christians, laid siege to Cyprus in 1570. St. Pius V then sounded the old reveille of the Crusades, but only two of the nations, Spain and Venice, hearkened to his call. In the words of an Elizabethan writer, "after three score and fifteen dayes battery and many assaults, the Turkes having spent an hundred and fiftie thousand shot of great ordnance, Famagosta was taken" and Cyprus was lost to Christendom. Don John of Austria, aged twenty-seven, "his eyes quick and shining, with a lovely proportion of all his limbs," as a Jesuit of the period described him, had already sailed to his rendezvous with the Papal and Venetian fleets at Messina, but St. Pius V, on whose bowed shoulders rested the hopes of Europe, bemoaned the absence of France, of Portugal, of the Empire, of Poland, from the ranks of the Holy League. He would send embassies to those tardy nations, and so it came about that in the high summer of 1571 St. Francis Borgia, then in the last stages of pulmonary disease and gravely afflicted with gout, carried the fiery cross to three remote and preoccupied kings. His letter to Father Antonio Araoz of 4 June 1571 discloses what he felt about the mission: "As I did not deserve to see my Father Araoz in Rome when I desired it, there is all the more reason for my not losing the pleasure of seeing him in Spain, where I hope we shall meet soon, if God gives me life and strength. His Holiness requires me to serve him by making this journey in company with Cardinal Alessandrino, his Legate. Your Reverence can guess how astounded I was to receive such marching orders. Little use as I am for important negotiations, I am even less for this one owing to my age, now past sixty-one, and to my many and chronic infirmities, some of which are highly incompatible with life on the road.

But the obedience due to the Vicar of Christ our Lord has put a seal on my lips. Indeed, it has given me an appetite for whatever hardships may be involved and will carry me contentedly over land and sea. I wanted to tell your Reverence this so that you may pray to our Lord to give me grace to carry out my orders in His service, and also to bring the pair of us together, which is one of my keenest desires." [1]

While Francis was being fêted on all sides in Spain, even by the Inquisition, which graciously removed his name from its *Index of Forbidden Books,* eight of his sons, under the leadership of Father Christopher Rodriguez, an intimate friend of the Grand Admiral, Don John of Austria, sailed as naval chaplains with the three fleets of the Pope, King Philip and the Doge "for the Islands Echinades, about midway between Lepanto and Patras, . . . little islands or rather obscure rocks scarcely appearing, but now to be made famous throughout the world by the most notable battell that ever was fought in those seas." [2] The Jesuits and their brave Franciscan, Dominican and Capuchin companions were in the thick of the tremendous fight all through the five fateful hours of history which it lasted, tending the wounded, Christian and Moslem alike, absolving the dying, inspiring with new courage the exhausted champions of Christendom. Not a single sailor, soldier or galley-slave died that memorable October evening without the comfort of the sacraments. [3] It was a marvellous and unexpected victory, but it did

[1] M.H., *Sanctus Franciscus Borgia,* v, 582–3.

[2] Knolles, *The Generall Historie of the Turkes* (London 1603), pp. 876–7. Cited in Tenison, *Elizabethan England* (1933), ii, 85. Miss Tenison's ten volumes, quarto, sumptuously produced and illustrated, are a magnificent if one-sided monument to the glory of the Virgin Queen. Among many interesting and previously unknown facts unearthed by the compiler is that the Queen ordered special prayers to be said every Wednesday and Friday in the diocese of London for the Knights of Malta, whose order she had suppressed in England, during their glorious stand against the Turks in 1565. But though England in general and Lord Burghley in particular watched with keenest sympathetic interest the preparations for Lepanto, Elizabeth ordered no prayers on this far more critical occasion, the explanation of course being that St. Pius had meantime unfortunately issued his sentence of deposition against her.

[3] M.H., *Sanctus Franciscus Borgia,* v, 412–16; Sacchini, *Historia Societatis Jesu,* pars tertia (1622), 336–7. The Sicilian Jesuits made a modest contribution to the fighting forces of Christendom in the shape of three hundred indigenous

not finish the Turks because the Catholic kings to whom the Pope appealed were too mean-spirited to follow it up with a general and decisive crusade. The King of Spain resented the Pope's gentle protests against his continual encroachments on the rights of the Church; the King of Portugal was bent on his own private crusade in Africa; the King of France and his mother, Catherine de Medici, cared for none of these things; and the Emperor of Germany pleaded the necessity of minding his Protestants.[1]

After a fruitless visit to the corrupt court of the Most Christian King at Blois, Cardinal Alessandrino and St. Francis turned sadly homewards with little to show for eight months of incessant talking and journeying.[2] The big guns that had boomed in their honour at Bayonne were a sort of ironic commentary on the failure of their mission, sound and smoke signifying nothing. Francis reached Ferrara in a completely exhausted state on 19 April 1572, to learn there that Don John of Austria's new expedition against the Turks had been recalled by King Philip because the French were threatening to invade Milan and Flanders. "They say," reported Nadal from Rome, "that one hell is not good enough for the person responsible" — *non li basta un inferno,* a sentiment heartily shared by Jerome himself. For more than four months St. Francis lay between life and death at the Jesuit house in Ferrara, though the good Duke Alphonso, who loved him and was his relative, had used every persuasion to coax him into the comfort of his palace. Early in September, he begged to be carried to Loreto, his last little pilgrimage,

---

bandits whom they had converted and persuaded to turn their murderous abilities against the Turks. Don John of Austria afterwards presented the crucifix which he had used for his standard to the Fathers of the College of Palermo (Aguilera, *Provinciae Seculae S.J. ortus et res gestae,* Palermo 1737, pp. 187–95).

[1] Emperor Maximilian II was himself half a Protestant.

[2] Except the famous "alcuni particolari," some secret promising news for the Pope, which Ranke and Acton interpreted after their fashion to mean that the Pope, a great saint of God, was plotting with the loathsome Charles IX to bring about the Massacre of St. Bartholomew. Baumgarten and other Protestant scholars have poured on this mean and completely arbitrary theory the scorn which it deserves. While pretending friendship with Spain, Charles IX, one of the vilest characters in history, conspired with the rebels in the Low Countries, with the Protestant princes of Germany, with Elizabeth of England, and even with the Turks, to destroy the one remaining bulwark of Christendom against Islam.

and then to Rome that he might greet many dear friends there before he died. Every yard of the long journey was a new torment. He desired his half-brother, Tomás, who accompanied him, to keep others at a little distance from the litter lest they be distressed by the moans he was unable to stifle. Such thoughtfulness had characterized him all his life. The end came on the night of 30 September, two days after his arrival in Rome, and an autopsy then revealed a final detail of his heroism. All along, the doctors had treated him for disease of the lower organs, whereas it was dreadful abscesses of the lungs that caused his pain. And he had never breathed a word of complaint or refused the perfectly useless and often nauseating remedies prescribed for him. This was in tune with the last two lines of his spiritual diary, added on 7 February 1570: "Desire to shed my blood for the love of Jesus whenever it may be for His service." [1] He was one of the sweetest, dearest, noblest men our poor old world has known.

Francis, the great-grandson of a notorious Pope and a famous King,[2] was succeeded as general of the Jesuits by a man of origins so obscure that he appears to have had no family name and was called Everard of Marcourt, or adjectivally, Everard Mercurian, after the humble little Luxembourg village of his birth.[3] Forty-seven professed fathers took part in his election, of whom twenty-six, a clear majority, were Spaniards, but they chose this non-Spaniard, wrote the decidedly Spanish Bobadilla, "with so much consolation and joy both inside and outside the Society that it was manifestly the work of the Holy Spirit." One of the best pleased of any was the new Pope, Gregory XIII, who deprecated national monopolies of office in the Church.[4] He signified his satisfaction by withdrawing the

---

[1] M.H., *Sanctus Franciscus Borgia,* v, 721, 887.

[2] Alexander VI and Ferdinand the Catholic.

[3] Some people in those days used to say, as possibly some people still imagine, that poor men such as Mercurian were not wanted in the Society of Jesus. To one good bishop who made this criticism Nadal replied with a friendly challenge: "It would take your Lordship too long to investigate the cases of all the Jesuits in Europe, as I have done, but you could easily carry out such an inquiry among those in Rome. Believe me, my Lord, you will find that scarcely one in fifty of us ever had had anything of this world's goods" (M.H., *Epistolae P. Nadal,* iv, 160).

[4] There have, in fact, been only five Spanish Generals out of a total of twenty-

hampering regulations of his predecessor with regard to choir and early profession.[1]

As in the second general congregation so in the third, which, after a small tempest or two raised by a few aggrieved Prosperos, closed in great peace and harmony on 16 June 1573, the problem of manpower again came to the fore. In Europe no less than in India it was a problem that taxed the wits of superiors to solve. In the middle of Mercurian's seven years' reign the Jesuits were 3905 in number, but these had to meet the demands of 210 insatiable colleges and missions. That meant an average of nineteen men to each place, which seems a reasonable number until we remember that a good

six, St. Ignatius included, and after St. Francis Borgia no other Spaniard was elected for 115 years. One Spanish province remained unrepresented at the election of Mercurian because its three delegates were captured and imprisoned by the Huguenots on their way through France. Father Martin Gutiérrez died in the prison clasping to his heart a little cross he had fashioned for himself out of candle-grease. Father Gil González, the Provincial, was badly wounded by the heretics, but the French Jesuits succeeded in ransoming him and his companion, Father Juan Suarez. Interesting letters in which those two describe their dreadful experiences may be read in Father Luis de la Puente's well-known *Life of Father Balthasar Alvarez* (English translation 1868), ii, 18–26. The reason why Spaniards predominated in the third general congregation was that they abounded in most provinces outside Spain and were freely chosen by Germans, Frenchmen and Italians to represent them. The Jesuits as a whole sat very lightly indeed to the nationalism which had begun to infect the minds of all European peoples and to dye their histories with blood. In those days, an English Jesuit, Father Adam Brock or Brooch, was rector of the Polish college in Vilna, a Scotsman, Father Edmund Hay, who spoke bad French with a Highland accent, ruled the Jesuits of Paris, while another from Caledonia stern and wild, Father William Crichton, did the same by the Jesuits of Lyons. Both Scots were present at the election of Mercurian. Two years after that event, an Irishman, Father Richard Fleming, succeeded the great Maldonatus as professor of theology at the Collège de Clermont and nine years later was appointed first chancellor of the new Jesuit University of Pont-à-Mousson in Lorraine. The only land of Jesuits in which one never reads of a foreigner coming to the top is Spain, except of course in such enclaves as the English and Irish colleges founded by Jesuits of those nations for their persecuted fellow-countrymen at Salamanca, Valladolid, Seville and other places.

[1] The Pope's desire, presented at first in the shape of an order, for the election of a non-Spaniard, was not wholly spontaneous but due in some measure to a petty intrigue of the Portuguese Father, Leo Henriques, who disliked Polanco and wanted to make sure that he would be excluded.

third at least would have been still in their training and not available at all, and that the colleges swarmed with youth. To give a few instances, Clermont in Paris was very much in the position of the Old Woman who lived in a Shoe. It had no less than 3000 pupils, and the Rector, Father Edmund Hay, was at his wits' ends to know where to put them or how to provide masters for them. He did everything in his power to keep the numbers down, but he might as well have tried to stop the flowing of the Seine. The names of Maldonatus and Mariana and the fame of the dead young genius, Pedro Juan Perpiñá, all three Spaniards we observe, were too great an attraction.[1] It was the same story in Spain, where the college of Seville had 900 pupils, Córdoba 800, Valladolid, Palencia and León 600 apiece, Monterrey 400 studying grammar and another 200 *minimos* learning to read and write, while, to jump the Atlantic, Lima and Mexico, the capital of New Spain, each catered for several hundred youths in 1576. In fact, primary and secondary education became almost a Jesuit monopoly in Spain under Mercurian, not at all by the wish of the fathers themselves but by the astute management of the *Ayuntamientos* or corporations of the towns, who, as the new schools charged no fees for tuition, were thus saved all cost and responsibility.[2] But the Jesuits were not on this account spared the labours of higher education and had flourishing theological and philosophical faculties at Salamanca, Alcalá, Barcelona (140 students), and other places. To man all their existing far-flung redoubts seemed to some fathers of the third congregation a sufficiently arduous task to justify legislation prohibiting the acceptance of new colleges or missions for a number of years. But this radical solution was rejected by the majority who contented themselves with prescribing that the General must do all in his power to solve the problems of the present before committing himself to others of the future.

So Father Mercurian, a quiet, gentle, sagacious man, began the rule of his twenty provinces, stretching from Japan and China west-

[1] Fouqueray, *Histoire de la Compagnie de Jésus en France,* i, 431. The opposition of the University to Maldonatus because he was a foreigner, led by that extravagant nationalist and enemy of Aristotle, Ramus, obliged him to retire from his chair in 1576. But, as mentioned above, the impenitent Jesuits put on an Irishman in his place.

[2] Figures from the *Litterae Annuae* of the colleges in Astrain, *Historia,* ii, 197.

wards to Peru. His secretary was the remarkable Mantuan, Antonio Possevino, fresh from ten years of incessant battling with the Huguenots at Paris, Avignon, Bayonne, Rouen, Dieppe and other French places.[1]   If we may believe the Governor of Dieppe, writing to Father Oliver Manare on 6 January 1570, Antonio must have been a most persuasive orator: "In five days during which he gave forth and preached the pure and holy word of God, about 2500 of the 6000 Huguenot persons we still have in this place were unexpectedly and as it were miraculously converted and have now returned to the Catholic religion."[2]   Mercurian also was very familiar with France and its troubles, for he had been official "visitor" of the three Jesuit provinces there immediately before his election as general.   As ever, the outstanding matter of interest for the Society of Jesus continued to be the fierce, implacable conflict between the University of Paris and the Collège de Clermont. It may well be of interest to more than Jesuits. The centre of the storm was Maldonatus. Every word spoken from his chair by that great teacher received the attention of many jealous eyes and ears. In 1574, while treating of original sin, he broached the subject of the Immaculate Conception of the Blessed Virgin, expressed his own firm belief in the doctrine,[3] and at the same time deprecated as inexpedient the custom common in French universities, especially Paris, of requiring undergraduates to swear that they held it as an article of faith. This piety of Paris was far from having a purely religious or theological explanation. At first, the University had determinedly opposed the doctrine of the Immaculate Conception, but finding that its original *bête noire*, the Dominican Order, was doing the same, it turned about and began to champion our Lady's privilege. At Basle, in 1439, that is, two

---

[1] Portuguese and Spanish opposition to Polanco, partly on account of his supposedly Jewish blood, may have had something to do with his retirement from the post of secretary, which he had filled with so much distinction for a quarter of a century.

[2] "En cinq jours qu'il a exprimé et presché la pure et sainte parolle de Dieu, es environ six milles personnes huguenots qu'avons encore en ce lieu, il s'en est inopinément et comme miraculeusement converty et ja revenus en la Religion Catholique environ de deux mil cinq cens" (Fouqueray, *Histoire*, i, 660).

[3] From the very first the Jesuits had constituted themselves defenders of this doctrine, and continued without a single exception to be among its foremost champions until the solemn definition of Pius IX in 1854.

years after the famous Council there had degenerated into a schismatical conventicle, the Paris theologians, who were so prominent in the anti-Papal debates, petitioned for a definition of the doctrine. A decree of the thirty-sixth session of the pseudo-Council was then issued, in which the schismatical prelates, usurping the functions of the Pope, delivered themselves as follows: "We define and declare that the doctrine of the Immaculate Conception is to be approved, held and embraced by all Catholics as pious and agreeable to ecclesiastical worship, Catholic faith, right reason and Holy Scripture, nor is it permissible for anyone in future to preach or teach to the contrary." [1] The men of Paris read this as a *de fide* definition, and ever afterwards the Immaculate Conception was regarded as an obligatory article of faith by the stalwarts of Gallicanism. Then comes this insufferable Spanish Jesuit openly denying it to be such and in the process casting aspersions on the Council that had given France her charter of liberty against the tyranny of Rome. It was not to be endured.

At a meeting of the Paris Faculty of Arts, held on 12 December 1574, the Rector of the University, Jean Deniset, denounced Maldonatus in unmeasured terms as an impious innovator and scorner of tradition, bent on driving France into schism. Next day the culprit was peremptorily ordered to appear and give an account of his teaching before the principal members of the four Faculties of Theology, Law, Medicine and Arts. He replied, as another father informed Mercurian, that he would obey when he came under the jurisdiction of the Faculties by the incorporation of the Collège de Clermont in the University, as the Jesuits had so long desired and been as long refused. If they had any complaint against him, let them apply to the Bishop of Paris or to the Parlement. Thereupon, the four Faculties pooled their resources of money and influence to bring the Jesuits down. Maldonatus was declared by a unanimous vote to be a rebel. He had appealed to Caesar, to Caesar he should go. But when the University denounced him to the Bishop, Mgr. de Gondi, they forgot that they were no longer dealing with the compliant Eustache du Bellay. Pierre de Gondi, afterwards cardinal, had a mind of his own. He listened patiently to the charge of the Sorbonne doctors, studied carefully the lecture notes of Maldo-

[1] Mansi, *Concilia,* xxxix, 182.

natus, questioned the defendant personally, and then pronounced in solemn form, 17 January 1575, sentence to the following effect: "We say and affirm that John Maldonatus, priest of the Society of Jesus, delated to us for ventilating false doctrine in his lectures, has taught nothing heretical or contrary to the Catholic faith and religion." [1]

Worsted on that point, the University men soon returned to the charge with another. No closer students of the Jesuit Professor's words and works were to be found in all France. They weighed his every sentence and phrase, hoping to find in them something short of orthodoxy. By May 1575 the Rector of the University believed that his search had been successful. Six years earlier, while treating of Purgatory, Maldonatus had discussed the question of its duration for any particular soul. "Without rashness," he declared, "we can decide nothing for certain on this point. . . But I would willingly subscribe to the opinion of those who think that nobody remains in Purgatory longer than perhaps ten years. For if in this life we pay the debt of temporal punishment owing for our sins by such brief and easy penances, who can believe that the extreme pain of Purgatory will last so very long?" In saying this, Maldonatus pointed out that the opinion to which he inclined was that of his master, the great Friar Preacher, Dominic Soto, and of the University of Salamanca, where he had made his studies. He did not hazard a personal opinion at all, but merely said that if it were permissible to hold one he would range himself with Soto and the Salamanca school.[2] At a meeting of the four Faculties held on 3 June 1575, the Rector of the University who presided denounced Maldonatus in set form for having publicly taught that "the souls of the

---

[1] Prat, *Maldonat et l'Université de Paris* (1856), pp. 349–60. Like all his brethren of that and subsequent ages before the definition of 1854, Maldonatus, as may be seen in a dozen passages of his works, believed wholeheartedly in Mary's Immaculate Conception, but he refused to take his cue from the Council of Basle or to anticipate the Holy See in declaring it an obligatory belief of Catholics when the Council of Trent and Popes Sixtus IV and Pius V had expressly left the question open.

[2] The reader might like to have Soto's words: "Responsio ergo *forte* est quod clementia Dei non fert multo tempore amicos suos a suo conspectu cohibere, et ideo sapientissima ejus providentia fuit illas poenas ad eos expurgandos instituere quae brevi tempore possent animas illic perpurgare. . . Quapropter crediderim nunquam aliquem in Purgatorio viginti annis exstitisse, imo, ut mea fert opinio, nec decem. . ." (*In IV Sent., d.* 19, *q.* 3, *a.* 2.)

faithful departed remain in Purgatory not longer then ten years." The Faculty of Arts reaffirmed its belief in the Immaculate Conception, "contrary to the opinion of Maldonatus," but courteously remitted the question of Purgatory to the Faculty of Theology; the Faculty of Law followed suit; the Faculty of Medicine omitted the pious profession of faith made by the others, but expressed itself indignant with the "novelties" of this man Maldonatus; and finally the Faculty of Theology promised to give the united front its opinion on the ten-years' question after having studied it "avec sa maturité ordinaire."

Of course the theologians found against Maldonatus, but this time they and their legal and medical brethren were not going to be such fools as to appeal to the Bishop who had proved a broken reed on the last occasion. They knew a safer tribunal and would bring Purgatory before Messieurs of the Parlement. Maldonatus at once protested against this attempt to ape the ways of England, but Mgr. de Gondi did not content himself with anything so mild as a remonstrance. He immediately threatened to excommunicate the entire University and to anathematize the Rector in particular, if they dared without his authority to proceed against a priest whom he had approved. The Faculties then reassembled in hot haste. Some were for braving it out and all were wild with indignation. The majority, however, thought it more prudent to appeal to Cardinal de Bourbon, the protector of the University's privileges, against "the saucy insults and iniquitous threats of the Bishop of Paris." The Cardinal, who was a diplomatist and besides knew that the appellants had no case, advised them to end the long conflict and to regularize the situation by incorporating the Collège de Clermont in the University. At the same time, he requested the Jesuits to supplicate once more for this favour, which they were only too happy to do. But the University men turned deaf ears to the peaceable counsels. They persisted in their plan to invoke the judgment of the Parlement, whereupon, as a warning shot across their bows, Mgr. de Gondi excommunicated the dean and "syndic" of the Faculty of Theology. Without hesitation, the brave dons returned his Lordship's fire. Leaving Maldonatus alone for the moment, they prosecuted the Bishop before the bar of the Parlement, which, sitting *in camera,* pronounced him to have exceeded his powers and quashed his sentence. In deference to the wishes of Cardinal de Bourbon, the triumphant doctors next summoned before them the Jesuit Provincial, Claude Matthieu, the new Rector of Clermont, Odon Pigenat, and the two professors of theology, Maldonatus and the Scotsman, James Tyrie, from Drumkilbo in Perthshire.[1] They were asked the same question that had been put to Paschase Broet and Ponce Cogordan ten years earlier, "Are you monks or secular priests?" When they tried to explain that they were neither, but clerks regular, a new form of the religious life approved by the Holy See, the doctors refused to listen to such quibbling. Monks they must be, or seculars. If monks, they were precluded by venerable statutes from teaching in the University; if seculars, the privileges and exemptions which they claimed fell to the ground. They might choose which horn of the dilemma they pleased and hang or impale themselves on it as soon as ever they liked.

Meantime, it became known at the University that the Pope was getting restive, so a group of the more implacable adversaries of the Jesuits decided to enlighten his Holiness on the situation. Their extraordinary letter is mainly an expression of thankfulness to God that they are not like the rest of men, extortioners, unjust, as also are those Jesuits and their patron the Bishop who undermine belief in the Immaculate Conception, and teach a ten-years' limit to the pains of Purgatory *in order to get into their own hands endowments bequeathed for Masses for the dead*.[2] This last gloss on the surmise

---

[1] As mentioned in an earlier chapter, Tyrie, a graduate of St. Andrew's, became a Jesuit with his friend, Edmund Hay, at Rome in 1562. His quality may be deduced from the offices to which he was appointed, Rector of Clermont, Assistant for France and Germany, one of the Committee of Six who drew up the first edition of the *Ratio Studiorum*. Among those with whom he engaged in controversy were John Knox, Andrew Melville and David Buchanan. Melville and Buchanan were generous enough to praise both his ability and his courtesy. He died in Rome in 1597.

[2] "Votre Béatitude n'ignore pas quelles contradictions nous avons essuyées de nos jours dans notre doctrine. . . L'Espagnol Maldonat, de la societé des Jésuites, a débité avec beaucoup d'animosité et d'aigreur, et dicté à ses auditeurs bien des choses capables d'ebranler la foi avec laquelle les Francais ont cru jusqu'à présent l'immaculée conception de la Vierge Mère de Dieu; ce que l'Université toute entière n'a pu ni dû supporter. . . Ainsi les Jésuites, d'après certaines rumeurs, auraient irrité contre nous et Rome et le Saint-Siège. . .

of Maldonatus reveals the bitterness of the controversy.   Maldonatus
himself maintained a dignified silence and even desisted from lecturing, but his Clermont brethren were not such models of meekness.
They addressed a vigorous apologia to the Pope, so vigorous that it
shocked Father Mercurian, who heavily censored it before presenta-
tion at the Vatican and reprehended its writers "for the sharpness of
their language about certain persons commonly regarded as good
and learned men in Rome." [1]   The following short extract is a fair
specimen of the incisive tone of the letter: "The grievance of the
Faculty of Theology, Holy Father, has nothing to do with the Conception of the Blessed Virgin or with the duration of the pains
of Purgatory.   They lament because we seem to diminish their
authority by our championship of the dignity of the Holy See;
because in the judgment of thinking men they no longer enjoy a
monopoly of greatness; because they are unable now to domineer
in the sphere of theology, absolving and condemning according to
their own sweet will; because they think that some people may get
to heaven for whom they had not opened the gates.   But what riles
them most of all is that our school is crowded, with a consequent loss

---

Nous cependant, selon notre coutume, nous restions dans le silence, attendant
notre secours d'en haut. . . A la vérité, nous sommes des serviteurs inutiles,
cependant Dieu a fait par nous ce qu'il a voulu.   Que de terribles tempêtes les
nôtres n'ont-ils pas fermement repoussées et bravées depuis trois cent ans!   Que
de grands théologiens ne sont pas sortis de notre école, comme du cheval de
Troie, pour gouverner les Eglises!   Combien n'en sort-il pas encore tous les deux
ans!   Quelle gravité, quelle pureté dans nos statuts ou nos décrets!   Quelle
sévérité, quelle solidité dans notre doctrine!   Nous ne sommes à charge à aucune
Eglise; nous ne détournons pas les héritages; nous ne cherchons point à faire
tomber dans nos pièges de monastères ou d'autres bénéfices ecclésiastiques pour
en jouir sans en avoir les charges; nous ne dirigeons point au nom de Jésus les
consciences des princes d'après l'opinion qui réduit à dix ans les peines du
Purgatoire, comme pour dire qu'il n'y a aucun danger, aucun dommage pour les
fondateurs, morts depuis longtemps, à enlever les biens ecclésiastiques aux
monastères, ou à d'autres, pour les transformer en commendes, les appliquer à
d'autres usages profanes, ou à d'autres œuvres de piété, ou à des collèges. . .
Nous ne nous vantons pas nous-mêmes, Très-Saint Père.   Nous sommes les
balayures, les ordures du monde. . . Mais nous apprenons à ne supporter nulle
part ni la fausseté, ni l'abus, ni la dépravation de la doctrine" (Prat, *Maldonat et
l'Université de Paris,* pp. 379–87, from D'Argentré *Collectio Judiciorum,* ii,
445 *sq.*).
[1] Fouqueray, *Histoire de la Compagnie de Jésus en France,* i, 585.

of pupils and profit to themselves. If they are moved by piety and concern for the honour of the Blessed Virgin, why do they try to prevent youths and men receiving the sacraments at our hands? Why does Pelletier, their ringleader, inveigh in private and preach in public against the Sodality of the Blessed Virgin, which the Holy See has approved and which flourishes among us with so much fruit of souls? Why do these men refuse to admit to the Sorbonne any of our students who belong to the Sodality?" [1]

Mention of the Sodality is a good excuse to leave the tiresome old quarrel behind. This world-wide organization, which is the nearest approach the Jesuits have made to the monastic institution of third orders, began very simply at the Roman College in 1563.[2] A Belgian priest, Jean Leunis, invited a number of students to join him every evening in one of the lecture rooms to recite a few prayers and listen to a short selection from some spiritual book. Next year, those young men and boys to the number of seventy placed themselves under the special protection of the Mother of God and drew up their first set of rules, whereby they contracted to do their best at their studies, to hear Mass daily, to go to confession once a week and to Holy Communion at least once a month, to spend a quarter of an hour in meditation each evening after schools, on Sundays to chant Vespers together, and to visit hospitals to console the sick, or to engage in some equivalent practice of charity. Leunis was such a sweet, humble saint of a man that his plan prospered exceedingly. It appealed to the instinctive chivalry of youth, bringing them near to the never-failing magnetism of the Virgin Mother, which even sceptics such as Henry Adams and John Ruskin recognized to be the most humanizing influence the world has ever known.[3] Similar

---

[1] Prat, *Maldonat et l'Université de Paris,* pièces justificatives, xiii, 592–601. The letter, which is in Latin, is signed by the Provincial, Claude Matthieu.

[2] The idea was not entirely original, as various sodalities and confraternities for youths and men had been earlier established by Jesuits at Perugia, Valladolid, Ferrara, Florence, Padua and other places. These, however, were not strictly sodalities of the Blessed Virgin.

[3] "Not to dwell too long upon it," wrote Adams in his famous autobiography, "one admits that hers is the only Church. One would admit anything that she should require. If you only had the soul of a shrimp, you would crawl, like the Abbé Suger, to kiss her feet." His charming book, *Mont-Saint-Michel and Chartres,* published in 1913, was written entirely to glorify the Blessed Virgin.

sodalities were soon established in the various Italian colleges outside
Rome. Another Belgian, the indefatigable Father Francis Coster,
propagated them in the Netherlands and Germany, as did Coster's
friend, St. Peter Canisius, in Switzerland. The Jesuits of France,
Spain and Portugal quickly followed suit, until by the end of the
sixteenth century it might be said as a general rule that wherever
there were Jesuits there were Marian sodalities, even in Japan and
Peru. By the year 1576 they numbered thirty thousand members,
each a boy or man dedicated to his personal sanctification and the
service of his neighbour. Omitting canonized Jesuits for whom
the new organization constituted their first novitiate, we find St.
Francis de Sales, St. Peter Fourier, and the Capuchin, St. Fidelis
of Sigmaringen, prefects respectively of the sodalities at Clermont,
Pont-à-Mousson and Fribourg, before 1600. They were only the
first of a long list of sodalist saints and *beati*. One observer of the
time went so far as to say that the sodality at Clermont had become
the common seminary for the Carthusians, Capuchins and Minims.
At a later date, Pope Benedict XIV, who though a Jesuit product
was no great lover of Jesuits, declared that it was "almost incredible
what results had sprung from this pious and praiseworthy institution
for the faithful of every condition." And so said Pope Pius XII
only yesterday.[1]

Maldonatus resumed his lectures for a few months during the
summer of 1576 to prevent Clermont from being injured by the
lying stories of his adversaries that he had been officially silenced or
had lost his spell-binding power. Men came in such crowds to
hear him, nobles, magistrates, college professors, prelates, monks and
friars, even doctors of the Sorbonne, even Pelletier himself, that
no hall was big enough to contain them and he had to hold his
enormous classes in the open air. It is said bishops and other eminent

---

[1] In the middle of the seventeenth century some sodalists of Clermont, re-
named at the wish of its great benefactor, Louis XIV, the College of Louis le
Grand, established themselves under their Jesuit director, Père Bagot, in a house
of the rue St. Dominique as a little community devoted to work among the poor
of the city, very much in the style of the first Brothers of St. Vincent de Paul.
That was their situation and only ambition when the Jesuit missionary from
Tonking, Alexandre Rhodes, made his appearance among them and set their
hearts on fire with a new great purpose. They became under Père Bagot's
guidance the pioneers of the famous and heroic Société des Missions Étrangères.

personages who could not be present employed copyists to take down his words. One of the greatest Catholic Scriptural scholars of our age, the German, Karl Cornely, considered his *Commentaries on the Gospels* to be the best work of the kind ever published.[1] That good judge of learning and character, Michel de Montaigne, who had already written his *Essais,* delighted in the Father's company. Together they discussed the merits of the waters at Spa, where John had been for a course. A little later in Rome they discussed a more interesting topic. "Master Maldonatus asked me my views on Roman customs, especially in the matter of religion," wrote Montaigne in his *Journal de Voyage,* "and found that his opinion corresponded exactly with mine, namely that the common people of France were incomparably more devout than those here, but the rich and those about the Court somewhat less so. He further told me that when people, and especially Spaniards of whom there are a great number in his college, spoke of France being entirely lost to heresy, he maintained to their faces that there were more truly religious men in the single city of Paris than in the whole nation of Spain."[2] Plainly, Maldonatus was not a man who bore grudges. He died as he had always prayed he might do, suddenly, sitting in his chair at the Roman College, 5 January 1583, when he was just fifty years old.

[1] Maldonatus and his junior brother in religion, Cornelius à Lapide, share the distinction of having had their Scriptural works translated into English and published in many volumes by a group of Anglican and Scottish divines.

[2] The statement, even if a little exaggerated by its reporter, bears out a contention of Abbé Bremond in his *Histoire du Sentiment Religieux,* that the purest spirit of Christianity flourished in France even during the horrors of the Wars of Religion. He adduced as an instance of what he meant "the quiet University of Pont-à-Mousson, founded in 1572, one of the strongholds of the Jesuits. About 1580 several of its students destined to rank among the leaders of the coming spiritual renaissance received the Divine spark — Pierre Fourier; the future reformer of the Praemonstratensians, Servais de Lairuels; Didier de la Cour, the future reformer of S. Vanne and initiator of the more famous reform of S. Maur; Didier's collaborator, Claude François; and, somewhat later, Philippe Thibaut, who was to reform the Carmelites." A few pages further on Bremond dilates on the extraordinary spiritual influence which radiated from the Jesuit college at Avignon, started by Antonio Possevino in 1565, under the leadership of Père Péquet, director and inspirer of the Provençal apostles, César de Bus and the remarkable convert from Calvinism, Jean Baptiste Romillon, co-founder with Bérulle and Condren of the French Oratory (*Histoire,* English trans., ii, 1–18).

At this period, the Roman College, already in process of being transformed into the Pontifical Gregorian University, was climbing steadily to the summits of its renown. " 'Tis a marvellous thing," wrote the admiring Montaigne in his travel book, "what a place this College holds in Christendom. I think there never was such another among us. . . *C'est une pépinière de grands hommes en toute sorte de grandeur.*" Among the great ones were two who, though not yet at the height of their powers, cannot well be passed over, even in so brief and general a record as this. The Tuscan, Robert Francis Bellarmine, canonized and declared a Doctor of the Church in 1931, has already had 939 pages devoted to him in the English language, so he may forgive us if we confine ourselves here to a brief account of some fresh evidence about his mind and character that appeared since he went into the Church's Calendar. A nephew on his mother's side of Pope Marcellus II, he was born a "poor gentleman" at Montepulciano in 1542, and eighteen years later became a Jesuit, against the wishes of his father, who thought his prospects of promotion would be better among the Dominicans. Heaven gave Robert a happy disposition and an excellent intelligence served by a marvellous memory, but to balance those favours a delicate physique which suffered grievously from the Spartan regime of the Roman College. He went there in 1560 and spent three years of torment listening to lectures on Aristotle from a certain Father Peter Parra, not otherwise known to fame. Robert's chronic state of illness did not impair his natural cheerfulness and sturdy independence of judgment, if we may judge by the notes and comments which he made on his lectures. One set of notes concludes with the following sally which may find an echo in the hearts of other men groaning on lecture-room benches: "Lectures on the second book of the *De Anima* came to an end on Thursday evening, that being April 22nd in the year of our Lord 1563, on which day the professor fell into a fever, etc., thanks be to God." Alas, writes the genial modern editor of the notes, the professor got over his fever all too soon, for he was back in his chair again on 26 April, delivering himself morning and evening until the lectures on that one work of the Stagyrite attained a total of 128. They were very thorough in those days, and also refreshingly independent. The brightest luminary of the College, Francisco Toledo, the future cardinal, had already made a great reputation at Salamanca before he became a Jesuit, but that did not in the least abash Pedro Parra or his pupil, Robert Bellarmine. "Observe," wrote Robert in his notebook, "that Master Parra's exposition of Plato's opinion is excellent. This is Master Toledo's reply, but you can elude it and remain steadfast in the way of Master Parra by this consideration. Do not desert from your professor's opinion which is beautiful enough for you." He writes a long marginal note of his own to supplement what Parra had said on the fifty-second question, and concludes: "This addition will put Question Fifty-two to rest, and it will be enough for it and for you also!" When the famous problem of essence and existence came up for discussion, Father Parra mentioned the view that there is only a grammatical difference between the two concepts, one being signified by a noun and the other by a verb. Many metaphysicians consider that this is a deadly error, subversive to all sane thinking. In a spirit of pure mischief young Robert wrote in the margin: "This third opinion which comes from Durandus gives me much satisfaction and I shall gird myself to defend it. *Vale!*" One of his bugbears through life was Lorenzo Valla, that brilliant fifteenth-century humanist, hedonist, grammarian, enemy of Aristotle, and canon of St. John Lateran. Robert privately enters the lists against the man and, having castigated him for his pernicious views on the Donation of Constantine and other matters, adds the following flourish: "So we conclude this question by warning grammarians not to dare to contradict philosophers. Otherwise overthrow awaits them, as this our Lorenzo Valla has been overthrown and retires from the present disputation covered with shame." On one occasion, Parra, bending towards his audience, said, assuming their profound interest, "But you will ask me, Gentlemen, how *many* modes are there?" In his notebook weary Robert wrote, "How I burn with desire to know how many modes there are!" The Arab philosopher, Averroes, against whom St. Thomas had contended, still remained the chief cock-shy of young metaphysicians. Bellarmine chooses to call him "the black Arab" or "the black Doctor," but a certain note of affection creeps into his raillery. One of the black Arab's sins was to deny that the intellectual soul is the *form* of man.[1] Robert's private

---

[1] This and the monopsychism or theory of a universal soul from which it sprang were widely maintained by rationalizing humanists in the sixteenth

comment on the denial ran: "If the good Averroes, good, I say, not learned, wants to be a beast, why, let him, and the Lord bless him. But we don't!" At one juncture, Father Parra announced that he proposed to follow the order of Averroes in dealing with Aristotle's text rather than that of certain Greek and Latin writers. Robert wrote in his book: "For the nonce we, too, are disposed to become Arabs, though in other matters we certainly will not be Moors." Averroes had a theory that it is impossible for two material bodies to touch. Robert anticipated Dr. Johnson's famous refutation of Bishop Berkeley's [1] idealism with his comment: "Let a good sizable rock fall on the head of Averroes — then I ask him whether two bodies can touch." Robert's attitude to Padre Toledo, "cujus via non semper erat via Parrae," is at once reverent and singularly detached. He stood by his own professor resolutely, but he knew that at the end of his course he would have to face the "Doctorem Famosum," and so took a keen interest in his theories, which he studied in notes borrowed from one of the Doctor's disciples. Montaigne spoke of Toledo's "extraordinary ability," and Robert respected it so much that, while teaching boys the following year (1567) in Florence, he copied out for his own use all the great man's voluminous commentaries on the *Summa* of St. Thomas. But he would not have been Robert Bellarmine from Montepulciano had he swallowed his Toledo whole. One of his marginal jottings, written in 1563, takes this form: "So says he, . . . but let not his arguments frighten you, my Robert!" Opposite another specimen of Toledo's wisdom he writes: "To my mind there is much that is doubtful here, for this author certainly seems to confuse the object of physics with the object of metaphysics." [2] Robert was twenty-one when he thus

---

century. The fifth Council of the Lateran anathematized both as "damnatissimas haereses" in 1513. So Averroes was by no means a dead issue in Bellarmine's time. Nor is he to-day.

[1] "After we came out of the church, we stood talking for some time together of Bishop Berkeley's ingenious sophistry to prove the non-existence of matter. . . . I observed that, though we are satisfied his doctrine is not true, it is impossible to refute it. I never shall forget the alacrity with which Johnson answered, striking his foot with mighty force against a large stone, till he rebounded from it, 'I refute it *thus*' " (Boswell, *Life of Dr. Johnson,* chapter xvii).

[2] The Dutch Jesuit, Father Sebastian Tromp, Professor at the Gregorian

matched his wits with those of the famous Doctor, and at twenty-one, in the presence of many cardinal and other dignitaries, he defended the whole course of philosophy against all comers, the formidable Toledo included. Afterwards, he was publicly crowned with a circlet of bay-leaves in the ancient Greek way, and became officially, "Il Maestro Roberto."

The new Master went off then, broken in health, to teach boys for four years at Florence and Mondovì, during which time he succeeded in keeping discipline without ever once invoking the power of the rod. More than once he denounced the brutal floggings which in that tough age were regarded as a Divine ordinance for the curbing of insolent youth. His reputation for eloquence must have gone before him to Florence, as he received an invitation to preach in the Duomo a few weeks after his arrival. We need not attach too much importance to the Jesuit Rector's enthusiastic report that the Archbishop, who was present, regarded the sermon as the finest he had ever heard, but it certainly is extraordinary to discover so young a man, all untonsured and without a single lecture in theology to accredit him, in that famous pulpit. After that beginning, he never stopped preaching till he died. He preached in the market-places of towns, along country roads, in monastery chapels, in little village churches, in the cathedrals of great cities. Few men of his age can have poured out so many words, and such simple, kindly, encouraging, humorous words, which welled spontaneously out of the abundance of a heart deeply in love with God and man. He was the least stern of mentors in the pulpit, as he was the least frowning of saints in the intercourse of daily life. One who lived long by his side bore witness that "a sort of sanctified merriment" was the chief note of his conversation. Mgr. Pierre Camus, the Boswell of St. Francis de Sales, knew this other Saint also and described him as being "d'humeur forte gaye." That gay humour, under which lay the deeps of his private austerity and intimate union with God, flashed again and again, even when tired and full of headache he sat up of nights in Florence transcribing Toledo's interminable dis-

University and a scholar who wears his immense learning and splendid critical faculty with the easiest air, was the first to draw attention to the importance of those *juvenilia* of Bellarmine (*Archivum Historicum Societatis Jesu,* iv, 1935, 234-52).

quisitions. Toledo seemed to think that theology was essentially a speculative science. "Not in the opinion of this copyist, by name Robertus," runs the comment, and indeed never was there a more practical theologian than the same Robert. Against another argument which Toledo claimed to be final and conclusive, he writes: "In the small judgment of Robert transcribing these lines it concludes nothing whatever." On a subtle point regarding the Divine essence, Toledo adduces a proof which he thinks to be *convincentissima*. "Weigh these matters, Robert," soliloquizes Bellarmine, "for to-day, Sunday, August 13, 1564, at half past two, shortly before dinner, I consider Durandus to be absolutely right, especially because I do not like the solution and reason given by the most learned Toledo."

A couple of years' formal study of theology at Padua, interspersed as always in this man's life with numerous sermons, followed the period of schoolmastering, and then, in 1569, Robert was launched on the public career of preaching and teaching which made his name, even in his lifetime, known the world over. But it is not his seven years' achievement in Belgium, where he did more than anyone to scotch the incipient Jansenism of Baius and lectured on St. Thomas so brilliantly that Dr. Allen at Douay procured his notes to have them dictated to his English students,[1] nor is it his subsequent famous *Course of Controversies* in Rome, nor his archbishop's crozier or cardinal's hat, which endears him to us now, but rather the chivalry so marked in all his encounters with the Church's foes, and the almost extravagant charity of his heart. "The walls won't catch cold," he said, as he ordered the red serge hangings of his house to be taken down and made into garments for the poor. As Cardinal and subsequently Archbishop of Capua, his few little valuables were nearly always in pawn, his ring, his silver candlesticks, his inkstand, sometimes even the mattress off his bed. Never a poorer cardinal lived than this one, because he gave everything away. Some may think that that was very foolish of him, but there is folly and folly. His harassed majordomo, Guidotti, strongly disapproved. "Whenever my Lord Cardinal went out for a walk or visit," he wrote, "he scattered alms right and left as usual. Every morning a perfect

---

[1] The Library at Lambeth Palace contains four large manuscript volumes of those notes, obviously confiscated from Catholics in the days of persecution.

flood of begging letters were passed on to me, each with a note in his Lordship's hand, saying, 'Please give such and such a number of *scudi* to this person.'   One fine day I got a note bidding me give thirty *scudi* to buy out of the army a soldier who had deserted from his regiment.   I thought this was too good and wrote back to say that I had no money in hand, that if his Lordship went on at this rate we should soon be bankrupts, and that the soldier could go back to his regiment or find work.   If he were going to pay the fines of all such blackguards he would soon have his hands full.   His answer to me was that I should not be so terribly cautious and strict about the merits of a case, that if we gave freely and generously, God would save us from bankruptcy, and that if I had no money in the house I could pawn something and get it that way." [1]   It is easy to see why an old cardinal, referring to Robert's small stature, described him as "the biggest little man in the world."

Bellarmine's colleague and friend, Francisco Suarez, was born to titles and wealth under the shadow of the Alhambra, Granada, in 1548.   Poor little rich boy, he was actually put to the study of law at the University of Salamanca when he was barely thirteen years old.   Three years later, during the Lent of 1564, one of the most electrifying preachers of the sixteenth century, the Jesuit Juan Ramirez, made such a profound impression on the anything but saintly undergraduates that within four months two hundred of them had joined various religious orders.   Among those affected was the sixteen-year-old Suarez, who decided to join the preacher's order, one of no less than fifty similarly resolved and the only one of them all to be rejected.   To this day it is not quite certain why the Jesuits of Salamanca refused him.   Apparently, they did not consider him sufficiently intelligent. [2]   But Francis was a determined youth and walked the eighty miles to Valladolid to appeal in person from the Rector of Salamanca to the Provincial of Castile.   Once again he was examined and once again the four examiners declared him

---

[1] The references and texts are given in abundance in the English Life of St. Robert published in 1928.

[2] In the following century the French Jesuits rejected Claude Martin, the son of Venerable Mary of the Incarnation, on the same grounds, and he became famous among the Benedictines.   On the other hand, the Benedictines rejected no less a person than Bourdaloue.

unsuitable, but something in the demeanour of the frail, blue-eyed boy so much impressed the Provincial that he decided to accept him anyhow. While bowing obedient, if astonished, heads to this verdict, the grave fathers of Salamanca provided against future trouble by requiring their unwanted novice to sign a paper expressing his willingness to be a lay brother, dedicated for life to dusters and brooms, should his superiors consider him unfitted for studious avocations. Those cautious Castilian Jesuits required almost all their applicants except those already priests to sign a similar formula, and the following year we find the famous theologian, Gregory of Valencia, though he was then a bachelor of arts, admitted only on the same condition. So the provision was not specially designed to protect the Society of Jesus from Francis Suarez.[1] Francis signed without a moment's hesitation.

Like Bellarmine, but for a very different reason, Suarez was submitted to only the briefest of noviceships. After three happy months in the seclusion of Medina del Campo, he returned by order of superiors to the harder noviceship of the Salamanca schools that the question of his fitness for the intellectual life might be decided without delay. Even the kindly Provincial who had received him began to doubt and described him to Laynez as a "mediocre subjecto." A few months' test, and report confirmed his worst forebodings. Francis had virtue in abundance but no brains. Though he listened with desperate attention to the explanations of his professor, though he glued himself to his text-books in his room, though he was favoured with extensive special coaching, he could make neither head nor tail of the metaphysics for babes which the others assimilated so easily. Even that minor logic which has been described as neither an art nor a science but a dodge was to poor Suarez the darkest of mysteries, a labyrinth without a clue. Eventually, after much prayer and searching of heart, he decided that he was meant to be a menial in the house of God and applied for a lay brother's status. But the prefect of studies to whom he opened his soul, the saintly Martin Gutiérrez,[2] encouraged him to persevere a

[1] De Scorraille, *François Suarez* (Paris 1913), t. i, 47. This is a thoroughly scholarly and critical biography, based on original materials.

[2] St. Francis Borgia considered this man whom the Huguenots killed in 1573 easily the most valuable Jesuit in the Castile province.

little longer and to beseech the help of the Mother of God, the *Sedes Sapientiae.* Francis thereupon redoubled his efforts, at first as fruitlessly as before. But one day something happened to him in class. He who had been teased for his dumbness at disputations suddenly spoke, and to such effect that the lordly professor himself on his high chair, with distinctions burgeoning from him like buds in May, came very near to being silenced. Whatever the explanation, and those who witnessed the dramatic change regarded it as a plain miracle, Suarez had arrived. His sudden flowering may have been due to some unfathomed psychological cause, analogous to the phenomenon of those strange cactus plants which bloom gloriously in a night after an age of green quiescence. But the cactus flowers quickly perish, whereas Suarez's new-born ability developed at such a pace that within five years he was in a professor's chair himself, discoursing on his old enemy, metaphysics, with the subtlety of a Duns Scotus, who also is known to have had a retarded development. Indeed, in this line, Francis, the "mediocre subjecto," stands second to no giant of the past, however great. For more than forty years he continued to be the most famous professor in Spain and Portugal, years of ferocious intellectual activity, of endless battling with critics, of a search for truth that had the quality of a crusade. During half the period he held by royal command the first chair in the great University of Coimbra and became involved, as did Bellarmine, in the tremendous tug-of-war between the Dominicans and the Jesuits on the subject of efficacious grace. To write a book of theology in those breezy times, and Francis wrote a score of heavy tomes, was indeed to give a hostage to the real distinction, for every syllable of it was certain to be scrutinized by merciless eyes round the campfires of Bañes and Molina. Pope Paul V condemned one of Suarez's countless theories, but the same Pope afterwards conferred on him the title of "Doctor Eximius," and an excellent doctor he surely was. His *Defence of the Catholic and Apostolic Faith against the Errors of Anglicanism* had the distinction of being solemnly burned by order of King James I in front of St. Paul's Cathedral, and a good blaze it must have made, being more than half a million words long. Suarez's own joy of this majestic and temperate work of controversy was that it had, to his knowledge, brought about the conversion of a single Englishman, who devoted himself to the service of God among the Dominicans. His *Disputationes Metaphysicae,* two thousand octavo pages in double columns, is a Mount Everest among books, soaring sublimely into regions where the majority of mankind would feel very short of breath.[1] More within our humble compass, though perhaps not much more, would be the treatise, *De Legibus,* which placed Suarez in the front rank of the world's famous disputants *de jure belli et pacis.* In this colossal encyclopedia of law, to quote an eminent English authority, "he has put on record with a master's hand the existence of a necessary human society transcending the boundaries of states, the indispensableness of rules for that society, the insufficiency of reason to provide with demonstrative force all the rules required, and the right of human society to supply the deficiency by custom enforced as law." [2]

The bishop who authorized the book burnt by King James described Suarez as "the common master of his age and a second St. Augustine." Thomists *pur sang* would die at the stake before admitting such an encomium, because Francis, though a devout disciple of St. Thomas, had a mind of his own and took the liberty of differing from the Master now and again. It seems to be a crime for which he will never obtain forgiveness. He would not have minded, caring so little as he did what men thought of him. *"Todo por mejor"* he used to say on all occasions, everything is for the best. During his twenty years at Coimbra he rose invariably before dawn so as to spend ninety minutes in prayer before his first lecture at

[1] The modern historian of scholasticism, Maurice de Wulf, describes it as "undoubtedly one of the ablest, fullest and clearest repertories of scholastic metaphysics." The novelist, Canon Sheehan, who was an amateur of these profundities, wrote of the book: "The student who some day will take down Suarez's *Metaphysics* and give it to the world in strong, resonant, rhythmical English, will become one of the intellectual leaders of his generation" (*Under the Cedars and Stars,* p. 38). So far, and it is a good many years old now, no student has accepted the challenge.

[2] Westlake, *Collected Papers on International Law* (1914), p. 28. At the great Empire Exhibition held in Glasgow in 1938 and reported to have had fifteen million visitors, the League of Nations' Union set up a Pavilion of Peace in which it hung portraits of Grotius, Puffendorf, Westlake, and other illustrious jurists. Among them was the portrait of Francis Suarez, secured in the year 1605 by the stratagem of a wily publisher. He plotted with an artist to disguise himself as a waiter at a dinner to which Suarez, the shyest of men, had been somehow inveigled.

half-past six. He then wrote and studied for three hours, said Mass at eleven o'clock, and towards noon ate his first bite of the day. Mass was deferred so late that he might come to it completely undistracted. His daily division of labour worked out at six hours of prayer and ten of study. Frail in body, he suffered intensely from rheumatism, neuralgia, gastritis and recurrent lung trouble, but he never relaxed any of his customary austerities and to the end of his days fasted three times a week. That end came on 25 September 1617, and surely flights of angels must have winged him to his rest, for never did saint or theologian write about those glorious messengers of God more finely or lavishly than he.[1] His last words were: "I never could have believed that it is so sweet to die." Like most Spaniards, he had a touch of melancholy in his disposition, but this was offset by the exquisite courtesy which was native to his character, and by his profound confidence in God. "His books, his chair, his pen, to-day as yesterday and to-morrow as to-day, without ever seeking, without ever taking either relaxation or diversion or repose, *voilà toute sa vie.*"[2] Storming cities or finding Americas was much better fun than that and perhaps not more heroic. He felt the strain and boredom of it, too, for he wrote to a friend in Mexico from Coimbra: "As for myself, I am always turning my millstone, always grinding out these scholastic aridities. No doubt death will find me thus occupied, for I feel that it cannot be far off now. But if so doing I am doing the will of our Lord, I ask nothing more of this life and nothing better."

While Suarez slaved at his millstone and produced his sober objective masterpieces on every aspect of theology and the religious life, some of his Spanish brethren, with the individualism characteristic of their nation, created uneasiness in Rome by intemperate preaching, propaganda for mystical prayer, and even outright criti-

---

[1] His treatise, *De Angelis,* runs to 1099 pages, with double columns and 660 words to the page, or about 725,000 words in all. How was it possible to spin such an enormous web? First, because he so much loved the angels that he scarcely knew how to leave off writing about them, and secondly, because the great theologian is like the great artist or poet who distinguishes a hundred delicate shades in the glory of the setting sun for two or three visible to less schooled and sensitive eyes.

[2] De Scorraille, *François Suarez,* t. ii, p. 304.

cism of the Jesuit constitutions. These were a few of what Father Astrain calls the "tribulaciones de la Compañía en tiempo del Padre Mercurian." His seven volumes are full of such tribulations. Take, for instance, the case of the rather attractive young Savonarola, Padre Miguel Gobierno, who mounted the cathedral pulpit of Valencia in 1574 and, mentioning no names because no names were necessary, preached a terrific denunciation of the Viceroy of the Province, in the Viceroy's presence, for his constant encroachments on ecclesiastical immunities. Now, this man, the Marqués de Mondéjar, was dreaded far and wide for his volcanic temper. His feelings can, then, easily be imagined while he listened to the brave Miguel discoursing on the Parable of the Talents and all the time driving shaft after shaft, with the deadly precision of a *banderillero,* into his Excellency's skin. At first it seemed that he would be satisfied with nothing less than the head of Gobierno on a dish, but he did not enjoy Herod's facilities and had to be content with ordering the man's immediate banishment. At that point, the Archbishop of Valencia, Blessed Juan de Ribera, who was the chief sufferer from the Viceroy's aggressions, advised the Jesuits not to obey, whereupon the furious Mondéjar seized all the ecclesiastical property within his reach. Blessed Juan then put Valencia under an interdict and peace was not restored until King Philip took strong measures and poor Father Mercurian had humbled himself and his Society to the dust before His Majesty, the Archbishop and the Viceroy.

The trouble about prayer was caused by two of the saintliest Jesuits in Spain, Antonio Cordeses, the provincial of the Toledo brethren, and Baltasar Alvarez, who had been for six years the favourite director of St. Teresa. They both strove to introduce among their brethren, without much regard to individual capacity, a form of affective prayer not entirely in accordance with the methods taught by St. Ignatius nor very well adapted to the missionary and apostolic life which was half the *raison d'être* of the Society of Jesus. In November 1574, Father Mercurian addressed the following sober words to Cordeses: "Our Father Ignatius laid down complete self-denial as the foundation of the edifice of solid virtues which our Institute demands, because the mortification of our appetites and the abnegation of our own will and judgment are a principal part of the Christian life, . . . according to the words of Christ our Lord, *abneget semetipsum.* Your Reverence, I am sure, will see that prayer is not an end in itself with us nor our principal avocation, as in some other religious orders, but rather a universal instrument which we use with other exercises to enable us to acquire virtue and perform our ministries, according to the end set before us by the Society. We have seen in the past that many among us who made prayer their principal study did not thereby become more mortified and self-denying men, but rather were extremely difficult to handle when superiors desired to dispose of them for the greater glory of God in some way unacceptable to their private judgment." [1] Very likely, in writing that last sentence Father Mercurian had Antonio Araoz in mind, but Antonio Cordeses was a totally different type and promptly and completely capitulated. That ended the danger in the Toledo province, but there remained Castile, where some foolish Jesuit disciples of Baltasar Alvarez had begun to say that the method of prayer taught by St. Ignatius was merely a "perambulator for babies." Baltasar's biographer, the saintly Father Luis de la Puente,[2] himself well known for his decidedly mystical bent, describes the behaviour of those imprudent disciples in the following words: "They spoke of prayer in terms far away from the thought of their master; they said or did things which led those who were well instructed and zealous to form no good opinion of the method that they followed nor of the master to whom they attributed it. It was a still graver matter that certain ignorant or indiscreet persons appeared to despise the use of mental prayer by means of deductions, affections, petitions and colloquies, as taught by the Blessed Ignatius in his book of *Spiritual Exercises.* These, said they, are but perambulators, good enough for children until they have learned to walk, and that is all; for when they can walk they are allowed to go as they please. The Holy Ghost will not be tied to rules and methods of prayer; He bloweth where He wills and as He wills. Hence these imprudent persons, more presumptuous than experienced, wanted everyone to follow the road they took them-

---

[1] Astrain, *Historia de la Compañia de Jesús en la Asistencia de España,* ii, 188.

[2] Though greatly drawn to the Dominicans, this famous spiritual writer became a Jesuit in 1575 largely owing to the impression made on him as a student by the modesty and charity of Suarez.

selves, and turned them away from the path ordinarily used by the faithful." [1]

Now, though Father Alvarez was the last man to disdain *The Spiritual Exercises* — in fact, he was the first man to introduce the custom of annual retreats according to those *Exercises* among his brethren — he certainly strayed from the beaten track by his insistence that, given good-will, mystical contemplation might be attained by all. It is a piquant circumstance that when, years before, as a young priest of twenty-five, he was charged with the direction of St. Teresa at Avila, just as she was entering on the most extraordinary phase of her life, he had tried every means in his power, including very harsh treatment, to keep her to the discursive prayer advocated by St. Ignatius. But the more he tested her, the greater did her obedience and humility appear, until he, who was so truly humble himself, clearly recognized that her visions and revelations were of God. Then he became her devoted champion against a host of critics and, as she testifies in her Autobiography, "suffered all kinds of trouble" on her behalf. In 1567, while exercising the functions of rector and novice-master at Medina del Campo,[2] Baltasar was himself raised to the prayer of quiet and union about which he had been so suspicious in his dealings with Teresa. He could not have chosen a worse period for his initiation. Ever since the Middle Ages, Spain had been troubled by heterodox mystical doctrines derived from Islam and associated with Averroism. In the sixteenth century these had developed into the heresy of the Alumbrados, or the Enlightened Ones, who taught that the human soul can reach to the contemplation of the essence of God in this life, that for those so privileged sin became impossible and the indulgence of carnal desires a matter of indifference, that external worship and the reception of the sacraments are superfluous, that the highest perfection attainable by the Christian consists in the elimination of all activity, the loss of individuality and complete absorption in God, and, in particular, that prayer so understood is the only duty, a duty dispensing from obedience to superiors or any other possible hindrance. Doctrines

[1] *The Life of Father Balthasar Alvarez*, c, xli.

[2] Among the pupils of the Jesuit college at Medina del Campo from his fifteenth to his nineteenth year (1557–61) was Juan de Yepes, now famous as the great Carmelite Saint and Doctor, John of the Cross.

so anarchical and destructive of morality no less than religion almost justify the rigours of the Spanish Inquisition. Unfortunately, however, the Inquisitors and their great backer, Melchior Cano, tended to smell Illuminism in any writing or teaching which went beyond the simplest exposition of the Ten Commandments. In spite of frequently renewed Papal approbation, Cano continued to the end of his stormy life to accuse St. Ignatius and the early Jesuits of the heresy. Melchior's own only spiritual work in Spanish was a little treatise against the Seven Deadly Sins. He entertained the profoundest suspicion of ascetical books in the vernacular. If people wanted to write on spiritual subjects let them stick to Latin, for so they would be less likely to do mischief. *The Index of Forbidden Books* issued by the Inquisition in 1559 was largely of Melchior's inspiration. Besides the works of St. Francis Borgia and the Catechism of Archbishop Carranza, to which allusion was made in an earlier chapter, it contained also three Spanish treatises of Cano's fellow Dominican, the great ascetical writer and foremost opponent of Illuminism, Luis of Granada, and one book of Blessed John of Avila. The Inquisition also kept a wary eye on Teresa of Jesus, but had to confine itself to threats as she was wise enough to publish nothing in her lifetime. Another nun asked the famous Augustinian, Luis de León, to make her a Spanish version of the Canticle of Canticles, and when that charming man obliged he paid for his kindness with five years of imprisonment. This was what the excellent historian of Christian spirituality, M. Pourrat, calls "the rout of the mystics." [1]

In 1574, the very time when the disciples of Baltasar Alvarez were ventilating their provocative exaggerations of his teaching on prayer, the Inquisition issued another edict against the Alumbrados. No wonder, then, that Baltasar's Jesuit superiors became alarmed. He was at the time rector of the college in Salamanca, and the Provincial of Castile, that good Juan Suarez who had been captured by the Huguenots in 1573, required him to compose a little treatise on prayer "in conformity with the truth and the spirit of the Church." He complied immediately, writing what such a good judge as M. Pourrat considered to be "one of the best refutations of the false Spanish mysticism of the time." His own mysticism

---

[1] *Christian Spirituality* (English trans.), iii, 1927, 108–13.

was absolutely orthodox, but he erred in thinking that the prayer of quiet might be attained by all and in endeavouring to foster it among his young Jesuits without sufficient regard for the old and sure ways indicated in *The Spiritual Exercises*. The climax of this little internal controversy came in 1577, when Father Alvarez was roundly condemned, and forbidden either to practise or to preach his mystical doctrine, by the well-meaning but brusque and insensitive visitor to the Castile province, Diego Avellaneda. Among many orders received by poor Baltasar was one that "he must not waste his time on Carmelite nuns"! Father Mercurian, who had nothing to go by except the reports of local superiors with the Inquisition very heavy on their minds, endorsed all Avellaneda's proceedings, Father Alvarez bowed his humble misunderstood head to the storm, and thus were the Jesuit mystics routed until in a more serene atmosphere at the century's end Father Claude Aquaviva, the greatest General the order ever had except St. Ignatius, restored their right-of-way by a wise and balanced letter on prayer addressed to all his sons.[1]

---

[1] Astrain, *Historia,* iii, 181–96; Pourrat, *Christian Spirituality,* iii, 113–18; *Epistolae Praepositorum Generalium ad Patres et Fratres Societatis Jesu* (Ghent 1847), i, 250–2. (The gist of Aquaviva's ordinance, dated 8 May 1599, is contained in the following sentences: "Quod si modus orationis attendatur vel materia, qui se jam saepius piis illis commentationibus exercuerunt, longoque usu facilitatem in orando sunt assecuti, illis nec certum argumentum nec ratio singularis videtur esse praescribenda. Spiritus enim Domini, qui laxissimis habenis ferri solet, per innumerabiles animorum illustrandorum et sibi arctissime devinciendorum vias, quasi freno, sic finibus denotatis non est coercendus: et nos, ut non minus pie quam prudenter bonae memoriae P. Natalis in hunc sensum aliquando pronuntiavit, divino Doctori par est quidem obsecundare, sed non licet antevertere. Quare ut absurdum foret, et prudentiae legibus alienum, Societatis nostrae hominibus penetranda naturae divinae mysteria, infinita per omnem modum Dei supremi attributa pervestiganda, . . . peculiari penso dictare; ita foret absurdissimum, illis commentandis, quasi nostro repugnantibus Instituto, cuiquam interdicere." At this point the General refers to the danger of illusion in the higher forms of prayer, and continues: "Neque tamen ea re veritati reluctandum est, aut testatissimae Sanctorum Patrum experientiae refragandum, et habenda despicatui contemplatio, vel ab ea Nostri prohibendi, cum illud, plurimorum Patrum sententia suffragioque perspectum sit et exploratum, veram perfectamque contemplationem potentius et efficacius altera qualibet piarum meditationum methodo, superbientes hominum animos frangere atque contundere, pigritantes ad obeunda Superiorum mandata vehemen-

The censure of Father Alvarez's method of prayer, dictated by a temporary emergency, was so far from implying any censure on the man himself that shortly afterwards Father Mercurian appointed him provincial of Toledo. If we may accept the evidence of his novice, Luis de la Puente, he must have made an ideal superior: "If his subjects wished to speak to him, they were not obliged to wait his convenience or to seek a favourable opportunity. Whenever they presented themselves, they were welcome. His kind manner convinced them of it, and they had as much love as veneration for him. If to try them, he sometimes assumed a severe countenance, he quickly returned to his usual sweetness. His friendship for them was accompanied by sincere esteem, which showed itself in his manner of treating them in public, and especially before seculars. He always spoke well of them in their absence. Continually occupied about them, he watched them carefully, and if anyone appeared sad he told him that a servant of God should always be joyous: and he more easily forgave some excess of joy than the least mark of sadness. The faults of those who sinned through ignorance or weakness only excited his compassion. Instead of severely reproving them, he encouraged them by his kindness to repair their fault and avoid a relapse. Through his pity for these imperfect souls, he entreated the Provincial to send them to him in preference to others, that he might exercise his sweet charity towards them; and God to reward him gave him a wonderful facility in changing them."

Even more revealing are the rules which Father Baltasar drew up for his own guidance in dealing with his subjects. If compared with those formulated by Father Nadal,[1] it will be seen at once that the same spirit pervades both lists because it is the only genuine and authentic spirit of the Society of Jesus: "The office of a superior is to serve souls for whom Jesus Christ has given all His blood; to serve them, I mean, as a servant serves his master, for the love of God. . . To act thus, he need only consider that God, in making him superior, did not intend to make him a lord over his brethren. He has placed them on his head instead of under his feet, and consequently they have a right to his services. This is, in fact, what faith teaches:

---

tius incitare, et languentes ad salutem animorum procurandam ardentius inflammare.")

[1] See above, pp. 147-9.

'I am not come to be ministered unto but to minister,' said our Divine Master. A superior should be affable and accessible so that his subjects may be convinced that their importunity is not troublesome to him, and that they may have recourse to him with as much confidence as consolation. Why should he not sometimes tell them that he is glad to see them come to him, and that the avowal of their weaknesses will never diminish his love and esteem for them? This point is of great importance for superiors, preachers and confessors, for how many thousands of souls perish from not daring to make known their interior sins! . . . If he desires to gain the hearts of all, which is indispensable for the good he wishes to do, his disciples must see that he loves them and is pleased to be with them; but let him beware of showing particular friendships, for this would be a rock on which his vessel would break. . . He must establish a very exact discipline, but instead of commanding imperiously, he should set about it humbly and meekly, saying, for instance: 'Do you not think that such a thing is an abuse, or that such a manner of acting has its inconveniences?' It is quite certain that this method is more persuasive, and conducts to our end more easily. . . In keeping up obedience, he must show the feelings of a father, that his sweetness and meekness may lighten the yoke of his firmness. Nevertheless, there are occasions when it is better to yield and give way than to insist. Whenever the superior cannot subdue a rebellious will without risk to the general peace, charity requires that he should overlook the obstinacy of the culprit, acting towards him in a spirit of love, bearing with him as God bears with him, until this good Master visits him by His grace. . . Let him never, in any case, allow himself to reprove the guilty when he feels irritated. . . Let him practice benignity and mercy, for his own weakness obliges him to it, and it is written that we shall be treated as we have treated others." [1]

[1] De la Puente, *The Life of Father Balthasar Alvarez*, xxiii. In a long letter, *De felici Progressu Societatis,* which Claude Aquaviva addressed to the superiors of the whole order shortly after his election as general in 1581, we find exactly the same sentiments: "Hoc itaque primum cupio insculpi cordibus nostris, familiam hanc universam, tam Deo caram, impositam esse super humeros et capita nostrum omnium, quibus haec pascendi cura credita est. . . Neque enim, qui in Societate praesunt, eo contenti esse debent, ut obediat subjectus, et hoc aut illud quod ipsi injungitur qualicumque modo praestet. Sed illud max-

There is one other ascetical writer whom we must briefly salute before coming to an end, Father Alphonsus Rodriguez, author of *The Practice of Christian and Religious Perfection*. That book needs no advertising. It became and has remained an institution among Catholics throughout the world almost since it was first published more than three centuries ago. It speaks to-day in at least twenty languages, including Russian, Arabic and Chinese. There have been forty-two different reissues of the Spanish original, and in France it was so much appreciated that even the Jansenists felt it necessary to sponsor a translation, which appeared in 1673, with a dedication to Mgr. de Gondren, Archbishop of Sens, a patron of Port Royal and as determined a foe of the Jesuits as ever existed. The first Englishman to quarry in the Spanish mine was Anthony Hoskins of Herefordshire, whose *Abridgement of Christian Perfection* appeared at St. Omer in 1612, three years after the publication of the original at Seville. The complete Rodriguez in three volumes did not find an English dress until just before the "Glorious Revolution," when Father Francis Sanders, a Jesuit and later confessor to James II in his exile at Saint-Germain-en-Laye, had it printed in London. Though only a translation of a translation,[1] this work enjoyed widespread popularity in Britain, Ireland and America until well on

---

ime spectari oportet ut id magna cum perfectione in Christo exsequatur: ad quod praecipue conducet si subditi vere intelligant se a Superioribus diligi, qui suis se filiis patres, matres, nutrices, medicos, denique omnia omnibus pro cujusque necessitate, exhibeant necesse est." And much more to the same effect. This letter would open the eyes of any who think that the Society of Jesus is, or ever has been, governed autocratically on a sort of military pattern.

[1] Father Sanders availed himself of the labours of Abbé Régnier-Desmarais, secretary in his time of the French Academy, who in 1675 and the following years had reintroduced the complete Rodriguez to his fellow-countrymen, partly, it would seem, as a counterblast to the Jansenist effort of 1673. Owing to his position as an Academician and author of an official French grammar, the good Abbé was somewhat disconcerted by the homely style of Rodriguez, as he explains in his preface: "Le style de l'original que j'ay traduit, estant, générale- ment parlant, un style negligé et familier, qui descend mesme quelquefois jusques dans le style bas; et cela ne s'accommodant gueres avec le goust de notre Langue; je me trouvois embarasé entre ce que je devois à l'un et à l'autre. . ." He was a conscientious translator and found a means of preserving the familiar semi-colloquial tone of Rodriguez without detriment to the dignity of the French language.

into the nineteenth century, being reprinted frequently at such diverse places as Kilkenny, Philadelphia, Glasgow, Dublin, New York, Manchester and London. In the judgment of M. Pourrat, "few works have had such a deep and wide influence." [1] Despite his reserved attitude to mystical prayer, for which he has been criticized but which was due to the circumstances of his time and country, Rodriguez remains to this day the favourite spiritual director of thousands both inside and outside monastery and convent walls. He aimed his book primarily at Jesuits — *dirigido á los Religiosos de la Compañía,* the title runs — but the Catholic world at large took it for its own. In an Apostolic Letter addressed by Pope Pius XI to the Superiors-General of all religious orders and congregations of men on 19 March 1924, his Holiness commended by name three authors as of particular value for the spiritual training of their subjects, St. Bernard, St. Bonaventure and Alphonsus Rodriguez, whose works, he added, "so far from having lost their virtue and power through the lapse of time seem to-day more effective than ever." [2]

But though his book is so well known, the author himself remains to most people a very dim figure, literally the shade of a great name. Even in Spain itself he has often enough been confused with his contemporary, St. Alphonsus Rodriguez, a Jesuit lay brother canonized by Pope Leo XIII in 1888. The uncanonized Alphonsus has himself to blame for the mistake, as he was the most retiring of men and did everything in his power to keep his history a beautiful blank. He was born, the son of a doctor in modest circumstances, at Valladolid in 1538, and became a Jesuit nineteen years later, without being, as he confessed to Nadal, in the least thrilled by the step — *sin ningunas consolaciones.* Some other concrete details of his past which he admitted to the same questioner in 1562 were that he had once found a half-crown (*medio real*) and kept it, though he knew the owner; that he used to pray a good deal as a boy but knew nothing of mental prayer; that he seldom went to the sacraments; that he liked study but had little ability for it, *especialmente para metaphisicas;* and that he was a bachelor of arts. On being asked by Nadal how he felt about remaining a Jesuit, whether he was prepared for perfect obedience, and what inclinations he had in the

[1] *Christian Spirituality,* iii, 213.
[2] *Acta Apostolicae Sedis,* xvi (Rome 1924), 142.

matter of mortification and trial, the young Alonso answered "I want to persevere until death in the Society, to obey, with the grace of God, in all things, however hard and difficult, and to keep the rules very perfectly. I am very anxious to be submitted afresh, as if I had but recently entered the Society, to all the mortifications and tests provided for in the constitutions. I would greatly like superiors to chasten and humiliate me very much, as I am in sad need of such treatment, being extremely immortified. I particularly desire to receive instructions about prayer, in the practice of which I am very ignorant and slack." Finally, Nadal wished to know whether, *supuesta la indiferencia,* Alonso had any preferences with regard to the field of his labours, India, Germany, or elsewhere. To this question he replied as follows: "I have an inclination to go wherever I might give God our Lord better service. I would gladly go to the ends of the earth (*al cabo del mondo*) for that. My ambition, with the divine favour, is to have the parts and qualities necessary for undertaking great and difficult enterprises, and to be appointed to such by obedience. But at present I lack any sort of equipment and have small hope of ever acquiring it by my own efforts." [1]

Such was Alphonsus Rodriguez's self-portrait at the age of twenty-four. Eighteen months later, the man who thought himself so undisciplined and ignorant of the ways of God was appointed by Laynez, on the advice of Nadal, master of novices in Salamanca. At twenty-eight, we find him rector and professor of moral theology at the College of Monterrey, with eight hundred small boys and grown men looking to him for their ABC and their lectures on the *Secunda Secundae* respectively. [2] Practically nothing is known of his activities during those years, or during the six which followed in his native Valladolid, or during the thirty afterwards in the difficult province of Andalusia, where he was sent in 1585 to undo the harm wrought among the young Jesuits by a group of harsh and unsympathetic superiors. Those rigorists, Father Mercurian complained,

[1] M.H., *Epistolae P. Hieronymi Nadal,* ii, 532-3.
[2] Astrain says that at Monterrey every child in the town who could stand on his feet (*tenerse en pié*) was packed off by his relieved mother to the Jesuit school. The teaching of those abecedarians was usually done by lay brothers or bigger boys, except the catechism which the priests on the staff kept in their own hands. Monterrey was a seminary as well as a primary and secondary school.

lacked the "suavidad y amor paternal" which ought to prevail in the Society of Jesus, and Alphonsus Rodriguez was uprooted from his own province of Castile to supply for their deficiencies. He began then a sort of Thirty Years' War of exhortations on behalf of the true spirit of St. Ignatius, out of which he built without sound of hammer or axe his *Ejercicio de Perfección y Virtudes Cristianas.* Between the lines of that book, with its great insistence on union and fraternal charity, we can read something of the stresses and strains to which the Society of Jesus in Spain was subjected in its author's day by a small clique of men inheriting the disruptive spirit of Antonio Araoz.[1] We can read, too, some traits of the author's character, his sense of humour, his geniality even when dealing with the most solemn topics, his generous encouraging spirit, his very obvious love of his fellow-men, his whole-hearted devotion to the order which he joined without any consolation. He had his faults as both man and author. He was so painfully shy that he could only with the greatest difficulty be induced to speak to strangers, unless they happened to be Jesuits. Otherwise Alonso used to hide in his room.[2] As a writer, he does not show himself very critical of his sources and he seems to have borrowed a good many of his stories, without much regard for their authenticity or even likelihood from the unpublished *platicas* or "talks" of his predecessor as novice-master, Father Gil González Dávila, the provincial of Andalusia. Like nearly everybody else in his wonder-loving age, he gave ready credence to far-fetched miraculous tales from such collections as *The Spiritual Meadow* and *The Golden Legend* and used them freely to confirm his teaching. Though he is an excellent *raconteur,* full of vivacity and colour, a modern reader might well wish some of his tall stories removed, as that of the poor monk who was beaten black and blue by angels, to Alonso's apparent satisfaction, because he had dared to argue with God in exactly the same way as the Psalmist does and as God commended Job for doing. But these are small defects compared with the general attractiveness of his "encyclopedia of asceticism," which caused the Cardinal Archbishop of Valladolid to describe it as a "bewitching book" at the

[1] This sad chapter of Jesuit history is dealt with at great length by Astrain in his second and third volumes.

[2] Astrain, *Historia,* iv, 745–6.

centenary commemoration of Rodriguez's death in 1917. One fancies that Alonso himself would have preferred Abbot Chapman's little tribute: "For Ascetics, I like old Rodriguez — he is very sound."[1] With that Benedictine feather in his cap, we may leave him to his age-old task of initiating ever so amiably new generations into the secrets of Christian perfection.

The story of his namesake, St. Alphonsus Rodriguez, is soon told. He was born at Segovia in 1531. Forty years later, after the death of his mother, wife and children, he wound up his business affairs and entered the Society of Jesus as a lay brother at Valencia. Then he was sent to Palma in Majorca, where he spent the rest of his long life, most of the time minding the college door. He had no history beyond that, even among his brethren, if we except his influence on the future apostle of the negro slaves, St. Peter Claver. In all the huge archives of the Spanish Jesuits of the period, Father Astrain was able to find only two tiny references to this man, their greatest glory, one saying that he was "very exemplary" and the other calling him a "very good religious." His life was the apotheosis of hiddenness, a hiddenness perfumed with all the virtues taught by the other Alphonsus, but which enclosed, too, the highest mystical graces, making the humble, simple-hearted old doorkeeper the unknown peer of St. John of the Cross.[2]

This book has already strayed a little beyond the limits set for it, which was the year 1579, a period in the history of Jesuit expansion

---

[1] *The Spiritual Letters of Dom John Chapman* (London 1935), p. 234.

[2] St. Alphonsus died at his post in 1617, aged eighty-six. In the years 1885-7, immediately preceding his canonization, three little volumes of spiritual autobiography, written by him at the command of his superiors, were published for the first time. A marvellous light, the very splendour of Heaven itself, streams from their simple, unstudied pages, for the old man, who believed himself to be the last and least of men, communed face to face with Jesus and Mary in his poor cell, the cell that didn't even boast a chair. He penned his account of these things seated on the plank that served him for a bed. As another, and now very famous Jesuit, Gerard Manley Hopkins, wrote:

> "God (that hews mountain and continent,
> Earth, all, out; who, with trickling increment,
> Veins violets and tall trees makes more and more)
> Could crowd career with conquest while there went
> Those years and years by of world without event
> That in Majorca Alfonso watched the door."

bristling with toothing-stones. One can see them very plainly in the following lines of the great enigmatic Robert Persons addressed from Rome on 19 March 1579 to his fellow-Jesuit and countryman, William Good, then serving the Pope in Sweden:[1] "Reverend and loving father, . . . Because never as yet after your departure I could have leasure to wryte to you at large, I mean to cumber you with this long Letter. . . First therefore touching our Society, God be thanked, it proceedeth every day more and more in spirit and charity one towards another, and in greate fervour of desire to advance the honour of God, and to suffer for the same. . . Missions since your departure hath byn dyvers of importance, namely two or three to the East Indies, wherehence, and especially from Japonia, we have had letters of great consolation. And amongst these Missions was one Englishman, that is Thomas Stevens, a young man of great fervour and a reasonable talent, whom I would have diverted towards a certayne North India,[2] but the lett you shall know after. To the

[1] As mentioned already, William Good, Fellow of Corpus Christi College, Oxford, and Canon of Wells, became a Jesuit at Tournai in 1562. After his return from Ireland in 1570, Good was stationed at Louvain, and there reconciled Robert Persons, Fellow and Bursar of Balliol College, Oxford, to the Church, whereupon the convert abandoned his medical studies at Padua and went to Rome to enter the Society of Jesus. In 1577 Father Good went with the Jesuit secretary, Antonio Possevino, on a Papal mission to Sweden and Poland.

[2] Meaning England. Thomas Stevens, a Jesuit worth a separate book to himself, was a Dorset man and educated at Winchester. He entered the order in Rome in 1575 at the age of twenty-six, and had Henry Garnet, the Gunpowder Plot martyr, and Robert Persons as companions at the Roman College. Fired by reading the letters of St. Francis Xavier, he begged to be sent to India and sailed from Lisbon with a fleet of five ships on 4 April 1579. After landing at Goa, the first Englishman of any quality to set foot on Indian soil, he wrote an account of the eventful voyage to his father, a prominent London merchant, which caused a great stir in commercial circles and was printed by both Hakluyt and Purchas. Off Madeira a daring English cruiser hove in sight and dogged them all the way to the Canary Islands. "The English ship was very fair," wrote Thomas, his sympathies divided between his religion and his country, "which I was sorry to see so ill occupied." For forty years, until his death in 1619, this charming and devoted man laboured among his Hindu flock in Goa or on Salsette Island. While at Goa he rendered signal service to many of his Protestant fellow-countrymen who had come out after him and fallen foul of the Portuguese authorities. "Not only was he the first Englishman to visit India, but he was the first and only Englishman to write a great poem in an Indian language, . . . the *Christian Purana,* an epic in the Konkani dialect of Marathi spoken by his flock. . . Its

West Indyes also there hath byn three or foure Missions, and that in good multitude, for that there came therehence from two divers countryes two Fathers of ours, demaunding with great instance both of the Pope and of our Generall fresh aydes, for that there was of late divers greate Countryes newly descryed, ready to receve the Gospell. . . Also there hath byn a Mission into Mesopotamia and Syria, and a part of that is diverted to Constantinople, God prosper them. The late Mission to Cracovia into Polonia at the King's earnest request, you have heard of I thinke, and F. Stephanus Hungarus, who commendeth himselfe to you, expecteth here to depart every day . . . to found a Colledg presently in Transilvania. . . In the mean space he hath not byn idle here, for he hath labored with the Pope for the erection of a Seminary for his Nation. . . The like Seminary is said to be concluded for the Flemings, and this good Gregory's purse is extended to every nation. But now you will say, here are Missions for all Contryes but only for England which seemeth to be abandoned above all others. To this I answere, that you perhaps are much in falt of this, who had not solicited the cause when you were heere and had more help than I now have, or can looke for. But yet I tell you, that had not the enimy cast in an impediment, . . . you had heard good newes perhapps before this tyme, and we myght have chanced to have pulled you out of your furres in Suetia. . . Now it is enough for Father Darbishire and me if we can keep our Englishe men of the Company together, and from other Missions, which also we shall not be able to do long, for albeit our Superiours do not gladly grant any Englishe man to any

---

subject is nothing less than a versified account of the whole Bible story. . . The poetry of this remarkable work, comprising ninety-five cantos and eleven thousand *slokas* or couplets, is really of a high order, and the author must have known Sanskrit to write as he did. . . Father Stevens was only indirectly connected with British enterprise in India. But his famous letter largely influenced the merchants of London in their decision to send a band of picked adventurers to report upon the commercial possibilities of the East Indies" (Rawlinson, *British Beginnings in Western India,* Oxford, the Clarendon Press, 1920, pp. 23-7. This is an admirably impartial, learned and delightfully written book. Father Stevens is passed over in stony silence by that useful monument of modern materialism, the fourteenth edition of the *Encyclopedia Britannica,* which finds room to celebrate the feats of an American cyclist called Thomas Stevens. However, he is given his due in the *Dictionary of National Biography*).

other Mission, for desire they have to reserve them for England, yet the multitude of us dayly encreasing (for there hath entered at Rome 8 or 9 this yeare, besides divers in other places) and also many Englishe men dayly for the greate zeale and desire they have to suffer somewhat for Christ, demanding instantly underhand and privily . . . to be sent in other Missions, seeing England is shutt from them." [1]

England, as everybody knows, did not remain shut much longer, nor did China, into which sealed Empire Father Matteo Ricci was just then preparing at Goa to make his famous incursion. To the college at Goa in that same *annus mirabilis* of Jesuit history, 1579, came Abdullah Khan, envoy of the mightiest monarch of the East, Akbar the Great Mogul, with a firman from his master courteously inviting some of the fathers to visit him at his court in marvellous Fatehpur Sikri for some discussions on religion. The two chosen amid great excitement for the mission were the warm-hearted, Mohammed-hating Spaniard, Antonio Monserrate, who twenty years before had enjoyed himself teaching small boys at Lisbon, and Rudolfo Aquaviva, son of the Duke of Atri in the Kingdom of Naples. Antonio has left an attractive pen-picture of Rudolfo. "Rudolfus," he wrote, "was of a very sweet disposition and so simple that he judged everyone after his own heart. . . He was perpetually conscious of God and seemed to dwell in his presence. . . Lest he should become weary, he used when journeying to sing gently in a low voice small prayers, or ejaculations, as we say. He was entirely forgetful of himself and slept very often whole nights with his clothes on, just as when at work, and that either sitting in his chair, or if he lay down overcome by fatigue, in a position calculated to torture his body and inflict pain rather than favour rest. He wore a hair-shirt, disciplined himself, and very frequently fasted. . . He had given

[1] The remainder of this huge letter is concerned with the troubles which had broken out at the English College, Rome, owing to the favouritism shown by its first Rector, the Welshman, Dr. Maurice Clenock, to the few students from the Principality as against the many English students. This famous contention, in which some of the future beatified martyrs played a lively part, was the "Impediment" referred to by Persons. His fine report to Father Good with its vigorous English and independent orthography has been published twice by the Catholic Record Society, in ii (1906) and xxxix (1942), the latter carefully edited by Father Leo Hicks, S.J.

himself into the keeping of the Virgin Mother of God, and used to take pleasure in singing softly in her praise little extempore songs which he improvised. It delighted him to wear old wornout clothes and shoes. His mind was so continuously fixed on God that he often forgot what he was about, and could not remember where he had left his hat, his spectacles, his books, and the like. . . He was a marvellously patient man." [1]   Aquaviva and Monserrate, Ricci and his companion Ruggieri, Persons and Campion, their names beckon to enchanted Sikri, to Peking under the last of the Ming Emperors, and to Shakespeare's London. Then, too, there was the tremendous epic of the faith in Japan about to unfold in all its suffering and grandeur. It is a sad point at which to end a book, on the threshold of great events, but an end has to be made somewhere.

[1] From Monserrate's *Commentary on His Journey to the Court of Akbar,* translated by J. S. Hoyland (Oxford 1922), pp. 192-3.

THE TROUBLES OF A HISTORIAN

FIVE years after the death of Laynez, when his successor, Borgia, was General, there entered the Society of Jesus a young Italian named Francis Sacchini. He came from Perugia, a place that has always known its own mind. After many years teaching the classics in Rome, Francis, then an established scholar, was appointed to continue the official history of his order at which the Florentine, Nicholas Orlandini, had been working when death took the pen from his fingers. Nearly thirty years earlier, on 25 July 1577, Father Simon Rodriguez, one of the first six companions of St. Ignatius and the founder of the Portuguese Jesuits, signed his name with the shaky hand of old age to a little record of early experience, exacted by his superiors, which he entitled, *The Origin and Progress of the Society of Jesus*. Simon had had a chequered career in the same Society, but of this he said nothing in his book, which exhales only the sweetness and the freshness of youthful memories. The missing story was supplied by Orlandini in his manuscript from what might be called the Roman point of view,[1] and that story Sacchini published at Antwerp in 1614. But there was also a Portuguese point of view and it made itself felt with no little eloquence when the lordly tome came into circulation. Whatever his faults, Simon Rodriguez was a lovable character, the idol of the Portuguese Court and the hero of hundreds of Jesuits who were given some reason to regret the good days when Plancus was consul on the arrival out of Spain of two stern martinets to replace him and reform the republic. According to Portuguese tradition those two men, Diego Miron and Miguel Torres, bore no affection to their new country, but found a native collaborator in the person of aristocratic Father Luis Gonçalves da Câmara, whom Rodriguez had reduced for his severity to the brethren from being rector of the grand college in Coimbra to charge of the college kitchen. Father Luis, a

---

[1] It is told in English from the same point of view in *The Origin of the Jesuits* (1940), pp. 242–51.

scion of the high Portuguese nobility, is also alleged to have been somewhat jealous that a mere commoner like Father Simon should enjoy so much popularity with the great ones of the land.   It is not at all impossible.   Simon's defenders, who include all Portuguese Jesuits to-day,[1] maintain that his disgrace at Rome was principally due to the tendentious reports of those three men and to their habit of making him the scapegoat for everything that went wrong in their own management of the province.[2]

That was the background of a little-known episode of Jesuit history which deserves remembrance here because it concerned the lives of two of the patriarchs, and is besides a good example of the integrity of a historian on whom subsequent writers about the Jesuits have had to depend for much of their information.   Sacchini defended his publication of Orlandini's paragraphs on Rodriguez in a long letter to a Portuguese father, dated 6 March 1616.   "God knows, dear Father," he begins, "how sorry I am that what is narrated in the *History* about Father Simon should have so deeply distressed the brethren in Portugal.   My conscience is my comfort, for I can say in all sincerity that I have a special affection for a Province that has deserved so well of our whole Society, giving it so many eminent sons and bringing it so much credit in every part of the world.   So far was I from desiring in any way to detract from the good name of your Province, that I rather strove to the best of my ability to praise and commend it.   Many were the prayers which I made to God while engaged on that narrative, and I certainly took all the pains in my power to tell the story, as far as conscience permitted, without offence to a single soul.   As your Reverence has now very kindly informed me of the distress of the fathers, I shall tell you here what I think may bring them consolation."   It may very much be doubted whether it did, for it consisted of three shattering replies to the fathers' threefold complaint.

The first complaint was that the narrative spoke falsely, to which

---

[1] And notably their very learned and impartial historian, Father Francisco Rodrigues, whose third fine volume appeared in 1939.

[2] The Portuguese case was very effectively and charitably stated in a letter of Father Balthasar Tellez to Father Nathanael Southwell, an English secretary of the Society of Jesus in the seventeenth century (M.H., *Epistolae PP. Broeti, Jaji Codurii, et Simonis Rodericii*, 817–21).

Sacchini answered: "I say only this. If the facts are called in question, then in the entire *History* there is nothing beyond question nor even probable, for nothing in it rests on such manifold and solid authority. Call the facts narrated in doubt, pitting against them the memories of a few old men who can have been only mere children at the time of their occurrence, and the whole credit of our *History* collapses. Indeed, all human credit is undermined at a stroke, for whom shall we believe if we doubt such witnesses?" He cites eighteen witnesses, including St. Ignatius, Polanco, Laynez, St. Francis Borgia, Nadal, King John III and Cardinal Henry of Portugal, and the two Portuguese martyrs, Gonçalo da Silveira and Blessed Ignatius Azevedo. It was a formidable list but not the end of his evidence, for he continues: "I beg your Reverence to be satisfied with this as an answer to the first complaint, lest I be compelled to exhume more corpses from their sepulchres which are better left undisturbed. Corpses rarely smell sweetly, you know! As to the second head of complaint, that even if true the facts should not have been revealed, my answer is that a historian, saving the rules of historical writing and also saving his own conscience, has no choice in the matter. Let him who thinks differently abound in his own sense; this is what I think and I could not think otherwise. Since it is of the essence of history to relate outstanding events, whether good or bad, which illustrate the condition of an organized society, or which, in the case of a biography, enable a true judgment to be formed about an individual person, the publisher of a history containing nothing but favourable material wants to throw dust in his readers' eyes.[1] By the very fact of undertaking to write history he makes a profession of telling both the bad and the good, and so it follows that by concealing the bad he is believed to affirm its non-existence, since, had it existed, he was under an obligation to reveal it. . . Should anyone be unwilling to set down aught save the good, then let him call his book, not History, but Select History. From all this it is plain that when we gird ourselves to write history properly so called, and all the more if it deals with religious and sacred events, we must observe the essential laws with the greatest strictness

---

[1] Compare Dr. Johnson's opinion: "The value of every story depends on its being true. A story is a picture either of an individual or of human nature in general: if it be false, it is a picture of nothing" (Boswell's *Life,* chapter lvii).

and scrupulosity, that truth may be preserved and defended. . .
Think how much harm would be done to the whole human race,
and how many errors would be spread abroad, if a historian had the
right to tell only one side of his story. Why, there never has been
a famous highwayman or heretic who did not do some morally good
deeds in his life, occasionally magnificent deeds, and suppose that
somebody professing to write the life of such a person should keep
silent about robberies, heresies and other crimes, while narrating only
things bravely, wisely, or even piously done by him, as that he respected the honour of virgins and was devout to the Mother of God,
might not such a writer cause future generations to hold the highwayman for a saint?"

Having made that protestation, Sacchini next adduces nine different reasons why it is incumbent on historians and biographers to
paint their heroes in honest colours, warts and all. Some of these
are an anticipation of the maxim that history is philosophy teaching by examples, and here perhaps the good Father is more sanguine
than we can be about the capacity of one generation to profit from
the mistakes of another. But he continues in a vein of argument
which, while immediately intended for his Jesuit brethren, has a
bracing tang absent from the platitudes of the "pious" school of
hagiography. "We take comfort, meaning encouragement," he says,
"from the knowledge that if trouble of the kind recorded should
happen in our days, it also happened in other days before us, nor
were those old times so much better than our own. Our Society
grew up from the beginning in the midst of domestic as well as
external storms, and so we conceive a good hope that as our fathers
prevailed through adversity, God will give us also increase in time
of trial. . . To wish to persuade the world that our Society never
was touched by a breath of scandal, would be, as Father Nadal says,
the extravagance of pride, seeing that there were scandals among the
Apostles and first deacons, nor should we succeed in the attempt but
only render ourselves ridiculous. . . In our *History* we do not, when
they deserve it, spare the reputation of cities but describe their
evil habits, nor of nations but set down their barbarousness, nor of
princes but tell of the plots and persecutions which they have engineered against us. Why, then, should we spare our own brethren
and seek to cover up their failings? Is not that to use different

weights and measures, which is an abomination in the sight of God?[1] All history, sacred or secular, has the same tale of imperfection to tell, so why should we want our history to be something special?"

At this point Sacchini cites St. Augustine on Psalm xcix as a witness for the defence, and begs his correspondent to bring the passage to the notice of the aggrieved fathers. How pleased he would have been had he known that just then, on the other side of the Alps, St. Francis de Sales, the Augustine of his own age, was voicing very similar opinions about the vandalism of the whitewashers who try to prune or prettify the great rugged, battle-scarred, travel-worn, toil-weary saints and servants of God.[2] He concludes his apologia with a moving personal statement: "I entreat the fathers to believe that if there is sin in what they allege, it is not a sin of prejudice or ill-will. What had we to gain by an exhibition of such malignity, we who waste away and die over our books in order that by paying the debt of obedience and deference which we owe to the whole Society we may obtain from God the forgiveness of our sins and the salvation of our souls? If, then, our work is faulty or wanting in any respect, it is to be attributed to our ignorance and little skill. We neither knew nor could do any better. Much more gladly, you may be sure, would we have written a story containing nothing but what was well and fair, for we are members of the same body and sons of the same mother, who must needs feel the pang of a common family sorrow. If you will consider the whole matter carefully you will see that goodwill is not lacking. Much that might have been dealt with at greater length is only briefly indicated, and instead of criticizing the conduct of Father Simon we dilate on the good deeds and virtues of others of Portugal, that the esteem of our readers for your province may be in no way affected. Of set purpose we mention that discipline suffered a collapse, not in the province as a whole, but only in one college and among its more youthful members. We

---

[1] Proverbs xx. 10.

[2] "There is no harm done to the saints if their faults are shown as well as their virtues. But great harm is done to everybody by those hagiographers who slur over the faults, be it for the purpose of honouring the saints, . . . or through fear of diminishing our reverence for their holiness. It is not as they think. These writers commit a wrong against the saints and against the whole of posterity" (St. Francis de Sales, Œuvres, Annecy ed., x, 345 sq.).

add an encomium of this very college, tell how discipline was immediately restored, and by other arts endeavour to sweeten the story,
to the limit permitted by the equity of historical interpretation. . .
As for Father Simon's good name, you need have no fear. We know
what is written about the Apostles, and of other great men history
records that they all had their ups and downs. Besides, in succeeding volumes the good work which he achieved and the virtues
which he exemplified remain to be recounted, proving him worthy of
the distinction of founding so admirable a province. . . Forgive my
prolixity, dear Father, and help me with your prayers to carry out
henceforth my heavy, irksome task to the greater glory of God, to
the honour of our fathers now reigning with Christ, and also, if
possible, to the general consolation." [1]

When he came to deal with Laynez in his book Sacchini mentioned as a matter of interest that he was of Jewish lineage. The
fact seemed to him to enhance the General's greatness, but in Spain
it was thought to be a poisonous libel on his memory.[2] In 1622,
when the second volume of the *History* containing the offending
passage appeared, the Spanish Jesuits rose *en masse* to denounce it.
The General of the time, Father Mutius Vitelleschi, was overwhelmed

---

[1] M.H., *Scripta de Sancto Ignatio de Loyola,* i, 701–7. The Portuguese province which contributed 271 Jesuit martyrs to the total of 907 needs nobody's
apology.

"Não faltaram Christianos atrevimentos
Nesta pequena casa Lusitana,"

had sung the great national poet of Portugal, Camoëns — Christian endeavours
shall not be wanting in this little house of Portugal, and the Jesuit "sons of
Lusus" certainly played their part. Towards the close of the sixteenth century
there were in the province 591 members of whom more than a third were preparing for the missions at the College of Coimbra. Long after the time when
Simon Rodriguez could fairly be considered responsible, the province continued
to suffer from internal dissension, due primarily to differences between two of
the very men who are alleged to have been the authors of poor Simon's downfall, Fathers Miron and Gonçalves da Câmara. Both were outstanding Jesuits,
but that did not prevent them from embarking on mutual hostilities. Gonçalves da Câmara admitted that the Spanish Miron was a "good and holy man,"
who, however, was bringing the province to ruin. More detached brethren
thought that the same might be said of Gonçalves da Câmara (Rodrigues, *Historia da Companhia de Jesus na Assistencia de Portugal,* i, Porto 1938, appendix,
531 *sq.*).

[2] See above, pp. 118–21.

with protests, one of which, from the province of Toledo, may serve
as a specimen of the rest: "The Province of Toledo, united in a congregation, unanimously petitions our Reverend Father General to
see to it that what is written in the second volume of the *History of
the Society* about the ancestry of Father James Laynez is deleted.
We beg for the removal of so great a slur on the sweet memory of
so great a Father. Let there be no mention of it whatever in the
second edition, and in this first we ask that Father General would
immediately cause the page containing this foul blot which damages
the whole Society to be cut out and replaced by another asserting
the purity and nobility of the Father's lineage. We give a few of
the many reasons which may induce his Paternity to grant the petition. First, what the *History* discloses about the birth of this great
man is false, as witnesses of the utmost probity who have investigated
the matter testify. Secondly, even if true, it would serve no useful
purpose but cause the greatest harm and be downright sinful to
brand a General of the Society and one of its founders with that
infamy. Thirdly, the vile imputation is not confined to our Father
Laynez alone but reflects on all his kin. . . Among others, the Mar-
quess of Almazán who is not ashamed to count the Father among
his relatives is deeply offended by it. . ." The petitioners advance
three other arguments, hint that Sacchini ought to be heavily punished for his temerity, and say that they would like their personal
detestation and repudiation of his libel to be made known in a public
document. Obviously in the golden century of Spain *limpieza de
sangre* was not a laughing matter to be dismissed with a light reference to the gardener Adam and his wife.

Sacchini's answer to his embattled critics is so refreshing in its open-
mindedness, so charged with the spirit of the genuine truth-seeking
historian, that it deserves to be rescued from oblivion. "Verily I am
a luckless miserable fellow," he begins, "and scarcely could there be
a more wretched creature. For who will spare a little sympathy for
one who manages to offend everybody? Many a year now have I
been sweating over my books, fondly hoping by my labours and
torments to please God in the first place, then our fathers now in
Heaven with Him, and after that the present and future Society, as
well as my neighbour in general. And behold the result, the evil
fruit of my honest endeavours. I have gravely offended God, vil-

lainously degraded and disgraced a most eminent and saintly man now reigning with Him, wounded the Society itself by fixing on it a foul blot and dishonour, and even contaminated my neighbour with infamy. . . O Father of mercies, in Thy infinite goodness forgive me! And may the good fathers of Spain listen with patience to what their wicked son, if son he may be called, has to say in his own defence, so that though condemned unheard, he may not be punished without a hearing."

The apologia which follows is in seven parts corresponding to the allegations from Toledo. As for the truth of his report which the Spanish fathers so flatly deny, he wishes with all his heart that he could accept their evidence and take upon himself alone whatever odium and affliction may have been caused by his words. They would not find him slow to make them all the reparation in his power, for he is not so hardened in conscience or devoid of the fear of God as lightly to imperil his immortal soul. But he has his conscience as a historian also to think of. "I therefore declare," he continues, "that what is revealed in the *History* is so certain as to leave no possible room for doubt in the mind of any prudent man acquainted with the proofs on which it rests. The first proof is that the fact was known throughout the Society from the beginning. I have been hearing of it for thirty-five years, and never until now have I come upon anyone who doubted it. Many of our older fathers have read my *History* and not a man of them regarded the statement about Laynez as news to him. Indeed, I have been widely congratulated for not having passed it over. Cardinal Bellarmine and his confessor, Father Fabius, together with five former assistants to the General, all men well versed in the study of our origins, had not the slightest doubt about the truth of the story. Nor had the assistants who revised the *History* nor Father General himself. Father Antonio Possevino expressly asserts its truth, and Father Ribadeneira plainly signifies the same in several places. While Father Garcia Alarcón, an assistant, was on a visitation of the provinces of Castile and Toledo he addressed to Father General a memorial giving reasons why the decree about the non-admission of New Christians should be modified. In this he wrote as follows: 'Our holy Father Ignatius admitted men of Jewish extraction who by their sanctity and learning have rendered our Society illustrious and at the Council of Trent preserved its institute inviolate.' None but Laynez can be in question here, for though there were other fathers at Trent on him alone fell the responsibility of defending the Society in the Council. Let the older fathers still happily among us be asked for their opinion and I guarantee that they will answer in my sense. Why, the Province of Toledo itself at a former congregation held in the year 1600 signified the same thing when petitioning for a modification of the decree about New Christians! Who, then, will believe that a story so old, so widely known, and so consistent is wholly without foundation? Why should it be told of Laynez rather than another unless it be true of him? Why if false has no one ever taken the trouble to confute it?"

Such is Sacchini's first proof, but he has four others equally effective. One of them has to do with happenings in Rome in 1564, a stormy year for the Jesuits. Carlo Borromeo, the twenty-six-year-old nephew and Secretary of State of Pope Pius IV, was then on very intimate terms with the fathers, especially the procurator of the Society, John Baptist Ribera. The Pope and his other relatives had wanted Charles to marry after the death of his elder brother, but he instead secretly took Holy Orders and began to lead a life more devout and austere than was considered appropriate for a Secretary of State. Pius, though a good man, was easy-going and unascetic. He did not like the way his nephew was shaping. At the time, the secular clergy of Rome were in arms against the Jesuits because the Pope had decided to give them charge of the new seminary which he was about to establish in the City. Borromeo's sudden trend towards the desert gave the opposition the opportunity it needed. The Pope had it explained to him that the change in his nephew was due entirely to Jesuit influence, whereupon he became angry with the fathers and bade them leave his Secretary of State alone.[1] There followed a spate of rather vicious libels against the order in one of which a certain titular bishop scornfully threw Laynez's Jewish pedigree in his face. The Jesuits answered the other charges levelled against them but this one they passed over in complete silence, which Sacchini reasonably maintains they would not have done had they been in a position to refute it. Similarly, when in Spain King Philip and his nobles showed themselves inimical to

[1] M.H., *Polanci Complementa*, i, 451–2.

the Society of Jesus on this and other counts, Nadal, far from denying the charge, maintained that it was a mean and unworthy thing to frown on any man because of the accident of his birth. For all that we had to do with it, any of us might have been born wart-hogs or rattlesnakes. Finally, in his list of proofs, Sacchini cites a letter, now lost, from Laynez himself to the chief critic of his blood, Antonio Araoz: "May our God never permit that the favour of kings, the flattery of nobles, the prejudices of nationalism, the conceit of private judgment, or disdain for another's flesh as though one's own were compounded of different and finer clay, should cloud your Reverence's recognition of the bonds of union and esteem which ought to govern the relations of a good religious with his superior, even though that superior be of Jewish stock." As Araoz had no superior but Laynez himself the evidence here seems conclusive.

Having shown the Spanish fathers to be in error on the main question, Sacchini counter-attacks them vigorously with regard to their other grievances. Even if true, they contended, he had no business to give the story publicity, and it was wicked of him to fasten such an infamy on one whom all reverenced as both a General and a founder of the Society of Jesus. Here we have again the old theme of a plurality of founders, propagated by Bobadilla. "The Society recognizes only one founder, Ignatius," replies Sacchini, "but waiving that point, I deny that Laynez has suffered any indignity from what I said of his birth. True, if that was all that I had re-counted of him, there might be reason to fear for his reputation in the eyes of the unthinking multitude, but since I tell so much of his wisdom, his prudence, his piety, his magnificent conduct of affairs, the shadows, so to call them, cast by his origin are utterly dissipated in this blaze of glory. Great virtues are not discredited by a man's birth, but rather is his birth graced and commended by his great virtues. How many philosophers, conquerors and kings of antiquity were of obscure or base lineage, not one of whom suffered in glory and renown because of his lowly birth. In all nations virtue was so highly esteemed that it sufficed of itself as a patent of nobility. And if this was so amid the darkness of paganism, what will not be its dignity in the light of Christian truth? In that light, as St. Gregory Nazianzen says, nobility is reckoned, not by pedigrees, but man by man. Did his birth in the land of Hus detract from the patience of

Job? Was the wisdom of Solomon less because he was born of her who had been the wife of Uriah? Are the Apostles demeaned by their fisher-folk connections? Is God an accepter of persons, He who made both little and great and from one man drew out the whole human family? Why, even sin itself of the gravest kind has been no bar to the fame and veneration of the penitents who afterwards attained to the highest sanctity. So far, then, from the chance of his birth obscuring the glory of Laynez, it rather enhances the beauty of his virtues, as colours are set off by their accompanying shadows. To deny this is to think too meanly of this great man's reputation, as though fearful that if all were known it must suffer some eclipse."

After that fine bombardment of questions our author adduces no less than ten good reasons why it was necessary and advisable for him to give the information which the Spanish fathers impugned. The origins of a great man are a subject of legitimate public interest which a historian has no right to suppress. Moreover, in the case of Laynez the information is essential to a proper understanding of the attitude of such critics as Bobadilla and Araoz. History is a record of fact and cannot afford the luxury of satisfying all tastes and prejudices. It must take the rough with the smooth as it finds it in life itself, whose complexities it is its business to reflect. For a historian to conceal an inconvenient fact would be to render his other facts suspect and to destroy the authority of his book, which a Jesuit historian could afford less than most of the fraternity, owing to the wide variety of fancies held about his order. To secure the trust of his readers he must be prepared to give them hostages in the shape of facts either really not redounding to the credit of his brethren, or innocent in themselves but capable of misrepresentation by prejudiced minds. To the unprejudiced mind Laynez's Jewish affiliation must seem an additional merit, as of a handicap nobly surmounted. What a sweet disposition of Providence it was, says St. Bernard, speaking of his dear friend, St. Malachy, that the rude barbarism of Ireland should have brought forth such a charming fellow-citizen of the saints and member of the household of God! [1]

[1] The reference is Sacchini's. Neither he nor St. Bernard knew anything about twelfth-century Ireland, but they meant no harm. Bernard's Burgundy at the time was every bit as "barbarous" as St. Malachy's country. After reading

But there are broader issues of Christian charity involved in the question. The Jesuits were not founded for the sake of Spain alone, but, so far as in them lay, to help all nations and men, without regard to birth or station. St. Ignatius regarded Jewish blood as a privilege rather than a disgrace. God forbid that his sons should think disparagingly of the race which gave them Jesus and His Mother: "The fathers of Toledo contend that by revealing the Jewish origin of Laynez I have inflicted a wound on the whole Society. How so, pray, when none but themselves felt any wound? My book has been circulated in all our provinces and read at table in many refectories, but only from Spain has come so much as a syllable of complaint. And where, anyhow, is this infamy of which they speak? St. Epiphanius, that great light of the Church and opponent of heresy, was a Jew on both sides. So was St. Julian, archbishop of no less a place than Toledo itself, and still its patron. And how many saints and doctors besides were of that same blood of the Saint of Saints! The Church glories in such men and so should we glory in our Laynez, whose so-called stain is an ignominy only to vulgar and prejudiced minds. It is our duty to make war on such prejudices and destroy them. Why this fear where there is no cause for fear? Is it an ignominy to find Christ our Lord, however late in the day? What stain remains in the new man who has put on Christ and become a temple of God, a son of God, an heir of God and co-heir of Christ? Must we blush to have the same mind as the Apostle of the Gentiles? It is he who forbids the wild olive to boast against the broken branches of the true olive, into which through no merit of their own the alien shoots have been grafted.[1] Armed with this

---

the letters of the twelfth-century Popes, Adrian IV and Alexander III, to the English King, Henry II, about Ireland and the Irish and his devout Majesty's very proper and commendable conquest of that wicked people, one is irresistibly reminded of what Mrs. Moloney said as she came away from the Archbishop's eloquent sermon on the beauties and joys of married life: "Ah, 'twas a fine sermon his Riv'rince is after tellin' us; an' I wish I knew as little about it as he does." It is true, however, that the Irish marriage customs of St. Malachy's time were not always in accordance with the laws of the Church.

[1] "For if thou wert cut out of the wild olive tree which is natural to thee, and, contrary to nature, wert grafted into the good olive tree: how much more shall they that are the natural branches be grafted into their own olive tree" (Romans xi. 24).

thought, how can any man who loves Christ be offended by the return to Him of His own racial kith and kin? But I am not pleading the cause of the New Christians. I merely wish to indicate that I in no way repent of what I wrote about Laynez. As a Christian, his Jewish blood was not an ignominy but an ennoblement, for he was not a wild shoot, as each of us is, but a fallen branch of the good olive grafted again sweetly and fitly into the parent stock." [1]

[1] M.H., *Lainii Monumenta,* viii, 831–55.

forbidden city by Philip II, 15; congregation in, 25 ff.
Romillon, Jean Baptiste, 282 n.
Romulo, Signor, 24
Rosas, Gulf of, 116
Rose of Lima, St., 228 n.
Ross, Bishop of. *See* Sinclair, Henry
Rotunda, Church of the, 26
Ruffach, Jesuit centre at, 169
Ruggieri, Michael, S.J., 308
Ruskin, John, *al.*, 280
Russia, 55

Saa, Manuel da, S.J., 68
Sacchini: *Historia Societatis Jesu,* 16, 136 n., 269 n., 309 ff.
St. Andrea, Jesuit novitiate in Rome, 183
St. Angelo, Castle of, 69, 105, 154
St. Anthony, college of, Lisbon, 224
St. Augustine, church, Paris, 99; city, 216 ff.
St. Cloud, 62 n.
Ste. Barbe, College of, 99
St. Germain-des-Prés, Benedictine abbey of, 48, 87 n.
St. Jacques, Collège de, 34
St. Omer, Jesuit centre at, 183
St. Paul, College of, 252
St. Quentin, capture of, 22
St. Roch, College of, Lisbon, 224
Sainctes, Claude de, 93
Salamanca, 33, 68, 77, 128, 139, 212-14, 216 f., 272 n., 273, 276, 288 f., 296, 302
Sales, Francis de, St., 6, 65, 281, 286, 313 and n.
Salmeron, Alfonso, S.J., 13 and n., 29, 33, 39, 56, 71, 76, 91, 96, 105, 107 and n., 108, 109 n., 112, 129, 143, 153 ff., 186 ff., 238 n., 266; correspondence of, with Laynez, 77-84, 188
Salzburg, Archbishop of, 177
San Salvador, 229
San Vicente, 229 ff.
Sanchez, Pedro, S.J., 217, 222
Sanders, Francis, S.J., 300 and n.
Santa Maria della Strada, 6, 9 n., 74 n.
Santa Maria Maggiore, 230
Santiago, the, ship, 231 f.
Santo Domingo (Haiti), 217 f.
São Thomé (India), 252

Saracens, 115, 254, 257
Saragossa, 47, 143
Sarate, Pedro de, 120 and n.
Sarpi, Paolo, 104 and n.
Saverne, Jesuit centre at, 169
Savoy, 37
Schipman, Father, S.J., 147
Scotland, 185 ff.
Sebastian of Portugal, 124, 132-3, 136
Sedeño, Antonio, S.J., 219 f.
Segovia, 139, 304
Segura, Juan, S.J., 211, 219-21
Selestat, Jesuit centre at, 169
Selim II, Sultan of Turkey, 268
Sens, Archbishop of. *See* Gondren
Seripando, Cardinal, 102, 105 f.
Serpe, Gaspar, S.J., 134 n.
Servites, 108
Seville, Archbishop of, Grand Inquisitor, 80 n.
Seville, College of, 272 n., 273
Sforza, Guido, Cardinal, 24
Sforzas, the, 4
Shea, John Gilmary, 216 n.
Siena, 70, 91
Siliceo, Cardinal. *See* Guijarro
Silveira, Gonçalo da, 208-9 and n., 214, 224, 237 n., 251, 311
Silvestrine monasteries visited by Bobadilla, 24-5
Simancas, 12
Simonetta, Cardinal, 102
Sinclair, Henry, Bishop of Ross, 195, 197 f.   :
Sixtus IV, Pope, 276 n.
Société du Collège de Clermont, 61
Sodality of the Blessed Virgin, 280-1
Sokotra, Nestorian Christians of, 252-3
Solano, Francis, St., 229 n.
Soldi-Gnechi. *See* Organtino
Somaschi, the, 3 n.
Sorbonne, la, 34, 45, 47, 49, 275, 281
Soto, Dominic, O.P., 34, 276
Soto, Peter, O.P., 34, 76 n., 107 n.
Soury, Jacques, 232
Southey: *History of Brazil,* 234
Spa, 149, 183
Spain, 11; power of, 4; prejudice of, on racial purity, 7, 118-19; impoverishment of, 9; anti-Semitism in, 118 ff.;